The People Maintenance Manual

Living Well-guidelines for health and fitness

THE JOY OF LIVING LIBRARY

The People Maintenance Manual

Living Well-guidelines for health and fitness

Mitchell Beazley Publishers Limited London

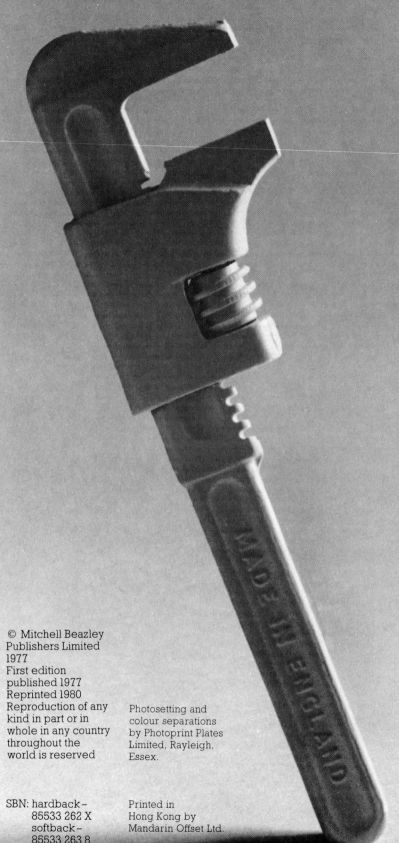

Photosetting and
colour separations
by Photoprint Plates
Limited, Rayleigh,
Essex.

SBN: hardback –
        85533 262 X
        softback –
        85533 263 8

Printed in
Hong Kong by
Mandarin Offset Ltd.

CONTENTS

The People Maintenance Manual
was edited and designed by
Mitchell Beazley Publishers Limited,
87-89 Shaftesbury Avenue
London W1V 7AD

Editor	Jack Tresidder
Art Editor	Barry Moscrop
Assistant Editors	Ruth Binney
	Tony Livesey
	Sally Walters
Designers	Len Roberts
	Ayala Kingsley
	Lyn Cawley
Picture Researcher	Jackum Brown
Editorial Assistant	Bridget Alexander
Production	Elsie Day
Executive Editor	Paul Bradwell

CONSULTANTS AND CONTRIBUTORS

DR IAN ANDERSON, MBBS, MRCS, LRCP, Clinical Assistant (Cardiac rehabilitation), Kent and Sussex Hospital, Tunbridge Wells

DR CHRISTOPHER BADCOCK, BA, PhD

PROFESSOR ARNOLD E. BENDER, BSc, PhD, FIFST, FRSH, Professor of Nutrition, Queen Elizabeth College, University of London

COLIN BLYTHE, Researcher in Food and Nutrition Policy, Earth Resources Research Limited, London

EDWARD R. BRACE, Fellow of the American Medical Writers' Association

DR MALCOLM CARRUTHERS, MD, MRCPath, MRCGP, Honorary Senior Lecturer, Institute of Psychiatry, London

ELIZABETH EVANS, PhD, Research Assistant, Queen Elizabeth College, University of London

HUMPHREY EVANS

STEPHEN FEBERY

THERESA FRANKEL, Research Nutritionist, Zoological Society of London

DR JOAN GOMEZ, MB, BS, MRCPsych, DPM, Senior Psychiatric Registrar, Westminster Hospital, London

PROFESSOR P. J. LAWTHER, MB, DSc, FRCP, Director, Medical Research Council Environmental Hazards Unit; Professor of Environmental and Preventive Medicine, St Bartholomew's Hospital Medical College and the London Hospital Medical College

CHRISTOPHER MACY, BTech

RUSSELL MILLER

ELISABETH MORSE, BA, MSc

PAMELA MUMFORD, Lecturer in nutrition, Queen Elizabeth College, University of London

ALISTAIR MURRAY, MSRG, Director of the City Gymnasium Fitness Research Programme, London

PAULETTE PRATT

JOHN RIVERS, Research Nutritionist, Zoological Society of London

DR F. D'SOUZA, BSc, PhD, Research Fellow, Zoological Society of London and Visiting Lecturer, London School of Economics, Department of Anthropology

DR BERNARD STONEHOUSE, MA, DPhil, BSc, Chairman of the Post Graduate School of Studies in Environmental Science, University of Bradford, Yorkshire

ROBERT WALLER, BSc, ARCS, Statistical epidemiologist, Medical Research Council, Environmental Hazard Unit, London

PROFESSOR J. S. WEINER, DSc, MRCP, Professor of Environmental Physiology, University of London

Index: SUSAN WILSON

Foreword

The galvanizing force of physical activity...

Most people take more trouble over their cars than their bodies. They would not feed their cars the wrong fuel, nor let them miss a servicing when it is due, nor let them grow rusty, but they neglect their own bodies without a qualm. The majority of adults and even children are physically unfit and alarmingly content to be so. The stresses of modern life are not balanced by adequate physical activity, and this has contributed to much ill-health and disease. This book aims to help people to see the dangers and do something to redress the balance. It covers many aspects of health, but I choose to emphasize physical activity as the field I know best.

Heart disease has increased to an alarming extent in the past twenty years, at progressively younger ages in both men and women at the time when their services to the community and to their families are greatest. History gives us insight into the health problem if we look at man's early development. Our recent ancestors spent most of their lives walking, riding and doing manual work, while our more distant ancestors doubtless chased sabre-toothed tigers and mammoths. For all of them, exercise was a compulsory part of life. But before the turn of the last century sedentary work had become vastly more common. If we study the way a child develops, we see clearly that his mind unfolds in harmony with the unlocking of an active body. It is through the galvanizing force of ceaseless physical activity that children first explore the world and come to terms with their environment. Time spent in physical activity greatly improves their academic performance, and what is true for the child is also true for the adult.

Quite apart from fitness, there are immense benefits in terms of fulfilment and happiness if everyone has the opportunity, at present open only to a few, to choose a wide variety of indoor and outdoor recreational activities. As the Greeks understood so well, the mind and body cannot really be separated; a mental tranquillity can result from the cathartic experiences of sport. The sense of well-being felt by those who acquire and maintain physical fitness should not be denied by those who have no inclination to acquire it. Perhaps fitness fanatics are bores, but this does not mean that the facts, such as they are known, about health and exercise can be ignored. We can now say with confidence that regular physical activity along with weight control and avoidance of cigarette smoking are sound common-sense recommendations for reducing coronary disease. There is no contrary argument that is at all intellectually respectable.

I can recommend this book for everyone who wishes to take an intelligent interest in positive health. Outstandingly it does two things: first, it provides in a lucid and readable style powerful arguments for a change in habits; second, for those who simply do not know where to start along the path to fitness, it will prove a guiding light.

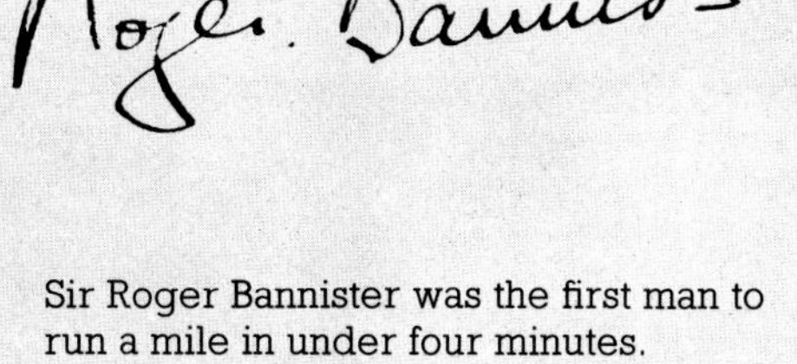

Roger Bannister

Sir Roger Bannister was the first man to run a mile in under four minutes.

9

CHAPTER 1 Who are you?

Knowing your strengths and weaknesses is basic to health.

The average human body is extraordinarily tough: looked after with respect—which means balanced measures of exercise and rest, fun and work, food and mental stimulation—it can do just about anything you are likely to demand of it, and a good deal more besides. But there are limits to the body's endurance. How much you enjoy life (and how long you live to enjoy it) depends largely on understanding what these limits are. The body's needs are much more subtle than they seem.

What the body can do: our genetic legacy

In the long process of evolution, we have altered our biology far less than we have our environment.

Despite the outward differences that exist between members of the human species, our bodies are all remarkably similar biologically. What is more, the logic of body design has hardly changed for thousands of years. Civilization has enabled man to alter and control his environment vastly without adapting much physically. As a result it is sometimes hard to remember that the human body evolved to meet quite different needs from those of most people now. To understand what the body can do and what it can't do, it has to be seen in the context of evolution because staying healthy depends partly on running the body as it was meant to be run.

Kept in ideal condition, the body is a fairly impressive mechanism—agile, balanced, flexible, strong and durable. It had to be so because when early man first walked on two legs more than three million years ago he faced formidable physical odds against surviving long enough to reproduce (on average, he

could expect to die at about the age of twenty). A considerable physical effort was involved in meeting his most basic needs—finding food, water, shelter and a mate, and avoiding predators. His unprotected body had to endure extremes of temperature; our capacity to sweat and our comparative hairlessness were significant factors in enabling man to remain active in hot conditions. Physical endurance was also needed to walk or trot for long periods once man became a meat-eater.

Our teeth and digestive systems show, however, that our bodies are adapted mainly to a vegetarian diet. We are not suited to slowly digesting big but infrequent meals. Man became a meat-eater not because meat was vital to his survival but because it was a conveniently concentrated form of nutriment. Once he had organized himself into hunting groups his extended diet left him with more spare time. Periods of intense hunting activity could be alternated with quite long periods

Evolution in action

The three vital links in the chain of human evolution have been the development of upright posture and controlled gait, hands capable of skilled manipulation, and a large brain. The ten-pin bowler can control his movements well enough to crouch, stride and accurately hurl a heavy object to a selected mark with the aid of his binocular vision. This apparently simple action involves an ability to combine two different types of hand grip, which is the basis of man's unique manual dexterity. In the power grip, objects are held between the palm and undersurface of the fingers. In the precision grip (used in a modified form by the bowler to hold and guide the bowl) the thumb and index finger are opposed. The use of sport as a means of relaxation itself reflects man's sophisticated brain.

of sedentary socializing. (A look at the human buttocks dispenses with the idea that man was never designed for a partly sedentary life.)

Our capacity to eat both bulk foods low in calorific value and concentrated foods high in value is typical of the versatility that characterizes us physically. It is this versatility, rather than any obvious physical superiority, that sets man apart from animals with whom he shares basic structural, fuelling, pumping and plumbing systems. Like other primates, man has eyes set well forwards in the head, providing not only stereoscopic vision but also the ability to assess speed and distance accurately; a constant body temperature—now 37°C (98.6°F); insulating fat and hair; a small number of offspring born after a long gestation period and needing a long period of nursing; and hands with mobile digits. His development of a thumb that can be placed in opposition to all his other fingers and the combination of that manual

dexterity with hand-eye co-ordination and neurological development gives him his only real physical edge over all animals.

A racehorse is twice as fast as man, a cheetah three times as fast. A roe deer can maintain over a distance of 32 km (20 miles) a speed in excess of a sprinter's best. Kangaroos put to shame man's jumping efforts and no male human has yet fathered more than 36,000 young, which a rabbit has been known to do! We have a long lifespan, but even here the tortoise is longer-lived.

In addition, man's upright posture, although it has conferred the enormous advantage of freeing the hands, has also caused some physical problems. Strains on our abdominal musculature, backbone and circulatory system have made us prone to hernias and slipped discs.

Man does score heavily, though, on adaptability. He is the best physical all-rounder. He can climb, walk, trot on his hind legs, jump, dive and swim. He is

more widely distributed geographically than any other species and almost any male can breed successfully with almost any female. Some of the outward differences between people reflect environmental adaptations. The colder the climate the more body fat we have—Eskimos tend to be about 18 kg (40 lb) heavier than Latins. Long, narrow noses serve to moisten inhaled air in dry conditions and dark skins protect against excessive humidity.

But all the evidence points to the fact that, increasingly over the past 50,000 years, man has learned to survive not by continuing to modify his body but by using his greatest asset of all—his large and complex brain—to alter his environment. Because society is now changing at an accelerating rate, we need to remember that the most fundamental needs of the body have not changed and in particular that the process of evolution did not intend our bodies to be overnourished, mentally overstressed or physically underworked.

Recognizing your own body type

Slope-shouldered or classic athlete, built like a tank or made to pass through keyholes, what counts is to be at ease with yourself.

A good deal of the advice commonly handed out gives the impression that if only we slim hard enough, eat the right food and train strenuously enough then we will all end up looking like Greek gods, able to excel at any physical or mental task set before us. The impression is quite false. Certainly, we can all improve our health, shape and performance, but to very different extents. Some people who have never run farther than from the top of the station steps to the door of a train can become capable sportsmen; others must resign themselves to leaving spectacular physical achievements to athletes.

Although we have all inherited a similar basic physiology (allowing for the major differences between men and women), we all vary greatly in build. Even within a normal range, there can be variations of thirty per cent in height and sixty per cent in bulk. There can also be a difference of several hundred per cent in endurance and strength. But the real key to those differences is a matter less of height or weight than of body type. Your general body type is something that you are born with—and stuck with for life.

An American psychologist, William Sheldon, devised a useful system of categorizing people in 1940. He defined three basic body types—the endomorph, the mesomorph and the ectomorph. The endomorph is rounded, heavily built and with quite a lot of fat (though not necessarily obese). The mesomorph is the classic, well-muscled athlete. The ectomorph is thin and angular, with not much muscle and not much fat. By using a one-to-seven scale for all three shapes it is possible to describe a person's physique with reasonable precision. Four-four-four means an equal share of each attribute—average for endomorphy, mesomorphy and ectomorphy. The marked ectomorph comes out as one-one-seven, since he has only a token quotient of the other two descriptions. Most people fall somewhere on a scale between the three extremes.

Sheldon's description is of basic body shape and it stands whatever you weigh and however fat you may be. A fat ecto-

morph is not an endomorph—he is a fat ectomorph who should lose some weight.

Each body shape has its own particular advantages, but mesomorphy is the most generally useful in an all-round physical sense. Mesomorphs who have a lot of muscle are good at exerting power over short periods, whereas a two-four-four man with equal proportions of meso- and ectomorphy will be less strong but have greater endurance, as he has less muscle to carry around. Professional strongmen have to be high on mesomorphy but have a fair quotient of endomorphy, too—say four-six-two. Someone who is higher on endomorphy than on mesomorphy may be strong, but too much of that strength may have to be used in transporting the extra bulk to allow top physical performance.

A difference in levels of physical achievement between men and women is inevitable. Although there can be all sorts of modifications according to the particular chromosomes involved, most women have smaller hearts and lungs than men and in relation to body weight they have a lower proportion of muscle and a higher proportion of fat. Their lower centre of gravity makes them generally less speedy than men and their metabolism is lower—by one-fifth or so.

Athletic performance is a useful measure of women's physical potential since it is well documented. It is striking that women champions are narrowing the gap between their performances and those of men; women were twenty-five per cent slower than men over 800 metres in 1945 but in 1976 the gap had been almost halved. There is still no reason to believe that the performance levels will ever coincide; what is happening is that thanks to changing social attitudes more women are now being trained and encouraged as men are, and are therefore realizing their potential.

If you are of the endo- or ectomorph type then you should bear two things in mind. On the one hand you need not feel that because you are not built like an Olympic champion there is no point in maintaining your physical fitness. Everybody can and should keep up a reasonable level of fitness as an aid to coping with ordinary life without undue strain or fatigue. On the other hand you should not aim to push your body beyond what it can reasonably achieve. If you are an endomorph you can keep your weight as low as possible, but you cannot turn yourself into an ectomorph or a mesomorph any more than a retriever can be turned into a poodle. Tales of seven-stone ectomorphs being transformed into men who could hold up the earth are myth.

Whatever shape you were born with, you can be physically fit, but what you need to do to achieve fitness will be dictated by your shape. Extreme mesomorphs need a lot of exercise—much more than extreme examples of the other two types. Endomorphs and ectomorphs should not strain to match mesomorphs in sport. Where they can succeed is in sports that require skill and practice: fencing, tennis, squash. Ectomorphs, for all their lack of strength, have the great advantage that their health is normally the best. By the same token, the stressed mesomorph is often in the worst position.

The body shapes at large

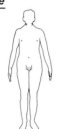

The endomorph
Well rounded, with soft contours and a large stomach, often apt to overeat.

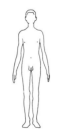

The ectomorph
Lean, angular, fairly frail, with more stamina than muscle, but long-lived.

The mesomorph
Muscular, full of energy, but needing exercise to stave off stress disease.

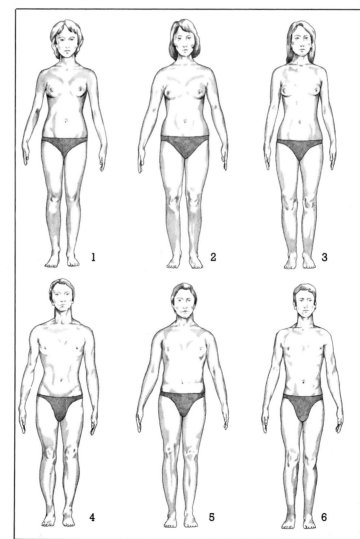

1 2 3

4 5 6

The favourite body
The adman's ideal physique is usually the tall, lean type with broad shoulders and narrow hips. In 1971 the Consumers' Association organized a survey in Britain which largely confirmed the popularity of this meso-ecto-morphic shape. But many people, particularly the middle-aged, prefer a more endomorphic version. A range of 12 average body shapes of equal heights was offered for each sex and people were asked which they liked best. Whereas (1) was the favourite female shape, some middle-aged women liked (2), as did many older men. Third favourite was (3). Of the male shapes, (4) was much the most popular with women and was also the favourite with men, followed by (5). Many young women preferred (6), but fewer men.

How your body affects your behaviour

Research tends to confirm old beliefs that the way you are built indicates the way you may react to life.

Human behaviour is more influenced by basic body shape than might be thought. Each body type has certain associated behaviour patterns, though the link is far from hard and fast. Apart from a slight tendency to become more endo-mesomorphic as you grow older, your body type is fixed throughout your life. Your personality, however, at least as it shows itself in your day-to-day behaviour, results from a mix between your basic constitution and your circumstances. Personality is obviously more complicated than the shape of arms, legs or torso: it can easily be shown that A is physically more mesomorphic than B, but B, although he is less aggressive than A, may more than make up for it with a stronger desire to dominate. (Both are mesomorphic personality characteristics.) Similarly C may be more ectomorphic, more introverted and more sensitive than D. But D may be more neurotically reactive, partly making up the balance and disguising the difference.

So the following three outlines apply only to those with a high score on one of the three basic body types. Most people will not fit one exactly, but will be a more or less complicated mixture. Any attempt to categorize human personality must be treated as entertaining and sometimes revealing theory rather than scientific fact.

Endomorphs are marked above all by being relaxed. In extreme cases their relaxation is total. It affects the whole body, action and life-style. As the features are rounded, so is the movement of the body smooth and deliberate. Breathing and heart beat are slow, full and regular. The endomorph reacts slowly, and can appear more passive to the energetic mesomorph and the reactive ectomorph than he really is. None the less, there is a strong element of complacency, a tendency to make the best of any situation regardless of the future. At times this can appear to others as infuriating indifference. The other side of the coin is tolerance, an acceptance of people, customs and situations. This means that endomorphs are usually companionable.

Those who seek positions of power sometimes deliberately adopt a commanding stance, with shoulders back and head up. The mesomorph has no need of such artifice: this is his normal posture. His trunk is erect with a straight spine, the chest forward and the stomach (unless he is obese) in; even the facial expression can appear set. Everything gives the appearance of preparedness for action.

The mesomorph often has a deep and abiding desire to dominate, to be important, to wield power. When on a winning streak this trait can manifest itself in an expansiveness and generosity superficially reminiscent of the sociability of the endomorph. When difficulties arise, however, the difference becomes clear. The endomorph becomes if anything more sociable, and may shrink from action. Action, however, is the mesomorph's refuge from distress—more and more of it, activity for its own sake.

The marked mesomorph tends to be highly competitive and abounds in drive and enterprise. He is aggressive, usually in the best sense of the word. He is comparatively untroubled by pain. The army seeks mesomorphs because of their

Harold Wilson (endomorph) **Henry Kissinger (endo-mesomorph)** **Winston Churchill (meso-endomorph)**

Physique and politics

In the management of national affairs every capability is required sooner or later. It is not surprising, therefore, that all body types are represented among leaders. Harold Wilson was known throughout his leadership as the compromiser, the pacifier; he is also a marked endomorph. Slightly less endomorphic is Henry Kissinger, who made his reputation as a negotiator.

As an endo-mesomorph one would expect him to impose himself in a more obvious fashion than Harold Wilson and indeed he appears to have done so.

The vigorous, dominating nature of the classic mesomorph has of course thrown up many political leaders, of whom Stalin is a textbook example. With a level of aggression that quickly turned to ruthlessness, with a contempt for those apparently less bulldozing than himself, courage in combat. These characteristics can turn to callousness in circumstances where they are not appropriate.

The mesomorph's body build is an essential element in athletic success—but so is his liking, even need, for physical exercise. A love of adventure goes with this need, but it can merge into a love of risk. The mesomorph is often a daredevil and a gambler.

The typical ectomorph, slender and sensitive, is extremely, even overly, responsive to all stimulation, both from within and without the body. He is easily startled. He tends to be fussy about his diet, preferring food of good quality with a high proportion of protein and not much bulk. He is more likely to suffer from digestive problems such as constipation. He is extremely sensitive to pain and winces easily. His inner awareness makes him something of a hypochondriac.

Externally he can be hyperaware. He has sharp eyes and ears and misses little of what goes on around him. This can lead to problems, especially when combined with a tendency to neuroticism, as the individual ends up trying to deal with input from several sources at once. He is easily distracted. His reactions are fast, sometimes too fast, causing him to stumble over himself.

As a result of these traits the ectomorph is usually a highly controlled person who needs an orderly life to function at his best. His posture is often tense and his movements unspontaneous; he may hunch his shoulders. In conversation the ectomorph may appear ambiguous, hesitant or withdrawn when in fact he is probably more aware of events than everyone else. In times of crisis he is likely to seek solitude.

The ectomorph tends to do well in intelligence tests and exams and to be quick to absorb new information.

Joseph Stalin
(mesomorph)

John F. Kennedy
(meso-ectomorph)

Charles de Gaulle
(ecto-mesomorph)

Woodrow Wilson
(ectomorph)

he fitted the type to perfection. Churchill, a meso-endomorph, was in no way lacking in determination or drive, but being essentially conservative he was more inclined to keep the world as he knew it than to change it—perhaps a reflection of his partial endomorphy. John F. Kennedy, the meso-ectomorph, distinguished himself by a combination of energy and introversion, a man with drive who tempered it according to firmly held principles and ideals.

A remarkable number of meso-ecto-morphs or ecto-mesomorphs end up in positions of power. Their combination of drive, reflection, responsiveness and acuteness has obvious advantages in leadership. De Gaulle would brood for months (if not years) about policy and would present the results of his deliberation in oracular fashion. To a strong degree he had the ectomorphic trait of being a loner, coupling it with a daunting asceticism. Woodrow Wilson, a more marked ectomorph, was obsessed by an ideal, his devotion to which eventually drove him into isolation. Much more the scholar than De Gaulle, he was also more of a moral crusader: the League of Nations was his idea, but his inability to compromise and win over opponents to US involvement ironically led to his own country failing to join it.

Environment, life-style and health

A good life is easier to achieve than ever before. But it is not the same as an over-soft life.

Whatever your physical or psychological makeup, the biggest influence on your health is likely to be the way you choose to live. Because advances in medicine and hygiene have overcome so many of the infectious diseases that killed people a century ago, survival to the biologically predetermined lifespan (at least seventy years) has become normal in the West—and in some parts of the East. We work less and in better conditions than ever before; we are better fed, housed and doctored. But the fact that so many are not fit enough to enjoy life suggests that modern society has made it too easy for people to live the wrong way.

Environmentalists look back with nostalgia to pre-industrial society, when men lived within a stable social and moral order, ate organic food, lived outdoors and knew nothing of tobacco, let alone car exhaust fumes. Environmental problems are certainly a factor in modern ill-health. To the stresses of noise, crowding, constant change and a high level of sensory stimulation are added respiratory dangers ranging from carbon monoxide to harmful organic compounds formed by the effect of sunlight on the polluted atmosphere of many large cities.

Even so, most of the failings of our bodies are our own fault. There is increasing suspicion that the two great modern killers—heart disease and cancer—are related to a conflict between our life-style and our inherited physical structure. We would be less inclined to heart disease if we exercised more often and ate less rich food. Our teeth would be better if we ate less sugar. Even the air we breathe would be better if we did not react to stress by lighting up a cigarette. A host of minor ailments ranging from backache and headache to ulcers and hypertension could be avoided if we did not overfeed, over-stimulate and underexercise our bodies—and if we simply learned how to relax.

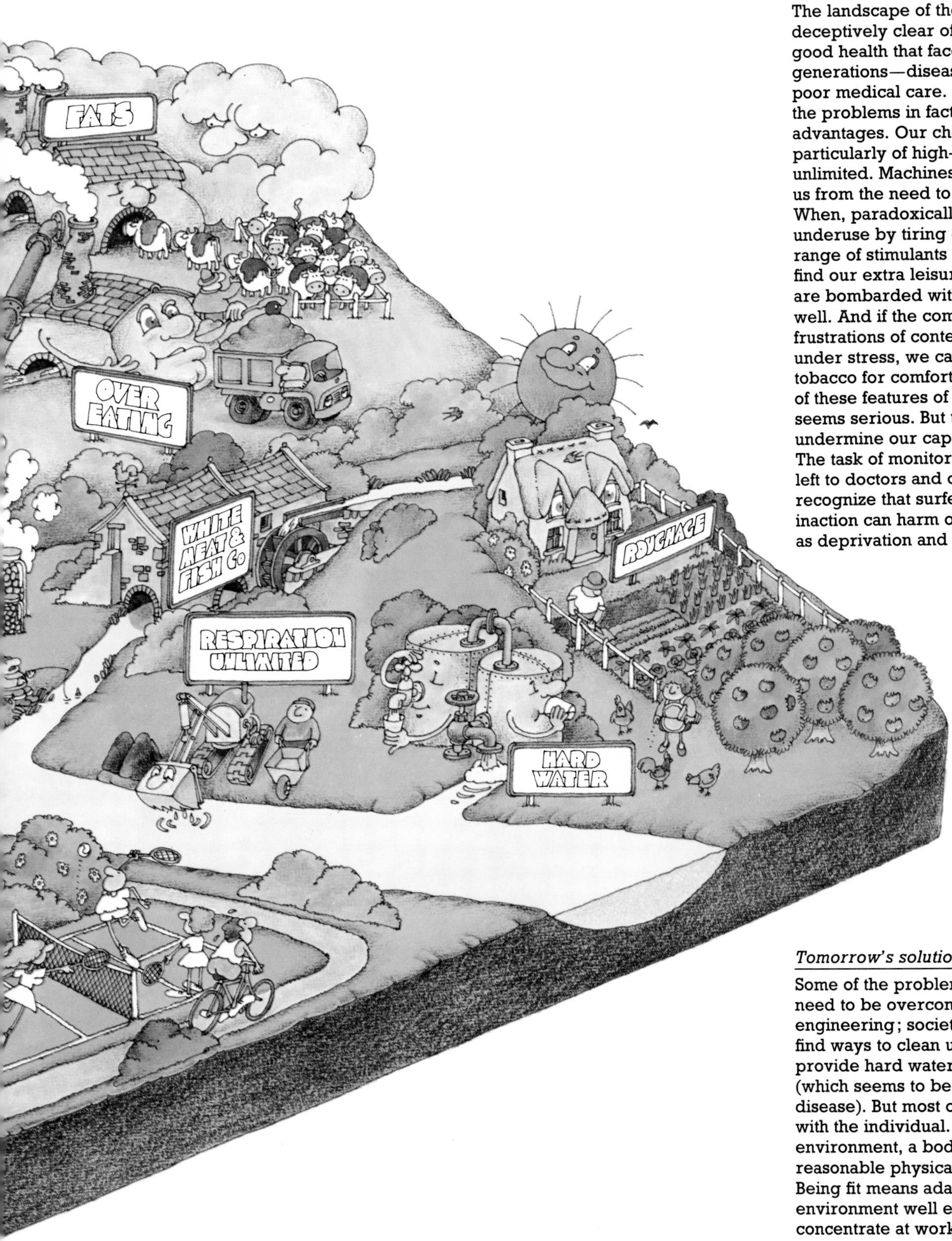

FATS

OVER EATING

WHITE MEAT & FISH Co

RESPIRATION UNLIMITED

HARD WATER

PSYCHAGE

The landscape of the Western world is deceptively clear of the obstacles to good health that faced earlier generations—disease, malnutrition and poor medical care. Urban pollution apart, the problems in fact often look like advantages. Our choice of food—and particularly of high-energy fats—is unlimited. Machines have largely freed us from the need to use muscle power. When, paradoxically, our bodies react to underuse by tiring quickly, we have a range of stimulants to pep us up. If we find our extra leisure time boring we are bombarded with mental stimulus as well. And if the complex social frustrations of contemporary life place us under stress, we can turn to alcohol or tobacco for comfort. Individually, none of these features of our environment seems serious. But together they can undermine our capacity to enjoy life. The task of monitoring them cannot be left to doctors and chemists. We need to recognize that surfeit and physical inaction can harm our bodies as much as deprivation and overwork.

Tomorrow's solutions

Some of the problems of modern life need to be overcome by social engineering; societies can, for instance, find ways to clean up pollution and provide hard water instead of soft (which seems to be related to heart disease). But most of the solutions lie with the individual. Even in the worst environment, a body that is kept in reasonable physical shape will survive. Being fit means adapting to the environment well enough to be able to concentrate at work, relax at play and have enough reserve energy to meet extra demands without fatigue. The main paths to fitness illustrated here— exercise, a balanced diet and reduced stress—are studied in detail in later chapters of the book.

Your work and how to stay healthy in it

The way you respond to work problems may determine whether you survive to enjoy your success.

Your occupation, how you respond to it and the conditions you work under all have a significant influence on your health. No one factor is decisive on its own: actors have a noticeably lower life-expectancy than farmers overall, but many actors will long outlive many farmers. The adjustment to work, the risk of occupational accidents and the general conditions of work will vary enormously but are equally powerful determinants. People at work may·run risks from lack of exercise, physical strain, stress, boredom, accidents or from long-term contact with hazardous materials.

Effective action against some of these dangers requires the concerted efforts of employers and unions. But in many cases individual workers can take sensible precautions to safeguard their health.

Anyone who has worked in a large office or workroom knows how quickly colds or flu can sweep through the staff. Taking sick-leave when necessary helps everyone. Bronchitis, too, may be linked with specific jobs or the social conditions that go with them: bank managers and doctors suffer less bronchitis than do men who dig holes in roads.

Sitting at a desk or work-bench all day long leads to problems, too. Working with

the brain is usually less boring than working with the muscles, but the long hours of mental stress and bodily inaction are potentially dangerous. All sedentary workers, from clerks to top executives, are more liable to coronary disease than their active colleagues. Smoking, diet and individual constitution all play some part, but there is plenty of evidence that physical inactivity is a prime factor. London bus drivers, whose work environment, income and life-style are similar to those of conductors, are more than twice as likely to suffer coronary thrombosis. Moreover they are more than twice as likely to die from it. Similarly, although less dramatically, post clerks are slightly more prone to heart attacks than postmen.

In each of these cases, the major factor making for greater safety seems to be exercise. The postman will walk a considerable distance every day and the bus conductor will have to climb the stairs to the upper deck many times each shift. If you do sit down all day, you should try to compensate with physical activities outside—perhaps taking up a sport or gardening—and by using every opportunity to move around at work, walking upstairs, for example, rather than waiting for the

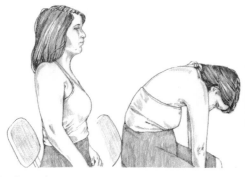

Taking the ache out of tension

Many people are unaware that their muscles are tense—aches and pains simply become part of living. However, it need not be so. Whether you are doing intricate needlework, driving for hours at a time or hunched over a typewriter or office papers, provided you are aware of where muscle tension builds up there are simple ways of relaxing. Here are some exercises that can be done without leaving your seat. The trick is actually to increase tension in the muscles concerned. Relaxation afterwards is then easier to achieve.

Back strain

Sitting in one position, even with correct posture, can cause an aching back. Slump down with rounded shoulders; straighten up·and repeat.

elevator; visiting a colleague in his office rather than telephoning him.

Planning your meals is important, too. It is not a good idea to skip a meal because of work pressure and then try to make up with a heavy evening meal. Light, regular snacks or meals lessen fatigue and keep the body's metabolic rate ticking over efficiently, reducing the likelihood of unused Calories piling up as fat. Workers need about 50 cl (1 pint) of liquid a day in winter and up to four times as much in summer. Rest breaks are another useful idea and even if they are not formally part of the day's routine many workers fit them in by turning to less demanding tasks.

Uncomfortable working conditions make for inefficiency and are a potential source of harm. Lighting should be bright enough to prevent eye-strain without producing glare. Machinery and job routines should be arranged to avoid unnatural body positions. A properly designed seat can protect truck drivers from the ill-effects of continual vibration. Surgeons use forearm supports for lengthy operations and machinists can often benefit from similar devices. The individual worker may adapt standard office furniture by tilting the work surface, using a cushion or footrest—

anything to prevent backache and poor circulation in the legs. Air hostesses and salesgirls should wear support tights and put their feet up whenever possible to lessen the risk of varicose veins. A manual labourer can learn the best ways of lifting heavy weights—the strain should be on the legs, not the back.

Mental stress at work can be more difficult to identify and cope with. Apart from the role it plays in heart disease, stress may produce physical disabilities such as indigestion, diarrhoea, headaches and possibly stomach ulcers. Contrary to the myths about ulcers being a complaint reserved for executives, they are widespread throughout the population. Stress may also contribute to semi-physical conditions such as alcoholism and mental illnesses such as anxiety and depression.

Taken to the extreme, stress levels play a significant part in life-expectancy. Actors, journalists and musicians are poor risks (but not as bad as coal-face workers, who simultaneously risk accidents and lung disease). Teachers live slightly less long than farmers, whereas doctors, who should know how to look after themselves, overcome their undoubtedly high stress levels and outlive farmers.

Many people like to feel that a job extends their capabilities to the full. But overreaching a physical and mental limit—and it varies greatly from one individual to the next—can bring problems. The idea of indispensability is among the most dangerous of all. Exercise, well-planned holidays and moderation in eating and drinking help to maintain physical and mental fitness. The development of strong interests outside work is the best antidote to obsessive fascination with a job.

Signs of anxiety or depression, shortness of breath or continual tiredness are warnings that you should avoid or change the stressful situation. Sharing the workload with someone else is one solution, shedding some responsibilities—perhaps by asking for an "antipromotion"—may be another or, as a more positive alternative, you may be able to arrange to go on a training course that will broaden your capabilities. Boredom—whether of the understretched executive or the lonely wife at home—may mean looking for ways to extend the job or find substitute activities. The worst situation of all—being answerable to several people with poorly defined areas of responsibility—can be improved by asking for exact instructions or requesting a transfer.

Long-term threats to health may stem from the materials used in a process or the working conditions themselves. Miners and other workers in dusty surroundings may contract pneumoconiosis, in which lung damage makes breathing difficult; chimney sweeps used to suffer cancer of the scrotum; many chemicals are poisonous—mercury and lead compounds particularly so. Even the solvents in typewriter correcting fluids carry some risk. Other materials—vinyl chloride, the starting point for PVC, and some forms of asbestos—are linked with cancer; high noise levels may gradually produce a serious degree of deafness.

Once again, dealing with these dangers has to involve employers, unions, scientists and legislators. Sometimes less dangerous chemicals can be used, sometimes safer manufacturing methods can be found or special clothing and handling apparatus introduced. But the individual worker must understand and follow these safety regulations—arranging for clean overalls because ingrained oil can cause skin diseases and even cancer; wearing protective clothing where provided; using air-filter masks and earmuffs where conditions make them advisable.

It is your responsibility to notice risks to your health at work. No job is perfect, no set of working conditions is perfect. But common sense says that you should enjoy your work on the whole and, overall, feel better for doing it.

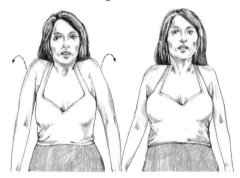

Shoulders

Sitting upright, circle shoulders in a forward motion, either one at a time or together. Continue the exercise for at least ten seconds.

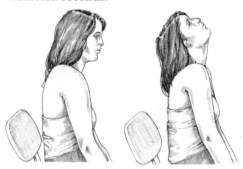

Tension in the neck

Bend head back and look up to the ceiling; hold for two seconds, then let your head fall forwards so that the chin touches the chest.

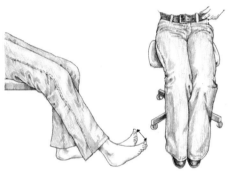

Thighs and legs

Pull thighs tightly together, then relax. Raise toes upwards hard. Repeat both exercises a number of times. Drivers can do them at traffic lights.

Arms and hands

Holding a steering wheel for a long time can cause tension, as can needlework or typing. Clench fist, raise arm and tense biceps. Relax and repeat.

The mysterious unity of mind and body

Health is a two-way process. Physical and mental links are closer— and stranger—than we often think.

Self-punishment without pain

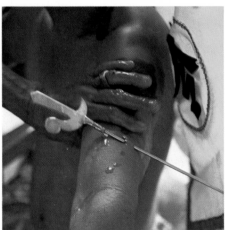

An Eastern medium lances the skin of his arm without causing either bleeding or pain *(above)*.

Whipping with knives, a Muslim ritual, draws blood, but is not felt at the time *(below)*.

When we talk about physical fitness and mental health, we tend to separate the two. We still think, as our ancestors did, of two separate parts to a human being, with the mind sitting up in the head, like a pilot in his cockpit, controlling the machine below. In fact, mind and body are inextricably intertwined. Achieving a state of "mind over body" is a familiar challenge—but body also influences mind.

One telling proof of this was recorded when two researchers persuaded some university lecturers and administrators to undergo hard, but not intensive, physical training. Half the men were reasonably fit to start out with, and half were grossly unfit. Many were worried that they would suffer heart attacks under the strain. But after four months all could run several kilometres quite comfortably and swim or play tennis or squash for half an hour.

The really important change, however, was the dramatic improvement in personality the men showed. At the start, those who were fitter were more emotionally stable and more imaginative, more self-assured and more self-sufficient than their fellows. At the end, those who had started unfit had gone a good way to catch up in their stability and imagination scores, but had overtaken by a very long way on self-assurance and self-sufficiency. Body was influencing mind. Physical fitness can thus make us all less neurotic, more imaginative and often more independent.

More has been known for longer about the unexpected ways in which the mind can control the body. Hypnosis was known to the Ancient Greeks, but was forgotten until rediscovered by Anton Mesmer during the 18th century. Hypnosis has a bad reputation, mostly because it is un-reliable as a general phenomenon—only ten per cent of people are deeply hypno-tizable, and another thirty or forty per cent moderately "suggestible". Hypnosis also suffers from a bad image because of popular fears about the "power" of the hypnotist. But such fears—that someone could be hypnotized to commit murder, for instance—seem baseless. People will not do what they genuinely do not want to do (unless a firm rational framework is built up for the entranced subject). For similar reasons, hypnosis has not provided many cures for behavioural problems.

Hypnosis has been notably successful, however, as an anaesthetic. Some mothers have had babies under hypnosis with either very little chemical anaesthetic or none at all. Even major surgery has been carried out under hypnosis alone.

The opposite of anaesthesia can also be produced. If the hypnotist tells a woman that he is going to burn her arm with a cigarette, and then touches her with the end of a pencil, a round burn mark will appear, which has been known to turn into a blister. Something very strange is going on here, which we do not yet understand.

Indeed, traditional Western science has been all too ready to ignore such phenom-ena. Understanding in the West of the more subtle interactions of mind and body was long obstructed by the orthodox medical belief about how the nervous system controls the body. The nervous system was said to be divided into two—the voluntary and the involuntary. The volun-tary system is made up of the brain and the nerves through which it controls the striate muscles—those that move the body about at will, as do, for example, the biceps in the arm.

The involuntary system, over which it was thought we had no direct control, seemed to have little connection with the brain. It controls the "smooth" muscles of the body and the various glands. Smooth muscle forms a wall round many internal organs, such as the stomach, and also all the blood vessels. It moves food through the body and controls things like flushing, heat loss and sweating. The heart, a muscle on its own, is another organ controlled by the involuntary nervous system.

The body and its involuntary nervous system is in many ways in command of itself—so much so that it can almost be said to have a mind of its own. This, indeed, is the basis of the lie detector. When you are under stress you sweat more, even if only a very little, and the electrical conductivity of the skin soars. Telling a lie induces a little stress in all of us—enough to show on the electrical record of changes in the skin's conductivity. Our voice can deceive; our skin cannot. An experiment showed how certain the body's own knowledge of reality is. Subjects were given a series of electric shocks and told that they would vary in intensity. All the subjects said that the shocks diminished in strength. In fact the shocks remained at the same level, and the response of the skin, recorded elec-trically, showed that the body "knew" this although the mind did not.

"Body knowledge" is a part of everyday life. Through much of our lives we undergo more or less permanent stress. Most jobs and much of family life involve hostility and frustration. We learn to cope with this through an elaborate system of social and personal controls. But the body knows, and reacts accordingly. High blood pressure, increased heart rate, recurringly and ab-normally high adrenaline levels, and raised skin temperatures (which may cause eczema) have all been identified by doctors and psychologists as the results of living under prolonged periods of stress.

There were thus two systems, we were taught—one that responds to our every command (within reason) and one that was

Mental causes		Physical causes

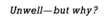

Unwell—but why?

Physical factors— inadequate diet or illness—are not alone in inhibiting growth. Children deprived of affection will not reach their physical potential either. Happier circumstances can induce faster, if limited, growth.

Diseases of the nervous system, venereal disease and addiction to alcohol are all causes of impotence. So, too, are psychological factors, such as ignorance and fear of rejection.

Backache, one of the commonest and most disabling of all afflictions, can be caused by lifting things incorrectly. The same symptoms may be felt by a woman longing for but unable to have children.

Asthma is a disorder of respiration often caused by sensitivity to one of many substances. Mental factors such as anxiety may, however, be largely or wholly responsible and may require a psychological remedy.

Skin complaints may be inherited or caused by disorders of the blood or by parasites. Blood samples will reveal such factors. But in many cases the cause is entirely psychological, stress being the most significant factor.

automatic, beyond the reach of our mind and will. So when stories of the strange feats of shamans, yogis and dervishes filtered through from distant cultures, they were dismissed as travellers' tales.

The discovery of biofeedback is changing all that. Using new electrical techniques to bring us information direct about how these various inner "automatic" parts of the body are functioning, researchers have found that we can learn to control blood pressure and heart rate, to relax individual muscles, even to control the working of the brain. This indeed is "mind over body".

Biofeedback is placing a tool in our hands to help the body meet the demands the conscious mind places upon it in facing up to modern life. This technique gives a person immediate information about his heart rate, blood pressure or state of muscular relaxation. Applied to the muscles, biofeedback has helped people both with general anxiety and with anxiety cramp of particular muscles, which they may have to use in an important task. People who have used it have found not only relief from tension in the head and chest or from "panic knots" in the neck and legs, but a most blessedly peaceful mental state.

It is control over the blood vessels and the heart, however, that is the most astonishing feat of biofeedback. If a person is given a light or a sound signal every time the blood pressure drops or the heart slows, and is instructed to keep the signal going, then he can learn to lower his own blood pressure and heart rate at will (although he has no idea how he does it).

All this shows that some at least of what we have thought of as bogus magic is not bogus at all—but it is not magic either. It does seem possible for a yogi in a trance to slow down the functioning of his body so that he does without food, water or air for long periods. It is possible for a dervish to pass a sword through both cheeks, and withdraw it later, without any bleeding.

We also have the beginning of an explanation for faith healing. Sceptics say "no broken leg was ever mended at Lourdes", and they may be right. But they are probably so anxious to counter the "superstitious" aspect of such cures that they are not prepared to acknowledge the cures that may come from the operation of bodily mechanisms that we are only just beginning to discover.

It is both startling and reassuring to realize that the mind is as susceptible to training as the body is. It has come as a revelation to thousands of people that they can, with the right information and the right techniques, exert far more control over their emotional state—with all the mass of effects this can have on the body—than they ever thought possible.

Growth: from embryo to adult maturity

The process is social as well as physical.

Human growth is fastest in the embryo, which between the third and fifth weeks doubles in size to reach about 1.5 cm (0.5 in) in length. This is a burst of growth that will not be equalled during the rest of life; it is equivalent to a toddler growing to a tall adult in the space of two weeks. The body's rate of growth diminishes; there is a spurt during puberty, when both height and weight increase rapidly as the newly active sex glands secrete the hormones that bring physical maturity, but in late adolescence this tails off and finally all growth comes to a halt.

The process of maturation has a practical fascination for parents. They can compare height and weight at each age with tables of normal values to assess progress. It is just as simple, but more interesting, to plot

the rate of change in growth. A growth-rate curve shows up well the extraordinary—though usually minor—differences in the rates at which individuals in a family mature. If plotted accurately, at short enough time intervals, it can even show how an illness such as measles slows growth, and how this is followed by a catching-up period as the body readjusts.

To decide accurately how well a child is progressing, a doctor will assess the shape of the body—the distribution of fat and muscle as well as the size and proportion of the limbs. He will assess sexual maturity (a valuable guide in girls is the first menstrual period, or menarche, after which they have on average 5 cm [2 in] left to grow). He will look at the teeth, and examine X-rays of the skeleton to see which bones have ossified and which are still growing.

The most important factor in growth is heredity: tall parents usually produce tall children, and short parents, short children. But firm prediction is a dangerous business. Whether the potential height is reached is never certain: many factors play a part. Illnesses may retard growth. Malnutrition or lack of vitamins will influence the result (a danger now almost totally absent in the West). Exercise is vital, although growing children rarely

need much encouragement in this respect.

A baby's consciousness of himself as a distinct entity, initially blurred, is usually well established by the age of three. Between three and five years, infantile sexuality makes its appearance along with an erotic fixation on the parent of the opposite sex. At around six or seven the sexual precocity of the earlier years disappears and the child shows a marked advance in his adjustment to reality. He usually becomes better behaved, acquires social graces somewhat more easily, and begins to develop interests and emotional links outside the family. Both boys and girls react to their previous attachment to the parent of the opposite sex by denigrating each other, so that a boy sees girls as beneath contempt and a girl thinks of boys as rough and unlikeable. The partial emancipation of the child from emotional dependence on the parents makes formal education possible, as well as instilling some sort of self-censorship.

With the coming of puberty, at anything between eleven and fifteen, the suppressed sexuality of childhood stages a dramatic reappearance. Masturbation is common in both sexes and failure by the child to accept it as normal—perhaps in response to parental disapproval, or the

Towards maturity at different paces

Boys and girls develop at different paces. A girl of 14 may be sexually mature, a boy's development is incomplete.
At five or six, boys tend to be rather aggressive, girls more co-operative.
Boys form groups, their interest focused

on competitive, self-assertive activities. Girls of this age are usually more introverted, often going about in pairs. By the age of ten, girls will play at adult

female roles, such as nursing; boys, needing to assert their masculinity, despise such activities and create more active, outgoing groups.

lack of reassurance in some other way—has been shown to correlate strongly with neurotic disturbances later in life. In both sexes, but especially in girls, there is a new concern with appearance. The crises prompt a return of the emotional conflicts and sexual rivalries of the earlier period, producing the moody argumentativeness and insubordination of many teenagers.

Later, between the ages of fifteen and twenty, antagonism towards the parents often takes the form of adherence to political or religious beliefs which enable the adolescent to act out his more conscious contradictory feelings about them. Even if this does not occur, all adolescents as they approach maturity have to emancipate themselves from their parents if they are to establish the responsible one-to-one relationship, especially with the opposite sex, that we regard as the principal sign of true maturity.

Average heights
(10 cm = 3.93 in)

2 years 6 years 10 years 14 years 18 years 22 years

	Girls	Boys
2 years	86 cm	86 cm
6 years	112 cm	114 cm
10 years	135 cm	137 cm
14 years	157 cm	160 cm
18 years	160 cm	173 cm
22 years	160 cm	175 cm

Male and female—how we grow

At two years of age a child is, on average, almost exactly half its final height. By using the table opposite it is possible to estimate, at any age between one and 17, how tall a child will ultimately be. Such predictions, however, are subject to numerous hazards; illness, for example, may retard growth and some children tend to grow in spurts.

	Boys	Girls	How tall when adult?
1	42	45	This table provides a guide to a child's final height. Take the child's present height; add two noughts. Next, divide this figure by the number in the column against his or her nearest birthday. For example, a boy of nine years has a height of 137 cm (54 in). Add two noughts to this figure —that is 13,700 (5,400)— and divide by 75. This gives his ultimate height of 182 cm (72 in).
2	50	53	
3	54	57	
4	58	62	
5	62	66	
6	65	70	
7	69	74	
8	72	78	
9	75	81	
10	78	84	
11	81	88	
12	84	93	
13	87	97	
14	92	98	
15	96	99	
16	98		
17	99		
Age in years	Average percentage of ultimate height		

By 14 girls look more mature than boys. They may wear makeup and show an interest in the opposite sex, idolizing pop stars and going out with boys a little older than themselves. Boys of 14, on the other hand, usually hero-worship other males, often sportsmen. They are still playing games in groups, although now this is more likely to be a sport, such as football. By 18 they, too, will dress to attract the opposite sex. Girls are more likely to get married than boys at 18 and have usually lost the competitiveness they may have had at school. Both sexes have now reached sexual, although not emotional, maturity and take the first, often faltering, steps towards a full, adult relationship.

Life-crises: challenges to adaptability

Crises are an inevitable part of human existence. If they are properly understood we can emerge from them all the stronger.

Times of stress

Some of life's milestones and crises are highly personal, but others—marriage, parenthood, illness, death of spouse and retirement—are common to most of us. Here are some differing responses by two very different personalities.

On his marriage, Mr A is tempted to spend too freely, thereby incurring future problems.

Parenthood imposes strains, not least financial. Anxiety causes a deterioration in Mr A's work.

Mr A develops ulcers and worries about them, aggravating the condition.

Perhaps the most traumatic crisis in anyone's life is the one we have all survived—birth itself. A new-born baby is not the insensitive, mindless bundle of flesh and bone it was once thought to be, but a responsive, developing human being. To emerge from a warm, safe and utterly dark womb into the glaring surgical lights of a delivery-room, and perhaps to be greeted with a stinging smack on the buttocks, may be the most violent emotional shock that most humans will experience during life. But other great trials face us all.

Adolescence automatically brings a number of challenges which, taken together, form a second major life-crisis. Adolescents find themselves painfully unsure. They will soon be expected to be adults, to choose professions and to prosper in them, to marry and undertake financial, sexual and social responsibilities; but as yet they are not fully equipped to master these hazards. Moreover, they are simultaneously plagued with more immediate problems, such as school examinations and adjusting to their own sexuality. To cope with this combined crisis they are in need of guidance from adults, usually parents; but because they are so near to maturity, they often find it mortifying, even impossible, to admit this, thus compounding the problem. Adolescence is a life-crisis that most people, with varying degrees of success, do no more than muddle through.

It is middle-age, however, that usually brings some of the harshest crises of life. In his twenties a man establishes himself (he is likely to become a parent and hold a responsible job), but he is still only a learner and subject to authority. In his thirties he will have advanced to a more senior position and may no longer be a subordinate. These years may well bring crises of their own (such as promotion, or otherwise, at work), but essentially, although he may often look back, he has a sense of steady advancement. Then, at about the age of forty, he realizes beyond denial that life for him is now half over. He becomes increasingly conscious of a younger, thrusting generation that will be alive when he is dead. And he often has to reconcile himself to the demoralizing certainty that he will never achieve some of his ambitions.

It is tempting, but profitless, for people to continue to cling to false hopes. But if these dreams are abandoned new effort can be invested in realistic ambitions. It may no longer be possible to become chairman of the company, but it may easily be possible to start a smallholding, for example, or to control a business, even if on a smaller scale.

For women, too, middle-age is a critical turning point. Children will leave home to make their own lives and a mother may feel that the main purpose of her life has gone with them. Moreover, she will know that the menopause approaches and may fear—wrongly—that she will become less attractive sexually or less interested in sex. This is no longer the case, for today hormone replacement therapy can alleviate many of the physical symptoms of menopause—irritability, headaches, nausea, hot flushes and vaginal dryness. However, the emotional problems (such as inability to accept that she is no longer fertile) must be honestly faced. Women with grown families should realize that they have the opportunity to find new interests and perhaps to take up former careers again. The native women of highland New Guinea, for example, seem to understand this need and cope with this particular crisis more satisfactorily perhaps than do Westerners. When her children leave home, a woman sets out on what is known as an "adultery tour"—her opportunity to have one last fling before returning to her husband and assuming the status of a senior woman of the village.

Again, retirement — withdrawal from money-earning work—poses considerable problems in the work-orientated Western world. An entirely new life-style has to be adopted, usually involving loss of former work colleagues, reduction in income and possibly a change of home. It is wise, therefore, that in early middle-age at latest men and women should start thinking about how they wish to spend their later years and prepare for them so that the change from full-time employment to leisure is a gradual rather than an abrupt process. Retirement need not then be, as the novelist V. S. Pritchett called it, "a fatal assault on the ego".

The death of a husband or wife often provides the most agonizing crisis of life. For a young person to lose a parent is painful, but with life stretching far ahead the anguish passes with time; to lose a partner, on the other hand, not only removes a life-long companion and support but is an awesome reminder of mortality. Many people cannot adjust to this blow;

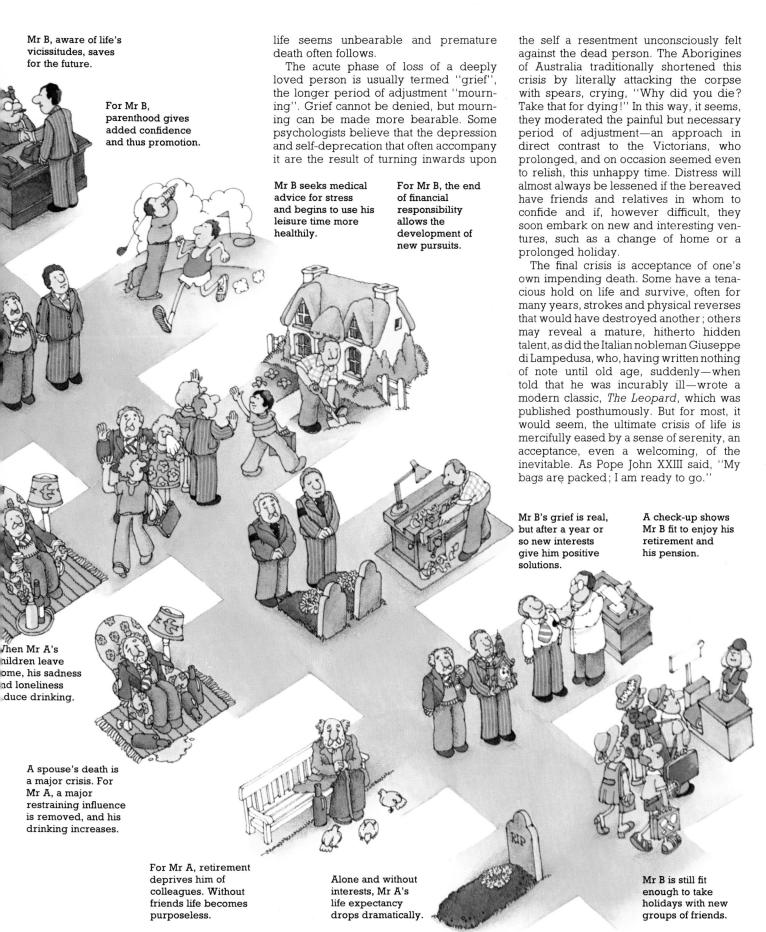

Mr B, aware of life's vicissitudes, saves for the future.

For Mr B, parenthood gives added confidence and thus promotion.

Mr B seeks medical advice for stress and begins to use his leisure time more healthily.

For Mr B, the end of financial responsibility allows the development of new pursuits.

When Mr A's children leave home, his sadness and loneliness induce drinking.

A spouse's death is a major crisis. For Mr A, a major restraining influence is removed, and his drinking increases.

For Mr A, retirement deprives him of colleagues. Without friends life becomes purposeless.

Alone and without interests, Mr A's life expectancy drops dramatically.

life seems unbearable and premature death often follows.

The acute phase of loss of a deeply loved person is usually termed "grief", the longer period of adjustment "mourning". Grief cannot be denied, but mourning can be made more bearable. Some psychologists believe that the depression and self-deprecation that often accompany it are the result of turning inwards upon the self a resentment unconsciously felt against the dead person. The Aborigines of Australia traditionally shortened this crisis by literally attacking the corpse with spears, crying, "Why did you die? Take that for dying!" In this way, it seems, they moderated the painful but necessary period of adjustment—an approach in direct contrast to the Victorians, who prolonged, and on occasion seemed even to relish, this unhappy time. Distress will almost always be lessened if the bereaved have friends and relatives in whom to confide and if, however difficult, they soon embark on new and interesting ventures, such as a change of home or a prolonged holiday.

The final crisis is acceptance of one's own impending death. Some have a tenacious hold on life and survive, often for many years, strokes and physical reverses that would have destroyed another; others may reveal a mature, hitherto hidden talent, as did the Italian nobleman Giuseppe di Lampedusa, who, having written nothing of note until old age, suddenly—when told that he was incurably ill—wrote a modern classic, *The Leopard*, which was published posthumously. But for most, it would seem, the ultimate crisis of life is mercifully eased by a sense of serenity, an acceptance, even a welcoming, of the inevitable. As Pope John XXIII said, "My bags are packed; I am ready to go."

Mr B's grief is real, but after a year or so new interests give him positive solutions.

A check-up shows Mr B fit to enjoy his retirement and his pension.

Mr B is still fit enough to take holidays with new groups of friends.

Ageing: the inevitability and the choice

The physical decline of ageing starts in your 20s, but your capacity to enjoy life fully can last almost as long as life itself.

The militant voice of old age

Maggie Kuhn, an astringent septuagenarian, leads a small group of Americans, the Gray Panthers, in a fight for the rights of the elderly. She campaigns for a much more positive attitude towards the aged and more medical care.

Medical science has made no breakthrough that will extend the potential maximum lifespan of human beings. The ageing process is as great a mystery as life itself. What medicine has achieved is an increase in the average life-expectancy. Because so many fatal diseases can be cured or prevented, more people than ever before in the developed nations can look forward to fulfilling their biblical potential of three score years and ten.

This also means that more and more people have to confront the problems of old age—and the problems are undeniable. Physical decline is inevitable; and the social position of old people, in the West at least, tends to be fraught with difficulties as well.

The process by which the protein composing muscle bulk is daily broken down and rebuilt continues throughout life. But, with age, muscle tends to deteriorate at a faster rate than it is remade. Age brings a decline in body weight: between the ages of twenty-five and seventy, muscles decline from nineteen to twelve per cent of body weight.

The physical decline of old age is the result not just of the decay of muscles but of a diminished capacity of the lungs to take in the oxygen needed to power the muscles. This process starts in the twenties, which explains why a thirty-five-year-old athlete, though his muscles may be in just as good a condition as a twenty-five-year-old rival's, will normally lose in a race. Other bodily changes—for instance in the brain, kidneys, liver, uterus, spleen and pancreas, which all lose with age a varying but perceptible part of their bulk—are uncontrollable. Such abilities as resistance to stress and to temperature

change worsen. The brain shrinks. The rate of decline is in part a matter of heredity: if you had four long-lived and slowly ageing grandparents, your chances of maintaining your vigour into a long old age are higher than if your grandparents succumbed comparatively early.

But whatever your inherited chances, there are ways of ensuring that, physically at least, you can live a more enjoyable old age. The best way, open to everyone, is exercise. Exercise stimulates the build-up of muscle, even in age. It is never too late to take up exercise (for details see pp 154–5) and some sixty-year-olds undertaking a training course after cardiac trouble, for instance, have within the space of a few months become fitter than they had been since they were in their mid-thirties.

The fact that the brain shrinks as a result of irreplaceable cells dying off often seems proof to laymen of declining mental powers. Not so. The capacity of the old to learn is not necessarily impaired. Much more crucial than brain size is the maintenance of an adequate blood supply to the brain. Recent experiments in both long-term and short-term learning among people aged sixty and upwards have shown that they can perform just as well as young students, especially in tasks demanding steady application.

There is no reason, indeed, to stop learning. In this the most important factor is attitude. Given the will and the encouragement, an old person can succeed

Preparing for leisure

Late in life, you could have time on your hands. Those who prepare for this in their 30s and 40s usually find it easier to fill their new leisure time creatively. Activities such as gardening, painting, rambling and reading can remain strong interests.

on a personal scale, and sometimes even on a national scale. One example is Alfred Wallace, a retired Cornish fisherman, who in his seventies and without any previous training took up painting. His remarkable pictures are now in many modern collections. But the point is not Alfred Wallace's success, but his use of his own resources and his continuing interest and hope in life.

It is a tragic fact of Western life that too many people lose interest and hope when they retire. Behind the terrible problems which retirement can bring is the problem of lack of previous constructive use of leisure. When a man or woman has spent his or her whole life working, without the opportunity to cultivate special interests, retirement comes too late. Those who have made the time for interests other than their job are often glad to have more of it.

These are a minority. Yet their determination and resourcefulness is a pointer to the future. The aged's only defence against dereliction and the habitual indifference of those around them may well be to rely on their own potential strengths. After sexism and racism, "ageism" is the next battle to be fought—so, at least, argues Maggie Kuhn, the leader of the US Gray Panther organization. Society must be forced to come to terms with its treatment of the old, and the attitudes by which they are excluded from social, working and leisure activities.

To such problems medicine has had little to contribute. There are still many

Old, active, fit and talented

A lifelong athlete, Scotsman Duncan Maclean, alias the "Tartan Flash", was still sprinting 100 yards almost daily—even at 91.

Helen Bradley, English illustrator and author, began to paint when she was over 60 to show her grandchildren her life as a child.

After he retired at 75, Bryan Latham began to study for an arts degree. He completed the course in 1975 at the age of 81.

Fred Streeter started a series of BBC gardening talks when he was 58. Forty years later, he was still lecturing to listeners.

theories about the causes of ageing. One theory suggests a build-up of faults in the genetic code according to which cells reproduce themselves. Another theory suggests that the immune system protecting the body from disease becomes less sensitive and begins to identify the body's own cells as invaders and then attacks them. Degeneration thus becomes ever more rapid.

It is quite clear from a study of those societies in which people do reach quite exceptional ages—100 and more—that diet and activity are essential factors. The Hunzas of Kashmir, the Abkhasia of Georgia and the people of Vilcabamba in the Andes, all of whom accept ages in excess of 100 as

practical, lead active lives on low-Calorie diets. The fact that numerous centenarians from these societies enjoy an active sex life is probably an indication that they are sufficiently active and healthy to enjoy sex rather than a suggestion that sex keeps you young. These centenarians are normally still engaged in physical labour at the age of 100 plus and their diet gives them roughly half the Calorie intake of the average Briton or American. Among the Abkhasia obesity is treated as a serious illness.

The moral is clear: eat sparingly, stay active, believe in a long life and you have a real chance not only of lengthening your life span but of enjoying it too.

What a doctor sees at a routine check

Part-psychologist, part-detective, the family doctor is trained to assess both the body and its owner, who may be maintaining it carelessly.

People who think they are healthy give little thought to their physical well-being: they simply take it for granted. When they are forced to confront the idea of their own mortality—when an apparently healthy friend of their own age suddenly drops dead, for instance—they may be shocked into action. They may swear to cut down on rich foods, or promise themselves that they will exercise more. They may even call their doctors for an overdue check-up.

Acting from fear—and perhaps acting too late—is clearly no way to run a healthy life. It is not simply a matter of prevention being better than cure. A cure may not be possible at all if a body has been misused over too long a period. For this reason thousands of companies around the world keep an eye on their personnel with annual physical check-ups. Medical screening centres, long established in the US, are now beginning to emerge in Europe as well.

There are two main methods of screening, both designed to discover any hidden defect in the way the body is functioning. A technique that is being used increasingly is a questionnaire—often one suitable for computer storage—itemizing every conceivable aspect of health. Family history, personal history, past diseases and history of any present complaint are all covered and the information can act as the basis of follow-up studies in later years. A more common check-up procedure is the direct personal interview by a doctor.

The number of questions and tests at a medical interview can be a little unsettling at first for an averagely healthy person. It may all sound more ominous than it really is. For the patient the best approach is complete honesty. Nothing he can tell the doctor will surprise or shock him anyway. And doctors develop a surprising ability to read between the lines. The text and illustrations that follow are the abbreviated record of a fairly typical interview. They show what range of questions to expect at a check-up and the kind of variations that often occur between the thought bubbles of a doctor and his patient in the surgery.

John Hardy is an archetypal business executive. He is forty-seven. He has been prompted to come in for a check-up because a forty-five-year-old colleague collapsed and died during a game of golf some three weeks earlier.

The doctor first introduces himself, offers a chair, makes some comment about

the weather to put the patient at ease and after taking some preliminary details begins his questions:
"Do you mind if I ask you some questions about your family?
"Are your parents still alive?"
"My mother is seventy-six and in reasonable health. My father died when he was sixty-two—heart trouble, I think."
"Any brothers or sisters?"
"A younger brother and a sister. My older brother died from a heart attack last year at the age of fifty-one."
"Are you married?"
"Yes, it's my second marriage. My first ended in divorce twelve years ago. My present wife had been working for me and we married quite soon after the divorce came through."

During the opening few minutes of the interview, the doctor has been glancing

rapidly at the patient's hands, skin and eyes, looking for obvious hints of diseases such as thyroid or liver complaints. There are no signs of anything too serious, but Hardy looks pale and overtired. The doctor notes indications of past emotional stress and the early death of father and brother—sufficient to indicate a family history of heart disease.
"Have you ever had any serious illnesses?"
"No, I don't think so—oh, I had to swallow

barium about eleven years ago after a bout of indigestion, but I went on a diet and haven't had any trouble since."

The doctor wonders if the barium meal was given to check on a suspected ulcer: it happened about the time of the divorce. Again he suspects previous stress.
"I see you are an assistant managing director. Are you having any special

problems at the moment?"
"Well, hard work's never frightened me. I worry about the company's future, though; we're expanding into some new areas I think we should stay out of."

The answer suggests to the doctor that bright young men are coming up the promotion ladder and threatening the patient's job position.
"Do you travel much in your job?"

often takes a long time to drop off."

The doctor has begun to come to some tentative conclusions. Slight self-deception over food; some vague worries; difficulties over sleep; fairly heavy smoking and drinking. These are typical reactions to

"A week-long trip twice a year. No worries there—I have a wonderful secretary."

The doctor wonders if his patient is having an affair—often a significant stress factor. In fact the patient's thoughts reveal a six-month-old affair with his secretary which has already caused some traumatic scenes with his wife.

"Do you smoke?"

That doesn't sound too much of a problem, but if it has been a way of life for twenty years or so, it could contribute to liver and heart trouble.

"What about your appetite?"

"Well, I like my food, but I try to be careful. I eat very little, but don't seem to lose any weight."

The doctor can see that Hardy is slightly

stress and often precede a heart condition.

"Do you take any exercise?"

"I wish I had time to do more. But I keep in fair shape playing golf and cutting the lawn at home."

"Do you suffer from any aches and pains when you exert yourself?"

"My wind isn't what it was. I get some shortness of breath running for the train, but no pain."

"That's fine, Mr Hardy, I don't think I need to ask anything else. Perhaps I could have a look at you now. Would you strip to the waist, please?"

"I'm afraid I do."

"How many?"

"Too many—about thirty cigarettes a day."

The doctor recalls a scientific paper he has just read estimating that smokers admitting to fifteen cigarettes a day usually smoked twenty. An admission of twenty or thirty a day usually meant forty. Hardy's nicotine-stained fingers could make this a case in point.

"How much do you drink?"

"It's difficult to say. It depends on business and pressure in general—I suppose I tend to drink more if I'm under pressure."

Again this is a defensive, vague answer. It may indicate a potential problem of alcoholism.

"Is that spirits, wine or beer?"

"Well—wine at lunch-time and a couple of whiskies in the evenings—then at the weekends I'll usually have some beers.

overweight and suspects large business lunches are partly to blame.

"How do you sleep?"

"It varies—once I am asleep I'm OK, but it

The physical examination usually begins with the doctor recording his patient's height and weight. He notes whether there is any blueness to the skin colour (an indication of heart disease) and he may use calipers to measure skin-fold thickness as an assessment of obesity. The condition and shape of a patient's nails, skin creases of the hands and corners of the eyes can give clues to the condition of the cardiovascular system.

(Continued overleaf.)

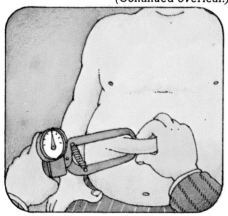

What the doctor sees/2

Hardy's eyes are examined through an ophthalmoscope, not to check on vision but because the eye is the only place in the body where blood vessels can be observed directly. A guide to the rate and

rhythm of the heart itself is provided by the pulse. This can also reveal hardening of the arteries which, in advanced cases, can be felt as if they were pieces of wire.

Hardy's blood pressure is recorded on a sphygmomanometer, which has a mercury scale linked to an inflatable cuff that the doctor places around the upper arm, puffing it up tightly to cut off the

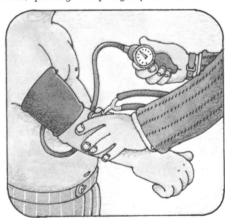

blood flow momentarily. As he releases the pressure slowly he listens through a stethoscope pressed to an artery at the elbow and notes the pressure level at which the pulse reappears. He also records the passive pressure of the blood in between the pumping actions of the heart. These two readings are called the systolic and diastolic levels. A good average would be 120/80 mmHg. Hardy's reading is a high 145/96.

As the doctor continues his check of Hardy's cardiovascular system, he notes the general shape and expansion of his patient's chest, as well as the size and position of the heart. He does this by percussing the chest wall with his fingers and then by using the stethoscope to detect any malfunction of the heart valves,

manifested by a noise or murmur. The pattern of the murmur in relation to the heart sounds is a good indication of the state of the valves.

Hardy's heart beat has a thrusting

character, indicating some enlargement. But a check of his ankles shows no signs of the swelling that could be an indication of early heart trouble.

The doctor then moves on to Hardy's respiration system, assessing the state of his lungs by tapping with two fingers to sound his chest (a low sound would indicate congestion). Through the stethoscope, he can listen to the sounds of the air coming into and being expelled from the lungs and check for any differences from the normal orchestration of breathing.

A check of Hardy's alimentary system

begins with his teeth and mouth. The doctor uses a spatula to press down his tongue so that he can see the back of his throat and his tonsils.

During examination of Hardy's abdomen, the doctor feels for his liver to see if it is abnormally enlarged. He also checks the spleen and kidneys and notes that no abdominal organs are ruptured. He examines the testicles to make sure there is no swelling and then makes a rectal examination of the prostate gland.

The doctor then turns his attention to his patient's central nervous system, assessing

his general muscle tone and suppleness as well as testing reflexes, usually by tapping the leg just below the knee cap. He examines the nose and ears, using an auroscope to look at the ear drums. A

blood sample checked by a laboratory will give a wider range of information, possibly confirming some of the problems indicated during the physical examination. A urine sample is checked for sugar and albumen to ensure there are no tendencies to diabetes.

Finally, a chest X-ray is taken and as there are already strong indications of

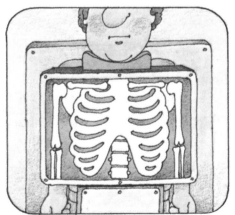

heart trouble an electrocardiogram is made of Hardy's heart beat to measure the activity patterns of the heart muscle. The ECG traces a graph that usually reveals any heart strain or disease and is of major importance if there is any suspicion that the blood supply to the heart itself is poor— a condition that results in pain (angina) after exertion. In Hardy's case the reading is slightly abnormal, showing early symptoms of heart disease.

With all this information at hand the doctor can sum up Hardy's state of health and advise him what to do about it. He tells him he must make some changes in his lifestyle. It has too many of the danger factors that add up to coronary risk. He is a smoker, his weight is about 9 kg (20 lb) more than it should be and his blood pressure is close to the upper limit of normality. He also has a family history of heart disease. Taken together, these factors suggest that he has a higher than average chance of having a heart attack during the next few years. Although at present it is coping well enough with the extra burdens it is carrying, his heart is slightly enlarged. This means that its efficiency has already been impaired.

Although anxiety rather than prudence has prompted Hardy to come in for the check-up, he is surprised and dismayed. Noting his depression, the doctor takes a few minutes to reassure him.

He tells him there is no reason to feel that he cannot live a normal, active—and pleasurable—life. The changes he needs to make are relatively minor ones. He strongly advises Hardy to cut down his smoking drastically and, if possible, to give it up altogether. He tells him how to lose some weight and reduce the level of

fats in his blood by keeping to a diet that contains very little animal fat. He also advises him to take more regular exercise but not to rush into any kind of strenuous programme. It is simply a matter of a few sensible adjustments. At this news, Hardy's gloom lifts and he leaves the surgery feeling the check-up was well worth the hour it has taken.

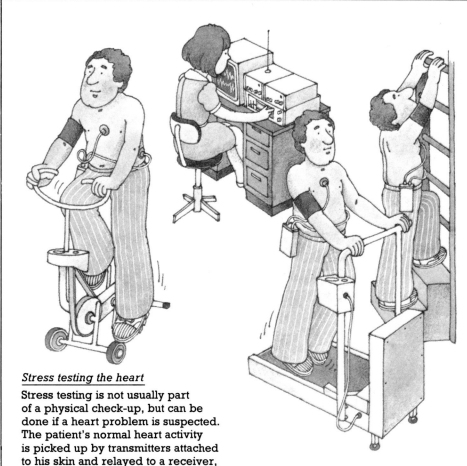

Stress testing the heart

Stress testing is not usually part of a physical check-up, but can be done if a heart problem is suspected. The patient's normal heart activity is picked up by transmitters attached to his skin and relayed to a receiver, where it is transferred to a visual print-out, or electrocardiogram, on a monitor. This is compared with a reading taken as he exercises on one of the machines shown.

The patient pedals a cycle, climbs on and off a step in time with a metronome set at varying speeds or simply walks on a moving belt at varying speeds.

Stress test results

The electrocardiograms before and after exercise can show up any heart abnormalities. The heart tracings shown are from a healthy person and are of normal heart beats. Deviations from these shapes allow the doctor to see that the heart is faulty. Any pain the patient may feel as he exercises will also be interpreted on the write-out.

After two minutes' exercise

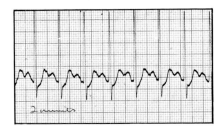

At rest

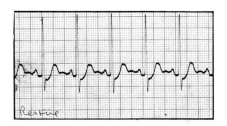

After six minutes' exercise

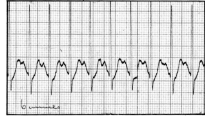

CHAPTER 2

Fuel for the system

The paradox of Western food: an excess of perfection.

Across the Western world, medical concern rises at the effects of eating too much rich food. The problem is a new one: never before has man had so wide a choice—or so regular a supply—of good food. The consequences surround us in a mass of ailments, from obesity to varicose veins and heart disease. But with even a basic understanding of what the body needs and how it uses its nutritional fuels, anyone can plan a variety of diets that will make eating healthy and enjoyable.

The elusive ideal of the perfect diet

The limited diets of remote peoples highlight the benefits—and dangers—of the West's varied foods.

Anyone seeking to understand the rights and wrongs of Western ways of eating may be baffled by two contradictory nutritional claims: that Western food is perfect; and that it is bad for you.

In fact, both these statements are true. Our industrial society does offer the most varied, the cleanest and the most readily available food supply in the history of the world. But our affluence poses a problem that we are fitted to solve neither by evolution nor by our own social development.

The quest for more than enough

From the limited local diets of prehistory to the modern supermarket cornucopia: man has continuously sought to extend the quality and range of his food supply. The diet of the hunting-and-gathering Kalahari Bushmen (right)—which includes nuts, roots, honey, lizards, impala and tortoises—is probably much like that of man's wandering ancestors.

Primitive cultivators use a staple crop—like millet—for about 80 per cent of their diet (right), which is supplemented by vegetables, fowl and grubs. Millet beer adds minerals and vitamins.

Medieval townsmen ate a wide range of meat, fish, fruit, cheese and vegetables (below). They also dried and salted meat and fish, which were stored in casks for times of shortage.

The problem is one of choice. The ability to choose well from such a range of food is not innate; it has to be learned, and few people are discriminating enough to make the best use of the potential offered. The problem may be put into perspective by looking at the varying diets of some non-industrial societies. In most such societies, there is little question of choice. People eat what is available. But despite the faults often imposed by natural shortages these diets are, in times of plenty, frequently appropriate to the body's needs in a way that our diet is not.

This is particularly true of the most "primitive" of diets, that of early man: there are today a few scattered communities of hunter-gatherers whose diet is probably similar to that imposed by circumstances on man's ancestors. Prime examples of these societies are the Bushmen of the Kalahari Desert in southwestern Africa. Although water is a continual problem in these arid regions, food is not. The women gather roots, berries, nuts, insects and grubs. The men go out almost daily, alone or with a relative or a dog, to hunt with bows and poisoned arrows. The poison may take a long time to act and much of the time hunting is spent tracking wounded game until the animal succumbs.

Other hunter-gatherers, like those few Hadza of northern Tanzania who still follow traditional ways, depend far more on vegetable foods than on meat for their daily sustenance. Hadza men, in fact, spend less time hunting than they do gambling. In their case gambling may be a social necessity—a means of distributing scarce resources, such as arrow heads, poison, stone pipes and pieces of metal, throughout the community. They depend on the women to gather the abundant vegetable foods.

Other societies which prefer a less nomadic way of life may get their food by the regular cultivation of those crops that grow best in the locality. In tropical forests, tribesmen tend fruit trees and grow root crops such as yam and cassava. More open areas, with a less humid climate, will support the cultivation of cereal crops. The produce of tropical root and fruit cultivation is not limited to a short harvest season,

but can be planted and harvested all the year round, ensuring constant crops.

Such communities have securer food supplies, but variety is more limited. Root crops tend to have a high carbohydrate content and a low density of other nutrients. Grain crops, on the other hand, are better nutritionally—but are more vulnerable to the vagaries of climate and therefore more subject to seasonal shortage.

A second type of cultivation is the "shifting" method, by which bush country can be used for growing grain crops—a way of life not in favour with the centralized governments of modern nation-states and one that is therefore rapidly vanishing.

Other peoples, such as the Nuer of the Sudan, have adopted an animal rather than a crop-based system. The traditional Nuer economy, culture and life-style is predominantly based on cattle, which provide them with milk, meat and numerous household goods. They even name themselves after cattle. But the dry savannah regions do not provide a rich vegetation and the meat diet has to be supplemented with grain (usually millet), fish and fruit.

Few Westerners would wish to rely on any of these diets. A seasonal shortage, amounting sometimes to starvation, may be a regular occurrence. Fresh vegetables and fruit may be available for only a few months of the year; wild game is a valuable source of supply but is always an uncertain one; and transport difficulties frequently prevent the effective distribution of supplies, such as surplus fish from coastal communities to inland areas.

Yet at their best such diets, which have often sustained cultures for centuries, tend to be appropriate to the nutritional and energy needs of the societies that developed them. If circumstances change, however, the natural controls vanish and the diet may become inappropriate. It has happened often enough, notably with the introduction of alcohol and sugar.

The problem is similar, if of longer standing, in the industrial world. About one-third of us—those who are overweight—have a diet that is simply inappropriate to our needs. From the consequences of our affluent life-style (detailed on pages 40–1) it is becoming increasingly clear that we must learn to select with care from the available food supply—to reintroduce consciously those controls that were once imposed by nature—if we are to match our health with the environmental changes we have created.

A world of choice

Today, refrigeration, canning, freeze-drying, world-wide trading and fast transport have given the developed world a variety of foods the year round. Food on the shelves of a British supermarket in September 1976, for example, included these products, originating on a wide variety of dates:

1 **Jamaican bananas (July)**; 2 **Hungarian plums (August)**; 3 **South African apples (May)**; 4 **Canadian packets of cereals (July)**; 5 **Irish peas (1975)**; 6 **American corn (1975)**; 7 **South American pilchards (1973)**; 8 **Dutch tinned carrots (1975)**; 9 **Indian tea (May)**; 10 **Ghanaian cocoa (1975)**; 11 **Brazilian coffee (January)**; 12 **Spices from the East Indies (1974)**; 13 **New Zealand lamb (March)**; 14 **Argentinian beef (May)**; 15 **English yoghurt (same week)**; 16 **French cheese (August)**; 17 **Danish butter (July)** and, 18 **Canadian frozen fish (April)**.

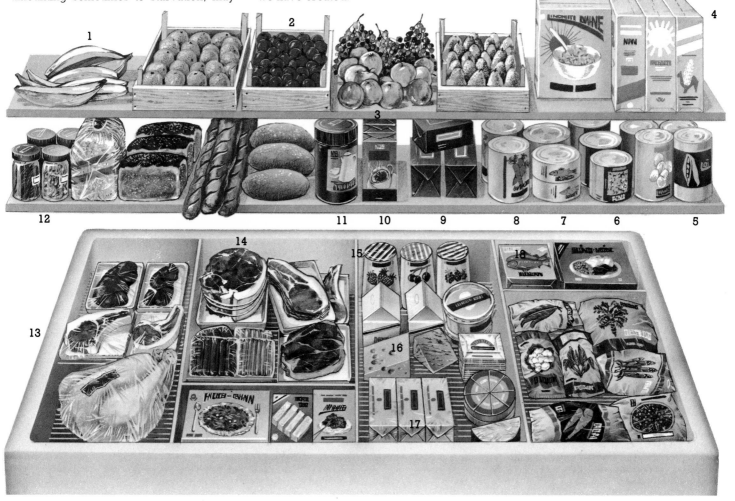

Body renewal —balancing the food intake

In rich nations, deficiency in any essential nutrient is comparatively rare, for the body has an amazing facility for supplying and balancing its own needs.

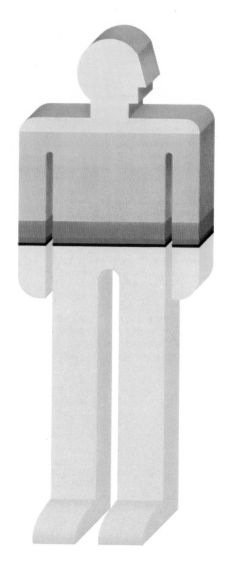

"Man", wrote the French gourmet Brillat Savarin, "is only the product of his own digestion." This sounds a cynical dismissal of man's mental capacities and the achievements of his civilizations, but it is nevertheless true in a limited sense. Physically, we are what we eat in that we cannot nourish our bodies with anything but food and drink.

But we do not change passively with the food we consume. Like all living organisms, our bodies try to maintain a constant, ideal composition. And whatever our intake—which amounts to about 35 tonnes in a lifetime—our bodies modify and rearrange the nutrients in an attempt to meet the ideal. Although the diet may cause small deviations, these are in a very narrow range.

Somewhat surprisingly, we do not know exactly what the ideal is, because the only ways of finding out are extremely complex. The most direct way is to analyse corpses—a macabre task that draws few researchers; the second, less direct, method is to experiment with animals, by depriving them of elements in their diet and extrapolating the results to human beings; and finally scientists can, in exceptional circumstances, use human volunteers.

This work has shown, first, that we are mostly made of water. Nearly three-quarters of the weight of a new-born child is water, and nearly two-thirds that of the average adult man. The proportion varies, for adipose tissue—fat—contains very little water (only about fifteen per cent). As the amount of fat rises in proportion to body weight from one-sixth (in a slim person) to one-half (in a fat one), so the relative water content falls.

Lean tissue, however, remains remarkably constant in its composition; if it varies it leads to malnutrition and disease. For example, of the 10.9 kg (24 lb) of protein in the average body only 2.2 kg (5 lb) can be lost without death occurring.

Next in volume comes fat. But this is also the most variable constituent, ranging from some ten per cent of body weight to fifty per cent in grossly overweight people. Some of this—about 1 kg (2 lb)—is essential; it consists of special types of fats, like cholesterol, that are vital to the body's structure. The rest is an energy store, and is not necessary for good health. One startling characteristic of extreme obesity is

The bodily constituents

◻ Stored fat	Water makes up 45 kg (100 lb) of the 73 kg (163 lb) weight of a 35-year-old man of average build. Fat and protein equal 23 kg (50 lb); the rest is minerals, vitamins and carbohydrates.
◻ Protein	
◻ Minerals	
◻ Carbohydrates	
◻ Vitamins, others	
◻ Water	

the amount of energy contained in the stores of fat. Chronically overweight people may store a million Calories—equivalent to months of normal food intake.

The other nutritional constituents of the body are much smaller amounts of minerals (six per cent), carbohydrates (a mere 1.5 per cent) and a mass of trace elements and vitamins in minute but vital quantities. Four grammes (0.14 oz) of the element iodine meets a man's needs for a lifetime, yet in some areas of the world the levels in food are so low that deficiency causes a characteristic neck swelling—goitre.

Calcium and phosphorus account for three-quarters of the minerals that our body contains, most of which is found in the bones. We need about 28 g (1 oz) of each every month, and a simple calcium or phosphorus deficiency is unknown.

However, a deficiency due to failure of the body to absorb calcium sometimes occurs. This can be due to items in the diet that reduce absorption. Calcium requires vitamin D for its absorption and so a diet adequate in calcium but short of vitamin D will result in a shortage of this mineral. Other substances in the diet may have some effect in reducing the amount absorbed, such as phytic acid in cereal bran. They can make part of the calcium insoluble so that it is not absorbed.

It is a similar story with iron. Anaemia is common, especially in women, not because of an absence of iron in our food (we need only an ounce every four or five years, easily provided in an average Western diet) but because of an inability of the body to absorb enough of it.

The body stores vital constituents with degrees of efficiency that roughly correspond to the quantities involved. Anyone refraining totally from eating or drinking would die very rapidly from dehydration. Although our body is about sixty per cent water we can only afford to lose ten per cent of this and our rate of water loss is so high (about one litre a day) that the average man would lose this in about four days. Relatively speaking, our reserves of vitamins are much higher; normally, we have enough vitamin A in our body to meet our requirements for two years, enough vitamin B_{12} to meet them for ten. Our stores of even the most rapidly depleted vitamins—thiamin or vitamin C—will meet our needs for more than a month.

The losses, however long-term, are nevertheless inevitable unless made good. They are the result of "turnover", the way in which the body continually dismantles and rebuilds itself. The turnover is measured in terms of a "half-life"—the time in which an organ replaces half its weight. Bone, for example, may seem fairly stable, but the calcium out of which it is built is constantly being replaced. The half-life

*One IU (International Unit) equals 0.0006 mg.

The value of a sandwich

A mixed meat and salad sandwich (*above*), with other balanced ingredients (*right*), if eaten three times a day, provides an adult with all his needs for weeks at a time, although adequate fluid would have to be taken also. Indeed, unless moderation is shown with the thickness of the bread and the amount of bacon and mayonnaise especially, this sandwich would provide rather too many Calories. As the normal diet is infinitely more varied, it is clearly quite difficult for anyone in the West to become undernourished or deficient in any essential mineral.

Weight (g)		Protein	Calories	Vitamin A (IU*)	Vitamin B_1 (mg)	Vitamin B_2 (mg)	Nicotinic acid (mg)	Vitamin B_6 (mg)	Vitamin C (mg)
100	Rye bread	9.1	243	0	0.4	0.25	1.0	0	0
10	Butter	0.06	72	350	0	0	0	0	0
100	Beef	21.1	164	0	0.05	0.22	5	0.3	0
50	Bacon	4.6	313	0	0.2	0.08	0.75	0.15	0
100	Lettuce	1.2	15	900	0.07	0.08	0.3	0.07	15
100	Tomato	1.2	21	400	0.06	0.04	0.6	0.1	20
10	Mayonnaise	0.11	72	30	0.0002	0.004	0	0	0
	TOTAL	37.4	900	1680	0.782	0.674	7.65	0.97	35

of bone is 180 days, that of liver a mere ten days.

Turnover accounts for almost all the body's demands. A child retains only a minute fraction of its daily intake as an aid to growth. As the child gets bigger, growth becomes less significant, but turnover increases and the bulk of the diet remains about the same. In growing from cradle to adulthood, a man can gain a net 10.9 kg (24 lb) of protein, consuming half a tonne of it to do so. From there until the grave he will consume one tonne more to cope with turnover, sustaining his early average of half a tonne every twenty years.

This may seem an inefficient way to work in mechanical terms, but it is extremely successful biologically. Our body selects what it needs from the food we eat to power its own continuous renovation.

The conversion of food into the structure of our body proceeds according to genetically programmed instructions of amazing complexity. It is this set of operations—collectively known as metabolism—that allows the body to convert a wide range of individual elements into a unified end-product. It may not seem so surprising that we can build our muscles from the steak we eat, for the steak is itself animal muscle. To most people it is, however, amazing to think that we can build muscle from a peanut butter sandwich or a boiled egg. It is equally extraordinary that we are able to build and maintain our brain not only without eating animal brain, but without eating anything apart from humble vegetable products.

This was the insight that Savarin lacked. We are not *simply* the product of our digestion: that is merely the process of breaking down food into its component chemicals and making them available to the body. What makes a body is the complete way these components are interconverted and reassembled.

The weight of a lifetime's food

During his lifetime (averaging 70 years) Western man eats 35 tonnes of food. This weighs the equivalent of 16,000 bricks—enough to build two three-bedroomed semi-detached houses. Yet, despite the consumption of this huge tonnage of food, a man of average build and height weighs in extreme old age no more than about 79 kg (165 lb).

The dietary ills of the affluent societies

Across the industrialized world, an ever-richer diet parallels the spread of once rare diseases. Heart disorders, in particular, are becoming common in the West.

In those societies that can afford it, medical science has all but eliminated the major infectious diseases so dreaded by our great-grandparents. Respiratory tuberculosis, cholera, typhoid fever and diphtheria are now almost unknown. At the turn of the century in western Europe, one in seven children died within twelve months of birth; the figure is now less than one in sixty.

Yet it is true to say that in most industrial countries a forty-year-old man has little more chance of reaching the age of seventy than he would have had in 1900. Modern men and women survive the hurdles of infancy and childhood only to fall prey at a later age to hardened arteries, heart attacks and strokes—the worst of the so-called diseases of affluence, which are in part related to bad eating habits.

Other less severe ailments cause widespread suffering to individuals and expense to the community. Several such diseases affect the digestive system—diverticulitis, constipation, appendicitis and certain forms of colonic cancer. Others damage the respiration—bronchitis, emphysema and lung cancer—and are almost certainly connected with high levels of air pollution and cigarette smoking. Tooth decay is a serious health problem in all affluent societies. Thus, the cost of dental treatment in the UK during 1973–4 was over £147 million, £70 million being for treatment of dental caries alone.

Many other ailments are the result of obesity. About half the adult population of the US and Europe is thought to be overweight according to the "best weight" figures for height and build most commonly used. Obesity (pp 52–3), which is a complex condition largely caused by overeating, but which may also be related to genetic makeup and is certainly related to the feeding regimes of early infancy, has a number of unwelcome side effects and carries a significant risk of premature death. Obese people have a higher incidence of metabolic disorders such as diabetes mellitus and are also more prone to kidney failure and to gall-stones. Finally, there are the purely mechanical consequences of carrying around too much weight: backache, varicose veins, impaired movement, breathing difficulties and arthritis of knees and hips.

Three elements—unwise eating, lack of exercise and smoking—figure prominently in connection with many of the diseases listed, and in particular with coronary heart disease, now the major cause of death in Britain, the US and most other industrial nations (with the odd exception of Japan, where strokes outnumber heart attacks). The way in which coronary heart disease is "caused" is not known with certainty, but on the basis of scores of studies it is possible to come to some intelligent conclusions. For instance, dozens of medical and insurance company surveys in all the countries concerned show a strong positive correlation between levels of fat consumption (particularly of saturated fats) and levels of heart disease in the community. There is also a high correlation between heart disease and diabetes, heavy smoking, high blood pressure, heart disease "in the family" and being significantly overweight. These are all considered major "risk factors" in coronary heart disease and we now know that all contribute to the complex overall picture.

Nobody can claim absolute certainty about the causes; but we cannot ignore the huge rise in the diseases of affluence. Most medical opinion throughout the world is now firmly in favour of making changes in our life-styles involving diet, exercise and smoking habits.

Of the dietary problems caused by "progress", one of the more straightforward case histories is that of fibre, which has been a steadily diminishing element in Western diets—a suggested cause of several modern diseases. The development of new milling techniques over the last two centuries enabled millers to produce white flour cheaply and in large quantities. In the making of white flour the fibrous covering of the wheat (the bran) is removed.

Added to this is the fact that consumption of bread (and also porridge) has fallen steadily over the years, so that it is estimated that between 1880 and 1960 consumption of cereal fibre dropped by ninety per cent. This is a large and relatively sudden change in a situation which, until so recently, had remained stable for many thousands of years.

Lack of fibre has been suggested as a contributory factor in several diseases, even coronary heart disease, though medical opinion on this is extremely cautious. On the role of fibre in one ailment, however — diverticulitis — there is near-total agreement.

Diverticulitis, which affects one in three

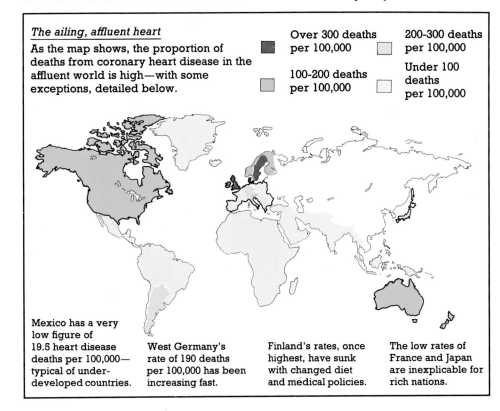

The ailing, affluent heart

As the map shows, the proportion of deaths from coronary heart disease in the affluent world is high—with some exceptions, detailed below.

Over 300 deaths per 100,000

200-300 deaths per 100,000

100-200 deaths per 100,000

Under 100 deaths per 100,000

Mexico has a very low figure of 19.5 heart disease deaths per 100,000— typical of under-developed countries.

West Germany's rate of 190 deaths per 100,000 has been increasing fast.

Finland's rates, once highest, have sunk with changed diet and medical policies.

The low rates of France and Japan are inexplicable for rich nations.

people over the age of forty and an even greater proportion of the elderly, occurs when small extrusions (diverticuli) form in the large intestine and become inflamed. The diverticuli probably form as a result of the muscular wall of the intestine contracting strongly over a relatively small bulk of faecal material and producing a high pressure which locally weakens the bowel wall. The condition can remain symptomless, but frequently the diverticuli become inflamed and, if untreated, this can have serious consequences, such as haemorrhage or perforation of the gut.

Lack of "bulk" in the diet can also give rise to ordinary constipation, which in turn may lead to piles and varicose veins as the sufferer strains to expel hard and slow-moving faecal matter. These common conditions are remarkably easy to remedy. Eating, for instance, about 40 g (1.4 oz) of bran a day, the equivalent of ten slices of wholemeal bread, can alleviate both diverticulitis and constipation by enlarging the faecal mass and by speeding up the "transit time"—that is, the time that elapses between food intake and its excretion from the body.

Many of the diseases of affluence are associated with the consumption of too much food in general and of certain foods in particular. These are detailed elsewhere in this book. But, paradoxically, eating too much food is no guarantee that we shall get all the nutrients we need. There are other deficiencies besides lack of fibre. There is evidence that some groups of people may be suffering "micronutrient" deficiencies, shortages of one or more of the vitamins and minerals which are essential to growth and metabolism. For the most part these deficiencies are not widespread, although fifteen per cent of women in Britain are affected by iron deficiency anaemia and the proportion is very much higher in some other countries (notably Sweden, where it has reached a level of twenty-five per cent).

Some of the blame for these essential nutrient deficiencies must rest on the type of diets now common in affluent countries, where a large proportion of our energy is derived from "empty Calories"—food such as sugar, some fats (hardened cooking fats) and alcohol, which supply large amounts of Calories but none of the vital proteins, vitamins or minerals.

Dangerous excess—animal fats, sugar and alcohol

Saturated fats, almost all from animal sources, are implicated in diseases of the heart and circulatory system. The "empty Calories" of sugar and alcohol contribute to widespread obesity, which may result in a variety of disorders and frequent eating of "indulgence foods" leads to dental caries.

Importance of fibre

Lack of cereal and vegetable fibre such as is supplied in the foods opposite leads to disorders of the large intestine and may lead to conditions such as bowel cancer.

Risks of unwise eating

The ills associated with affluent eating habits seem formidable when listed together, as they are around this portrait of an unfit man aged 45. Only a minority of people in fact suffer from any more than a few of these ailments.

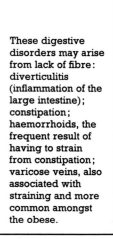

Obesity is associated with several problems: backache—from the strain and bad posture caused by carrying too much weight; renal (kidney) failure and gall-stones. Arthritis of the hips and knees comes in part from too much weight, unevenly distributed. Fallen arches or flat feet are also aggravated by too much weight.

A tendency towards gout is hereditary, but its onset is often associated with too much eating and drinking.

Recent research suggests that there may be some link between a diet high in saturated animal fats and the development of some kinds of cancer.

Dental caries (tooth decay) is probably the most common dietary disease of all.

Cardiovascular diseases affect the walls of arteries and the heart muscle and are linked with diet, as is cerebrovascular disease (a stroke), affecting the brain.

Diabetes mellitus is often hereditary but is linked to diet.

These digestive disorders may arise from lack of fibre: diverticulitis (inflammation of the large intestine); constipation; haemorrhoids, the frequent result of having to strain from constipation; varicose veins, also associated with straining and more common amongst the obese.

Calories: measuring "the fire of life"

The body regularly burns up Calories—but to control the process needs long-term planning.

The energy burners

The American footballers (*below*) are using up to 900 Calories each to power their tremendous bursts of activity during a two-hour match. Yet the spectators, waving and cheering, are using up Calories, too—about 250 each, or nearly a quarter as much as the sportsmen themselves.

Most Westerners are superficially aware of that new kind of malnourishment—eating to excess. Calorie counting has become an international obsession. Yet few laymen—even those who know they are overweight—could say exactly what it is that they are counting so carefully.

A calorie is a measure of heat. It is, strictly speaking, the amount of heat required to raise the temperature of one gramme of water by one degree centigrade. Food is actually measured in units of 1,000 calories—"large calories", kilocalories or Calories (spelled with a capital C). Confusingly, many popular publications speak of little-c "calories" when they mean capital-C "Calories", the style adopted in this book as it is the measure that is most familiar.

An odd way to measure food? Perhaps, but there is a sound practical reason for it.

In early attempts to measure the amount of food the body needs, researchers used straightforward units of weight or volume. But there was nothing straightforward about the answers. For instance, a man can maintain his weight on 226 g (8 oz) of peanuts a day, but if he eats only lettuce he needs 21.8 kg (48 lb) a day. If he drinks cow's milk, he will need 4.5 litres (8 pints); if he chooses sheep's milk, 2.8 litres (5 pints) are quite sufficient.

It seemed nonsensical; and remained so until the late 18th century, when the brilliant French chemist Antoine Lavoisier devised the theories and provided the facts that founded the science of nutrition.

In the course of his researches into the nature of heat and combustion, Lavoisier made two simple discoveries that together have had an effect on science comparable to the historical impact of the French Revolution, which brought his work, and his life, to an abrupt halt in 1794.

First, he observed that both a burning candle and an animal—in this case a guinea pig—use up oxygen (a word that he coined) and produce carbon dioxide. Air that will no longer support a candle flame will not support life, either. Then, he placed both candle and guinea pig in insulated boxes containing ice and measured the amount of ice that each would melt. In this way he could compare the heat they produced and showed that, for a given amount of oxygen used, both the candle and the guinea pig produced the same amount of heat.

Both, he concluded, must therefore be burning some fuel. Tallow was fuel to the candle; food must fuel the animal. However different they appeared, they were comparable in energy terms.

If we burn our food, therefore, we should measure it in units of heat, or Calories, the term officially adopted in the late 19th century. This done, man's food needs became simpler to understand. He needs nearly a hundred times more lettuce than peanuts to live because, when burnt (or eaten), peanuts liberate nearly a hundred

This apparatus—a container surrounded by a jacket of water—measures Calorie values by burning food. The energy released heats the container and its surrounding jacket of water. A thermometer is used to measure the rise in Calories.

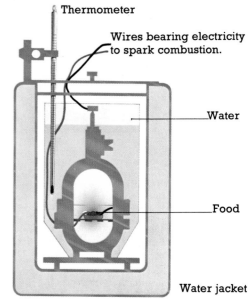

Thermometer

Wires bearing electricity to spark combustion.

Water

Food

Water jacket

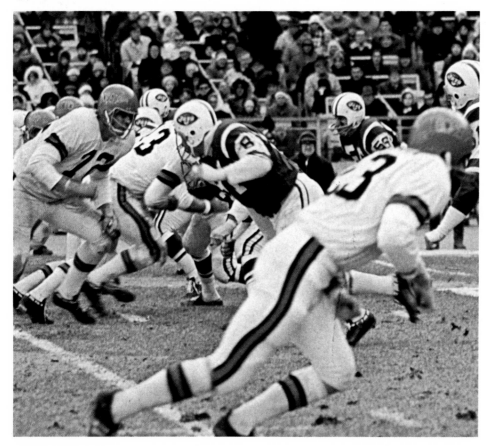

Idle v. active: the Calorie balance

The illustration (*right*) compares the Calories used in the typical daily activities of an active man and one who eats the same food but chooses a lazier way of life. Both need Calories to keep the body ticking over, but at the end of the day the active man will have used nearly 1,000 more Calories than his sluggish counterpart—who will gain an average of $^1/_2$ kg (1.1 lb) in weight about every five days.

times as much heat. (In this case—as with many similar ones—the difference is largely the result of varying water content: a lettuce is ninety-seven per cent water; a peanut only five per cent.)

How is the heat generated? And how is it used? Although the rate at which we burn fuel can vary enormously, we can never—until death—stop burning it up. Even when resting in a warm room we spend about a Calorie a minute. This minimal ticking over—the basal metabolic rate—accounts for about two-thirds of the energy we spend each day. Activity—work, play, leisure—accounts for the remainder.

For those who want to get rid of surplus fat, this is bad news. It means it is practically impossible to use up large amounts of stored food just by exercising more. On average, we use about 2,500 Calories a day. A brisk walk will use five Calories a minute—so a half-hour brisk walk every day will use up an extra 150 Calories. This is under 30 g (1 oz) of body fat!

You cannot, therefore, lose fat quickly. If you diet hard you may lose weight, but the loss will be mostly water, which is replaced rapidly when you try to re-establish a normal, regular diet. If you go on a starvation diet, you run the risk of cutting down on your essential needs for liquid and nutrients. Such diets are for extreme cases and should be undertaken only under medical supervision. (In these cases, the reserves of energy in body fat can be dramatically revealed. The record for a starvation diet—in which only liquids and vitamins are administered—is over a year.)

For would-be dieters, there is a corollary to this warning. The chances are that you became overweight quite slowly, perhaps over the course of years. The increase on a daily basis was minute, but even 30 g (1 oz) a week will add up to a very substantial amount. The increment can be lost again quite painlessly on a long-term basis by a small alteration in the balance between your intake and energy expenditure. For instance, to lose the Calories you have absorbed with a can of beer, you would need to play a hard game of tennis for an hour. But if you cut out only 30 g (1 oz) of sugar from your daily diet, you will achieve the same result.

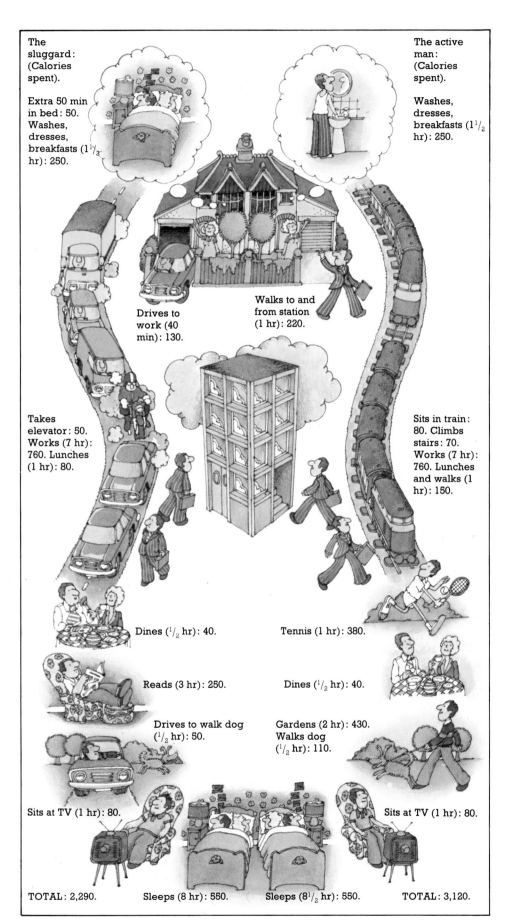

The sluggard: (Calories spent).

Extra 50 min in bed: 50. Washes, dresses, breakfasts (1$^1/_2$ hr): 250.

The active man: (Calories spent).

Washes, dresses, breakfasts (1$^1/_2$ hr): 250.

Drives to work (40 min): 130.

Walks to and from station (1 hr): 220.

Takes elevator: 50. Works (7 hr): 760. Lunches (1 hr): 80.

Sits in train: 80. Climbs stairs: 70. Works (7 hr): 760. Lunches and walks (1 hr): 150.

Dines ($^1/_2$ hr): 40.

Tennis (1 hr): 380.

Reads (3 hr): 250.

Dines ($^1/_2$ hr): 40.

Drives to walk dog ($^1/_2$ hr): 50.

Gardens (2 hr): 430. Walks dog ($^1/_2$ hr): 110.

Sits at TV (1 hr): 80.

Sits at TV (1 hr): 80.

TOTAL: 2,290.

Sleeps (8 hr): 550.

Sleeps (8$^1/_2$ hr): 550.

TOTAL: 3,120.

Carbohydrates: King Sugar's growing empire

The West has shunned starch and fibre in favour of sugar. It is time, many scientists suggest, to reverse the process.

Carbohydrates are the most fundamental of all nutrients. They derive from the process by which plants, using the sun as an energy source, capture carbon dioxide from the air. The compounds thus formed by photosynthesis are the prime sources of energy for cells in all forms of living matter.

For us, the most important carbohydrates are starch, sugar and fibre. Nutritionally,

they have had a chequered career. Until about 1950, nutritionists divided them into two sorts: available and unavailable. Available carbohydrate could be digested and, whether it was sugar or starch, one form of available carbohydrate was regarded as much like another. Unavailable carbohydrate—fibre, like the husks' of wheat germs—could not be digested by humans; it passed through the bowels unchanged and was therefore regarded as of no significance except as roughage. Some nutritionists announced airily that fibre-based breakfast cereal contained less goodness than the packet.

But since then there has been a very great change. The different forms of available carbohydrate are known to differ widely in their effects, and unavailable carbohydrate is now seen to be more complex and more important than was previously supposed.

To understand the change and its significance demands a quick survey of how carbohydrates are made. All carbohydrates in our diet are built from combinations of single molecules of different

sugars (in the chemical meaning of the word; the sugar we put in tea or coffee is properly called sucrose). Of the many one-molecule sugars—or monosaccharides—the best known is glucose, sometimes called dextrose or grape sugar. Fructose, from fruit, is another. These in combination build other, more complex, carbohydrate molecules—disaccharides, with two molecules, of which sucrose (glucose joined to fructose) is one; and polysaccharides, complex chains of which starch and fibre are the best known. Another is cellulose, found in grass; cellulose is very similar to starch, but the difference is enough to make it indigestible to man.

Both the disaccharides and the monosaccharides from which they are formed are small molecules as nutrients go. They dissolve easily in water and are readily digested or absorbed unchanged. They all taste sweet, but in differing degrees. Fructose, for example, is almost twice as sweet as sucrose, which in turn is 1.3 times as sweet as glucose. (By comparison, saccharine is some 500 times as sweet as sucrose.)

Sharing out the sweetness

Average sugar consumption is 50 kg (110 lb) a head annually in developed nations. Half of this is taken in tea and coffee. The rest comes from food to which sugar has been added, both as a preservative and—mainly in soft drinks and candies—simply to satisfy the demand for sweetness.

50 per cent in tea and coffee.

50 per cent in processed foods.

It is sweetness that has made sugars prized, with dramatic consequences. Until recently, sweetness was a rarity in our diet. A hundred years ago, Europeans consumed per head 2 kg (4.4 lb) of sucrose a year. Now, we eat it in staggering amounts. In Europe and the US consumption is running at about 50 kg (110 lb) of sugar per person per year. (In the West, this is now stabilizing; but sugar consumption parallels national income, and consumption in developing countries is still doubling about every twenty-five years.)

Another side to the dietary change in the West is that we now eat much less starch. Even at the beginning of this century about ninety-seven per cent of the carbohydrate we ate was starch. Now it is only forty per cent.

Nutritionists were slow in appreciating the importance of this change because of the chemical similarity of starch and sugar. In terms of nutrition, however, there are many differences. Starch is composed of simple sugars, but in long branching chains that make them more stable. They do not break up in the mouth, nor do we taste

Supplying demand from unlikely sources

The rise in sugar consumption in Western nations—most notably in the UK *(bottom)*—is partly due to the addition of sugar to a wide variety of foods, some of which *(below)* taste anything but sweet.

	% sucrose
Ham and tongue pâté	1
Mustard	4
Baked beans in tomato sauce	4
Peanut butter	7
Dried tomato soup with rice	20

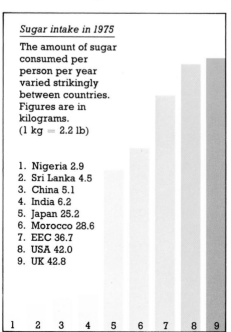

Sugar intake in 1975

The amount of sugar consumed per person per year varied strikingly between countries. Figures are in kilograms. (1 kg = 2.2 lb)

1. Nigeria 2.9
2. Sri Lanka 4.5
3. China 5.1
4. India 6.2
5. Japan 25.2
6. Morocco 28.6
7. EEC 36.7
8. USA 42.0
9. UK 42.8

the sugar molecules that make them up.

The nutritional shift away from starchy foods to sugar is of great significance. Although the slimmer might say of potatoes that they are "only starch" (in fact, their starch content is seventeen per cent) they are for most of us the source of between twenty-five and fifty per cent of our vitamin C. Although bread itself is regarded by some with anathema, it is an important source of protein, calcium and B-vitamins. Sugar, however, provides nothing but itself; it has what the nutritionist calls "empty Calories"—it is an energy-producing food with all the goodness removed.

Some scientists feel that the situation is a lot worse. Sugar, they believe, is specifically dangerous in a way distinct from most other carbohydrates. Our increasing consumption of sugar has been blamed for obesity and heart disease as well as tooth decay.

Everyone accepts the latter indictment and, while the first two remain controversial and the subject of research, they command impressive support. Impressive enough, indeed, for any sensible man to admit that however harmful or harmless 50 kg (110 lb) of sugar a year might be, most of it is definitely unnecessary and at best unwise.

Nutritionists are also concerned with a more recent change in the type of sugary carbohydrate we eat. Because of the cost of sucrose, food technologists have for some time been looking for a good, cheap substitute. They have at last found one in fructose, which—following the recent invention of new production techniques—can now be derived from maize starch.

Finally, fibre: most of the fibre in our diet is also made up of simple sugars, but joined in such a complex way that we cannot digest it. The removal of this fibrous component of our diet was one of the earliest achievements of food technology. There is fibre in the husks of wheat, in the cellulose of vegetables and in the pectins of fruit—all elements eliminated in modern processing techniques.

Taken as a whole, dietary fibre seems to be good for us. Doctors have cured people of diverticular disease by feeding them fibre, after previous treatments involving the elimination of fibre had failed.

Many nutritionists claim that dietary fibre protects against heart disease and against piles. True, the renewed interest in the subject is less than a decade old and some claims may prove to be exaggerated. But nobody suggests that fibre does any harm, and it is worth while making every reasonable effort to consume this roughage. It is easily obtainable as bran, or in wholemeal bread (which, in addition, contains more B-vitamins, minerals and protein than does refined white bread).

New sugars for an expanding industry

Until recently sugar cane from the West Indies and home-grown sugar-beet cornered the Western market. A possible alternative source of sugar—cereal starch, usually maize, split chemically to produce a syrup—was no real competitor, despite a ten per cent price advantage. The syrup, mostly of dextrose, was one-third less sweet than sucrose, which had to be added to give the required sweetness. In 1965, however, a way was found to convert much of the dextrose in maize into much sweeter fructose. The resulting high fructose corn syrup, produced commercially in the US since 1972, is as sweet as sucrose, cheaper and—though not yet available in powdered form—is more suitable for use in a wider variety of foods such as soft drinks. In 1974 the US was providing about a fifth of its sugar needs as corn syrup. Although almost all production so far is in the US, the discovery of new sources of sugar means that countries with a starch source can in the future fulfil their own needs. It is estimated that because of its relatively low cost, one-quarter of the consumption of sucrose in Western countries will be replaced by fructose syrup by the end of the 1970s. Its use should spread to the developing world, and the soaring graph of world sugar consumption is not likely to level off for many years.

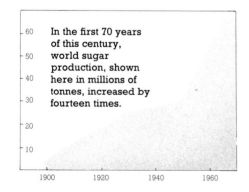

In the first 70 years of this century, world sugar production, shown here in millions of tonnes, increased by fourteen times.

Sweetest sweetener

A western African fruit called the Serendipity berry contains a substance 1,500 times sweeter than sucrose, which makes it the world's most concentrated natural sweetener.

Proteins: an army of specialists

If you are worrying about protein, don't: you get it from almost any food, and consume twice as much as you really need.

Proteins are essential parts of all living things. If the body is seen as a chemical factory, the proteins, of which many thousands have been discovered, are the workers. Some carry chemicals here and there; others place chemicals together to spark reactions; yet others may be quite specific in their function, remaining fixed (as muscle fibres do) to perform a special task. Our flesh and blood are proteins; so are our liver, kidneys, heart and lungs; so are the enzymes that carry out the digestive processes, the digestive tract itself, hair, fingernails and some hormones.

As befits so flexible a set of chemicals, proteins come to us from any living thing we eat—from plants, which make their protein from the nitrogen of the soil, and from animals. Indeed, in any reasonable diet, we automatically get enough.

Although all living material contains protein, which means that most of our foods

do, some foods contain more than others. Cabbage and lettuce are only one or two per cent protein, while peas and beans, which are the seeds that store the protein for the plant's next generation, contain as much as twenty-five per cent. Animal foods like meat, eggs, fish and cheese are very rich in protein—twenty to thirty per cent—which is why they are often called protein foods; cereals like wheat, maize and rice contain less, about ten per cent, but are still good sources. While root crops like potatoes, carrots and beets contain only around five per cent protein or less, they still make a useful contribution to the diet because we eat them in large amounts.

It may seem strange that rhubarb and rice, liver and lobster can all be converted into human body proteins. This is because all proteins, whatever their source, are made from the same twenty basic units—the amino acids—in varying proportions. After a meal the proteins are broken down to liberate these amino acids, which pass into the blood and are rebuilt into whatever we need.

It is obvious that a fast-growing child needs to eat protein foods—it is building new flesh and blood and tissues. But it is not so obvious why an adult who has finished growing should need to eat protein every day. The reason is that there is a continuous breakdown and replacement going on as the body routinely services its own organs.

An adult loses, and therefore needs to replace, about forty grammes (one and a half ounces) of protein a day. While a young child will not need quite as much as this for

replacement, since it has a smaller body, it needs extra for growth; so the child's needs are not much less than an adult's.

There are occasions when the need is greater—in a very young child, for instance. If the adult should be getting about five per cent of his Calories in the form of protein (which would provide him with his minimum physiological needs) a young child needs about eight per cent and the infant in the first few months of its life needs ten to twelve per cent.

A woman has slightly greater needs when she is pregnant because of the new baby being formed, but this is only a fractional amount each day. Similarly, if she is breast-feeding the baby she needs extra protein to help produce the milk.

In many illnesses the need for protein is much higher than forty grammes a day.

With all the different proteins in the diet it would seem likely that some foods contain the amino acids in proportions more suited for human needs than other foods. This is in fact so: protein is measured not only by quantity, but also by its quality.

The measure of a food's usefulness to the body in terms of protein is termed its "biological value". The figure of forty grammes a day needed to replace human tissues refers to a perfect protein—one in which forty grammes of the food protein equals forty grammes of human protein. There are only two of these in nature. One is human milk; the other is the hen's egg. Their amino acids fit our needs precisely: the biological value is 100 per cent.

Meat is not quite so good and we need fifty grammes (about two ounces) of meat

The protein quality of foods

The illustration shows the amount of any one of 12 foods we would need to eat to derive all our weekly protein need of about 280 g (10 oz). Protein value is measured by the total amount of the amino acids and by their variety. Most foods contain some protein, but some are better in quality because they contain more of the eight amino acids that the body cannot make itself. A balanced diet, with varying smaller quantities of the foods listed, would provide ample weekly protein.

Steak:	Frankfurters:	Mackerel:	Cheese:	Eggs:	Milk:	Yoghurt:
2 kg (4.4 lb)	3 kg (6.6 lb)	1.5 kg (3.3 lb)	1.5 kg (3.3 lb)	48	11 litres (19 pts)	16 cartons

protein a day, or fifty grammes of fish or cow's milk protein. Cereals are a little farther removed from our needs; if we had to rely solely on them for our protein we would need seventy to eighty grammes (three ounces) of cereal protein a day.

These figures refer to the protein, not the food itself. Meat, for example, is about twenty per cent protein (the rest is fat and water), so to get fifty grammes of the meat protein we would have to eat 250 grammes (about half a pound) of meat. In the case of bread, which is about ten per cent protein, we would need to eat about 700 grammes (almost two pounds) a day.

In prosperous countries nearly everyone gets about twice as much protein as he really needs, so there is little chance of anyone going short. The only foods that might lead to a deficiency are the fats, sugar and refined starch that have been separated from the original plants. These low-protein foods are disproportionately high in Calories. It is theoretically possible for someone to eat so many candies, so much sugar and so much fat that there is not room left in the diet for ordinary foods. Such a person might get down to the minimum levels—about five per cent protein instead of the ten to fifteen per cent the Western diet usually supplies. But they would rapidly become unhealthy for reasons other than protein deficiency.

Nor do we need to worry about protein quality. While it is true that the biological value of egg protein is 100 per cent and that of bread only fifty per cent, we do not live exclusively on any one of these foods. By the time we have eaten the hundreds of different foods that go to make up the ordinary diet we find that the amino acids in one protein balance out those in another, so that the average diet has a biological value of seventy-five per cent.

Even in those developing countries where the diet is based not on cereals, which are good sources of protein, but on foods like cassava (manioc root), sweet potatoes and plantains, with only three or four per cent protein, nearly everyone also eats beans, which are a rich source of protein (they are called "poor man's meat"), so that there do not seem to be many people who are getting enough in the way of Calories without at the same time getting enough protein.

Mixing proteins for quality

Most nations have foods—like the Scotsman's haggis and the American's peanut butter sandwich—whose constituents would individually be poor protein sources but which in combination are of high quality. The reason is that eight of the 20 amino acids that our bodies need must be supplied in the diet. Some foods, such as eggs, have all these amino acids. Other foods, although good sources of protein, are relatively deficient in one or more of these: lysine, isoleucine, leucine, methionine, phenylalanine, threonine, tryptophane and valine.

Haggis is principally made from blood and oatmeal. Blood lacks isoleucine; oatmeal has some. The combination produces a useful protein source.

In a peanut butter sandwich, the bread lacks lysine but is rich in methionine. Peanut butter is the reverse. The two together make a good source of protein.

Bread: 6 kg (13 lb)	Popcorn: 4 kg (8.8 lb)	Soya beans: 1 kg (2.2 lb)	Peas: 6 kg (15 lb)	Potatoes: 5 kg (12 lb)

Fats and heart disease: the cholesterol link

Dire warnings about the risks of eating fats need not come true: there are simple ways of eating well in safety.

Man may not need meat, but he unquestionably likes it. Most people, when given the chance, choose to eat meat rather than just vegetables alone. With increasing affluence, therefore, the nations of the world have consumed increasing quantities of animal products.

This does not mean there is more protein in the diet—so often used as a justification for indulging in juicy steaks or hamburgers. Animal protein merely replaces vegetable and cereal protein. What it does mean is that there is a dramatic jump in fat consumption. The fat is not merely where you can see it, as in butter or around the edges of steak, chops and bacon. There is invisible fat in all animal products—in eggs, milk and even lean beef, ten per cent of which is fat.

It is on this dietary revolution that many nutritionists blame the West's epidemic of heart disease, a complaint virtually unknown a century ago and now the cause of more than half of all deaths among people in the advanced industrial countries.

Fats constitute a vast range of oily chemicals found in all living things. About the only thing they have in common is that they are all soluble in ether, but not in water. In terms of human nutrition, ninety per cent of fat consists of chemicals called fatty acids. These define but are not the same as fats, although the two are often confused. Some of the fatty acids—the "essential fatty acids"—are vital to the workings of the body. Others are not essential, and act mainly as energy stores.

As with any set of complicated substances, there are several other ways fatty acids can be classified. One such classification is that which divides them into saturated and unsaturated. These two terms—now well publicized in the debate about animal fats and heart disease—refer to the number of hydrogen atoms in the fatty acid molecules. The more hydrogen atoms there are, the more saturated the fatty acid is. A fatty acid with one fewer hydrogen atom is termed monounsaturated: an acid with two or more fewer is termed polyunsaturated. There is a whole spectrum of such fatty acids, ranging from almost totally saturated ones like those in lard, to highly unsaturated ones, like those in fish oil.

In broad terms, though, the difference between them is immediately evident. Saturated fats, like lard and butter, are solid at room temperature; unsaturated fats, such as the oils of maize and sunflower, are liquid. This is because saturated fats come from warm-blooded animals, whose composition is adjusted so that it is just liquid at their body temperature. Unsaturated fats, on the other hand, come from plants and also from fish, which have a much lower body temperature; their fat naturally remains liquid at a lower temperature than does saturated fat.

All animals have a small requirement for some polyunsaturated fatty acids, the "essential fatty acids" that the body cannot manufacture for itself. But in man the requirement—less than 30 g (1 oz) a week—is supplied by so many foods that a deficiency hardly ever occurs.

What then is all the fuss about? Why

Fit on a fat diet

Until recently, Eskimos have followed their centuries-old practice of using fish and seal (both extremely high in fat) as a basic diet. However, since marine animals are cold blooded, their fat is less saturated than that of warm-blooded creatures. It is assumed that it is for this reason that Eskimos have not been as prone to heart disease as those in more developed areas. But with the coming of Western foods, deaths from heart disease have increased.

should anyone be advised to cut down on saturates and instead eat polyunsaturates?

The answer involves that villain of popular nutrition, cholesterol. Cholesterol is a special kind of fat—one of the few that does not contain fatty acid. It is a natural and important constituent of the body—used, for instance, in building brain tissue and sex hormones. It is made in the liver and is normally transported in the blood to the tissues where it is needed. We make about 30 g (1 oz) of cholesterol a month in the body. We do not need to consume any more of it to supply our needs, but we get, on average, about 7 g (0.25 oz) more from our diet. This is known as dietary cholesterol and is found in all animal foods in small amounts (most dramatically in eggs). It usually makes up less than one per cent of the weight of the fat in our diet.

It seems probable that the saturated fats and the extra cholesterol in animal fats interfere in some way with the body's regulation of its cholesterol supply. Too much of it gets into the blood stream. Once there, it begins to fur up arteries. In places, a fatty streak develops, which ulcerates, and finally forms scars that make up an atherosclerotic plaque.

Until scarring occurs, the process is reversible. Thereafter, degeneration can be stopped but complete repair is not possible. If nothing is done, the plaque gradually enlarges, and more plaques develop. Then, characteristically in middle age, a blood clot builds up around one of the plaques, drastically narrowing the artery. If that clot blocks an artery supplying blood directly to the heart, the heart is starved of oxygen, and goes into spasm. At best, it is damaged and recovers; at worst it stops beating.

It is this process that has been identified in numerous medical reports from industrialized nations as a prime cause of heart disease and heart failure. Communities that consume little dietary cholesterol and little saturated fat do not suffer from heart disease. But in the West, the plaques that lead to heart attacks are found in some form in most thirty-year-olds, in significant numbers in twenty-year-olds, and even, occasionally, in children.

The actual causal relationships between fats and cholesterol in this process are not yet known for certain, but much evidence suggests that the overwhelming factor in the development of the plaque is the level of blood cholesterol. The less cholesterol we consume, and the more we replace it with unsaturated fats, the more likely it seems that our blood cholesterol will stay at its ideal level. In the young (children most especially, but also adolescents and even the middle-aged) such a change in diet will almost certainly help prevent heart disease in later life.

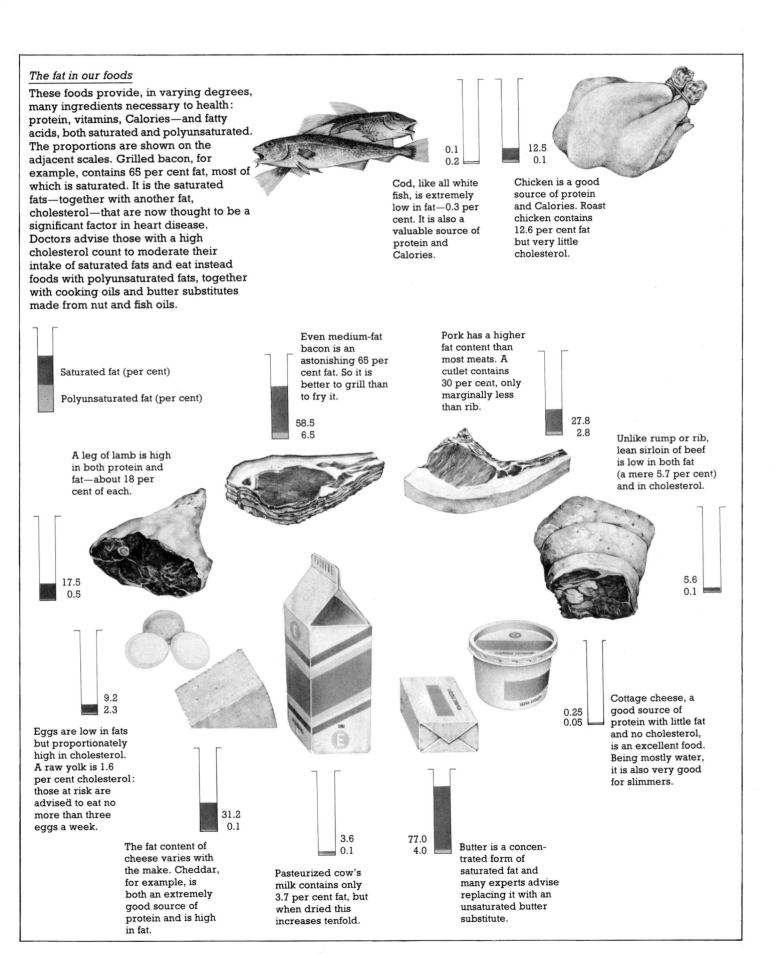

The fat in our foods

These foods provide, in varying degrees, many ingredients necessary to health: protein, vitamins, Calories—and fatty acids, both saturated and polyunsaturated. The proportions are shown on the adjacent scales. Grilled bacon, for example, contains 65 per cent fat, most of which is saturated. It is the saturated fats—together with another fat, cholesterol—that are now thought to be a significant factor in heart disease. Doctors advise those with a high cholesterol count to moderate their intake of saturated fats and eat instead foods with polyunsaturated fats, together with cooking oils and butter substitutes made from nut and fish oils.

0.1
0.2

Cod, like all white fish, is extremely low in fat—0.3 per cent. It is also a valuable source of protein and Calories.

12.5
0.1

Chicken is a good source of protein and Calories. Roast chicken contains 12.6 per cent fat but very little cholesterol.

Saturated fat (per cent)

Polyunsaturated fat (per cent)

Even medium-fat bacon is an astonishing 65 per cent fat. So it is better to grill than to fry it.

58.5
6.5

Pork has a higher fat content than most meats. A cutlet contains 30 per cent, only marginally less than rib.

27.8
2.8

Unlike rump or rib, lean sirloin of beef is low in both fat (a mere 5.7 per cent) and in cholesterol.

A leg of lamb is high in both protein and fat—about 18 per cent of each.

17.5
0.5

5.6
0.1

9.2
2.3

Eggs are low in fats but proportionately high in cholesterol. A raw yolk is 1.6 per cent cholesterol: those at risk are advised to eat no more than three eggs a week.

31.2
0.1

The fat content of cheese varies with the make. Cheddar, for example, is both an extremely good source of protein and is high in fat.

0.25
0.05

Cottage cheese, a good source of protein with little fat and no cholesterol, is an excellent food. Being mostly water, it is also very good for slimmers.

3.6
0.1

Pasteurized cow's milk contains only 3.7 per cent fat, but when dried this increases tenfold.

77.0
4.0

Butter is a concentrated form of saturated fat and many experts advise replacing it with an unsaturated butter substitute.

Vitamins and minerals: vital in low doses

Perfect health needs only minute amounts of these essential substances. A balanced diet provides more than enough.

Sugar was once jokingly defined as the stuff that makes your tea bitter if you forget to put it in. Vitamins and minerals can perhaps be defined in a similar way ("they make you ill if you don't eat them") with one major difference: you can always avoid sugar, but it would be almost impossible to avoid getting an adequate supply of vitamins, even if the diet is deficient in other respects.

Yet many people are afraid of just that. Because vitamins and minerals are vital to health, many people believe that eating them to excess will make them feel extra well. It doesn't. Except in rare cases of medical need, that early morning multi-vitamin tablet or the daily mineral tonic contribute nothing to your health.

True, a small extra dose of most vitamins and minerals will usually do no harm. But occasionally a large dose will. One famous example is that of a group of Arctic explorers who ate too much polar bear liver—and suffered severely as a result of

an overdose of vitamin A. Polar bear liver contains up to 100 times as much vitamin A as calf liver, and a single moderate meal of it would provide enough to last a lifetime.

Of more immediate concern are the cases of vitamin A poisoning that occur in infants—overdose through ignorance, misguided enthusiasm or accidental access to the family vitamin pills. In infants, the iron tonics—which are of dubious benefit even to adults—can actually be toxic.

So why are packaged vitamins and minerals so vigorously sold? Mainly because of the effect they have on the imagination. Their tiny amounts seem positively magical in their effects. Our daily requirements for both vitamins and minerals amount, on average, to only about half a gramme each. Yet to be deficient in them is to invite an amazing array of diseases: beriberi, scurvy, night blindness, rickets, haemorrhaging, skin lesions and anaemia.

The existence of vitamins had been

Product pressure to buy vitamins

The chart (right) shows how easy it is in a balanced diet to obtain adequate vitamins. Consumers need not be overimpressed by the emphasis on vitamin-enrichment in supermarket food labels such as these:

Instant fruit drink—enriched with vitamin C. A small glass "will provide your daily need for this vitamin".
Rolled oats—oatmeal and "vitamin nourishment for the children". With

added B vitamins "vital for growth".
Vitamin-enriched crispbread—niacin "for skin and nerves", thiamin "for correct use of carbohydrates in the body" and riboflavin "for normal growth".

hinted at in the 18th century, when James Lind cured the British Navy of scurvy—which killed far more sailors than did Britain's enemies—by making compulsory the consumption of lemon juice. This revolutionized shipboard life, enabling voyages of many months to be undertaken without danger. But it was not until the 20th century that the relationship between scurvy and citrus fruits was defined.

Then, in the 1890s, a Dutch scientist called Christian Eijkman, working in Indonesia on beriberi, discovered that he could produce this disease in chickens simply by restricting their diet to the polished rice on which most of the people in the area were subsisting. If he added the polishings, or husks, the disease was cured. Clearly, there was something vital being omitted from polished rice.

A Polish biochemist, Casimir Funk, proposed that there was just one vital factor, which he suggested was a chemical called an amine. His term—vital amine or "vitamine"—stuck: even when a whole succession of factors was discovered, the name (without the final "e") was applied to them all.

From then on vitamins became a popular scientific craze. Between 1915 and 1945 more than fifty vitamins were identified, some correctly, most wrongly.

Terminological chaos ensued. The original "vitamine" was shown quickly to be two—one of which was fat-soluble, the other water-soluble. The vitamins were termed A and B. Soon, C and D joined the collection, but meanwhile B was shown to be of several kinds, which were naturally termed B_1, B_2, and on up to B_{20}. The same thing happened in turn to the other groups.

The numbers have now been reduced to twelve, but the effects of the early exuberance of classification are still with us. Of the series of Bs, only B_1, B_2, B_6 and B_{12} turned out to be separate vitamins, each of which is indeed needed. As the numbered chemicals became better understood, some acquired one or more names. Nicotinic acid, nicotinamide, aneurin, pellagra-preventing factor, vitamin P-P, antiblacktongue factor are all different names for the same thing. Vitamin H is the same as biotin or vitamin B, and ascorbic acid is vitamin C.

It is now known that vitamins are not a group of closely related chemicals. The only thing they have in common is that we need them in tiny amounts, so they are more frequently referred to by name than by letters and numbers. For example, vitamin B_1 is more often called thiamin and vitamin C ascorbic acid.

Vitamins are seen to be less earth shattering now than their mythology once suggested. The wise consumer trusts his food rather than his pharmacy to supply the vitamins he needs. A wise consumer is one who eats a varied diet and so obtains all the different vitamins. So while it is not usually necessary to take vitamin tablets, they can be regarded as an insurance policy if the diet is limited. If a person's diet is wrong enough to make the doctor diagnose a lack of vitamins, there is likely to be a deeper reason for the deficiency.

What is true for vitamins applies also to minerals. These, the salts in our diet, are not surrounded by so great a mythology as vitamins, probably because their discovery made less of a stir.

Some minerals are of practical importance. Iron deficiency anaemia, for example, does occur in women. An insufficiency of fluoride does decrease the resistance of dental enamel to tooth decay, and in some areas a lack of iodine in the food gives rise to goitre.

There is no evidence, however, that we need to institute a widespread programme of taking mineral supplements. Nor is there any but psychological value in the mineral waters and salt mixes so widely on sale as cures for everything from lassitude to rheumatism.

So if you eat a normal range of foods it is highly unlikely that you will be short of vitamins or minerals.

The booming vitamin industry

Affluent peoples consume vast numbers of vitamin tablets each year. In the UK in 1975 one-quarter of 1,500 tonnes of vitamins produced was sold as tablets.

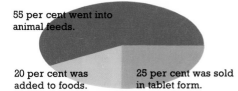

55 per cent went into animal feeds.

20 per cent was added to foods.

25 per cent was sold in tablet form.

A guide to your vitamin requirements			
Vitamins: Other names	Good sources	Daily requirement in mg (1 oz = 2.8 mg)	Facts of interest
A Retinol and carotene	Liver, fish oils, eggs, milk, butter, enriched margarine	0.75 (e.g. 2 eggs)	Toxic in excess as stored in the liver. Not destroyed in cooking
K Menadione	Green plants	Not established	Made by bacteria in the intestine
B_1 Thiamin	Yeast, liver, pork, wholemeal cereal	1.3	Requirement higher with increase in carbohydrate intake
E Tocopherol	Vegetable oils	30	
D Calciferol	Fatty fish, eggs, butter, enriched margarine	0.01	Also made by the action of sunlight on the skin
B_2 Riboflavin	Milk, liver, meat, yeast	1.4	Requirement higher with increase in protein intake
Nicotinic acid or niacin (no number or letter)	Liver, meat, nuts, legumes, yeast, wholemeal cereals	17	Can be made from the amino acid tryptophan
B_6 Pyridoxine	Most foods	2	
Bc Folic acid	Liver, green vegetables, yeast	0.4	Deficiency may occur in pregnancy
B_{12} Cyanobalamin	Animal foods	0.005	Dietary deficiency very rare
Pantothenic acid	Nearly all foods	10	Never a problem
C Ascorbic acid	Fruit and vegetables	60 (1 orange)	Much is lost in cooking
H Biotin	Liver, eggs, nuts, yeast, cereal, vegetables	Low	Some made by bacteria in the intestine. Deficiency never a problem

Obesity: the 20th-century disease

Being overweight may not be a cause of death in itself, but it is a proven way of shortening your life.

If you are overweight, you come within the definition of obesity. It is the most common nutritional disorder in modern Western society, where it affects about fifty per cent of the adult population. Its cause is simple: more energy is taken as food than is expended—or, more simply, you eat more than you need. The excess energy is laid down as fat.

Beyond this definition, however, matters become a little more complicated. By how much are you overweight? Direct measurement of body fat is difficult—it involves complex weighing procedures to assess the relative amounts of bone, muscle, fat and everything else. Body weight is usually taken as the basic criterion. Tables of "desirable" or "ideal" weights are based on the hard statistics of

The tubbiest twins in the world

Benny and Billy McGuire, US professional wrestlers, weigh an astonishing 300 and 259 kg (660 and 570 lb) respectively. They each eat about 1 kg (2 lb) of meat and drink a bucket of water daily.

life insurance companies, themselves related to the average survival rates of millions of individuals. The tables most commonly used are those published by the Metropolitan Life Insurance Company of the US. These were originally very arbitrary scales, relating to no more than weight and height. They were extensively revised after US military authorities used them to assess recruits—and found they were rejecting most of the athletes in their intake, because athletes tend to be abnormally bulky for their height. Since the weights will overestimate the degree of fat in muscular individuals and underestimate adiposity in women over sixty years of age, the tables now allow for three frame sizes—small, medium and large. But still the tables do not indicate how the classifications should be made. A variation of up to 20 lb is given for the desirable weight at any given height, and if the uncertainty of frame-size classification is taken into account the range becomes 30–40 lb. Obviously there is the temptation for people to classify themselves as large frame and judge themselves not to be overweight.

To gauge their frame accurately, women should measure their wrists—13.9 cm ($5\frac{1}{2}$ in) indicates a small frame, over 16.5 cm ($6\frac{1}{2}$ in) usually means a large one. Anything in between indicates a medium frame. A small-framed man would have the following measurements: chest 96.5 cm (38 in), shoulders 43.2 cm (17 in) and foot 20.3 cm (8 in). A large-framed man would have a chest measurement of 111.7 cm (44 in), shoulders 53.3 cm (21 in) and foot 25.4 cm (10 in). Again, anything in between indicates a medium frame.

Methods for determining the actual

amount of fat in the body are generally too sophisticated for routine diagnosis of obesity. One indirect method that has been developed is based on the measurement of skin-fold thicknesses at four critical sites on the body—biceps, triceps, the subscapular (under the shoulder blade) and the side of the waist. Doctors do this with precision calipers, but a guide may be had by pinching oneself between finger and thumb at these points. Any excess of fat indicates a need to lose weight.

However, there is a yet simpler way—look at yourself naked in a mirror. Assess yourself critically before you decide you are happy with what you see. If in doubt, jump—and see how much fat flops about. Or else think back to the time you were at your slimmest and healthiest, and compare your current weight with what it was then.

The result of this simple test is important, because being fat is dangerous, especially later in life. Although obesity is rarely given as the cause of death it is often an important contributory factor. Fat people die younger. Insurance statistics show that to be twenty per cent overweight results in a mortality one-third higher than for all persons at standard risk. To be 5 kg (11 lb) overweight appears to carry a greater health risk than smoking twenty-five cigarettes a day.

A number of conditions are associated with obesity. These include cardiovascular and kidney disease, diabetes (although of course not all overweight people are diabetic), and cirrhosis of the liver (especially in men, which may be associated with a high alcohol consumption). The obese, especially women, are more accident prone, presumably because they do not move briskly enough to avoid trouble and are more clumsy.

There are also a number of less lethal conditions associated with overweight, such as flat feet, varicose veins, hernias, osteoarthritis (especially of the knee, hip and spine) and bronchial disorders—all of which give rise to much chronic discomfort and pain. Obese women often find it difficult to conceive, and when they do become pregnant have a thirty-five per cent chance of complications.

However, it is encouraging to note that if a person successfully reduces weight, life expectancy improves and—in insurance terms at least—he or she becomes a normal risk.

Why people get fat is something of a mystery. There is no evidence that fat people necessarily eat more than thin people, or that their activity is so very different. Nevertheless, some fortunate people are able to maintain a constant body weight without consciously thinking about how much food they eat or the amount of exercise they take.

In part, this reflects the degree of precision with which energy balance is achieved in the body. Thirty-five tonnes of food is consumed in a lifetime, yet adult weight may fluctuate by only a few kilos. If there was a continuing error of only one per cent in food intake, body weight theoretically would double for some people every twenty years.

However, the need for precision is greater in some people than in others. Some are able to burn off their excess Calories while others lay them down as fat. In other words, some people are more efficient at converting food energy to body tissue. In experiments where volunteers have been deliberately overfed for up to seven months it was found that some of them gained weight easily, while others stayed the same even though they were consuming more Calories than the others. And the "easy gainers" found it harder to reduce their weight. Thus it seems that unconscious controls on energy output by changes in metabolic rate are probably of greater importance in the maintenance of body weight in man than conscious controls on food intake.

Can the differences be explained simply by differing metabolisms? Not quite. Energy expenditure is made up of basal metabolic rate (BMR); work done by the body in looking after its chemical needs and the heat produced by this work. In modern man BMR accounts for more than half the total energy expenditure. If all obese people had low BMR it would provide a convenient explanation for their condition—their "tick-over" would be very efficient and their energy requirements therefore low and easily exceeded. However, not all obese people have low BMR—there are some individuals who appear to consume less than their measured BMR and yet still put on weight. Such people probably depress their energy expenditure during the night in the same way as hibernating animals, but nobody yet knows how or why.

Also related to the problem of obesity is thermogenesis, the rise in the body's production of heat following the consumption of food. The scale of this is dependent on the nutritional balance of the diet and on the size and frequency of meals. But it appears that in some obese people the mechanism is defective and there is a lower than normal increase in heat production after meals.

Fat people are different from those of normal weight in many ways. It may be that different types of obesity exist which, when the primary causes are fully understood, will require different treatments. But in the meantime, effective treatments will be refinements of the basic slimming requirement—a lower Calorie intake.

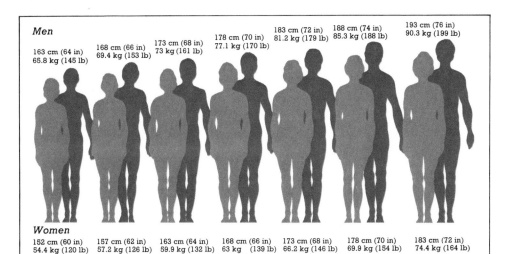

Men

163 cm (64 in)
65.8 kg (145 lb)

168 cm (66 in)
69.4 kg (153 lb)

173 cm (68 in)
73 kg (161 lb)

178 cm (70 in)
77.1 kg (170 lb)

183 cm (72 in)
81.2 kg (179 lb)

188 cm (74 in)
85.3 kg (188 lb)

193 cm (76 in)
90.3 kg (199 lb)

Women

152 cm (60 in)
54.4 kg (120 lb)

157 cm (62 in)
57.2 kg (126 lb)

163 cm (64 in)
59.9 kg (132 lb)

168 cm (66 in)
63 kg (139 lb)

173 cm (68 in)
66.2 kg (146 lb)

178 cm (70 in)
69.9 kg (154 lb)

183 cm (72 in)
74.4 kg (164 lb)

What we should weigh

The chart above shows average weights (in indoor clothing) for men and women aged 30 to 39 years of medium frame and at varying heights. But it is not height alone that determines ideal weight. Other factors include age. The weight of a man in early middle life (30-39 years of age) and of average height, 174 cm (5 ft 8$\frac{1}{2}$ in), should be about 80 kg (163 lb). Up to that age and for 20 years beyond he will put on a modest amount of weight; after 60, a slight fall is expected. A woman gains weight slightly throughout life.

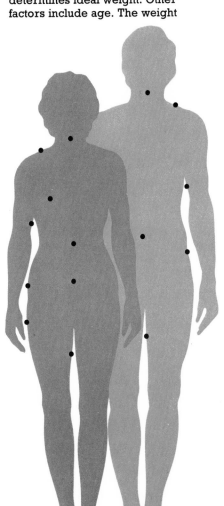

Are you too fat? A simple test

Doctors, using precision calipers, measure skin-fold thicknesses at four main sites—biceps, triceps, under the shoulder blade and at the waist. The amount of body fat related to the sum of these skin-folds is then read off from tables. This, however, is a medical refinement; it is possible to make a reasonably accurate estimate of one's own body fat by pinching at these points between finger and thumb. Any excess of fat will be immediately apparent— and is a sign that weight should be lost. Areas of the body where excess fat most readily accumulates on men and women are indicated by dots *(left)*.

Biceps

Triceps

Subscapular

Waist

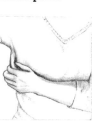

Fat children: danger signs for the future

Chubby babies were once much admired. Now plumpness is seen as the first step to adult obesity.

The difficulties of treating obesity in adulthood are great. It is, therefore, vital to prevent the condition developing in childhood, when eating patterns become established, and before too much fat has formed. The long-term results of the treatment of overweight children are poor and studies have shown an eighty per cent relapse. The only lasting solution is to be aware of—and act on—as many of the causes of obesity as possible. Parents worried about overweight children should always seek medical advice. The number of overweight children has increased considerably in recent years. Surveys have shown that twelve to fifteen per cent of children and adolescents in the US are more than twenty-five per cent overweight, while in Europe the figure is about seven per cent. The problem is serious because four out of five obese children stay that way, making up one-third of those who are overweight—and therefore at greater risk—as adults.

Obesity in early childhood is harmful emotionally as well as physically. In infancy, fat children have an increased risk of incurring respiratory disorders, and since eighty per cent of them are likely to remain obese in adulthood, they carry with them into adulthood increased risks of disease and death.

Both genetic and environmental factors are involved in the problem of obesity in children, but the two are difficult to separate. There is good evidence for a family tendency to the problem—nearly all fat, overweight children have one or both parents who are obese also. This seems to be more a reflection of eating habits than

Overweight parents tend to have fat children. This probably reflects family eating habits more than heredity.

of inherited body type: fat people tend to regard their condition as normal and unconsciously recreate this normality around them—they not only tend to have fat children but even fat pets, and they choose other fat people as friends.

Evidence for a genetic factor has been shown, however, in studies of adopted children and identical twins. The weights of adopted children show no relation to those of their adoptive parents, whereas those of natural children correlate well. The weights of identical twins brought up in separate families are closer than those of non-identical twins brought up together.

The significance of two other known facts about overweight children is still unclear. First, the pattern for obesity in childhood seems to be set very early in life, since children with the highest weight gain in the first few weeks of life tend to be overweight later. Second, obesity in children is usually associated with rapid maturation—particularly in girls, who tend to menstruate earlier if they are overweight. This is because menstruation generally occurs when a certain weight, 45 kg (100 lb), is reached rather than when the girl reaches a particular age. (The steady lowering of the age at which girls have their first period over the past century is partly explained by increases in the size and weight of children.)

The first nine months of a baby's life play a part in determining its future weight, for this is a time during which many fat cells are formed for life. These fat cells may later become empty, but they never disappear completely.

Overfeeding in infancy is one of the causes of obesity in childhood and sometimes is associated with the preference for bottle rather than breast feeding. While it is virtually impossible to overfeed a baby on breast milk alone, it is all too easy—and tempting to many mothers—to make up a bottle feed that is overconcentrated or to add sugar to pacify a restless infant.

There may also be a relationship between overfeeding and the thirst induced by over-rich foods. The baby becomes thirsty because it has been fed too concentrated a feed and cries; the cries are interpreted by the mother as an indication of hunger and the baby is given a further feed, so setting up a vicious cycle of thirst and overfeeding. Often, it is better to give a crying baby plain water than yet more food. Weight gain during the first few months of a baby's life is often taken by the mother to be a healthy sign. This is another reason why many mothers prefer the bottle to the breast, because artificially fed babies gain weight fastest. But there are limits in such weight gain beyond which the child's later health is set at risk.

Weaning from breast or bottle to solid foods is the next stage at which the baby can be overfed. The addition of cereal to the baby's diet too early (before the third or fourth month) raises its energy intake beyond its needs and encourages the formation of fat cells.

During and after weaning it is most important to give a child no more food than it needs or wants, as long as it stays healthy. A stomach encouraged to hold excess food will continue to "demand" an equal degree of filling and the food that cannot be used will be converted to fat. The mother seeking emotional fulfilment from the fact that her child eats all the food she has prepared and encouraging her child to eat against its will is probably doing more harm than good.

Children have no special need for sweet foods and if not encouraged to eat sugar will happily eat food that tastes sour or bland to a mother who is used to sugar. She should try to resist adding sugar to their food. Once children are eating regular meals with the family, always give them fresh fruit or sticks of raw vegetable such as carrot or celery to eat between meals rather than biscuits or sweets. This will help set children along the road to healthy eating, but unfortunately is no guarantee against their eating too many energy-rich snacks—sweets, chocolate, soft drinks, ice-cream, biscuits and nuts—later on. Many of these foods are particularly undesirable because they provide a great many empty Calories—that is, Calories with no associated vitamins and minerals. Parents should try to discourage such eating habits but, at the same time, find out whether their child is turning to sweets and other snacks—sometimes to the point of vomiting—because of some emotional disturbance.

Eating sometimes becomes a way of relieving anxiety. An eating pattern may be determined very early in childhood if a mother puts a bottle or sweetened dummy into the child's mouth every time it shows signs of distress.

After infancy there is no marked increase in fat cell formation until puberty. In girls the increase is gradual at this time while boys tend to put on weight between the ages of ten and twelve with a further increase later on in puberty.

Some excess weight in adolescents who have not been fat through the previous years of development is not usually a problem and should gradually disappear as long as their appetites are normal and they take plenty of physical exercise. During adolescence it is wise for parents to guide eating habits rather than nagging their children about being overweight, for it is possible to tip the balance in the opposite direction and encourage the self-induced starvation known as anorexia.

Obesity in childhood—fiction and reality

Billy Bunter, the fictional schoolboy, is a popular character because he can be laughed at for his size and the scrapes into which his greed lands him. In fact, a boy would suffer from such ridicule.

Breast or bottle feeding?

Plump babies (*above*) are no longer considered pictures of health. Their excess fat is often the result of an overconcentrated bottle feed. It is difficult to overfeed a breast-fed baby because in twenty minutes' feeding it will probably take only what it needs. Human milk has the following nutrient composition and bottle feeds should mirror these percentages:

Fat	Protein	Carbohydrate
11.8	1.5	7

To avoid overfeeding a bottle-fed baby it is important to know how much to offer at each feed. On average the advice is 142 gm (5 oz) per kg (2.2 lb) of body weight per day. A 5 kg (11 lb) baby would therefore need 710 gm (25 oz) in twenty-four hours. An additional check is to monitor weight gain. During the first three months this should be about 226 g (8 oz) per week.

Reducing: the commonsense way to slim

There is no magical way to slim. The key to success is to eat a well-balanced, low-Calorie diet.

People become obese because their energy input has been larger than their expenditure, so the cure would appear to be simple—to eat less and/or exercise more. However, it is all too easy to get fat and stay fat—Calorie-rich foods are readily available, activity levels are low and we live in centrally heated, air-conditioned environments usually surrounded by labour-saving devices.

It requires a lot of will power to stick to a reducing diet for a long time and it is no wonder that many people who are heavily overweight lack the will power and perseverance to stick to a restricted diet for the many months—or even years—necessary to lose their excess weight. It is important to find a diet that suits the individual's food preferences, and is socially and psychologically acceptable.

There is no magical way to make fat disappear overnight—the more overweight a person is the longer it will take him to lose his excess weight. The key to success is a regular, low-Calorie diet.

The aim of all slimming diets is to reduce energy intake below energy expenditure. The rate of weight loss will depend on the degree of energy restriction and how overweight the person is initially. A good target is a deficit of 1,000 Calories a day. At this level, weight losses, usually high at the beginning, will, over a period of time, average $\frac{1}{2}$–1 kg (1–2 lb) a week for most people. The rate of loss of fat will vary between individuals and between different parts of the body; fatty areas around the stomach, for instance, are often less tenacious than those on the hips.

What you eat is less important than how much you eat and when. The rate of weight loss depends purely on Calorie restriction and is independent of protein, fat and carbohydrate consumed. And there is some evidence that food should be taken little and often throughout the day rather than as one big meal, especially one late at night, because the food is used more efficiently in smaller amounts.

Reducing diets are either of the "set" type or of the do-it-yourself kind. The "set" diets involve very detailed information with instructions on all foods and amounts to be eaten at every meal. Such diets are very regimented and therefore offer the strong incentives some people need to slim; but they do not teach the obese to help themselves control their diets permanently.

Do-it-yourself diets take two forms, Calorie-counting and low carbohydrate diets, which are in effect two versions of the same thing. For the Calorie-counting method, the slimmer sets himself a daily intake target, say 1,500 Calories, and records the amount (preferably by weighing) of food consumed and its value in Calories (see *Appendix*, pages 194–213). Such diets demand a fair amount of application and knowledge.

The low carbohydrate diet in its simplest form restricts the consumption of carbohydrate-rich foods such as bread, biscuits and sugar. The principle of this diet is not that carbohydrate Calories are more fattening than those from protein and fats, but simply that carbohydrate-rich foods form a large proportion of our diet and by restricting the intake of these foods less food energy will be consumed overall. If the intake of carbohydrate foods is

restricted, it follows that the intake of associated foods is also reduced: if you eat no bread, you automatically eat less butter, too.

To meet the needs of the slimmer a large market has developed in recent years for so-called "slimming" foods. But no food is slimming since all foods contain Calories and to eat twice as much of a slimming food does not make it twice as slimming—as some people believe. Such misconceptions give rise to the misuse of these dietary aids when people eat them in addition to, rather than instead of, their normal diet.

The range of products available includes artificial sweeteners, starch-reduced breads and biscuits, slimmers' chocolate and complete Calorie-costed meals. Used correctly, they can be useful in a short-term slimming regime, but slimmers usually pay a high price for them—the evidence is that the size of the slimming-food market has tripled in value in many Western nations since the mid-1960s.

It is often hard for overweight people to accept the restrictions of a long-term low-Calorie diet, and there is a strong temptation to try short cuts. The main ones can be quickly summarized:

—Diuretics, which induce urination, are totally ineffective. The weight loss can be dramatic and immediate, but since it merely represents loss of essential body water the weight is quickly regained.

—Bulking agents such as methylcellu-

Reducing foods: fact and fiction

All these foods have at some time been claimed to have a magical reducing effect if consumed in quantity. Together, grapefruit, lemon juice, eggs, cottage cheese, celery, bran, steak and lettuce form a good basis for a low-carbohydrate diet, but no one of them can work alone.

lose act by swelling in the stomach to form an inert undigested mass, which gives rise to a feeling of satiety so the slimmer eats less. These agents are effective in reducing food intake if incorporated into the diet in high enough doses, but at these levels there is some danger of obstructing the intestine in a harmful way.

—Anorectic drugs, which depress appetite, are available usually only on prescription. Amphetamines, once commonly prescribed, are no longer used because of their addictive characteristics. Modern drugs of this type are effective, but only for short periods.

The ideal slimming drug would be one that increased energy expenditure by increasing heat production; an overweight person would then be able to eat normally and the excess energy would be burnt off. There are drugs that do this, but the effect is slight—a ten per cent increase in metabolic rate for an hour or two.

Exercise is a valuable adjunct to a reducing diet. But this, too, can have its problems. It must be begun very carefully, especially by the elderly or unfit. The amount of exercise required to lose 1 kg (2.2 lb) of fat is formidable—200 holes of golf, a 160-km (100-mile) walk, or 100 sets of tennis. But when you have become used to, and enjoy, regular exercise there are many side benefits. There is evidence that the efficiency of muscular work varies according to the amount of food eaten. The heat production following a meal is increased by exercise and the beneficial effects of exercise persist after the exercise has finished. Exercise can also play a very valuable role in stopping you getting fat in the first place.

Various exercise machines are available which supposedly help to reduce weight. Those that encourage physical work—like rowing machines—are fine. The passive exercise machines that stimulate muscles to contract and relax electrically may improve muscle tone but do not promote weight loss. The same is true for machines that are meant to reduce fat in particular places, such as belt vibrators and massagers. "Slimming garments", creams and other magical devices that promise effortless slimming will lighten only your purse.

The most successful way to get rid of excess weight at present involves the selection of a diet that suits the individual who may be helped by a mild anorectic drug, and the continual support of family and friends during the reducing phase. Thousands of people find that group therapy in slimming gives them similar support. It is difficult to lose surplus weight but even more difficult to adjust your appetite to a level that will keep your weight constant for life.

Danger drugs

Drugs injected to depress the appetite work by acting on the feeding centres of the brain. They should always be administered by a doctor.

The caffeine in coffee reduces appetite by filling the stomach with liquid and increasing its secretion, but it can impair digestion and provoke the formation of ulcers.

Smoking reduces appetite by acting on stomach secretion as caffeine does and by replacing the oral satisfaction of eating, but can cause lung diseases and increase the risk of cancer.

Most reducing pills have too little appetite-reducing content to work effectively and larger doses will act only over a short period.

Weight Watchers to the rescue

Of all the organizations set up to help the reducer, Weight Watchers can claim the greatest and most consistent success record. Weight Watchers helps new club members to work out the weight and diet that are individually right and then to lose the excess slowly, safely and permanently. The target is re-education about food so that members finish the course with a flexible but soundly based dietary regime. At weekly classes each member is weighed on a tested scale so that there is less chance of self-deception or solitary depression. The classes help in re-educating eating habits and provide the psychological back-up of group discussion. Weight Watchers says that because people have made a financial investment with them in losing weight they are much more likely to succeed in their reducing plan. As an added incentive free membership for life is offered to those who achieve the weight goal that has been set for them.

Social pressure and dieting struggles

Unless you inhabit a hermit's cell you are likely to find dieting difficult, since much of the pressure to overeat is social.

As anybody who has ever tried it will know, dieting is a struggle. The major pressures to keep on eating are, of course, appetite and habit. But there are other, more subtle pressures—external, social demands from family, friends and colleagues, and inner, psychological ones.

In most societies, the sharing of food is often an event of considerable significance. For instance, feasting expresses unity and friendship: the offering of food or drink—even if it is only coffee or a cocktail—is an offer of companionship that is hard to decline. In some societies—in particular in the Middle East—the laws that bind guest and host through food are stong.

In the US and Europe there are many examples of food being consumed for social rather than nutritional reasons. Two businessmen discussing a deal will have a three-course lunch and a bottle of wine because the sharing of the experience breaks down inhibitions rapidly. A housewife visited by a neighbour will offer coffee and perhaps a slice of cake. Two old friends meeting after an interval may have a drink together, persuading each other to accept unnecessary Calories of alcohol in the process of reforging the bond they once had.

To conform or behave tactfully on social occasions, people often eat more than they need. The most obvious conformity is eating three meals a day at a set time. Also, guests at a dinner-party may well eat more than they need just to please their host or hostess, or in a convivial atmosphere keep eating because others are accepting second helpings.

Pressure to conform is especially strong when people drink together—the obligation to keep pace with your companion's drinking, the demand that you accept "one for the road" even when you have decided to leave and have had all you want.

Originally such pressure arose for good reasons: if food was scarce and therefore valuable, to offer it was a true sign of friendship. Now people simply press food on each other because society has not come to terms with the superabundance of it in the West today. One way of getting round this problem is to ensure that you offer (and accept) only foods that are low in Calories—crackers and cheese, for instance, rather than peanuts.

The normal long-standing social pressures are compounded by another, newer one: advertising, which plays not only on basic urges for happiness but also on any unhealthy attitudes to food that may have been acquired in childhood. It is common, for instance, for children to be given food as a bribe to perform some chore, or as comfort when they are upset or hurt. There is a danger that a child habitually rewarded or silenced with food will, in adulthood, turn to food in times of stress or depression. Food can become almost a drug that is taken for emotional reasons in a subconscious effort to recreate the sense of security that food once provided. Of course the effort fails and often a vicious circle can be set up: because you are unhappy, you eat, and become fat; being fat makes you unhappy—so you eat even more and make yourself more unhappy.

The various external and internal motives that make you eat are legion. But they can be fought. If you are overweight, it is both helpful and instructive to keep a strict record of what you eat, when and where. Hidden motives for eating will suddenly become clear. People may realize for the first time that whenever they are angry they go out and eat, for example. Such recurring situations can be recognized, and then either confronted and resolved or avoided.

Few people whose motives for eating are emotional realize what drives them to food. "Because I feel hungry" means no more than wanting to eat, and hunger is not necessarily prompted by an empty stomach. A simple and conclusive experiment conducted by A. J. Stunkard, an American psychologist, admirably demonstrated this point. He invited two groups of people, obese and normal, to his laboratory. They arrived at 9 a.m. without having eaten breakfast. They then swallowed gastric balloons, small devices whereby the contractions of their stomachs—which indicate the degree of actual hunger—could be measured by observing the changing air pressure in the balloon. Every fifteen minutes the subjects were asked if they felt hungry. Those of normal weight showed what one would expect: when their stomachs contracted, they felt hungry and said so. But the obese ones reacted quite differently. The question itself aroused in them a desire to eat. They said they were hungry when their stomachs said they were not. This meant that the obese subjects had lost touch with their body's needs, and ate—as most fat people do—for social and psychological reasons or purely out of habit, with no idea when to stop.

It seems clear, then, that many people become overweight because they eat automatically. They do not necessarily enjoy their food. They are not interested in experimenting with new tastes. They eat the most familiar foods and the foods that are easiest to prepare—which are, all too often, the foods which make them gain weight. Bread, cake and biscuits need no preparation. Frying is the least difficult way of cooking, but the most calorific. The best way to control what you eat is, strangely, to take more interest in your food. Cook for yourself whenever possible, and prepare difficult dishes. This way you will register what you eat; even if you fail to keep detailed records of your calorific intake, you will eat critically and alertly—a first step to reducing your food intake and eating better.

Travelling heavy

Drinking on holiday, not to mention eating, can play havoc with a reducing programme. Unfamiliar food and new forms of alcohol are part of the fun of going to a new place. Because you are there to enjoy yourself, because your time is limited, it is tempting to put aside your normal dietary controls, with obvious consequences for your weight.

Overeating as a life-style

Eating and drinking are diabolically pleasant. Even worse is that food and drink are even more pleasant taken with friends. The result is that normal people with normal appetites stop off for the odd drink with a friend, eat one more course than they really want if dining out, drink two more glasses of wine than they ought at dinner-parties, eat cakes mid-morning and eat at parties just for the fun of it. The net result is a bit of extra weight and a bit more guilt. The guilt reduces the pleasure and the most comforting course then is to eat more.

Vegetarianism as a chosen way of eating

One method of reducing the dangers of an overrich diet is to avoid animal protein. Nutritionally, you have little to lose.

The economics of vegetarianism

In terms of land use, and leaving aside the cost of labour or machinery, it is more economical to use a field to grow crops than to use it to graze animals that will be slaughtered for meat. The illustration *(below)* shows how many people, for the same period, could be

Meat, poultry and fish were not originally part of man's diet. Our teeth evolved to deal with tubers and seeds, not flesh. Our digestive systems are those of foragers, not hunters. We cannot gorge ourselves on meat and then go without eating for days as many carnivores do.

Such evolutionary arguments may seem a thin basis for adopting a vegetarian diet today, however. The fact is that meat is a highly concentrated form of nutriment. It is also among the most appetizing foods in the average diet. Its flavours and smells are so thoroughly woven into the traditional Western way of eating that many people find the prospect of doing without it disheartening. Yet the evidence is that

supported by 4 h (10 acres) in terms of vegetarian proteins compared with meat protein. A 453 kg (1,000 lb) bullock eats 2,381 kg (5,250 lb) of plant food in its lifetime. Its carcass weighs only 254 kg (560 lb) and from this the consumer will be able to buy only 127 kg (280 lb) in prime cuts of its meat.

vegetarianism as a matter of individual choice is now spreading. For a variety of reasons, a habit that was once regarded as an eccentricity is gaining respect.

A vegetarian diet may be adopted for any one of three reasons—the philosophy of the individual, the range of foods that are available locally or the religious beliefs of a particular community. Religions can impose varying degrees of vegetarianism. The Ethiopian Coptic Church, for example, prohibits meat on more than 200 days of the year. Trappist monks abhor the taking of life and are entirely vegetarian. Of the major world religions, both Hinduism and Buddhism have similar objections to exploiting other living creatures for food. Strict followers of these faiths are wholly or partly vegetarian.

A form of enforced vegetarianism is common in many parts of Africa and Asia, where meat costs so much to produce that poorer people are seldom able to eat it. About eighteen per cent of the world's population (excluding China) eat less than 10 g (0.3 oz) of animal protein per head per day—equivalent to two small eggs or one cup of milk.

But with the spread of affluence, the amount of animal protein eaten in the average diet has been increasing. Vegetarianism in the West is therefore less a matter of economic necessity than of choice. The number of voluntary vegetarians in Europe and the US is estimated at several million. Some are motivated by aesthetic or moral ideas; they deplore the killing of animals and some of the methods of raising them for food. Some base their choice on economics; it is more efficient to use land for growing food directly than for feeding animals. Still others simply believe a vegetarian diet is more healthy.

An extreme form of vegetarianism is veganism. There are vegan societies in more than thirty Western countries and probably a few thousand members in each country. The Charter of the Vegan Society says that "Veganism is a way of living which excludes all forms of exploitation of, and cruelty to, the animal kingdom and includes a reverence and compassion for all life." In practice the vegan excludes from his diet not only meat, poultry and fish but also animal milk and its derivatives, eggs and honey. Soya-based plant-milks are substituted for cow's milk and are equally nutritious. Seaweed agars are used instead of gelatine, and arrowroot and soya are used as binding agents in cooking. Extending the vegan philosophy to clothing, vegans use plastic, rubber and PVC instead of leather jackets, belts or shoes.

How nutritious is a vegetarian diet? In poorer countries it is often accompanied by general shortage of food and assessment is therefore difficult. In affluent

**Soya feeds
61 people**

**Wheat feeds
24 people**

**Maize feeds
10 people**

**Meat feeds
2 people**

countries, however, research shows that a vegetarian diet can be nutritionally sound for all ages, differing from a normal diet only in the sort of foods supplying the essential nutrients. Vegetables, fruits, legumes and nuts are excellent sources of the vitamins and minerals man needs and vegetarians tend to have relatively high intakes of calcium, vitamin B_1 and vitamin C.

Since the quality of mixed cereal and legume proteins matches that of meat and fish proteins, vegetarian diets have protein values similar to those of mixed diets, provided adequate quantities are consumed. There is certainly a tendency for vegetarians to have lower Calorie intakes than people on mixed diets. This is largely because their fat intake is lower—an advantage in view of the association of high fat consumption with heart disease.

The lower energy content of vegetarian diets requires some adjustments in total food intake. For instance, to provide 2,700 Calories (the recommended intake for an adult man) a person would need to eat 6 kg (13 lb) of apples, or 11 kg (24 lb) of raw cabbage or 1.1 kg (2.5 lb) of wholemeal bread. Vegetable foods tend to have a higher water content, so that vegetarians automatically take larger quantities of water as part of their food, instead of additional liquid. Vegetables also have a lower fat content. However, if fat is required, nuts are more than fifty per cent fat, oils can be added to salads and vegetable fats can be used in cooking.

The vegan diet, with its protein-rich cereals and legumes and its vegetables is difficult to fault nutritionally except for the lack of two vitamins. The most likely problem a vegan will face is lack of vitamin B_{12}. Over the years this may cause anaemia and in extreme cases nervous disorders. The vitamin is made by bacteria in the animal intestine and is concentrated in the liver. It is not found in plants. However, as it is stored in the liver, anyone changing from a mixed or vegetarian diet to veganism is likely to have enough in their body to live on for about five years.

Vegan foods such as plant-milks are supplemented with B_{12} and many vegans take vitamin B_{12} tablets. The problem that occasionally arises of B_{12} deficiency in people on mixed diets is due to an inability to absorb the vitamin in the intestine and this may result in pernicious anaemia.

As there are no plant sources of vitamin D, vegans may also have to beware of rickets and poor bone development in their children. However, the vitamin is synthesized under the skin in the presence of sunlight, and if children get enough sunlight vitamin D deficiency is unlikely. Also the vitamin is synthesized in the food-manufacturing industry to be added to margarine and a number of proprietary preparations.

Adults do not need the vitamin in their diet, and in any case they will have large stores in their livers if they have been brought up on either a normal mixed or a vegetarian diet. The vegan children who have been studied are also perfectly healthy and well developed.

Good sources of fats

Although most vegetarian foods are low in fat, nuts are particularly rich sources. Pecan nuts are about 70 per cent fat and almonds and peanuts are about 50 per cent fat. Nuts are also excellent sources of protein and carbohydrate.

Good sources of protein

Most vegetables contain some protein, but only in small quantities. However, 100 gm (3.5 oz) of soya beans contains nearly twice as much protein as the same weight of chicken. Broad beans and dried lentils are also rich in protein.

Good sources of carbohydrate

Vegetarians have no difficulty finding starchy foods. Particularly rich sources are kidney beans (60 per cent carbohydrate) and raisins, dates and rice (70-80 per cent). Kidney beans are protein-rich too.

Jainism—a philosophy of restraint

The ethical basis of Jainism, an ancient religion and philosophy of India, is reverence for all life. Even vegetables are believed to have feelings. Strict Jain monks avoid eating not only meat but also vegetables growing underground (for example carrots, potatoes, turnips) and certain fruits, in case they inadvertently kill insects. For similar reasons they will drink only filtered water and will not eat or drink at night. On certain days the stricter Jains will not even eat green vegetables. Cloth masks prevent them swallowing flying insects and brooms are used to sweep away insects from their path.

Vegetarianism/2

If you think you might be fitter by giving up meat, it does not mean that you will have to face a dull diet, existing on endless meals of tasteless and textureless vegetables. Vegetarianism is an alternative that can offer a surprisingly tasty and varied diet—and save money as well. Cheap foods such as flour, oatmeal, potatoes, haricot and broad beans, soya, carrots and spinach provide between them enough key nutrients to meet everyone's daily needs and more.

Unlike the millions in developing countries whose vegetarian diet is close to subsistence level, vegetarians in the affluent world have a wide variety of foods that can replace the protein supplied in an ordinary diet by meat, fish, poultry, eggs and cheese. Some vegetables con-tain so little protein that a vegetarian would need to eat huge quantities to absorb the protein equivalent of an ordinary mixed diet. But other vegetable foods compare favourably weight for weight with animal protein. The best is textured vegetable protein from soya, followed closely by legumes such as kidney beans and broad beans. Other substitutes are nuts and seeds such as sesame seeds, pine nuts, pumpkin seeds, walnuts, pistachio nuts and coconuts, and whole grains such as millet, barley, oats, sorghum and rice. Lacto- and ovo-vegetarians will of course be able to substitute cheese and eggs as additional sources of protein. Provided vegetarians know about these high protein sources, and also that nuts will give them the fat that may be lacking in their diet, they should have no need to worry about essential nutrients.

What is involved in eating intelligently the vegetarian way? Polished rice, macaroni and products made from white flour should be avoided in favour of natural and whole foods—100 per cent whole wheat flour, wholemeal macaroni, wheat germ cereals, brown rice, unrefined sugar, fruits and vegetables with skins, sprouted pulses, and unrefined and cold-pressed vegetable oils. Whole foods eaten raw provide an excellent source of roughage often lacking in a meat diet. Examples are bread made from cereal mixtures, and muesli, the Swiss-style breakfast cereal made from raw oats, nuts, dried fruit and brown sugar with optional fresh fruit. Cereals mixed with legumes and nuts, for

The talented tomato
Tomato recipes show how versatile even a single vegetable can be.

Curried tomatoes
5.6 cl (2 fl oz) oil, 2 onions sliced in rings, 1 kg (2.2 lb) peeled and chopped tomatoes, 2 crushed garlic cloves, 2 finely chopped chillis or chilli powder, turmeric, coriander, fenugreek, root ginger, paprika to taste, a 150 g (5 oz) carton yoghurt.

Heat oil in a heavy saucepan, add onion and fry until golden. Add ginger, garlic and chillis and cook, stirring occasionally, for 4 minutes. Combine spices with yoghurt and add to the pan. Simmer for 10 minutes. Add tomatoes, bring to the boil, then simmer for 20 minutes. Serve on a bed of boiled rice.

Gazpacho
45 cl (16 fl oz) canned tomato juice, 3 chopped garlic cloves, 1 green pepper and 1 red pepper seeded and chopped, $1/_2$ cucumber peeled and chopped, 1 large Spanish onion chopped, 700 g (1.5 lb) tomatoes peeled and chopped, 8.5 cl (3 fl oz) olive oil, 2 tablespoons wine vinegar, salt and pepper, basil and marjoram to taste.

Purée all ingredients. Pour into a large bowl and refrigerate for one hour before serving. The soup should be as thin as single cream; if too thick add more tomato juice and adjust the seasoning. Serve with croûtons and garnish with chopped chives and parsley.

Green tomato chutney
1.5 kg (3 lb) unripe tomatoes peeled and sliced, 1 kg (2.2 lb) cooking apples peeled and chopped, 3 large onions chopped, 340 g (12 oz) raisins, 340 g (12 oz) sultanas, 1 heaped teaspoon dry mustard, 1 heaped teaspoon ground

example sesame, wheat and beans, give delicious meat substitutes such as rissoles and nut meats. Raw foods need not be boring. Different combinations of dried fruits, milled nuts, hedgerow plants, and herbs and spices "pep up" salads; oils made from sunflower seeds, sesame, maize, soya, cottonseed and walnuts provide unusual and delicious flavour combinations. Yoghurt, herbs, such as mint and parsley, and seasonings make a tangy salad dressing.

Food cooked the vegetarian way is washed (not soaked) and either steamed or cooked in minimal amounts of water for the shortest possible time to keep vegetables crisp and their essential vitamins and minerals intact. Gravies can be made with yeast products such as Barmene, and

hot cheese sauces can be made with vegetable margarine, plant milks, and cheese made from soya. Nut milks and creams prepared in a blender can be used diluted or in place of butter.

Lacto- and ovo-vegetarians have little problem in preparing balanced, tasty and attractive meals. Eggs are even better sources of protein than meat. Cheeses from Cheddar to Camembert make starters, main meals and desserts packed with protein and milk, and yoghurt can be blended with fruit to make fruit drinks.

Dried skimmed milk is one of the cheapest ways of improving the protein content of any dish. Adding 1 kg (2.2 lb) of dried milk powder to 4.5 litres (8 pints) of water gives a milk with twice the protein and calcium value of fresh milk.

ginger, 1 heaped teaspoon allspice, 1 tablespoon salt, 700 g (1.5 lb) soft brown sugar 57 cl (1 pint) vinegar.

Place all the ingredients in a large saucepan and bring quickly to the boil. Simmer, for about 2 hours, stirring until the chutney thickens. Ladle the chutney into jars, putting in a circle of waxed paper before sealing. Store in a cool, dark place.

Pipérade

6 ripe tomatoes blanched, skinned and chopped, 3 red peppers seeded and chopped, 3 onions chopped, 3 crushed garlic cloves, 6 eggs, 4 tablespoons oil, salt, pepper and basil to taste.

Fry onions and crushed garlic very gently in the oil for 15 minutes, without browning. Add the peppers and continue cooking gently until they are tender. Add the chopped tomatoes and a little salt. Simmer until the mixture is moist but not wet—about 25 minutes. Beat the eggs in a bowl and season with salt, pepper and basil. Stir them into the vegetable mixture and serve as soon as they begin to thicken. Serve garnished with parsley on fried bread.

Stuffed tomatoes

6 large tomatoes halved horizontally, 1½ tablespoons oil, 1 onion chopped, 2 crushed garlic cloves, 1 green or red pepper chopped, 227 g (8 oz) black olives stoned and chopped, 113 g (4 oz) grated cheese, 113 g (4 oz) cooked rice, salt, pepper and basil.

Scoop out tomato flesh into a bowl and place skins in a casserole. Heat 1 tablespoon of oil, add onion, garlic and pepper and cook gently for 7 minutes. Add remaining ingredients and cook for 3 minutes. Remove mixture from heat and spoon equally into each tomato half. Spoon a little oil on top and bake for 20 minutes.

A balanced vegetarian diet for a week

The menus given below show a typical weekly plan of vegetarian meals that could meet all the dietary needs of a family of four. The emphasis is on whole foods and a good supply of protein and fats from nuts, and dried and fresh fruit. Plamil is a milk substitute made from plants; Barmene is made from yeast.

Day 1

Breakfast: Half grapefruit each. Muesli. 60 g (2 oz) soaked raisins. 4 slices whole wheat toast. Butter or margarine. Barmene.
Midday: Lentil soup. Vitamin salad with 113 g (4 oz) roasted cashew nuts. Brown rolls and butter. Chocolate apples.
Evening: 57 cl (1 pint) tomato juice. Country pie and 170 g (6 oz) grilled mushrooms. Banana salad.

Day 2

Breakfast: 57 cl (1 pint) orange juice. Porridge with milk or Plamil and brown sugar. Soaked prunes. Toast, etc., as Day 1.
Midday: Onion soup. Cheese and apple salad. Pear and hazel-nut flan.
Evening: 57 cl (1 pint) apple juice. Savoury rice with a medium cabbage shredded and cooked. Vitpro in tomato sauce. Blackcurrant jelly.

Day 3

Breakfast: Soaked dried apricots. Weetabix (two each) and milk or Plamil. Toast, etc., as Day 1.
Midday: Mixed vegetable soup. Egg mayonnaise, mixed salad and baked potatoes. Coconut sponge with orange sauce.
Evening: 57 cl (1 pint) carrot juice. Butter beans in parsley sauce with spinach and beetroot. Date and apple compote.

Day 4

Breakfast: Fresh fruit. Scrambled corn. Toast, etc., as Day 1.
Midday: Tomato soup. Cole-slaw and nut rissoles. Ryvita with butter or margarine. Spiced fruit crumble.
Evening: 57 cl (1 pint) grape juice. Cheese and mushroom flan with savoury sauce, potatoes with chopped parsley and peas. Pineapple snow.

Day 5

Breakfast: Mixed dried fruit, soaked. Welsh rarebit with tomato. Toast, etc., as Day 1.
Midday: Potato soup. Cucumber salad. 227 g (8 oz) cheese, Ryvita and butter. Flapjacks.
Evening: 57 cl (1 pint) grapefruit. juice. Cashew-nut pie with cauliflower and roast potatoes. Fresh fruit salad.

Day 6

Breakfast: Bananas (1 each). Frugrains with milk or Plamil. Boiled eggs and toast, etc., as Day 1.
Midday: Celery soup. Brazil-nut and date salad with baked potatoes. Bakewell tart.
Evening: 57 cl (1 pint) pineapple juice. Savoury lentils with curry sauce, boiled rice and spinach or sprouts. Apricot cream.

Day 7

Breakfast: Pears. Shredded Wheat and milk. Toast, etc., as Day 1.
Midday: Mushroom soup. Cottage cheese and pineapple salad. Gingerbread and whipped cream.
Evening: Grapefruit and orange cocktail 57 cl (1 pint). 170 g (6 oz) almond pizza with peas and spaghetti. Prune whip.

Recipes for these menus can be found in *Vegetarian Review*, from The Vegetarian Society of the United Kingdom, London.

Processing: the nutritional question mark

Nearly all the food eaten
in Western societies
is processed in some way
or another. How does it
compare nutritionally
with fresh food?

All food preservation techniques aim to safeguard food from the decay that results from chemical change and attack by the micro-organisms—bacteria, moulds and yeasts—that make food not only unpalatable but potentially fatal (as in salmonella and botulinum poisoning). Preservation destroys micro-organisms by heat, chemicals or irradiation or inhibits growth by freezing or by depriving them of the moisture essential for their multiplication.

Food can spoil because of the chemical reactions that take place when it is exposed to oxygen in the air. This oxidization makes the fats in food rancid and turns proteins

and carbohydrates brown. In addition there are enzymes (natural substances in the foods themselves) that have a spoiling action, causing fruit to become overripe and inedible, for example.

Against the advantages of food processing must be weighed the disadvantages of nutrient loss. Quick freezing, in which food is rapidly cooled to and stored at −18°C (0°F), is the least nutritionally wasteful method. Freezing does not completely stop enzyme action so these enzymes are destroyed by a preliminary heat treatment, such as blanching in hot water. This leaches out some of the water-soluble

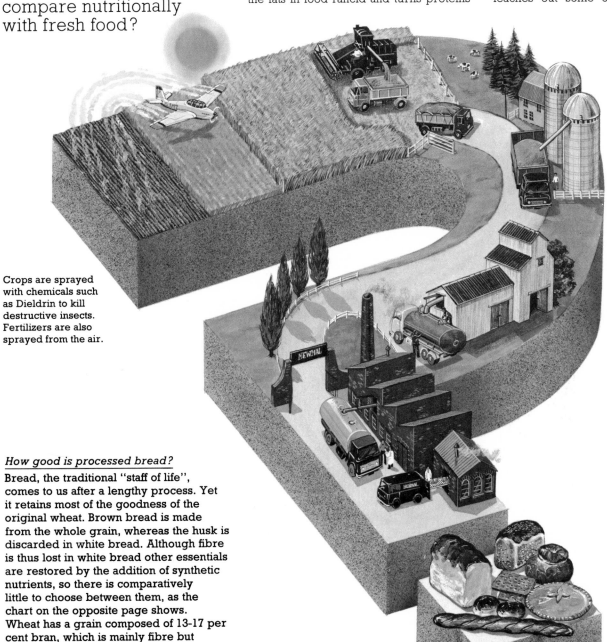

The ripe crop is cut and threshed to separate the grain from stalk and chaff.

After drying with hot air, wheat is mechanically lifted into storage silos equipped to weigh the wheat, clean it and dry it further if necessary.

Before milling, different wheat varieties are blended according to the intended fate of the flour.

In milling wheat to white flour the grains are passed through pairs of corrugated rollers and torn open. The endosperm is released and ground up. The bran is sieved off and the endosperm rolled to a fine powder. The germ, flattened by the rollers, is removed to improve storage qualities. Iron and B-vitamins are now added.

Crops are sprayed with chemicals such as Dieldrin to kill destructive insects. Fertilizers are also sprayed from the air.

Flour for factory-baked bread is mixed with water and vitamin C added to improve the dough. The dough is rapidly kneaded mechanically after the addition of yeast (rather than being left to stand while the yeast ferments), then shaped and baked.

How good is processed bread?
Bread, the traditional "staff of life", comes to us after a lengthy process. Yet it retains most of the goodness of the original wheat. Brown bread is made from the whole grain, whereas the husk is discarded in white bread. Although fibre is thus lost in white bread other essentials are restored by the addition of synthetic nutrients, so there is comparatively little to choose between them, as the chart on the opposite page shows. Wheat has a grain composed of 13-17 per cent bran, which is mainly fibre but has B vitamins and iron; 80–85 per cent carbohydrate-rich endosperm; and 2-3 per cent germ, containing proteins, B and E vitamins, minerals and fats.

nutrients, especially vitamin C, but other nutrients are well preserved in this process. Commercial freezing is so organized that peas, for example, are frozen within ninety minutes of harvesting and contain more vitamin C than the tired vegetables on the greengrocer's stall, which may have been picked a week or so before.

Canning kills decay-producing germs by heat sterilization, and the heating is continued long enough to cook the food. The can is then sealed to make it airtight and thus prevent food from oxidizing and from being recontaminated by bacteria in the air. Canning temperatures are not standard. Foods high in acid, such as tomatoes and pineapples, can be sterilized at the temperature of boiling water—100°C (212°F)—while those lower in acid, such as meat and fish, need to be heated under pressure to 121°C (250°F).

Although canning may keep food in an edible condition for decades—a plum pudding canned in 1900 and eaten over sixty years later was still in first-rate condition—the high temperatures on which success depends and the long cooking (up to fifty minutes) have some destructive action on nutrients. This applies particularly to vitamin B_1, which is partially lost from meat during canning, and vitamin C, partially lost from fruit and vegetables. Despite this, canned food is not much less nutritious than fresh food after it has been cooked and is certainly better than overcooked fresh food.

Recently a new fast-canning method has been introduced which cuts down the cooking time and thus vitamin loss. Many baby foods and some sauces are fast-canned, but in most foods enough enzymes remain even after fast-canning to allow

The nutrients in different breads

Nutrient	Whole wheat	Brown	White enriched
Protein per cent	12.0	11.8	11.1
Fibre per cent	2.0	1.9	0.12
Calcium mg/100 g	30	148	142
Iron mg/100 g	3.5	2.7	1.7
Vitamin B_1 mg/100 g	0.4	0.33	0.24
Vitamin B_2 mg/100 g	0.12	0.09	0.04
Nicotinic acid mg/100 g	5.7	3.5	1.6

some of the chemical spoilage to continue.

Air-drying, perhaps the oldest preservation method, is among the most destructive of nutrients, for it removes all the vitamin C and nearly all the vitamins A and B_1. Foods least harmed by air-drying are fish and meat; these are most valuable for their proteins, which remain unharmed.

Freeze-drying, in which food is frozen then carefully heated in a vacuum so that the ice is converted directly to water vapour, is an excellent processing method that deprives food of very few vitamins or other nutrients. It does change the texture of some foods, however; thus one of its most successful applications is to coffee, in which this factor is unimportant.

Another way of making essential water unavailable to bacteria and yeasts is to add a large amount of sugar. The sugar works by "holding" the water and this is the principle behind jam-making.

The processing and preservation of food with chemicals ranges from traditional wood smoking, salting and pickling to the addition of synthetic chemicals. In pickling, food is either allowed to ferment in salt and the mixture becomes acid enough to stop the growth of decaying micro-organisms, or vinegar is added with the same result. Chemicals added to food act to prevent this growth in the first place and stop fats turning rancid.

A vast number of chemicals can kill microbes or prevent food spoilage by stopping oxidation, but unfortunately most of these cause direct harm to the human body, even in small quantities. Most countries have strict laws governing the types and amounts of food additives. The most widespread of the preservatives generally thought to be safe include sulphur dioxide, used to keep fruit and vegetables fresh, sodium nitrite, put into ham, bacon and pork products, such as sausages, and proprionic acid, which is added to bread flour. Permissible antioxidant chemicals include butylated hydroxytoluene (BHT) and butylated hydroxyanisole (BHA), but the safety of all of them is under continual examination.

Chemical additives are clearly invaluable in making food available world-wide and year-round. Much more controversial is the use of chemicals to improve the colour, flavour, texture and supermarket shelf life of processed food. The problem is that large doses of every chemical, including vitamins, salt and many natural substances in plants can be shown to have harmful effects in experimental animals, so it is extremely difficult to prove that small doses are absolutely safe.

Among synthetic additives, the colouring agents derived from coal tar—particularly the aniline compound butter

yellow—the synthetic sweeteners called cyclamates and monosodium glutamate (MSG), the flavour enhancement common in Chinese cooking and used in processed protein foods, have all been shown to have adverse effects of varying degrees.

It is the concern of government food and drug laws to protect consumers from the potentially harmful effects of chemical additives. As a result, butter yellow, for example, was universally banned immediately it was found to cause liver damage and cancer when fed to experimental animals in high doses. Cyclamates, found to cause cancer in rats when administered experimentally in large doses, have been banned in many countries, including Britain and the US, but not in some others.

In most countries food manufacturers are legally bound to declare the contents of their products. In some, goods such as cream, yoghurt, bread and cakes are stamped with a date after which consumption is not advised or its sale forbidden.

Food technology and economic affluence have combined to provide the consumers of the 1970s with a vast number of convenience foods, none of which can be considered essential but all of which have been given an official seal of safety. Most people try to balance the advantages in time-saving and ease of storage against the relatively small risk of unforeseen dangers. Moreover, many unprocessed vegetables contain known poisons, but we have eaten them for centuries.

Buying and keeping for freshness
Canned foods Avoid dented cans or those with "blown" convex ends. Stored in a dry place will keep many years.
Bread Store in a dark but ventilated container or in a refrigerator.
Cakes and biscuits Keep in an airtight container in a cool place.
Cheese If packaged, use date stamp as buying guide. Will keep a week in refrigerator or covered in a cool place.
Dried foods, e.g. packet soup Will keep many months in a cool, dry place. Keep in airtight place once opened.
Frozen foods Avoid partially thawed produce, store as soon as possible. If not refrigerated, eat on same day. Will keep a week in a refrigerator freezing compartment, many months in a deep freeze. Follow storage instructions on packet.
Poultry, frozen Thaw thoroughly in a refrigerator overnight then bring to room temperature and cook at once. Remove giblets as soon as possible.

Cooking: a raw deal for vitamins?

Good cooking means adding flavour without losing the goodness. The rules are simple, but some experienced cooks break them every day.

Good cooking is not simply a matter of being able to present food in a way that looks attractive and tastes succulent. It involves treating the food in such a way that its nutritive value and the balance of the meal are not destroyed.

Cooking is essential only for foods that our digestive systems have difficulty coping with raw, such as meat and flour. The added advantage of cooking these and many other foods is that it improves flavour and palatability. The variety of ways in which food is cooked adds enormously to the enjoyment of eating. On a more practical health level, cooking kills harmful micro-organisms. Yet these advantages can be over-stressed. Too many people reject all raw food except "salad" and cook far more than they need, for longer than they should.

Good cooking and healthy eating start with choosing fresh ingredients and preparing them quickly and properly. Fruit and vegetables are the foods most likely to suffer from bad handling, for they are our major source of vitamin C, the most unstable of all vitamins. From the moment it leaves the soil a cabbage, for example, starts to lose vitamin C simply through the action of its own enzymes. Crushing during handling and chopping in preparation releases enzymes that speed this destruction; soaking the chopped leaves in cold water leaches out yet more vitamin C, along with useful minerals. Even before this, the outer, most vitamin-rich, leaves may well have been discarded as useless.

Another preparation practice to avoid is peeling, for this can remove some valuable nutrients—for example the protein in potatoes—that lie just under the skin. So scrub vegetables in preference to peeling them. Peeled fruit and vegetables benefit from the addition of lemon juice or vinegar, as these acid substances help slow the vitamin C breakdown and also stop food turning brown through enzyme action.

Other foods are less vulnerable, but still suffer from careless preparation. Leave enough fat on meat, for example, to help it retain its juices during cooking, and only salt meat just before cooking it, for salt will draw out valuable juices. Frozen meat should be thoroughly thawed, preferably in the refrigerator, then brought up to room temperature and cooked with no further delay.

Cooking applies heat to food either dry or through water, fat or oil. The last two boil at a much higher temperature than water and cook food faster with less nutrient loss. Heat and the way it is transferred in cooking has different effects on proteins, carbohydrates, fats, vitamins and minerals, and it is in these effects that the guidelines to good cooking can be found.

Proteins, found mainly in meat, fish, eggs and dairy products, undergo the greatest physical change when cooked. Many, such as those in eggs, coagulate when heated, but despite this are unaffected in nutritive value. Meat proteins react rather differently because they include collagen and elastin, the proteins that make raw meat tough and indigestible. Because they become even tougher when heated quickly, cheaper cuts, in which they are more abundant, should be casseroled or steamed long and slowly using moist heat, so that elastin is softened and collagen converted to soft, digestible gelatin. Better quality meat, conversely, needs less cooking.

Carbohydrates, which include starch found in foods such as potatoes and flour, are broken down by the heat of cooking and this makes them much more palatable and easier to digest. Plant foods contain the carbohydrates cellulose and pectin, which are constituents of roughage. Cooking softens both of them, so making fruit and vegetables easier to eat.

Fats melt when heated but lose little nutritionally when cooked. They are important in our diet as a source both of energy and of vitamins A and D. These two vitamins, especially abundant in oily fish such as herrings, are the vitamins least affected by cooking, because they do not dissolve in water and are destroyed only at very high temperatures.

Cooking can easily rob food of vitamin C and the B-group vitamins and some loss is inevitable. Both vitamin types are found in vegetables, but, as in preparation, the vitamin C in vegetables is the most vulner-

The versatile potato

The potato, a valuable source of energy-rich carbohydrate, also provides us with proteins, vitamins and minerals. Potatoes supply an average eater with about one-third of all his vitamin C, but should be carefully treated, however they are cooked, to preserve nutrients.

Scrubbed and boiled

Boiling the potato in its skin (*above*) helps maintain food value because there is a slightly higher concentration of nutrients such as proteins just below the skin.

Jacket baked

The potato (*below*) that is scrubbed and oven baked in its jacket retains a large proportion of its vitamin C, which cannot dissolve out.

able because it dissolves in water and is destroyed when heated. For "conservative" vegetable cooking to minimize vitamin C loss, use as little water as possible (and put a tight-fitting lid on the pan); put the vegetables into ready-boiling water, cook them for the shortest possible time, add salt only at the end of cooking, eat the vegetables as soon as they are cooked and use the cooking water as stock for soups and gravies. Even better, invest in a steamer, or try cooking vegetables in milk. Alternatively, stir-fry them in a large, open pan with a little oil as the Chinese do. If using frozen vegetables, do not thaw them: instead, tip them straight into boiling water.

The vitamin B in vegetables is less likely to be lost in cooking and they are not a rich source of vitamin B anyway. Most of our vitamin B comes from meat, but up to half the vitamin B_1 and up to one-third of the vitamin B_2 can be lost at the high temperatures of roasting. To help retain vitamin B, seal the juices of meat by brushing it with oil before grilling or frying and by quick-frying before roasting or casseroling. Cook tougher cuts at low temperatures or in a pressure cooker and always keep every drop of meat juice. If using meat from a can, heat it for an absolute minimum of time.

Minerals, the final food elements, are unaffected by heat, but many of them, like vitamins, are soluble in water and so are lost when food is boiled. Thus conservative cooking is the way to get the best out of food and prevent your kitchen sink being the best-fed mouth in the household.

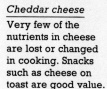

Green vegetables
Boiling leafy, green vegetables in too much water removes at least 60 per cent of their vitamin C and 30 per cent of B-vitamins.

Carrots
Cook carrots to conserve nutrients by baking in the oven, braising them in a little milk and butter, or stir-frying them.

Onions
Although often used only for flavouring, onions are a source of vitamin C.

Apples
Peeled, boiled and puréed apples not only contain fewer vitamins than the whole raw fruit but are less useful as a roughage supply.

Cheddar cheese
Very few of the nutrients in cheese are lost or changed in cooking. Snacks such as cheese on toast are good value.

Eggs
However they are cooked eggs retain their high vitamin and protein content.

Mackerel
Cheap, oily fish such as mackerel are a much-neglected nutrient source. Grill, bake or fry them and serve with the pan juices.

Ox liver
Liver, rich in iron, vitamins and protein, is among the most nutritious of foods, whether fried, grilled, braised, baked or casseroled.

Lamb chops
Make the most of expensive meat by grilling it and saving the juices for gravy, stocks or sauces.

Beef pot-roast
Cheaper cuts of meat are as nutritious as expensive ones if cooked long and slowly.

French fried
The chipped potato (*left*) gains some vitamins from the oil it is cooked in. The oil also adds to the potato's already high Calorie content.

Mashed
When peeled, boiled and mashed (*below*), then left exposed to the air, the potato may lose 90 per cent of its vitamin C.

Reheating destroys the remaining 10 per cent. Some other vitamins can be replaced if potatoes are mashed with milk and butter.

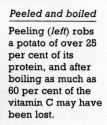

Peeled and boiled
Peeling (*left*) robs a potato of over 25 per cent of its protein, and after boiling as much as 60 per cent of the vitamin C may have been lost.

Food fads and dietary foolishnesses

Expensive health foods seldom have the advantages their mythology suggests. Man's only "natural" food is human milk.

Food is the one big business of immediate concern to everyone everywhere. It is also almost infinite in its variety, and the larger the choice the greater the possibilities of confusion, exploitation and self-deception. There are many special foods, special diets, eating regimes, pills and potions, a few of which are harmful; most are harmless, but in most cases there is nothing specially beneficial about them either.

A certain magic has long been attached to some foods—honey, for example. Honey is simply pure sugar with very small traces of vitamins and a few impurities, but the amounts of extra materials are so small that (apart from flavour) it is in no way superior to sugar.

The magic of honey leads to the even greater magic of royal jelly—the food of the queen bee—for which rejuvenating powers are claimed. It does indeed contain a number of vitamins, but you would need to eat great quantities to get any marked benefit from these. Royal jelly has long been recognized as a fraud, but there are still many people who want to believe in its supposed power. After all, there is nothing else that will rejuvenate you.

Biochemical salts are a collection of a dozen ordinary inorganic salts that, taken in various combinations, are claimed to cure many diseases. The names indicate the approach—ordinary table salt, chemically called sodium chloride, is labelled with its old Latin name of natrium muriate, and sells at hundreds of times the price of salt. Another one if not described as silicon dioxide would be called sand.

The Zen macrobiotic diet has been adopted in the West on a small scale in protest against the industry that has created "bad" unnecessary foods. Certain foods are designated Yin and others Yang (an acid-alkaline contrast), and the dietary regime consists mainly of seven diets in which these foods are balanced. The "ideal" diet is one of brown rice only, but it has been condemned by the American Medical Association as one of the most dangerous, since not only could it give rise to ill-health from malnutrition, but it could also lead people to avoid medical treatment because of the claims that it cures diseases (even cancer).

It is probably inevitable that apparently new dietary problems should be blamed on modern methods of food processing. Certainly processing, additives or long storage can bring about changes in food that may affect our health. But this does not mean that all food processing is suspect; on the contrary, the greater part is of proven benefit.

Doubts about the effects of processing have given rise to the "natural" school of eating. But what is natural except human milk? Although the human race has been eating vegetable foods for a long time, most of them contain known toxins.

The small amounts present are continually disposed of by the body with no ill-effects, but it can hardly be argued that all that is natural is both good and beautiful—or that the body cannot cope with substances that are harmful in some degree. Synthetic vitamins may not sound as good as natural ones, but they are identical.

"Naturalistic" thinking survives and its proponents tend to dislike all change. Pasteurization of milk, which certainly destroys part of the vitamin C and a small part of the B-vitamins, is of enormous benefit to mankind and has saved a great number of lives—but it is still opposed by some people.

Canning of foods is only 150 years old—really large-scale canning rather less—and so is still suspect as a "modern" process. Certainly there is some destruction of vitamin C in the canning process, but otherwise the food is not harmed. The argument should not be whether canned food is worse than fresh but whether it is better than not having such food at all.

Old processes have an air of respectability—smoking, drying and salting are

Brown sugar
The average sugar-eater will take in 3 tonnes of sugar in his or her lifetime. Since all of it is more likely to do harm than good, the arguments about the relative merits of brown and white tend to be somewhat academic. Clearly the best thing to do is to eliminate sugar from the diet. In fact brown is no better for you than pure white.

Brown bread
White bread is almost as nutritious as brown since bakers normally replace most of the vitamins and minerals lost in processing white flour. Processing also reduces an acid in wholemeal that can be harmful; wholemeal flour does contain more roughage from the grain husks, however.

Pasteurized milk
Pasteurization is known to destroy some of the B- and C-vitamins in milk, but it has also saved a great many lives.

traditional methods of food preservation and are therefore accepted by the "naturalists"; but the range of strange chemical substances deposited in the smoking of fish and meat would, if the process were invented today, surely lead to its banning until it had been thoroughly investigated.

Arguments over the harmfulness of refined sugar often miss the point. Sugar pushes more nutritious foods out of the diet and is implicated in many of our "diseases of affluence". But it is eating not refining that is to blame, since brown sugar offers no advantages over white.

Just as food processing is subject to criticism by the "natural" school, so are the methods by which food is grown. No farmer or gardener would deny that organic manure from animal droppings or composted vegetable matter is good for the soil, but what the out-and-out organic grower claims is that food is nutritionally better when grown without any inorganic fertilizers. This is completely untrue. No evidence has ever been put forward (after years of trying) that the nutritional content of foods grown on organic manure or compost is in any way superior to that grown with the use of inorganic fertilizer. The latter is often called "artificial" fertilizer, but this is incorrect. Plants absorb their nutrients from the soil in the form of inorganic salts—their "natural" food. Organic manure has to be broken down to inorganic salts by the action of soil bacteria before plants can use it.

The term "health foods", in that it implies that these foods are "healthier" than the

The honey myth
Honey is a good source of energy, but it works no miracles. It is no better or worse for you than refined sugar, whether brown or white.

Biochemical salts
If you think you need extra mineral salts note what you are buying: calcium sulphate is simply plaster of Paris.

The macrobiotic diet
The Zen macrobiotic diet divides foods into Yin and Yang. Yin foods are acid, Yang alkaline. Supposedly perfect is brown rice, which is both Yin and Yang in the proportions five to one, the ideal balance to be followed in all meals. In the macrobiotic regime (*macro* = great,

bio = energy) almost all foods may be eaten, but there is a strong emphasis on grains and, above all, on brown rice. In theory brown rice would be the sole food, but in practice 20 per cent is in the form of vegetables. A diet that is 20 per cent composed of meat is tolerated but is at the bottom of the scale.

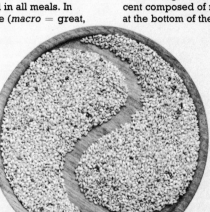

Yin foods:
mushrooms
cucumber
oranges
spinach
butter
cream
pears
peas
oats
pork
honey
melons
peanuts
yoghurt
potatoes
bananas
pineapples

Yang foods:
strawberries
herrings
pheasant
cherries
lettuce
shrimps
carrots
apples
duck
onions
chicory
salmon
sardines
pumpkin
chestnuts
watercress
goat's cheese

other kinds of food we eat, is a misnomer. Vegetables grown, for example, without the use of organic fertilizers, weed-killers and pesticides are not superior nutritionally to any others and are invariably more expensive. What you must decide, therefore, is how much you are prepared to pay to avoid the chemicals used in food production, some of them, such as the hormones used to fatten cattle, derived from natural sources.

Natural poisons
There are poisons in "natural" foods as well as in synthetic. Peanuts and cabbages contain a substance that may give rise to goitre, rhubarb has oxalic acid and cassava, a staple, cyanide. People have even been poisoned by potatoes.

What is in store for our stomachs

Synthetic elixirs will not keep us fit. The future of food is more of the same (less of the same if we are wise).

One thing is certain about the foreseeable future—we will not be living on pills. Many people imagine that one day man will get his food from nutritionally balanced, cheap, synthetic, precooked, flavoured pills—a technological elixir of life. The reason why that cannot happen is that we need on average about 400 g (14 oz) of carbohydrate, 100 g (3.5 oz) of protein and 100 g (3.5 oz) of fat a day (although this can be varied). The total is 600 g (21 oz) even if eaten in the dry state—a little much for pills.

A second certain statement is that we will eat foods very similar to those we eat now. This assertion is based simply on past experience—people change their food habits slowly, and even when they enjoy new foods these form only a very small part of their diets—they still get the greater part from bread or rice and traditional kinds of meat, fish, vegetables and fruit. The term "new foods" includes foods already eaten by some people but not, perhaps, widely known. Snails, Cornish pasties and avocado pears may be new to some but are common foods to others, who, in turn, might find cornflakes or instant dessert whips quite bizarre.

The expansion of traditional local diets

Food from oil and gas
Future animal feed may come from yeasts and bacteria grown on gas burnt off oil wells. Protein from bacteria grown on petroleum by-products is also promising.

Soya bean treatment
Before being eaten by humans, most soya beans are at present treated physically and chemically. The soya is first made into a slurry that is either fed into a "pressure cooker", puffed up as it extrudes and cut in pieces, or spun into a roll as shown. Flavour and colouring matter are added and the final product, often known as texturized vegetable protein (TVP), is made to resemble the meat it is intended to replace or supplement.

has paralleled the advance of transport, refrigeration and food technology and has accelerated with recent developments, but especially with the steady lowering of food prices.

The biggest change ahead is one that most of us may hardly notice. Enormous efforts are now being devoted to producing bigger and better yields. Ideally, mechanical harvesting needs plants that all ripen at the same time, with fruits at the same height from the ground, of the same colour and shape and size, so that they can be packed for supermarkets. The farmer wants a crop that will grow out of the normal season, ripen even in bad weather and be easily stored until the manufacturer wants it. Unseen by the consumers, much progress has already been made along these lines and more will follow.

One of the major changes that comes with affluence is the production of convenience foods. The trend towards ready-prepared, easily cooked or "instant" foods is likely to continue, but it is less likely that we will see a great expansion

of synthetic foods. We already eat synthetic vitamins and food that is synthetically coloured and flavoured, but the foods that make up the greater part of our diets, the proteins, fats and carbohydrates, are easier and cheaper to grow than to make in the factory. The only foodstuff that has ever been synthesized in the factory on a large scale is fat—about 100,000 tonnes were eaten in Germany during World War II.

A wide range of "primary" foods, including grass, straw, paper, sulphate of ammonia and krill, is now eaten directly, mainly by animals, but could be used to extend our diets. The problem is again one of cost. Grass is food of the ruminant, but we can extract the protein from the large amount of unwanted cellulose and eat it first-hand, as is already being done in some countries on a small scale. Straw, paper and sulphate of ammonia are being fed to animals and in turn we get the meat and milk. It is possible to convert the straw and the paper to sugars for us to eat directly, but it is simply not worth while. Krill is the name given to the small shrimps

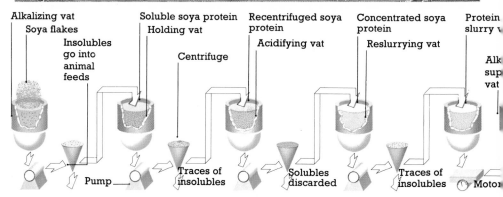

Alkalizing vat
Soya flakes

Insolubles go into animal feeds

Soluble soya protein
Holding vat

Centrifuge

Recentrifuged soya protein

Acidifying vat

Concentrated soya protein

Reslurrying vat

Protein slurry

Alk sup vat

Pump

Traces of insolubles

Solubles discarded

Traces of insolubles

Motor

on which whales feed. The Russians use a factory ship in the Antarctic to squeeze the shrimp meat out of the shell, cook it and freeze it. The product is sold mixed with cheese.

The two biggest current developments in food technology make no obvious difference to what is on our plate. The first is the production of yeasts and bacteria on a factory scale for animal feed. They are grown on petroleum by-products, gas flared off from oil wells and waste carbohydrate from food processing or even paper pulp manufacture. New sources of animal feed could make available to man much of the soya, fish meal and oilseed cake he now feeds to animals. But at present the American farmer can still grow soya bean protein cheaper than the chemical engineer can grow yeasts and bacteria, so the new process has yet to prove its economic worth. One thought for the future is that some 50 million tonnes of gas is flared off from the oil fields of the Middle East and could be used as an energy source for growing micro-organisms. The

yeasts and bacteria that grow on this material are 50 per cent protein and a rich source of vitamins.

A second and well-developed series of new products are the textured vegetable proteins based on soya that are being made to simulate meat; they are added to hamburgers, pizzas, sausages and pies. So, although this is a major change in food production, and even a change in the food we eat, if the food technologist does his job well we will not notice the change.

Much effort is being put into projects to make life easier for the food producer and consumer, again without much change in our eating habits. Have you had a hamburger with onions in small pieces that fall out of the bun? Well, the breeder is producing an onion with large rings—just what the consumer wants.

Do you like small potatoes, all the same size? You can now have them, marble-sized. You can also have seedless cucumbers that do not need peeling. Apples can be grown on short trees so that you can reach the top without a ladder. Even

cube-shaped apples may be used to save packing space: more efficient bees have been bred, oysters grown in "parks" and salmon in "cages". All these "new" foods may pass on to our plates unnoticed.

Much of the impetus to produce new foods comes from the rapidly increasing number of mouths to be fed. We want high yields of food from a limited area of soil. A steer weighing 1,000 kg (2,200 lb) put out to feed on grass will gain 1 kg (2.2 lb) of protein in a day. The same quantity of yeast growing on waste carbohydrate or petroleum hydrocarbons will produce 4,000 kg (8,800 lb) of protein a day. Finally, if bacteria could be grown in the same way it would produce the phenomenal amount of 10,000,000 kg (22,000,000 lb) of protein a day.

So we can expect to see better methods of producing animal feeds, better methods of producing cereal grain—ranging from the Green Revolution to Triticale—more instant, convenience, coloured, flavoured, ready-packed foods. But we cannot expect much change in our main foods.

Soya "meat"

Spun soya (*below*) resembles meat in texture. It has the protein equivalent of meat without the handicap of gristle and bone. A bland flavour makes it suitable to "pad out" certain foods (*right*).

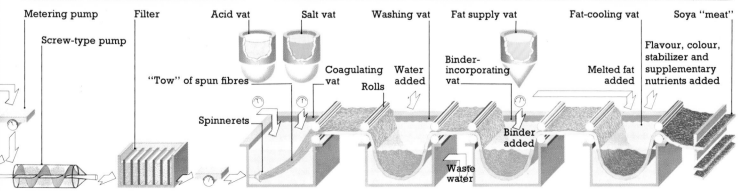

Metering pump
Screw-type pump
Filter
Acid vat
Salt vat
"Tow" of spun fibres
Spinnerets
Coagulating vat
Rolls
Washing vat
Water added
Fat supply vat
Binder-incorporating vat
Binder added
Waste water
Fat-cooling vat
Melted fat added
Soya "meat"
Flavour, colour, stabilizer and supplementary nutrients added

CHAPTER 3

Living
with
stress

Are we paying too high
a price for stimulus?

In the industrialized countries, most people live in an environment that combines rapid change and a high level of nervous excitement with limited physical outlets for tension. There is now increasing biochemical evidence that the resulting stresses can damage the body. Competitive people who find it hard to relax or whose aims in life are frustrated are particularly at risk from stress illnesses. We can all benefit from learning to detect the danger signals and to relax.

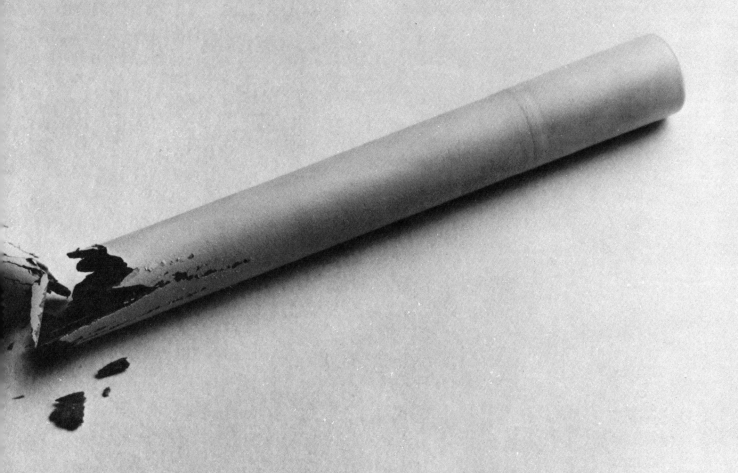

Stress: the charge that ignites us

To function well the human body needs stimulation. The risk comes when our responses are blocked.

The human body and mind are built to take stress. In fact they thrive on it. An experiment with some athletes showed how the body deteriorates when all stress is taken off it. They were made to lie on their beds for a fortnight. Their muscles began to waste away, their bones began to soften and their internal organs and their blood systems functioned less well. This is one of the reasons why hospitals nowadays make patients get up as soon as possible after an operation. Although rest was once supposed to assist recovery, too much of it actually sets the body back.

Mentally, too, we need stimulation and occupation. Sigmund Freud suggested in his book *The Pleasure Principle* that people try to regulate the amount of stimulation in their lives to the level that gives them the most pleasure—not too little and not too much. Experiments have shown that a total lack of stimulation is intolerable for more than a limited period. In fact, even animals will usually work to improve a boring environment.

In this sense stress just means stimulation, load of work. Our job here, and everybody's in everyday life, is to distinguish between normal light load, temporary and tolerable high levels of load and severe or permanent overload.

Stress has many sources. Bodily stress is produced by hard physical work, by strenuous exercise or by disease or wounds. Psychological stress is produced by emotional disturbance, by frustration and by anxiety. The remarkable thing is that the body reacts in the same basic ways to all kinds of stress. All are sensed by the body either as different forms of threat, or as a challenge to achieve something.

Biologically the origin of stress lies in survival. All organisms that live by hunting and which themselves are likely to be hunted—and man was originally one of them—need to be able to react in different situations either by making a big effort to catch their own prey or to escape being the prey of some other creature.

Psychologically, stress is caused by parallels of these situations. The businessman who is facing fierce competition in difficult markets is—despite the fact that he is probably well fed—in a worse position than the primitive hunter-gatherer whose prey constantly eludes him. The politician who lives a life of continuous uncertainty through the rivalries in his own party and the efforts of the opposition to overthrow his government lives a life in which psychological stress is non-stop. Both they and many others must tolerate high levels of uncertainty, which psychologists call non-closure.

In many human societies, and certainly in all urban civilizations, anger is endemic. In the home, at work, on the way to work or in shops we meet with behaviour in others that arouses our anger and aggression. The trouble is that we are not allowed to express it. We must bottle it up and be polite. So to the aggression is added frustration. Or else we may be unlucky enough to incur the wrath of other people who are less inhibited and who do vent their anger on us. When that happens our stress response goes up. Frustration on its own is also a common feature of modern life. When we cannot get our own way at home, when the man in front drives too slowly and we cannot get past, when the customer walks out without buying what we have just spent half an hour explaining and praising, when our boss turns down our best idea, then we are frustrated and under stress.

The many faces of stress

In engineering terms, a bridge is under stress whenever a lorry or car passes over it, but provided the weight of the vehicle is not excessive for the design of the bridge no harm is done. It is the same with humans. It is only when stress becomes extreme, or is of long duration, that the mind or body will suffer. A crowded train journey is a common, recurring example of stress. This may include a feeling of anxiety ("Will I be late for work?") as well as frustration and anger. More serious stresses cause more extreme results. A road accident, for example, is a shock that can leave even an uninjured person emotionally scarred. At an extreme, pleasant as well as unpleasant stresses produce the same bodily results in the short term. It is as stressful to begin a love affair or to win a large sum of money as it is to be caught in a travel hold-up or involved in an accident—although such stresses seldom do harm if a physical outlet is found for them.

Curiously, while we may appear on the surface to react to frustration with anger by shouting or complaining, our bodies actually undergo a fear reaction. And our behaviour is also altered, in the same way as when we are frightened or anxious.

High emotion is also stressful—sorrow and grief especially. Many studies have shown that people can literally die of heartbreak after their husband or wife has died. Depression is the most common reaction to bereavement, but susceptibility to physical diseases also increases.

Surprisingly, perhaps, pleasure is also stressful. If a mother who has lost her son in war—and already been through one period of stress—is suddenly confronted with him alive, she will be under very high stress and her body will react accordingly.

Even love is stressful. Just meeting the person with whom we are in love raises not only the spirits but the body's preparedness for action, as those who have felt their heart pound, their cheeks suffuse with blood, their eyes sparkle and their whole awareness of life and the world take a great lift will know. The act of making love itself is not only as strenuous as a mile run; it too, is accompanied by an alarm reaction in the body.

There is one thing that makes modern urban life more stressful than it was in the past, or still is in the country, whatever your state of mind or health—noise. Experiments with humans and animals show that simple noise causes an alarm re-action. Think of that as you try to read in the tube, or crawl in a traffic jam, or try to converse through the roar, clatter and whine of a machine shop or typing pool.

Just to show how wide a range of things can cause stress, at the opposite end of the scale complete isolation is also stressful. When people were shut alone in an all-white room, blindfolded, wearing loose pyjamas and hearing only a featureless hiss to cover any small noise made by their own movements, they reacted bodily as though they were being threatened. Many people hate solitude, and most of us are far more jumpy and alert when we are alone, especially at night when it is quiet, dark and mysterious.

Perhaps the simplest way of defining stress, then, is any deviation from the norm, whether physical or psychological, pleasant or unpleasant. The next step is to determine how much stimulation the body can safely stand.

How electronics can measure stress

Stress affects people in different ways and different stresses produce different results. Today, advances in electronics have made it possible to measure people's reactions to stress accurately, not only in the laboratory but in their everyday surroundings.

When a person is under stress certain changes take place in his body. Heart rate and blood pressure change; brain activity alters; stress hormones, more especially adrenaline and noradrenaline, appear in the body; free fatty acids may be mobilized from fat deposits into the blood stream; uric acid, another stress-related compound, appears in excessive quantities in the blood and, under these conditions, blood will clot more readily than during relaxed periods.

The latest and most efficient way of measuring stress is with pocket-sized tape recorders. The newest of these can be slowed down to record up to four body activities over a twenty-four-hour period. The activities recorded include heart beat. Every time the heart contracts it generates a wave of electrical activity, which can be picked up by two leads attached to the chest. The recording reveals the heart rate, whether it is beating regularly and whether it is short of blood because of diseases of the arteries. Such recordings are valuable because they give a picture of the heart under stress at any time.

Blood pressure is also recorded. This is a more difficult proceeding. A new technique uses a record of the pulse at the wrist. When the tape is analysed, this measure is compared with the recording for the heart and the result gives the pressure of the blood in the veins and arteries. This gives valuable evidence of the increase in blood pressure caused by activities such as driving, smoking, drinking coffee and sex.

The electrical activity of the brain can also be recorded. The technique has shown, for example, how fatigued pilots on intercontinental flights may show patterns of brain activity characteristic of short periods of sleep. The potential for studying fatigue in drivers, shift workers and so on is clearly immense. Stress technology has only one gap: it ignores emotion—possibly the most important stress factor of all. To gauge this we need, and will continue to need, the human contact of a doctor.

What happens to your body under stress

The primal response is to fight or flee. As the body prepares, some of the physical changes are dramatic.

The body's reaction to stress is to prepare for action. The whole system gets ready for violent physical activity, whether it is advance to achieve something or retreat to avoid something—in other words for fight or flight. The same basic changes, with modifications, take place for either contingency. They can be likened graphically to a country mobilizing for war.

The government, the cerebral cortex or conscious part of the brain, receives and analyses the incoming signals and interprets their meaning. When it receives information that mobilization is necessary, it instructs its alarm centre in the lower brain and brain stem to sound the general alert. The pituitary gland, which is attached to the hypothalamus at the bottom of the brain, releases an alarm messenger hormone (ACTH) into the blood stream. This is quickly carried to the adrenal glands, which sit just above the kidneys. These release two main hormones, adrenaline (or epinephrine) and noradrenaline (or norepinephrine), and cortisones.

The hormones mobilize reserves, direct transport away from areas "behind the lines" to front-line areas and direct communications and detector systems to concentrate on the source of stress. The heart speeds up, pumping blood round the body more quickly, bearing its supplies of oxygen and fuel for the muscles, while the blood vessels constrict at the skin and stomach to divert more blood supplies to the muscles and the brain. Breathing increases in speed and air passages in the lungs dilate to bring in more oxygen. The spleen contracts, releasing more red vessels into the blood to carry the oxygen. The liver releases supplies of sugar while fat or cholesterol is released into the blood from deposits in the body, skin and gut. That stress can increase blood sugar level has been known for over fifty years, since one of the first doctors to study stress, an American physiologist, Walter B. Canon, observed that a tense intercollegiate football match could raise blood sugar in healthy young spectators to the point where it overflowed into the urine, causing a temporary diabetes. Another stress indicator is the skin, which begins sweating ready to shed excess heat. The body's repair system is also set on alert, with an increase in fibrinogen and "platelets", which clot the blood and stop bleeding, and white blood cells called lymphocytes, which help to repair body tissues.

Some of these changes are quite dramatic. The heart beat can go up from a normal rate of about seventy beats per minute to 120, 130 or even more. One television reporter's pulse averaged 150 beats per minute during an evening's broadcasting. Car driving, even on the road, regularly produces heart rates of 160. Novice parachutists show pulse rates as high as 200 on occasions.

All these changes take a little time. The speed of modern life is such that the crisis—the screech of brakes, a sonic boom or a harsh word—is often passed before the body has fully reacted. Then we are left breathing heavily with heart pounding and with no opportunity for corrective action. Our early ancestors might have met a corresponding crisis by sprinting, either in pursuit of a deer, for example, or in flight from a sabre-toothed tiger. It seems likely that stressfully unresolved social situations rarely confronted early man. In later societies, warfare often provided an outlet for the bodily tension built up to meet threatening situations.

The same basic physiological reactions appear to underlie the response to totally different situations. The psychologist Stanley Schachter showed this when he injected a group of people with adrenaline, and then put some in fearful, some in angering and some in humorous situations; others he just left alone. All reacted

Fuel to burn

Tests sponsored by the British Heart Foundation show that competitive motor racing causes a driver's heart to reach 200 beats a minute, nearly maximum speed. Drivers also produce large amounts of the stress hormone noradrenaline, which tunes up their brains and speeds their reflexes but also supercharges their bodies. This is a healthy response when matched by strenuous physical activity. But the racing driver's relatively restricted movements do not burn up the extra fuel—which is why, after a race, the blood plasma of some drivers looked milky from surplus fat. Cyclists fare far better. Although racers get the same noradrenaline boost as car drivers, the physical exertion of pedalling uses up all the extra body fuel.

as might be expected, but more so. Those in the humorous situation laughed more than normal, those in the fearful situation were more frightened and those who were angered were more angry. The others just felt unaccountably edgy. All these responses were associated with similar bodily changes.

The differences that do show up in response to varying stresses are chiefly in the amount of noradrenaline, which seems to be higher in situations when initiative is possible—that is when you are angry and attacking or when you are enjoying something. Racing-car drivers reach very high noradrenaline levels. This too seems to be a relic of our past. Animals that hunt produce high levels of noradrenaline; animals that are hunted produce more adrenaline.

There are some situations in which pre-paring for action is pointless—there is nothing the body can do. This produces a freeze response. Many studies have confirmed how prisoners of war, often quite young and healthy men, have reacted to the crowded confinement and humiliation by just turning their face to the wall and dying. In such a condition of passive terror the heart slows rather than speeds up, and beats irregularly. This is what happened to a group of people whose reactions were measured while they watched the film *Clockwork Orange*. During the sex scenes they were pleasurably aroused, but during the violence they showed the slow, irregular heart beat of passive terror.

One well-known physical effect of stress is a lowering of sex drive. This is what you would expect when basic animal functions are involved. A man who is, in effect, out on the hunt or on the run cannot

afford to stop and indulge in the distractions and pleasures of procreation, especially since making love is itself such a strenuous activity.

Some research suggests that social stress can also act as a kind of population control. Crowded conditions are stressful and reduce breeding among animals; it is likely that humans are similarly affected. Both these factors—stress and overcrowding—may suggest why people usually find that their sexual capacity improves on holiday, away from the stresses of work and the crowded life in towns.

Under mild stress there may be a paradoxical increase in sexual activity in some people because of the general high arousal level. But this soon passes and stress is probably one of the most potent contraceptives, not to say killjoys, of the modern world.

Alarm—and the body mobilizes

Like a country being invaded, the body immediately prepares for action when challenged. Headquarters in the brain alerts hormone squads. The lungs provide more oxygen; sugar and fat reserves are released, heart rate increases and more blood is pumped to the muscles.

Overload: when the body can take no more

Dynamism can be pushed too far. When our defence systems are worn out, stress can be a killer.

If you take a piece of elastic or spring steel and stretch it just so far it will go back to its original shape or size when you let go. But if you stretch it past its limit of elasticity then it will go only part of the way back. Heavy stress overload has the same effect on the human body. It never recovers fully.

A Canadian doctor, Hans Selye, has analysed three stages of response to stress. The first is the brief period while we mobilize to meet the threat or challenge. The second is the process of actually confronting and coping with the stressful situation. If the stress continues for long enough, then the third stage, of exhaustion, sets in and the body can no longer cope. This period comes sooner when stress levels are very high.

In mild or temporary overload the body can cope quite well with additional stress from other sources. If you are putting up with a moderately bad situation at work, being stuck for two hours in a traffic jam or having a row with your wife or husband will not impose too much load. But as the basic stress level rises or lasts longer, then it becomes increasingly difficult to cope with all other forms of stress.

Experiments with animals have shown that the same distortion of the various glands involved in stress mobilization occurs in all kinds of stress overload and exhaustion. The adrenal glands become discoloured and distended, the thymus and lymph nodes shrivel and the stomach suffers bleeding ulcers. In a Swedish experiment army officers were kept at various kinds of demanding work for seventy-five hours non-stop. They were allowed to eat and drink normally but were not permitted stimulants, cigarettes or relaxing physical exercise. All the men showed severe emotional and biochemical reactions. A quarter of them developed dangerous heart-beat patterns, which took several days to return to normal.

Many people find high levels of stress pleasurable. Parachuting from aeroplanes or swimming deep under the sea bring all the alarm responses into play. Many other people who try these sports find them too stressful, but some take great pleasure not only in the experience itself but in over-

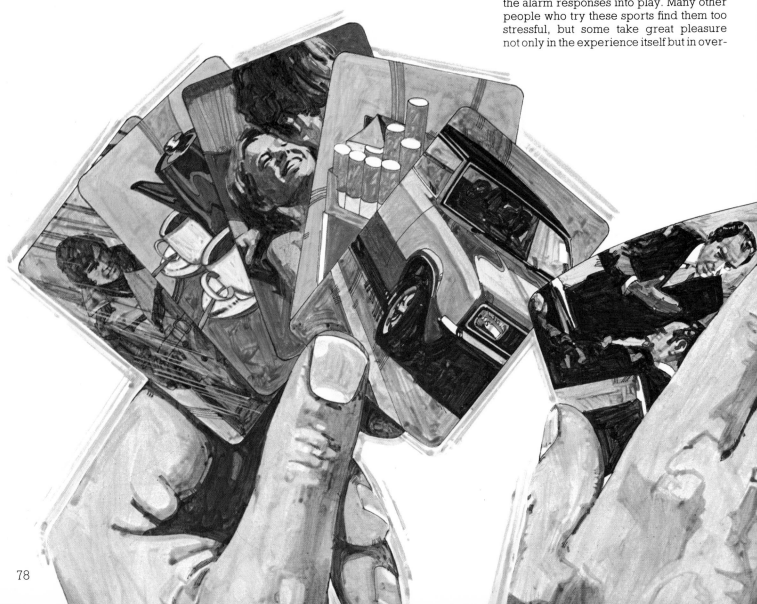

coming the anxiety that accompanies it.

It seems that many people actually become addicted to high levels of adrenaline and noradrenaline, especially the latter. Addiction, after all, is only the state of being habituated to an adaptation by the body to unusual stimulation. In sporting activity stress is normally fairly harmless, since high levels are reached only once or twice a week or month. But when an individual becomes addicted to stress at work—in other words to permanent overload—then he is in trouble.

In many people a curious sort of paralysis sets in, in which they are unable to take any sort of initiative. This is probably a version of the response that sometimes causes animals to "freeze". Most animals, if put into unpleasant surroundings or given electric shocks, will try to escape. If they are caged together, even quite gentle and friendly animals will "take it out on each other" with vicious fighting. Oddly enough, however, if they are conditioned to expect a shock after a signal such as a light or a buzzer, then they respond not by running but by freezing. Much human stress is like this: we have repeatedly to confront situations where we must be prepared for punishment, whether it actually comes or not.

Coupled with this may be a submissive

response that accompanies fear. Without realizing what he is doing, a man may defer to his boss when what the boss is looking for is initiative. Again, the rounded shoulders and anxious look may indicate a lack of qualities that in fact only await the right conditions to be fully usable.

Unlike animals, however, human beings are only too aware of the goals they set themselves and of those set for them by others. In this kind of situation, then, a man or a woman knows that something is wrong; they know they are falling short. But because the mechanism is at the unconscious conditioning level, they will not know why. And so they are set on a downward spiral of psychological incapacity.

Others, perhaps more robust individuals, may take flight from stress in other ways. Some are able to redirect the anger built up in the stress situation and obtain relief in that way. If there is trouble at work they will take it out on their wife or husband. In extreme cases, where all outlet is barred except one, murder may result. Still others escape from reality entirely into semi-delusional states of paranoia, ideas of grandeur or into a cycle of alternate mania and depression.

Two common drugs, nicotine and alcohol, are widely used by people suffering from high stress. Both produce feelings of

relaxation, and alcohol is potent in counteracting fear in approach/avoidance conflict situations (this basic mechanism is why it has such different effects in different people—it lets them do what they really want to). Yet both produce in the body symptoms of actual stress. Nicotine in particular immediately increases heart rate and raises blood pressure and levels of cholesterol and noradrenaline. So just when the smoker thinks he has taken some of the stress off he has actually increased it. Since high cholesterol levels are associated with heart trouble, many doctors have advised dieting or cutting down on smoking to reduce blood fat, but in cases of stress this is only a partial solution. Diet does not cause high cholesterol levels but simply makes the cholesterol supplies available. It is constant stress that calls on those supplies and does the damage.

Long-term high-level stress has physical effects that can be fatal. A permanently high heart rate and blood pressure can cause heart attacks, which are perhaps the commonest result of excess stress. The rapid, irregular beating of the heart, the strain on the blood vessels, especially those next to the heart, caused by the pounding and the pressure, coupled with the damage to the walls of the arteries and veins caused by permanent high levels of adrenaline and cholesterol—plus nicotine and alcohol if the sufferer has resorted to smoking and drinking—add up to a serious health hazard. The same factors can also cause strokes, when small blood vessels in the head succumb and burst, releasing blood among the delicate brain cells and damaging a wide area.

Stomach ulcers are another common result of stress. While blood is diverted away from the stomach, its content of hydrochloric acid, which normally helps to break down food during digestion, is increased. The stomach wall is simultaneously convulsed and attacked by the cortisone in the blood which the adrenal glands have released. In other people it is the intestine that suffers, causing colitis. Still others have a paradoxical rise in skin temperature, causing eczema, or experience an interference with their breathing, causing asthma.

Perhaps less common now than formerly, is death through sheer exhaustion. When people have driven themselves, or let themselves be driven, consistently hard over long periods, they can reach Selye's third stage. The body simply cannot cope with any stress at all and gives up, often quite suddenly. In the relatively affluent years since World War II, death caused directly by "overwork" has been rare. But when failure and frustration attend constant stress, then the danger level is very high.

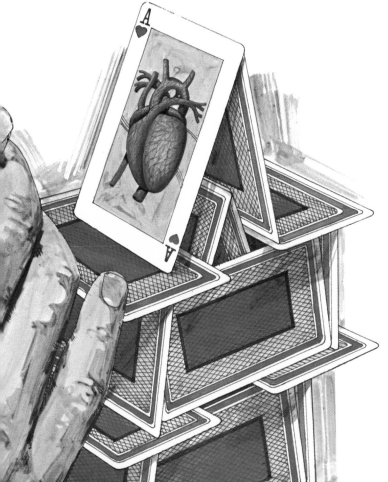

A hand of stress
Each of us builds a house of cards with our life stresses. The higher the house the greater the excitement—but also the greater the peril. Some crises are beyond our control (a road accident, for example, may be unavoidable), but there are major stress cards in our own hands. Car driving, cigarette smoking or coffee drinking are all activities that we can moderate or give up. The secret is to judge how much stress life events are likely to add to the card house. This indicates how many cards can be safely added from your "pleasure pack". Should the house be overloaded and collapse, the penalty may be a heart attack or other "overload" disease.

Are you under pressure and can you cope?

The signs of overload are not difficult to read. Here is a simple check-list. Keep your own score.

The activities that are stressful are often those that bring the most satisfaction or pleasure—a sense of achievement after dedicated personal effort. Coping with stress adequately is largely a matter of assessing your stress levels and then matching them up with your ambitions, your needs and your performance.

The drive to get things done is so strong in many people that they are often tempted to ignore the signs that indicate overload. A severe stress-induced illness seldom strikes without warning. If you are really concerned to enjoy the things you achieve it is only logical to plan a sensible compromise between your ambitions and your physical capabilities. This means being able to estimate the amount of stress in your life and to recognize the signals of tension and anxiety that can add up to a threat to your health, or at worst to your very survival.

Attitudes to work or leisure are just as hard to break as dietary habits. The changes that may be needed to reduce your stresses to a safer level are therefore unlikely to be made unless you have a picture of your individual stress patterns that is clear enough to be convincing.

The equation by which stress can be assessed is governed by three factors. The first is the number of stressful situations in your life; the second is your personality, which determines the way in which you will react to these situations; and the third is your life-style as it affects the capacity of your body to resist stress. Because of the links between these various factors it is not easy to allocate "stress scores" with any degree of precision. But completion of the questionnaires on the opposite page will provide at least a guide to whether you need to ease up on the load your body is carrying. The questions are designed by doctors and psychologists to give similar results in industrial countries as far apart as Sweden, the US and Japan.

Because stress shows itself in both body and mind, a good way to make a general assessment of your stress rating is to take a measured look at the state of your physical health and at your mental condition.

More than two of the following physical signs may well add up to a situation that puts your body at high risk from stress and demands expert medical attention: excess weight for your age and height (see tables on page 53); high blood pressure; lack of appetite; a desire to eat as soon as a problem arises; frequent heartburn; chronic diarrhoea or constipation; an inability to sleep, either because you wake up early or because you cannot drop off to sleep at night; a feeling of constant fatigue; frequent headaches; a need to take aspirin or some other medication every day; muscle spasms; a feeling of fullness although you have not had anything to eat; shortness of breath although you have not taken any exercise; a liability to fainting attacks, possibly preceded by feelings of nausea; an inability to cry or a tendency to burst into tears at the least thing; persistent problems with sex, such as frigidity, impotence or fear of intercourse; excess nervous energy that prevents you sitting still and relaxing.

More than four of the following mental symptoms, (or a total of four physical and mental symptoms) also qualify you for the high-risk category: a constant feeling of unease; constant irritability with family and work mates; boredom with life; a recurring feeling of not being able to cope; anxiety about money, either because you cannot pay your way or because you are driving yourself to satisfy your personal ambitions and/or to keep up with the Joneses; morbid fear of disease, especially cancer and heart disease; fear of death—both your own and that of other people; a sense of suppressed anger because you never allow yourself to lose your temper or vent your rage on something or somebody else; inability to have a really good laugh; a feeling that you are rejected by your family or that they do not care about you; a sense of despair at being an unsuccessful parent; dread as the weekend approaches; reluctance to take a holiday, either alone or with the family; a feeling that you cannot discuss your problems with anyone; inability to concentrate for any length of time or to finish one job before you start another; and a terror of heights, enclosed spaces, thunder-storms or similar situations that appear to pose a threat to your life.

The lists above may make daunting reading, but are designed to provoke remedial action rather than blind panic. If you see them as a challenge to do something positive, then this in itself may be a step towards taking the dangerous stresses out of your life.

Three ways to assess your stress level

A life events table drawn up by Dr Richard Rahe in America puts the death of a husband or wife as the highest stress factor. How many points did you accumulate during the past six months?

The stress of adjusting to change

Events	Scale of impact
Death of spouse	100
Divorce	73
Marital separation	65
Jail term	63
Death of close family member	63
Personal injury or illness	53
Marriage	50
Loss of job	47
Marital reconciliation	45
Retirement	45
Health problem of family member	44
Pregnancy	40
Sex difficulties	39
Gain of new family member	39
Business readjustment	39
Change in financial state	38
Death of a close friend	37
Change in line of work	36
Increased arguments with spouse	35
Large mortgage taken out	31
Foreclosure of mortgage or loan	30
Change in work responsibilities	29
Son or daughter leaving home	29
Trouble with in-laws	29
Major personal achievement	28
Wife starting or stopping work	26
Starting or leaving school	26
Change in living conditions	25
Revision of personal habits	24
Trouble with boss	23
Change in work hours	20
Change in residence	20
Change in schools	20
Change in recreation	19
Change in church activities	19
Change in social activities	18
Small mortgage taken out	17
Change in sleeping habits	16
Change in family get-togethers	15
Change in eating habits	15
Vacation	13
Christmas	12
Minor violations of the law	11

If you scored more than 150 points on this scale of life events during six months you are still safely behind the man who scored 468 without apparent damage. But you are under stress and your chances of falling ill are much higher than usual.

Your personality

Taking 5 as an average on each of the following questions, score yourself out of 10. Then get a close friend to confirm.

1. Eager to compete.
2. Driving, forceful personality.
3. Strive for advancement in work or success in sport.
4. Like getting things done quickly.
5. Anxious for public recognition.
6. Easily angered by people or things.
7. Time and deadline conscious.
8. Anxious for social advancement.
9. Accomplish many different activities.
10. Impatient when delayed or held back.

These questions were designed by two American doctors, Meyer Friedman and Ray Rosenman, who have related heart attacks to behaviour patterns. If you scored more than 50 you are probably a type A person and your risk of having a heart attack is about three times as high as that of a type B person scoring less than 50. Low scorers deal better with stress.

Your life-style

The higher you score on the life-style quiz that follows, the more likely you are to be healthy enough to cope with stress.

How did you feel yesterday?
Well—score 2; so-so—1; terrible—0.
If you did not take any medicine yesterday, not even an aspirin for a headache, give yourself 1 point.
If you have not had any illnesses during the past month, not even a cold or 'flu, give yourself another 1.
If you have not had any accidents during the past month—not even minor mishaps such as a cut finger or a scald, score 1.

How tired were you last night?
Pleasantly—score 2; a bit overtired—1; exhausted—0.
If you slept well last night, score 1.
If you did not spend more than an hour last night watching television, staring idly into space or dozing over a book, score 1. If you practise yoga or set some time aside each evening for a hobby or some other form of relaxation, score 1.

Are you eating too much?
Refer to the charts on page 53 to find your ideal weight.
If you are less than 6 kg (13 lb) overweight, score 2.
Less than 12 kg (26 lb) overweight—1; More—0.
If you take one spoonful of sugar or less in tea or coffee, score 1.
If you eat less than 226 g (8 oz) of butter a week, score 1.
If you do not average more than two large glasses of beer or a tot of spirits a day, score 1.

Do you get an hour or more of vigorous exercise in an average week?
Yes—score 2; half an hour—1. None—0.
If you play any sports, score 1.
If you are not mainly desk-bound at your job, score 1.
If you made love last week, score 1.

How many cigarettes a day do you usually smoke?
None—score 2; less than ten—score 1; more than ten—0.
If you have not smoked cigarettes for five years or more, score 1.
If you do not smoke a pipe, score 1.
If you do not smoke cigars, score 1.

To assess how healthy your life-style is, add up your score and multiply it by four, giving you a percentage.
If you scored 0-25 per cent your life-style is in need of urgent improvement.
If you scored 25-50 you could do better.
With 50-75 you can feel reasonably satisfied. Was it smoking that kept your score down?
With 75-100 you are doing well.
If your combined scores on the three sections indicate a high level of stress and a low capacity to deal with it, you had better safeguard your health either by changing your life-style or by adjusting some of your mental attitudes. It may not be possible to avoid situations of stress, but it would help to take a holiday, get fitter by exercising and cutting down on your particular "vice", and above all learn to relax.

The personality factor in stress illness

Go-getters live at speed. But survival takes stamina, too. In the long run, who stands the pace best?

How well we live with stress may depend at least as much on personality as on physical fitness. Overrich diets coupled with inadequate exercise may account in part for the spread of heart disease during the past half-century. But some researchers have been looking closely at behaviour patterns to see how far stress-induced illness depends on individual temperament. Their findings tend to support the popular idea that there is a strong link between coronaries and captains of industry. As the pace of life and the rapidity of social change accelerates, it is the natural pushers and go-getters who suffer most.

The simplest categories of personality in stress research are those proposed by Drs Meyer Friedman and Ray Rosenman in America, who have distinguished two main types of behaviour, A and B. The type A person suffers from "hurry sickness"; type B is realistic about what can be achieved and the time it will take. A-people

are those most liable to stress diseases. They move fast, talk fast and are impatient. Their speech is commonly emphatic and if you hesitate in the middle of a sentence they are likely to finish it for you. They are finger waggers, table bangers, teeth clenchers. They are highly time conscious, usually setting themselves several goals at once to be completed according to a strict schedule. They are punctual and intolerant of unpunctuality in others. They have to lead and they have to win. In short, they have drive.

Type B people are not necessarily lacking in force, nor are they necessarily lazy. They take a longer view than A-people and recognize that petty irritations *are* petty; simultaneously, and paradoxically, they are less worried about the future. Whereas the A-type has the edge in driving force the B-person gains by being relaxed and may well, if patience and methodical application are required, outshine the aggressive A. Classically, top salesmen are A-people, the top decision-makers are Bs. A-people are the ones who tend to ignore stress symptoms; what is worse, they are the ones who are most subject to stress. If asked to do a boring, repetitive task they are likely to rebel, but if they have to do it nevertheless they will bottle up their rebellion. If left free to originate and initiate they naturally work at a high stress level.

The classic career pattern of an A-type who does not learn to control and pace himor herself properly is that some real success is likely to come early because

of the high level of involvement and energy; but then stress exhaustion sets in and the body and the brain cannot cope.

The effects of exhaustion are generalized: interests outside work get dropped, the capacity to enjoy any activity other than work seems to disappear. But simultaneously work becomes less rewarding; more effort gives poorer results. Pessimism takes over, but there are periods of wildly unrealistic optimism. Effort is dissipated in the search for a quick answer, a magical solution. Colleagues seem dull or hostile and more and more time is spent criticizing them. There are physical responses too—headaches, muscle pains and a sense of being generally unfit. This feeling also has its dangers: a typical response is to eat more and thereby become more sluggish. Flexibility disappears and performance drops. This in itself increases stress. But there is no refuge in blowing a mental fuse by depression. The pressure must be kept up. The result is a body bombarded with adrenaline, noradrenaline, fibrinogen and cholesterol—a body in prime condition for heart disease.

A-people seem set on damaging themselves as much as possible. As they feel the need for some tranquillizing/stabilizing factor they smoke, which raises their blood cholesterol levels. As they realize that they are bad at relaxing they may well drink more heavily than is good for their health. Because of their habit of doing several things at once they risk more accidents. Even the digestion may suffer from eating too quickly.

Much of the trouble stems from personality features that cannot readily be changed. They can, however, be moderated and controlled. Just as a lazy person needs sometimes to whip himself on (or be whipped), a go-getter must sometimes slow down—or be slowed.

Restraint need not mean that you achieve less—that is, if you recognize that finger drumming and fuming at traffic jams is no kind of worthwhile achievement. The aim is to reduce the overload of frustration and—with luck—to lengthen your effective achievement span. There is no easy way forward; if you are a run-down A-type and are really determined to succeed you have to reconstruct some areas of your life. You have to be persistent.

The greatest weapon against stress is realism—the hallmark of the B-person. Set your targets and your schedules with a clear sense of what you know you can sensibly achieve. Look carefully at the possibilities of promotion: you may have been working hard for it, it may appear to be imminent, but will it actually be good for you? Is the most sensible thing to move sideways if you can from your current

Women under stress

Nobody who has real experience of it would suggest that running a home is a stress-free job. It is not, however, a killer. Women tend to react to stress by withdrawing, often into depression or "suburban neurosis" rather than by extending their aggression as A-type men will do—there are few power goals for a woman to achieve at home. Women are thus more prone to mental ills, but have a lower rate of heart disease than men. Women with careers, however, face higher risks than non-working women, especially when they run a home as well.

situation or would that be running away? Do you need to stay among people who irritate you—can you actually come to terms with them or would it be better to cut your losses? If getting to work takes a long, frustrating time consider moving house or changing to a more conveniently placed job. How much ego-boosting do you actually need and how much are you being conditioned into rivalry? Would your life be improved by earning more or by enjoying what you've already got?

Insulating your home against stress

It is all too easy to take stress home and pass it on to your family, and all too difficult to break the habit once it is acquired. If it is to be broken, it must be deliberate: sit down and unwind when you get home, remember to take home flowers occasionally, make time to play with the children, take up an interest or hobby, learn a relaxation method. It may seem artificial at first, but it quickly pays off—for your family as well as yourself.

Don't put your heart into your driving

There is a stress connection between cars and coronaries. Careful driving means more than just avoiding accidents.

The connection between driving and stress diseases is a simple consequence: driving encourages aggression, aggression leads to risk-taking, risk-taking is stressful. Skilful drivers can calculate the odds on any given risk, but they have to pay for those judgements with risks to their hearts, despite their relaxed appearance.

The aggression levels associated with driving are familiar: the build up of impatience as you sit behind a slower car, the thrill of being first away at lights or pushing a car round bends to the point where it is only just holding the road, the sudden surge of anger at all the other people who have caused a traffic jam when you are in a hurry. These are fairly extreme cases, but even if you are a stable, normal driver you are quite likely to be intimate with a machine called a Jaguar, a Hawk, a Rapier, Scimitar, Barracuda, Challenger, Falcon, Mustang or Avenger, none of which indicates an easy-going

intention. You may also feel that you do not drive aggressively—you don't actively wish anyone harm. This may well be true, but it would be surprising if you did not sometimes drive competitively.

Men are tempted by competitiveness more than women and they also suffer from it more in that women appear to have better physiological defences against the worst effects of stress. The person most at risk from driving is the competitive male, the type-A person, whatever his age. That person is likely to be risking heart disease from other aspects of his life-style too, but since the consequences of competitive, aggressive driving are readily observable it is worth paying attention to them on their own.

When tests were done on racing drivers before and after competition it was discovered that their heart rate was rising to 200 (maximum speed) and, more important, that high quantities of fat were

Passing a truck, Mr X sees a "Road Works" sign and drops back.

Stuck in a line of cars, Mr X calms himself by turning on the radio.

A truck suddenly enters from a side road. Mr X lets it through.

A three-hour highway journey will usually entail a number of hazards that call for quick decisions. Even a considerate, sensible driver is bound to suffer some stress, measurable in his pulse rate and in other physical and mental reactions. The graph of an average driver's heart beat shows the sharp fluctuation that occurred during a typical journey.

Despite the danger, Mr Y passes at speed on a narrowing section.

Fuming, Mr Y blows his horn although this achieves nothing.

Horn sounding, Mr Y swerves round the converging truck.

Drivers who regard motoring as a challenge or a race may harm themselves even if they arrive at their destination without visible damage. The incidents that would normally raise heart beat are multiplied and heightened by extra risks or tension and are reflected in sharper fluctuations in pulse rate. Such competitive driving also causes tension in other drivers.

being released into the blood. Because the drivers had not normally eaten before racing the necessary conclusion was that they were manufacturing this fat in their own bodies and thus there was a demonstrable link between very high stress levels and a risk of the fatty degeneration of the blood vessels which causes heart failure. The high rate of heart disease in occupations such as taxi driving points to the same conclusion.

A normal pulse rate is 70 to 80 and exercising the heart to its limit is unlikely to harm someone who is young and fit—200 is not in itself damaging. But tests on ordinary people driving their own cars in normal conditions showed rises to 110–150—levels consonant with moderate to heavy exercise—and to 180 in one middle-aged subject who had already had a coronary. A near accident produced an ECG reading indistinguishable from a heart attack, although the subject was a fit

young woman. The strain on the heart is therefore considerable to an unfit person, and whereas in exercise the fats would be burned up, in driving they remain in the blood stream.

How, then, can the motorist reduce or eliminate the danger without actually giving up driving? First—and most important—it is necessary to adopt a new attitude towards driving, to discard the desire to be first and fastest and to adopt instead an easy-going attitude. This is encouraged by the Institute of Advanced Motorists and goes a large part of the way towards solving the problem. It by no means entails dawdling or driving extremely slowly; what it does entail is driving well, within the legal and traffic limits, and thinking it better to travel comfortably and safely than to arrive a few minutes early.

It is also helpful to have radio or tape music available. This makes motoring

more enjoyable and traffic jams easier to bear. It also helps—and is not emasculating—to have automatic drive in preference to the manual gear-change so rich in sexual symbolism. A less competitive style of motoring inevitably follows.

Finally, it is desirable, where possible, to limit the total amount of motoring undertaken. Shorter distances, for example, should be walked or cycled. In other words, it is dangerous and possibly fatal to regard your car as a harmless substitute for your legs.

It would be wrong and unhelpful to overestimate the hazards of driving, but it is certain that driving for a couple of hours every day places the coronary-prone, middle-aged person in a situation that puts a variety of stresses on his heart. Some of them can be diminished, with a new attitude to driving together with such precautionary measures as taking more exercise and cutting down on rich foods.

Mr X hears a police siren but is within the legal speed limit.

Entering a roundabout, Mr X stops to let a fast-moving car through.

Traffic lights change. Mr X has to brake sharply but stops easily.

At the end of his three-hour journey Mr X arrives tired but not unduly tense. He has been in no danger and placed no severe strain on his heart. Once rested, he is ready for work or an evening out.

2 Hours

3 Hours

Speeding, Mr Y has to pull over and stop as he is waved down.

Mr Y makes the other car brake and let him into the roundabout.

Accelerating, Mr Y just squeezes through in front of crossing cars.

Thrusting through traffic, endangering other road users, Mr Y has travelled slightly further in three hours than the more considerate driver. But the extra ground is hardly worth the strain on his heart.

2 Hours

3 Hours

How to get the most out of your leisure

We all need holidays and look forward to them. Sometimes, however, we are disappointed and come back unrefreshed.

Leisure offers us our chief opportunity to unwind and most people quickly find out what suits them and what does not. The rule still is that a change is as good as a rest: a desk-bound clerk has more to gain from labouring in his garden than from collecting stamps, while someone who strains his muscles all week will usually find it more relaxing to spare them at the weekend.

If this is true of weekends and short breaks it is much more true of holidays. A man who overexerts himself in his job

The benefits of change
Sedentary workers, perhaps, are most in need of change. The person who works at the cash till of a supermarket has a repetitious task that involves little physical activity or initiative and a

benefits from a lazy holiday, such as a coach tour, and his wife will probably enjoy a hotel where she is looked after rather than having to look after others. This may seem self-evident, but it is surprising how many people take the wrong kind of holiday and fall into the trap of choosing one that is simply an extension of their daily routine. The salesman who spends his working days driving from one city centre to another may be tempted, because he has the use of the company car, to pass his holidays driving round the capitals of Europe, encountering the additional strain of coping with various languages, finding places to stay and, perhaps, learning different road rules. His wife, whose time is taken up with cooking and cleaning, may choose a caravan holiday, although this forces her to continue her usual chores under more primitive and difficult conditions. Neither will come back feeling rested.

To the extent that change has become something of a disease in modern society, some people may be unsuited to holidays that present any kind of challenge at all. If they are badly overstressed through a year of hard work they might do better with a "collapse holiday" where the

reasonably active holiday, hiking or cycling in the country, will be far more rewarding than a motoring or coach tour. The excitement of discovering new places will make a mentally stimulating contrast to ordinary working life.

batteries of life can be recharged. For them, a quiet country hotel or a cruise is probably best, or even a health farm.

For everyone, it is usually best to cut the lines of communication with friends and work colleagues. There is little point in a businessman holidaying abroad if he feels bound to telephone his office every day to check up on what is happening.

Sometimes, too, it makes sense to arrange separate holidays for children, unless they are very young. It helps give them a sense of independence and relieves tired parents of the need to mould their holidays around them.

In certain cases it is even beneficial for husbands and wives to take holidays separately from each other. This, of course, must be a matter of personal feeling: what is best for one couple may not be for another, but couples who have some independent interests can find this arrangement broadens their relationship.

Nothing ruins a holiday quicker than worry about money, anxiety about whether travel funds will last out and a need to estimate scrupulously the cost of everything. This situation can be more stressful than not having a holiday at all. A relaxing, rejuvenating and enjoyable holiday need

Holidays and children
Parents usually enjoy the company of their children, but a married couple may often find that, when the children are old enough, a holiday without them is more relaxing. The complete change

not cost a lot of money. A holiday nearer home or in more modest surroundings can be equally pleasant.

Physical factors should also be taken into consideration. If you react badly to the sun, it is asking for trouble to go to a hot climate. North Africa may seem exciting in brochures but it is no fun spending a fortnight indoors with sunburn.

A change of surroundings can upset people physically in other ways. Some who have become accustomed to sleeping through the roar of city traffic become insomniacs in the countryside. Conversely, people used to quiet can be tormented by traffic at a busy beach resort. If you find yourself in this situation, the only thing to do is to give yourself a few days to adapt (it does not take long) and meantime try to relax. If you are woken early, go for a morning walk, for example.

Change in diet or water can affect the digestive system. Many people on holiday get either diarrhoea or constipation— some even get first one and then the other. This is usually caused by a different amount of roughage, fat or some other ingredient in the diet. Just the stress of travelling can sometimes bring on these symptoms. Moderation in eating, par-

ticularly on the first few days of a holiday, will prevent the worst effects and it is surprising how quickly the body adapts to a new diet. People are often tempted to overeat on a package tour in order to get their "money's worth", to drink too much because the local wine is cheap, or to over-indulge in exotic dishes because they cannot easily be obtained at home.

Getting to a holiday location needs careful advance planning to avoid stress. A nervous flyer can have his holiday ruined, not only on the outward trip but by the constant thought that he has to endure the return flight. Trains and ships provide a pleasant, if slower, alternative. Again, driving can put a strain on the heart and people with coronary disease or high blood pressure should try to limit their motoring on holiday. If a car must be taken, the driving sectors should be made short, night driving should be avoided and tiredness must be recognized as a warning to stop as soon as possible.

A holidaymaker always knows whether he has enjoyed and benefited from his holiday as much as he had hoped. If he has not there is no point in repeating the exercise and the rule must be: try something quite different next year.

The stress of speed

Jet travel has the attraction of getting the holidaymaker to his destination quickly. Unfortunately, it also has drawbacks. Sitting cramped for six or more hours will slow the flow of blood, making clotting, as in a stroke, more likely, especially if aggravated by smoking, drinking and overeating. Since the coagulability of the blood is increased by emotion, the moments of take-off and landing can impose additional strain. This danger applies only to those at risk from coronary disease, but everyone is subject to "jet-lag fatigue". A man flying from London to New York, leaving at midday, will arrive at 3 pm New York time. But for him it is already 8 pm; he is tired and longs only for bed. He should respond to his "body clock" rather than the clock on the wall. There are four rules for holidaymakers who travel by jet: take an adequate rest after arrival; travel by day whenever possible; eat and drink in moderation and, lastly, move about the jet whenever space permits.

from the routine of domestic life may also encourage a couple to renew the more intense relationship they had as lovers. The children perhaps go to relatives or to a supervised camp where they can be with others of their own age.

Holidays for drivers

Driving long distances and for many hours, as the truck driver does, imposes considerable stress. Tension builds up over a working year and a holiday in direct contrast is desirable. A fortnight's

leisurely cruising on a canal, river or lake would be ideal, for it combines physical activity, fresh air and a con-tinually changing scene—a perfect change from the driving seat of a truck on congested roads.

Meditation: its relevance to the West

Meditation takes many forms. But all establish a link between health and spiritual peace.

Meditation has understandable attractions for a society living on its nerves and subjected to constant change. Its popularity in the West has increased rapidly since it became clear that this mainly Eastern method of relaxation has measurable benefits in relieving tension. It is now being used effectively to treat medical conditions such as raised blood pressure, migraine and tension headaches. Among a variety of physiological changes observable during meditation are a marked decrease in respiration rate and in oxygen consumption and a decline in concentration of blood lactate, a chemical that seems to increase when the body is under stress.

The word "meditation" comes from the Latin meditari, which means both to "reflect" and to "practise". This gives the idea of combining inward-looking thought and awareness of your own mind and body with a regular training process involving a certain amount of discipline.

In the East meditation is as old as recorded history. In China and Japan, particularly, meditation was closely linked with the religion of Buddhism in its various forms. In Zen Buddhism, for example, meditation is aimed at achieving a higher plane of consciousness in which physical needs are forgotten and man's spirit perceives essential truth. Many Buddhist monks can slip quickly into a state of serenity and peaceful alertness, and some can even survive burial for several hours, emerging wakeful and refreshed. But the religious content and the emphasis on mental concentration rather than relaxation make these forms of meditation forbidding to most Westerners.

What has gained far greater acceptance, particularly in America, is the form of meditation that originated in India called yoga. This stems from the Sanskrit word meaning "to bind" or "yoke" together. It has many forms, or schools as they are called, each with a different aim. The most

popular form in the West is Hatha yoga. The name is again derived from Sanskrit, and combines Ha, the female principle, and Tha, the male principle. This unisex yoga claims to enable both men and women to gain complete control of mind and body. It is the form described in greater detail on the next pages and, when you compare it with other schools, you begin to see why it is more acceptable in Western eyes.

The difficulty in practising Karma yoga, for example, is that you need to devote your life to selfless service and dutiful behaviour, aims that few people are interested in pursuing in our commercial society. The student of Karma is indifferent to both praise and blame, does not accept rewards for his work other than the satisfaction of doing the job well, and devotes his life entirely to the service of his fellow man.

Brakti yoga, meaning "loving surrender", demands of its followers that they be free of both guilt and egoism. They must be humble, unmoved by either happiness or sorrow, or given to any of the seven deadly sins. Unfortunately, sinners seem vastly to outnumber saints in our society and not many of us can face up to the detailed specifications required even to enrol for this school.

Juana yoga, the yoga of knowledge, is more related to the approach developed by Hindu philosophers 3,000 years ago, and is based on the idea of separating the subjective workings of the mind from objective consideration of things as they really are. By this means it is thought to be possible to master all desire by the development of wisdom, although the chances of achieving such idealistic self-control are remote for most people not brought up in this school.

Japa yoga, which requires a comparatively mild degree of mental discipline, introduces two ideas to aid relaxation which are often used together with Hatha yoga. These are to displace distracting thoughts from the mind by repeating a single-syllable word, the mantra, again and again. It usually contains the vowel "O" as in "Om" or "One". The other technique is to concentrate on deep, regular breathing called "prana", which not only cuts out many other bodily sensations but, by blowing off carbon dioxide from the blood going through the lungs, can give a curious all-over tingling, which to some represents an elating experience as well.

Finally there is Raja yoga, or King of yogas, which aims to take its disciples through eight highly spiritual stages. The last one is a state of bliss where the mind is freed of all earthly attachments, and the consciousness is absorbed in a unity with the whole, or "oneness" with the creator,

with nature and indeed with all creation.

More recently, followers of the Maharishi Mahesh Yogi claim that you can arrive at a similar stage by a less painful route, using Transcendental Meditation. The TM technique is based on selection of a personal mantra and concentration on it for twenty minutes twice a day. Physiological measurements provide only a limited guide to mental states. But in 1972, when a test was made in America on thirty-six people using this simplified technique, after only a few training sessions, all achieved similar brainwave patterns to those of meditating monks of long experience.

The methodical Germans have organized meditation by numbers, in the form of "Autogenic Training", which is described in a book of that name by Hannes Lindemann. In contrast with the complicated postures adopted by most students of yoga, all it involves is relaxing comfortably in a chair with the eyes closed. You then talk to one of your arms, telling it six times in turn that it is becoming relaxed, heavy and warm. Between each message you repeat to the rest of you that you feel completely calm and relaxed. These sensations spread to the rest of the body, so that you begin feeling calm, warm and relaxed all over. After ten to fifteen minutes you finish very much refreshed.

Another difference from yoga is that in Autogenic Training your thoughts are neither blocked by a mantra nor allowed to roam free. They are either concentrated on the relaxation messages, or on a positive resolution put in between them such as "I am very confident" or "I can succeed". This auto-suggestion seems to be effective for those who find the basic method acceptable.

Meditation, then, is not just one technique for relaxation or raising your thoughts to a higher plane. There is a wide range of methods, and given an interest in the subject you will have no difficulty in finding one to meet your needs.

Centring the thoughts

Buddhists, striving to achieve a higher level of consciousness in which they can perceive essential truth, aid transition to this plane by use of an object on which to concentrate, such as a mandala. Mandalas are symbols of the universe, varying a little but having an enclosing circle, usually an image of a deity and a tendency to arrangement in fours. The idea of creation as a wheel without beginning or end is a fundamental element in Eastern thought. This mandala shows the figure of the Bodhisattva Avalokitecvata, a compassionate deity and one of the most revered in Nepal.

Yoga: the physical path to serenity

The aim of yoga is to tap inner resources. You can do it without becoming a contortionist.

Not many methods of taking the stress out of life blend a mental and physical approach more successfully than Hatha yoga. Its method of postures and breathing exercises take up only a small part of a working day and its rewards are great—not only mental calm and relief from stress but improved health, increased vigour and a clearer, more alert mind. Yoga, literally union or fusing, aims to unite a tranquil mind with a healthy body so that the two can work together.

Yoga, practised for centuries in the East, is part of the Hindu religious philosophy that aims to merge the human spirit with the universal spirit. Many types of yoga have this aim, but Hatha yoga is most popular in Western society. Contrary to what many people believe, yoga is not a

regime of painful body contortions—when postures cause discomfort it is time to stop them. The postures do, in fact, aim to increase the mobility and suppleness of the body, but perhaps the most important part of yoga is that it is a way to deep mental relaxation.

This mental relaxation has produced remarkable results when used to help people with physical disorders. Dr Chandra Patel, an English practitioner, taught a group of patients the basic Hatha relaxation exercise. Then, with the help of instruction cassettes, the patients practised at home for at least one twenty-five-minute session a day over a period of six weeks. During the study period patients with high blood pressures of 165/101 mm Hg had reduced them to a much safer 146/90 mm Hg. High blood cholesterol levels, another stress indicator, had also fallen from 240 mg per 100 ml to 220 mg per 100 ml. Similar changes are commonly seen during meditation, relaxation and even sleep. What was remarkable about the yoga experiment was that the changes lasted between sessions and for as long as the patients continued to practise yoga, suggesting an overall improvement in the body's reaction to stress. Yoga also appears to reinforce good resolutions, such as cutting down on eating or smoking. A quarter of the smokers in Dr Patel's group gave up smoking and others reduced it.

Yoga does not suit everyone. One in ten of Dr Patel's "normal" control group had to stop meditating because they found it too upsetting. It is the same with most meditation techniques. Some people find that they are unable to relax because when they let their defensive tenseness and restless activity drop, underlying anxieties come welling up.

If you are not one of this minority group Hatha yoga may be your way to living with stress. To practise at home, conditions must be right. The room should be warm, not too bright and as quiet as possible. Yoga requires the discipline of setting aside about twenty minutes at least once a day and defending your yoga time and territory against all intrusion. A thickly carpeted floor is ideal for the sessions.

Making sure not to eat beforehand, you

The Perfect pose

Tension and anxiety are diminished, the mind stilled, the nerves soothed and the circulation stimulated in the Perfect pose. Breathing is controlled and the mind emptied of all interfering thoughts.

should start by lying on your back with feet apart and relaxed outwards, the arms away from the body with palms facing outwards; close your eyes and progressively relax all your muscles, from the feet upwards. Direct your thoughts to each region in turn and, concentrating on the spine, try to feel you are sinking into the carpet. Try to breathe with the diaphragm only, letting the abdominal wall rise and fall while keeping the chest wall still. This relaxed diaphragmatic breathing, called the "breath of life", or "pranayama", controls and quietens the mind. When fully relaxed you can start the meditation part of the routine. A mantra, a word such as "Om" or "One", repeated mentally and slowly in time with exhalation, helps to clear the mind of thoughts and worries. You will find that ten minutes spent relaxing your body and ten relaxing your mind in this way will itself leave you refreshed.

The yoga exercises shown are each designed to benefit a particular bodily function, to relax a specific part of the body and to induce mental calm. As you progress the postures become more complex (though ideally not more difficult) until you are able to achieve the Lotus, or Buddha pose, the hallmark of Hatha yoga.

Warm-up

After the initial relaxation routine, you should start with a warm-up that loosens and tones muscles in back, shoulders and legs and prepares the body for the *asanas* to follow. Stand with feet slightly apart, arms at sides. Exhaling, drop the trunk and head forwards, if possible with the backs of the hands resting on the floor.

Inhaling, stretch the spine, head and arms forwards and then up to the ceiling. For best effect, stretch well before coming upright into this second position.

Exhaling, take arms behind the ears. Clench fists and trace a circle behind, bringing fists into the small of the back. The knees may be allowed to bend slightly.

Inhaling, arch the spine, then, exhaling, flop into the first position. Repeat four times in an almost sleepy manner. Do not jerk, force or overstretch.

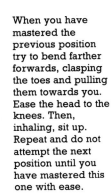

Posterior stretch

The objectives of posterior stretch are to strengthen stomach muscles, slim the waist, stretch muscles and tendons at the backs of legs, tone the body and aid the digestion. First sit with the legs outstretched and arms above head.

Exhaling and contracting the stomach muscles, bend forwards from the hips and ease the head to the knees slowly and without jerking. Try to clasp the ankles. Hold the pose, breathing deeply. Inhaling, sit up, arms above your head. Keep the back stretched while returning to the sitting position. Repeat.

When you have mastered the previous position try to bend farther forwards, clasping the toes and pulling them towards you. Ease the head to the knees. Then, inhaling, sit up. Repeat and do not attempt the next position until you have mastered this one with ease.

Try the previous position with forehead and nose on the knees and palms flat on the floor. Hold, relax, breathe deeply. Inhaling, sit up. Repeat.

The shoulderstand

This position improves circulation. Lie flat on your back, feet together, palms on the floor. Inhaling, raise legs and hips as shown.

Put weight on elbows and support back with your hands. Moving hands up the back raise legs and trunk to a vertical position. Tuck the

chin into the chest. Take hands from back and gradually rest them on thighs. Hold as long as comfortable. Support back with hands and roll down.

Yoga/2: Exercises

The Plough

This yoga position, or *asana*, firms the thighs, flattens the stomach and loosens the spine. Lie on your back with arms at your sides and palms on the floor. Inhaling, slowly raise legs and hips off the floor in a continuous movement. Tilt your legs over your head.

Gently raise more of your upper body off the floor. Exhaling, lower your toes to touch the floor behind your head. Do this slowly with control and with knees straight and together. Hold the position as long as is comfortable.

Curl your toes in, clasp your hands and give the spine and shoulders a stretch by pushing both feet and hands as far away from the body as you can. Do not roll over on the side of your neck. Do not try the next position until this one is mastered.

Bring knees down on each side of your head. Put arms round backs of knees and hands over ears. Hold. Return to position three then slowly to the floor.

The Fish

Start the Fish by lying flat on your back. Cross legs under you and grasp big toes. Lean back on elbows.

arch spine, drop the head back so that the crown is on the floor. Hold, breathing deeply, as long as is easy.

To come out of the pose, slide head back and relax your shoulders to the floor, then release and straighten legs.

The Cobra

Abdominal muscles and internal organs are toned, breasts firmed and posture improved by the Cobra. First lie face down, forehead on the floor with the arms bent and palms flat on the floor, fingertips and shoulders in line and legs straight.

Inhaling, lift head, shoulders and trunk, using back muscles, but keep hip bones on the floor. Hold. Exhaling, lower body to the floor. Relax then repeat.

Inhaling, repeat the second position, then arch the back and straighten the elbows using fingertip pressure. Close your eyes, hold; exhaling, lower body; repeat.

The Dog

Start the Dog in a kneeling position then rise on to your toes, keeping palms flat on the floor.

Walk forwards until feet are flat on the floor. Keep your head down and your chin tucked in.

Keeping palms flat on the floor alternately raise the right heel then the left. Repeat five times slowly and rhythmically, but do not move your upper body.

Raise and lower your heels together, still without moving your palms. Repeat five times. Throughout, you should feel ankle joints being well exercised. The Dog also firms upper arms and tightens thigh muscles.

The Bow

This pose tones and exercises the whole body, firms the upper arms and jawline and tightens abdominal muscles. First, lie face downwards, chin on floor, with your legs outstretched and together. Bend knees and reach back to clasp ankles.

Inhaling, pull on ankles, raise your knees, head, chest and shoulders off the floor to form a bow. Relax, repeat twice. Do not force to lift thighs.

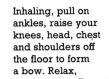

Once you can do the pose easily, rock back and forth on your abdomen four times, breathing normally. Look up to stretch throat.

92

Roll back to cross-legged position in one movement with body and head relaxed forwards. As you do so exhale sharply and loudly. Repeat five times without stopping. This *asana* is particularly good to follow back-bending poses or at any time when you feel back tension.

Spinal Twist

Sit erect with legs outstretched. Then bend your knees and put the right leg underneath the left with the right heel touching the left buttock. Bend left leg over right knee so that foot is flat. Take right arm over left knee and hold

left ankle with right hand. Place left palm behind hip. Inhale. Exhaling, twist to the left from the waist. Breathe deeply.

On each exhalation twist farther. Inhaling, return to front. Repeat, alternating legs and arms. Do every day.

Spinal Roll

Sit cross-legged, grasp right big toe with your left hand and left big toe with right hand.

Inhaling, roll back and over, gradually bringing the knees straight.

Extend your legs fully so that your toes touch the floor behind your head. Keep a tight grip of your toes, but not so tight that it stops you getting your toes right down to the floor.

Supine Pelvic

This posture firms and stretches the thighs, strengthens the spine, tones the pelvic area and makes ankles and insteps flexible. Kneel, separate your heels and sit between feet. Keep knees together and grasp your feet.

Lean back on to your elbows. Arch the spine and drop your head until crown rests on floor. Hold the pose, breathing deeply.

Sliding down, relax your shoulders on to the floor and put arms above your head. Hold and try to have your back on the floor. This posture can eventually become comfortable enough, but be careful at first not to strain the knees.

Relaxation pose and abdominal breathing

Always begin and end every yoga session with these. Lie with arms at sides. Clench fists and tense muscles, lifting arms and legs slightly off the floor. Hold for a count of three.

Exhaling, relax all facial and body muscles. Feel each muscle relaxing completely. Now inhale slowly through the nostrils so that your abdomen expands like a balloon, to a slow count of five.

Exhale through your nostrils, contract abdominal muscles to a slow count of five. Repeat eight cycles. Relax.

Pose of a Camel

Always take great care when you do this *asana*, which stretches thighs and abdominal muscles, strengthens neck, firms jawline and makes the spine more flexible. Kneel with hands on hips and if possible keep your knees and feet together. Push hips and chest forwards.

Inhaling, drop your head back. Put left hand round left ankle, then push hips farther forwards.

Put right hand round right ankle, arch your back and, breathing normally, hold as long as possible. Remember to push thighs, hips and chest forwards and upwards and to concentrate on rhythmic breathing while you are holding the pose.

Biofeedback: measuring the mind's power

You can relax and lower your stress level by mastering bodily processes that were once thought beyond control.

The scope for personal control of stress in modern life has been strikingly shown by developments in biofeedback—a process that enables body processes that are normally involuntary, such as heart rate, blood pressure, skin sweating or electrical activity of the brain, to be brought under conscious control. Until recently, such physiological versatility seemed possible only for yogis with years of practice. But now machines have been developed which enable people to "see" or "hear" a record of their own involuntary body processes and monitor any changes that take place. As a result, biofeedback has become a practical means of teaching people to manipulate body functions.

Stress tends to raise blood pressure and heart rate, increase muscle tone and skin sweating and lessen the amount of alpha wave activity in the brain. (Alpha waves are electrical waves of the brain associated with relaxed awareness.) Control of the underlying processes can reverse such effects, produce relaxation and thus reduce the harmful effects that anxiety can have on health.

The biofeedback machine supplies information both continuously and as rapidly as possible. This enables a person using it to know immediately when his efforts are succeeding and when they are not. Continuous information is far more useful in helping this learning process than short

Head over heart
The mind does not necessarily need the help of a biofeedback machine to exert control over involuntary body functions, produce relaxation and lessen stress and anxiety. Just sitting still in a quiet room and visualizing a tranquil scene can slow the heart beat, induce lower blood pressure and reduce other symptoms of stress. But machines help by measuring success—interpreting the heart rate as sounds, flashing lights or, in a more conventional fashion, as a trace (here shown as it is adjusted from a faster to a slower rhythm by means of mental concentration). Many yogis argue that biofeedback cannot be thought of as a quick alternative to control achieved through meditation. Despite this many people have found that, with the initial help of biofeedback machines, they can rapidly achieve a considerable control of involuntary body functions when away from the machine.

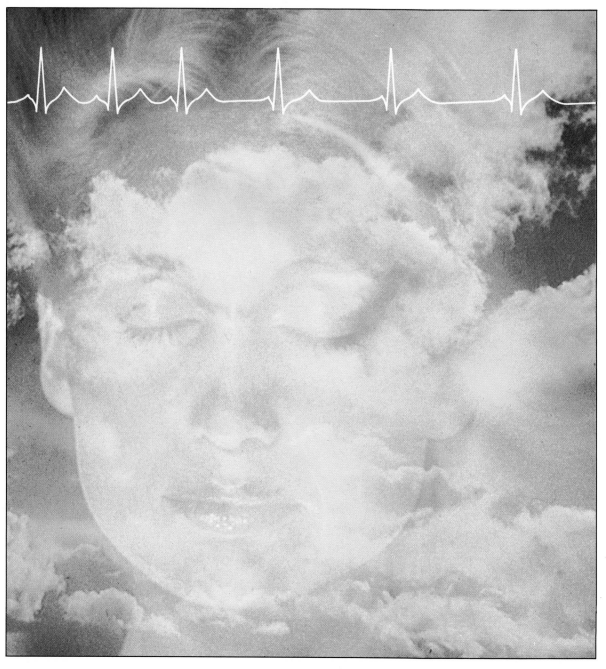

bursts of information at, for example, intervals of one, two or five minutes.

Eventually many people find they can achieve control without using a machine, but for any method of biofeedback to succeed the motivation must be right. The benefits of feeling less anxious or in better physical health are an incentive for some; others find it fascinating to discover how much self-control they can achieve.

Control over involuntary functions is gained chiefly by means of changes in activity of the higher levels of the brain. As a result of these changes, various parts of the "autonomic", or automatic (involuntary), nervous system are switched on or off. Such control can be exercised by using one of the meditation techniques or, with the help of biofeedback machines, by learning to increase the alpha wave content of brain activity, slow down pulse, lower blood pressure or warm the skin of part of the body by conscious thought.

The brain works in such a way that, with practice, merely thinking about a calm and peaceful scene and emptying your mind of worrying or distracting thoughts can produce some of these remarkable results. Certain patterns of deep breathing can also help produce relaxation effects, either by activating the calming, parasympathetic part of the autonomic nervous system or by blowing off anxiety-provoking carbon dioxide gas from the blood stream.

Gaining control of a bodily function through a new self-awareness and with the aid of biofeedback machines is not just a party trick. It is already being used in cardiac units particularly, as a means of treating stress symptoms. Patients with raised blood pressure are linked to a device that continuously reads their blood pressure. If the pressure rises above a certain level, either a light comes on or a warning bell sounds. By lying quietly and practising various relaxation techniques, especially visualizing scenes of great tranquillity such as a beach with a peaceful lagoon, patients learn to control their blood pressure further and further, thus keeping the light off or stopping the alarm bell from ringing. The result is often an effectively lowered blood pressure both during and between sessions.

Another use of biofeedback is to control rapid or erratic beating of the heart (palpitations). In one set of tests patients were connected to a machine that continuously recorded heart rate and beat regularity. The machine had lights of three colours. If a red light came on then the heart was over-revving or beating erratically; a green light meant too slow, while a yellow light showed that the beat was just right. Within a few sessions the patients learnt to drive their hearts at exactly the right rate and some were no longer troubled by palpitations even when away from the machine.

Tension headaches caused by stress have also been prevented by means of biofeedback. In trials conducted at McGill University in Montreal, people suffering from headaches were asked to sit in front of meters that registered the degree of tension in the muscles of the forehead. By watching the needle on their personal meter, each patient received moment-to-moment information about the tension of the forehead muscles. The patients themselves soon found ways to relax the muscles—and keep them relaxed. The results were even more dramatic when the reading was converted into a sound signal that switched off when the required measure of relaxation was achieved.

In the same tests some patients were split into two groups. One group was given accurate feedback information via earphones, the other inaccurate random information. The results showed most strikingly the beneficial action of good feedback. Within nine weeks all the members of the first group had lowered their forehead muscle tension to forty per cent of starting levels, while it remained at over eighty per cent in the second group. After three months of training the difference was even greater and many patients in the first group had either got rid of their headaches altogether, or were taking fewer tablets to relieve them, while those in the second group showed no significant improvement. The deliberate efforts to relax made by the patients in the first group had become automatic, confirming that biofeedback can have long-term benefits in teaching people to control their levels of stress.

If you feel that a biofeedback machine could help treat your stress symptoms, then why not suggest it to your doctor? Even without a machine it is helpful to try to relax on your own by means of tranquil thought and deep breathing. Another good way to monitor your progress is to keep a chart of your own body rhythms. By recording your sleeping, eating, physical and mental activities every day you will soon build up a picture of the stress elements in your life and a critical daily assessment will provide good accurate feedback on a non-mechanical level.

Again on a simple level, feedback techniques related to specific areas of stress and easily carried out at home are to tape record your own voice and play it back, to keep hour-by-hour records of your smoking habits or to make exact notes of your daily food intake. Control of your body starts from self-awareness. What biofeedback shows is that it may be a short step from there to control of some of the emotional strains of modern life.

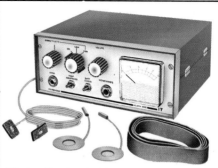

Biofeedback machines

The muscle tension meter or electromyograph (illustrated) is used to help treat headaches, tics, cramps and posture problems. Electrode pads can be put on any group of body muscles, for example those of the head and neck, and link up with a device that records the activity generated by tense muscles. The aim is to silence the machine by learning to relax the muscles.

The skin resistance meter, used to help control sweating, has electrode pads, which are wrapped around the first and second fingers on either hand. The machine operates so that the secretion of sweat on to the hands, which increases when a person is tense, causes a flow of electricity, which produces a screaming tone in a pair of earphones. Relaxation and reduced sweating will stop the noise. Migraine and high blood pressure have been treated with similar meters.

The alpha wave recorder measures fast-frequency alpha brain waves, which rise rapidly to a peak when people achieve a state of mind that is relaxed but receptive, especially during meditation. Electrodes are attached to the back of the scalp and behind one ear and wave peaks are recorded as clicks. The greater the alpha wave activity the more noise is heard in the earphones. Alpha wave training can help people who are overactive and have difficulty in concentrating, and it may also help treat insomnia.

The temperature meter records changes in skin temperature as sound signals. As a person relaxes muscles, skin temperature rises because more blood is allowed to flow near the body surface and the sound is reduced. As well as producing general relaxation these machines are used to treat migraine and to improve circulation to the hands and feet.

Sex: turning stress into happiness

The emotional and physical strains are far outweighed by the relaxed happiness that good sex brings with it.

Sex is the best-known form of relaxation. It is also excellent exercise. It requires no equipment, it costs nothing, it can happen almost anywhere. Anyone can enjoy sex—the young, the middle-aged, the old. It is for most people the greatest single source of pleasure, but for many a major source of stress, too.

The connection between sex and stress is two-way. Too much stress is likely to lead to a neglect of sex, for the simple reason that tension causes stress hormones to be secreted in greater quantity; the secretion of sex hormones reduces correspondingly. Conversely, long-term neglect of sexual activity means a gradual build up of tension. Yet sex builds its own tensions, and the stress to which prospective lovers are subjected before they gain release through sex can be enormous. Romeo and Juliet, unable to gain that release, found death the only alternative. Their case was extreme and anyway it was complicated by social factors, but most people have known high sexual tension.

Variety is the key to sex. An urge to have sex is a basic drive and is almost universal, but the forms it may take and the frequency with which it may occur are as varied as people themselves. For reasons that are mostly cultural most people in the West look for a one-to-one relationship, which they seek to maintain for the duration of their adult lives. If achieved it gives not only the benefits of sex, but also the security of fitting in with a pattern, of being "normal".

From this most intimate of contacts practised over a period of years under many different conditions the benefits are largely psychological. The confidence that comes of having made something difficult work; the satisfaction of solving individual problems; the deep knowledge of someone else and the greater understanding of people it gives; the security starting from your most private life that allows you to concentrate on external problems; the sense of risk and adventure in trusting yourself to someone else. A great deal of psychotherapy is directed at helping people evaluate themselves—to know what they are capable of, to accept their limitations—and this, in an amateur way, is just what people who are thoroughly relaxed together in an intimate, satisfying way spontaneously do for each other.

The success of a sex relationship normally depends on continued sexual activity to dissolve the stresses that are brought to the relationship from outside and those that are generated internally. From adolescence to old age, sex is normal. Sex, as Alex Comfort said in *The Joy of Sex*, "ought

The three Rs of sex
Recreation (*left*), Relationship (*centre*) and Reproduction (*right*) are the fundamental aspects of sex, each with its own stresses and rewards. There is often a progression through the three stages, though this is by no means inevitable. At all stages, though, the tension of sex is relaxed and resolved through it. It is, perhaps, permanent, deepest and most intimate sex that brings a deeper understanding of the people involved. It certainly resolves the tensions between two people and eases the stresses that they have contracted outside their relationship.

to be a wholly satisfying link between two affectionate people, from which both emerge unanxious, rewarded and ready for more''; it is that long-term release as much as the single orgasm which is the joy.

Sex is not just for procreation; nor is it just a way to an orgasm. The ordinary person spends a widely variable but significant proportion of his or her waking hours daydreaming about sex; these fantasies increase expectation and therefore need to be released. The consequences of not doing so are all too familiar to most people: sleeping becomes more difficult and less refreshing, tempers get shorter, concentration is diffused. Just as the urge is many sided, so is the release, and although orgasm is the most thorough of all releases a little affection, a thoughtful caress, can at the right time do more. It is the understanding of what each partner requires that is the key.

Understanding, patience, tenderness cannot be overemphasized. Not only are they the key to happy sex but to a durable relationship, too. It is generally accepted that a major influence on adult sex is the security, warmth and tenderness that a child receives from its mother. It is in that relationship that the normally fortunate child learns to trust another person, to give and receive love and, in retrospect, to appreciate the value of patience and caring. Even if that relationship is established it will still be strained by adolescence, when independence takes over from dependence, when the adolescent has to be self-assertive *vis-à-vis* the other sex. Parental frankness about sex and appreciation of its pleasures can be enormously reassuring; if a child knows what is going to happen, the first menstruation and the first ejaculation will not seem disturbing but will be welcomed as signs of increasing maturity.

Some of the same qualities that parents have to show children are necessary between adults: understanding when your partner really is too tired for sex or when, in fact, a little patience and gentle stimulation will result in sex that is rewarding for both of you; patience in changing sexual habits of your partner which do not suit you; allowing yourself to change to accommodate your partner's individual needs.

No relationship is all honey, harmony and roses. People fight, they get bored with each other, resent one another, find other people, have whims that amuse themselves alone. It is a common experience that it is the practice of sex itself which introduces many strains. Once the fruit has been tasted it is a rare person indeed who is not tempted to raid other people's orchards.

Sex can also become a weapon that one partner may use on the other to win a point. Then there are the anxieties of performance—thirty years ago Kinsey found that the American male peaks at an average of nearly three orgasms a week in the late teens and declines steadily to one a week at sixty; the average for women was steady throughout adult life at less than one a week. Another worry may be infertility—ten per cent of couples cannot have children. But caring sex is a solvent, and a particularly good one if it is used regularly as a creative way of dealing with stress rather than being kept on a shelf to be taken down and used when a relationship needs to be repaired.

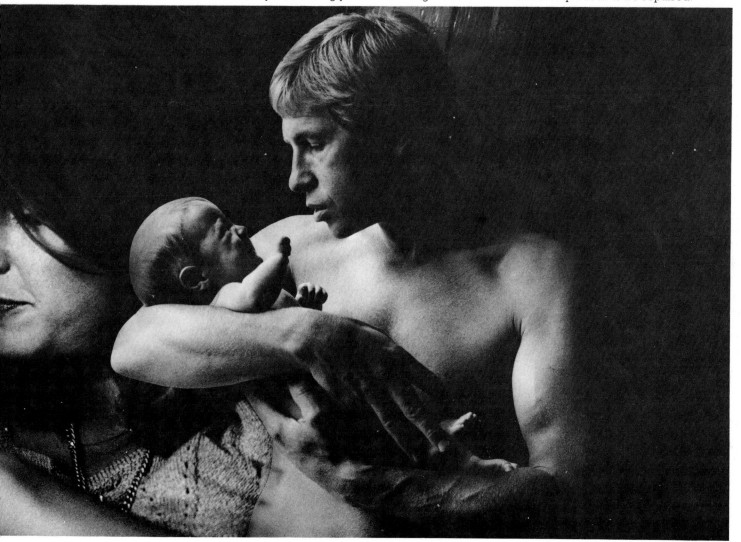

Sex: when anxiety spoils the game

If sex goes wrong it can cause despair and a whirlpool of increasing stress. Getting out of it is difficult, but it is not impossible.

If you don't look forward to having sex there is something wrong with your attitude, your circumstances or, less likely, with you. The plain fact is that a lot of people get in that situation at times, and the greater the suppressed desire the worse the frustration. There is a vein of masochism in just about everyone, and it is all too easy to accept frustration even though you know it is doing you harm. If you have lost sexual confidence, or never gained it, you have to work at it and learn, just as you learnt other skills.

What happens when a man becomes impotent, or a woman finds herself frigid? What happens when you get pregnant at the wrong time or you find you are a homo-sexual? What if you cannot get pregnant? What if you fall out of love with the one you are married to? These are the genuine stresses of sexual relationships and few people avoid all of them.

Very few men cannot get an erection, but on the other hand a great many men will seem impotent when under stress. For many the most stressful time of all is the first, but a new partner, an excessive set of non-sexual anxieties or advancing old age can have the same effect. The man is inclined to feel a fool, and it is up to his partner to reassure him in general and to make that failure seem trivial.

Women suffering frigidity are similarly placed; they can feel trapped and inadequate. The condition is less common than occasional impotence in men, but should be treated in a similar way. It is up to the man to give reassurance and be patient—actively patient—until the condition eases. Masturbation is often a great help towards knowledge of your own bodily needs and responses. Talking about the difficulty with your partner so that it becomes a shared problem is always better than concealment and pretence.

Finding yourself pregnant at the wrong time is one of the great nightmares. Many women will expect the man involved to "do something about it"—to marry if both are single, or to arrange for the termination of the pregnancy if local laws, social *mores* and medical facilities allow it. The first answer, as with all sexual stresses or dis-orders, is to talk the problem out at once in an attempt to come to terms with it one way or another. Certainly a woman needs a lot of resilience—as well as gentle, understanding support—to recover from the crisis.

Finding that you are a homosexual can cause enormous stress for both men and women, particularly if you are already committed to a family. It is difficult to accept because it means not only an alternative life-style but repression, too. "Coming out"—being publicly recognized as an active homosexual—is difficult for all but young exhibitionists. But it is essential to recognize that there is no need to change: if that is the way you are or the way you have chosen, the world today can and will accept it if you insist.

Infertility often strains an otherwise entirely successful relationship to the point of breakdown. Ten per cent of couples cannot have children at all and many more have some difficulty. Success is more likely in some sexual positions than in others, but if you are making no progress see your doctor. Much is known about infertility and you are more than likely to get some help. The vital thing is not to let temporary failure put you off sex.

Unwanted pregnancy and unwanted homosexuality are particularly dramatic sexual accidents; most people will get through life without them, though the odd pregnancy scare or the occasional homosexual urge in the adolescent/early adult experimentation phase will affect many. It is the longer-term worries that cause stress to most adults: how often to have intercourse, failure to achieve orgasm, the collapse of loving relationships.

For what it is worth, the available evidence on the frequency of intercourse between vigorous adult couples in settled relationships in Western industrial countries indicates an average frequency of between two and three times a week, tapering off with age. Because that figure is an average, a normal range would be between once a fortnight and every night.

The first generalization about orgasm is that women normally have fewer than men, although in theory most women are physically capable of having more orgasms than men. The male orgasm is biologically essential (for impregnation) whereas the female orgasm is not. Given that intercourse depends first on the male being aroused, given that there are occasions for most men when they reach orgasm rapidly,

Sex and understanding
Good sexual communication often means that you need to talk less, but if that sexual sympathy and understanding are lost it becomes imperative to talk the problems out.

it is not surprising that the female orgasm rate should be lower than the male's. The second generalization is that orgasm is not the be-all and end-all of sex. If, however, you do not get an orgasm more than once in a blue moon you are not getting the best out of sex and a good sex manual will indicate new ways of stimulation.

Few mature adults would disagree that keeping a durable relationship going on all levels is difficult. Equally, few would disagree that it is worth trying. Unfortunately, sex is an early victim of stress and we tend to let it go instead of holding on for dear life to its benefits. There is no easy way out: both of you will simply have to will the trust and desire back, though relaxing agents such as holidays and alcohol can be of considerable help.

Much anxiety is also expended on wondering what is normal and what is permissible. The short answer to both is that if you both enjoy it, if it hurts nobody and if it does not create anxiety it's good. Adolescents should be told that the same rule applies to masturbation. As a means of relaxing tension and developing sensuous capacity it is no more harmful than exercising any other part of the body.

Adolescents have on the whole the largest problems, for their attitude to shared sex must be conditioned more by hearsay than by experience. The social pressures in an adolescent group to demonstrate sexual success can be damaging, as can repressive family attitudes and social codes. The parental attitude should be that sex is a private matter but not a secret one. Nobody can teach sex, only the way to approach it.

It is your attitude, much more than your physiology, that will decide your sexual happiness. Your body cannot be anxious but your mind can. Sex eases anxiety but anxiety spoils sex. It is a chicken-and-egg game and the only way out of it is trust: if it is going wrong, trust yourself to get it straight again and trust your partner to do the same with your cooperation and help.

The stress trap
Poor sex or no sex builds stress and there is nothing easier than to let that stress feed on itself and grow.

Sleep: making sure you get enough of it

You may need less sleep than you think. But there are simple ways to stop keeping yourself awake.

Whether we are under stress or not, we need sleep. Without it, hallucinations start to occur and after about ten days with no sleep at all death can become a real likelihood. We know that on average a new-born baby spends almost two-thirds of its time asleep, that by the age of four or five the proportion has dropped to under half and that the average adult sleeps for about seven hours of the twenty-four. Some doctors believe that adults who regularly sleep more than seven hours are doing themselves harm because their body processes are becoming too sluggish. However, anything between four and eleven hours a night is quite normal. It is your life-style and your constitution that dictate how much you should sleep.

The mystery is why we need to sleep. The most plausible theory at the moment is that input of sense data to the brain has to stop for several hours a day to allow the brain to rationalize, disperse and store the day's intake. Consider how much information the brain takes in accidentally during the day—everything you see, hear, touch, smell may stir associations in the subconscious; if all these things are left unsorted, so to speak, in the brain the effect would be similar to a mail sorting office with the staff on strike.

We cannot be certain yet, but it seems that the process of rationalization that goes on in the brain is closely related to dreaming—indeed, dreams may represent the process itself. It is also likely that dreams may be useful to express parts of our waking urges that have to be repressed for social or cultural reasons—the erotic fantasy dream is an obvious example. Other dreams are probably prompted by sense data too strong even for sleep to block out: a familiar example is dreaming of bells when an alarm clock is ringing.

We have different levels of sleep: shallow, deep and "paradoxical". Shallow sleep is the first stage, in which breathing is light and the body slows down; people often change position in this stage—thirty or more changes are normal in one night's sleep. In deep sleep the body is thoroughly relaxed, growth hormones are released and the body replaces dead cells. In "paradoxical" sleep the level of relaxation is much the same as in deep sleep but the brain is much more alert. Breathing becomes irregular and the eyes can be seen moving rapidly under the eyelids. It seems that it is in this stage that dreaming occurs most profusely; if deprived of paradoxical sleep subjects will within a few days show marked behavioural disorders. It is in paradoxical sleep also that sexual dreams become prominent.

Babies will apparently spend up to fifty per cent of their sleeping time in the paradoxical stage, adults about twenty per cent. A cycle of shallow-deep-paradoxical sleep repeats itself throughout the

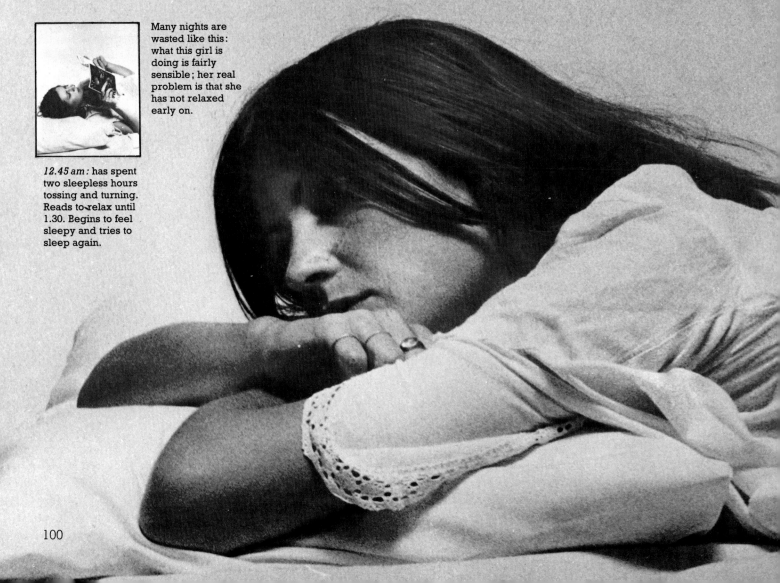

Many nights are wasted like this: what this girl is doing is fairly sensible; her real problem is that she has not relaxed early on.

12.45 am: has spent two sleepless hours tossing and turning. Reads to relax until 1.30. Begins to feel sleepy and tries to sleep again.

night—normally four or five times. The greatest objection to the use of sleeping pills (apart from the possibility of addiction) is that they appear to derange this pattern and to reduce the quantity of paradoxical sleep. A reduction in paradoxical sleep is probably a normal feature of ageing, though there is still doubt that the elderly need less sleep than the young or middle-aged: differences may well be due to the relative mental inactivity of many elderly people.

Catnapping—if you can manage it—reduces your night's sleep requirement considerably. By keeping fresh during the day you can easily cut your night sleeping time by half. In order to catnap, though, you must be able to relax very quickly and very efficiently.

A good method of relaxation is this: lie flat on your back with your arms beside you, the hands slightly away from the body. Starting from the feet think of each part of your body in turn and command it to relax. As soon as it has done so move on to the next part. If necessary, repeat the process from foot to head several times until you feel yourself going to sleep.

The commonest reason for not sleeping is that you believe you won't. Very few people have a good night's sleep every night of their lives and equally there are very few people who literally cannot sleep. In most cases not sleeping is attributable to straightforward causes: diet, anxiety, circumstances or simply lack of fatigue.

Circumstances are probably the most obvious of these factors. If you are sleeping in a noisy place you are less likely to sleep well than if your bedroom is quiet. You may think you have got used to sleeping with noise—indeed you may seem to sleep the whole night through—but the disruption will have its effect none the less. Dramatic changes occur in sleep if the noises are unfamiliar. The sound of the sea, for those who are not used to it, is notorious for ruining a good night's sleep. All you can do is make sure you are sleeping in a place that is as quiet as is reasonably possible. If you are going to stay there be patient and get used to the noises.

Bad beds are another common hindrance to sleep and stale air is no help either, but there is no need to sleep always with the window open. As long as the room remains fresh and pleasant you will have enough air.

The effects of diet are also straightforward. If you eat a large meal shortly before going to bed you must expect the more obvious manifestations of digestion to continue. A full bladder will soon wake you, cheese and coffee definitely act as stimulants to the brain (cheese has a similar chemical effect to that of amphetamines) and alcohol, like barbiturates, produces heavy but unrefreshing sleep.

The effects of anxiety are anything but straightforward, common though they are (more women lose sleep through anxiety than men, married men lose more than single men). The ordinary person must reckon to have periods when he or she will be worrying too much to sleep well. Usually the effects are no more serious than those of a common cold. But to perhaps halve your sleep for a few consecutive days once or twice a year is very different from losing sleep night after night for weeks at a time. Then you must do something to alleviate the source of stress: come to a decision if you possibly can; if not, learn relaxation. Pills, a last resort, cure nothing.

2.30 am: gets up, still not sleeping. Makes a hot drink and until 4 am writes a letter that she has been worrying about.

4.15 am: victory at last. The cause of anxiety is removed and general fatigue can now have its relaxing effect.

9 am: overslept. Feeling less than bright and knowing that she will be yawning over her work that afternoon.

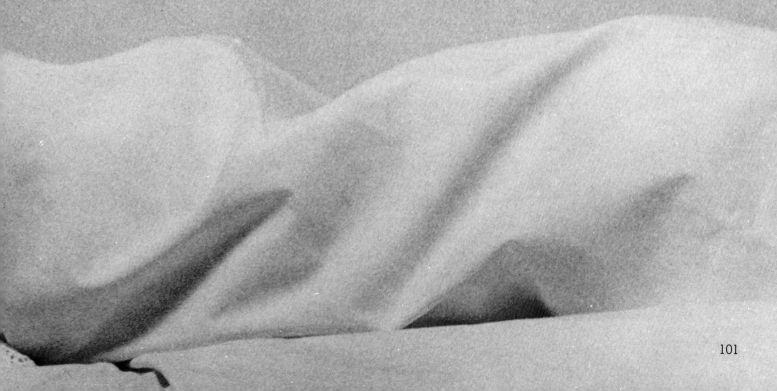

Psychotherapy: removing the mental block

While a doctor of medicine may treat the symptoms, emotional conflict often needs to be treated by a doctor of psychology.

OBSESSION

Obsession
Like many other psychological problems, obsession can be caused by anxiety. Someone with a true obsession feels compelled to repeat certain actions, such as turning round a certain number of times before closing a door, although such actions are very inconvenient and obviously absurd. Obsessions act to divert anxiety.

Phobia
People with phobias can become so afraid of, for example, mice, spiders, open spaces or crowds, that they panic and are sometimes physically sick. The phobia acts as a kind of protection to the mind from a deeper emotional problem with which a person cannot come to terms. Phobias need the help of a psychotherapist.

PHOBIA

Our minds are constantly under stress, not only from the outside—the environment and other people—but also from within, from our own emotional reactions. Emotional conflicts are unavoidable, but they are usually resolved without too much strain. It is when the conflicts are evaded or repressed that our minds and bodies are likely to suffer real damage.

Physical symptoms brought about by emotional stress are known as psychosomatic or psychogenic. They include ulcers, colitis, asthma, allergies, anorexia (undereating), overeating, headaches, stammering and, in women, menstrual disorders. It may be that even coronary heart disease and cancer—the great killer diseases of the century—are largely the result of deeply repressed feelings buried in the unconscious. Man, it seems, is disturbingly able to alter his body chemistry and we are still in the early stages of finding out how and when.

On the mental side, psychologists classify emotional disorders in many ways, but the main categories are *neuroses*, which, although they produce much suffering, do not interfere with a person's ability to cope

with most areas of life, and *psychoses*, which do cause serious interference and debility. The stresses set up by emotional problems can reveal themselves in a wide variety of personality disorders. The inadequate personality, for instance, is unable to respond to stress and instead of tackling problems does not even attempt to cope with them. The paranoid personality, on the other hand, is hypersensitive to stress and overreacts by being suspicious or jealous. The obsessive-compulsive personality avoids stress by indulging in a rigid daily ritual, for example of always dressing and preparing for work in exactly the same order every morning, down to the smallest detail.

Such personality disorders are only extreme examples of the patterns of behaviour many of us develop to cope with the stresses of life—the hungry infant cries for its mother's attention; the frustrated businessman works out his aggressions on the squash court. The trouble comes when the pattern of behaviour we adopt either prevents us from achieving our goals in life or does not resolve the emotional conflict it is intended to resolve. Our emotional

health then begins to suffer—and our bodies suffer with it.

Emotional health in adulthood depends on many factors, including psychological development in childhood and interpersonal relationships. But an important underlying factor seems to be the way in which we evaluate our own emotions. The first step towards solving an emotional problem is often to recognize what our real feelings are about a situation. If these feelings are repressed into the unconscious then permanent and damaging conflict can be set up.

Take the case of the fat girl who eats compulsively because she feels lonely and unhappy. Instead of facing up to the problem and trying to solve it, she represses it. She may rationalize: "I need the food to keep me going"; project the responsibility on to someone else: "My mother always made me leave my plate clean"; deny the situation: "I'm not overweight for my type of build"; compensate: "This new suit makes me look really slim"; react by avoiding the possible solution: "I'd buy some bathroom scales but you can never trust them"; or find another explanation

DEPRESSION

NEURASTHENIA

HYPOCHONDRIA

Depression

Everybody gets depressed at some time, but depression becomes a serious problem when it is semi-permanent. Such depression is often accompanied by feelings of anger on the one hand, with a despairing sense of inability to retrieve the situation on the other. The underlying anxiety may be so extreme that the person attempts suicide.

Hypochondria

The hypochondriac is persistently convinced that he is ill. This total preoccupation with health and fear of disease and death is one way in which people show extreme anxiety and dissatisfaction with life. The confirmed hypochondriac is difficult to treat because he is always changing his doctor as a result of mistrust or a disagreement.

Neurasthenia

Someone suffering from neurasthenia complains of constant weakness and fatigue, but as soon as things start to improve and his anxiety diminishes the fatigue vanishes. The person with such anxiety-produced inertia never has enough energy at difficult times to try getting to grips with his own problems and needs help from a psychotherapist.

for a disappointing incident: "That man is taking no interest in me, but I expect he's married anyway". In the same way, a man with an ulcer may have no idea what is causing his problem because he has not acknowledged to himself that he bitterly resents his boss.

What if candid self-assessment does not produce a solution to an emotional problem? If the conflict goes back far enough and is buried deep enough, the block may only be shifted by psychotherapy. This method of dealing with stress is often seen as a last resort, after less effective methods, such as drink and drugs, have been tried in an effort to ease the burden. The shrill claims of competing theorists in the field of psychotherapy may partly account for this reluctance. In addition, many people suspect that a course of analysis will be hard on their pockets, their time and their egos.

Yet modern psychotherapy has come a long way since Sigmund Freud founded the analytical method of therapy. One of the most significant changes is in the time-scale of treatment. Whereas a classic course of psychoanalysis used to take several years to complete, modern methods aim at a much speedier approach. Many people still start psychotherapy at the shallow end only to find that the final alleviation of their symptoms lies in the depths of more exhaustive treatment. But active therapy concentrating on current problems rather than childhood traumas often shows quick results.

A good psychotherapist is not one who lectures or advises, or tells you how to organize your life, but one who listens with an open mind and tries to give you the opportunity to resolve your own problems. He does not prescribe drugs or aversion therapy for your emotional problems; nor does he see you as an inferior human being. During the course of a treatment session that may last fifty minutes he allows you to say whatever comes into your mind, however frank, so that he can understand your individual troubles and, using knowledge derived from other cases as well as yours, give practical advice and guidance.

As well as one-to-one relationships, between patient and psychotherapist, many people find help in group therapy.

It takes different forms but is aimed basically at encouraging people to help themselves by sharing their problems and feeling less isolated. Encounter groups, which have been tried by an estimated two million people in America, use a wide range of face-to-face methods to break through people's defences and get them to express their genuine feelings. At a still simpler level of self-help, people who do not want to put themselves into such challenging situations can often vent their anxieties simply by talking them out with an understanding person, as priests and family doctors have long known.

Whatever form it takes, psychotherapy involves a highly individual journey back through the barriers erected against feeling, often as a result of stress. These barriers may involve the body as well as the mind and, for this reason, lasting help with emotional problems must ultimately involve healing "the whole man". Rather than using tranquillizers to block the effects of emotion on the body, or trying to argue yourself out of a problem, the best way to deal with emotional conflict is to come to terms with your inner self.

CHAPTER 4

Exercise at your own pace

How to look and feel better
without being a fitness bore.

Unlike a machine, the body wears out
faster when it is idle than when it is used.
But maintaining adequate fitness does not
call for the kind of masochistic regime
that makes exercise seem hard work. The
difference between keeping your body in
good working order and letting it clog
up and run down will be only forty
minutes a week if you follow the
programme in this section of the book.
The charts on pages 122–3 show you
how to use the exercises progressively
and safely.

Exercise: why should we bother?

We can lose our innate strength and agility as muscles and body tissues deteriorate and wither with disuse.

It is easier not to exercise. It is easier to take an elevator than it is to climb the stairs. It is easier to be driven than to walk. It is easier to leave a coin on the pavement than it is to bend and pick it up. It is easier to wait for the next bus than it is to run for the one that is just leaving.

But by taking the easy path you could be sacrificing your health, for the body deteriorates through lack of use. Physiotherapists and physical training instructors have an adage that nicely describes this fundamental truth. "If you don't use it," they say, "you lose it." If we exercise we feel better, eat better and even look better. The reverse is true in all cases if we do not.

Evidence is the feeling of weakness most people experience after an illness that has required a period of bed rest. It is natural enough to ascribe the blame to the illness itself, but the truth of the matter is that you are weak because you have been lying inactive in bed, not because you have been ill.

What happens is that your body adjusts to the demands you make on it. If you lie in bed for a week, your muscles, heart, lungs and circulation quickly adapt to the situation. Their efficiency decreases drastically because they do not need to be particularly efficient to supply your energy requirements. Even your bone marrow will stop producing so many red blood cells because fewer are being destroyed by activity. When you get up and start moving around, your body cannot immediately readjust to the new demands you are making (it takes the bone marrow about three weeks, for example, to catch up with the normal production of red blood cells) so you feel physically "washed out" until the balance begins to be established again.

This balance between energy supply and demand can be upset just as radically in the opposite direction. If you have not taken any physical exercise for years and suddenly decide one morning to go on a lengthy run, your body will leave you in no doubt that you have asked too much of organs accustomed to a more sedentary life. Worse, you could place an intolerable strain on your heart.

Lack of exercise affects the working of your body in four main areas: the strength of your muscles; the flexibility of your joints; the efficiency of your heart and lungs, and the circulation of the blood. All of these are interconnected and help produce the side effect that is the visible result of inactivity—fat.

Excess fat and cholesterol are formed when your body takes in more Calories than it uses. If you consume 2,500 Calories a day and only use 2,000, the extra 500 Calories will be stored as fat. In about two weeks, you will have put on as much as a kilogramme (2.2 lb) in weight (7,000 Calories = 1 kg, approximately).

The best way to use up excess Calories, and prevent putting on weight, is a combination of diet and a balanced programme of exercises. With regular physical activity to burn up most of the excess, you need only make a very small adjustment in your diet in order to balance intake and expenditure.

So exercise can control your weight, strengthen your heart and body and reduce the likelihood of an early death from a heart attack. But why should being physically fit make you feel better emotionally? Or, indeed, why should it help you cope with the stress of modern life?

Although it is far from being proved beyond scientific doubt, most doctors agree that the agent responsible for improving your mental state as you become physically fit is the powerful hormone noradrenaline. It is believed to act as a general stimulant, increasing alertness, reducing fatigue and helping concentration. Excessive amounts of this stimulant can be harmful if not coupled with physical activity, but when balanced by proper exercise, noradrenaline can tone up the body and produce the physical glow and mental tone we associate with good health.

Where high spirits start

The impulse that makes a man vault a gate when he could have climbed over it sedately—or opened it—is the mind's response to a fit body. Without exercise, you won't feel like jumping anything. Four main parts of your body may let you down.

Muscles become smaller unless they are adequately exercised. Some of them can virtually disappear in a matter of days (like the vastus internus, a pear-shaped muscle in the knee, which will wither to the size of a toothpick after only a week of bed rest). Apart from affecting your physical strength, weak muscles will not pump sufficient blood to adequately exercise the heart.

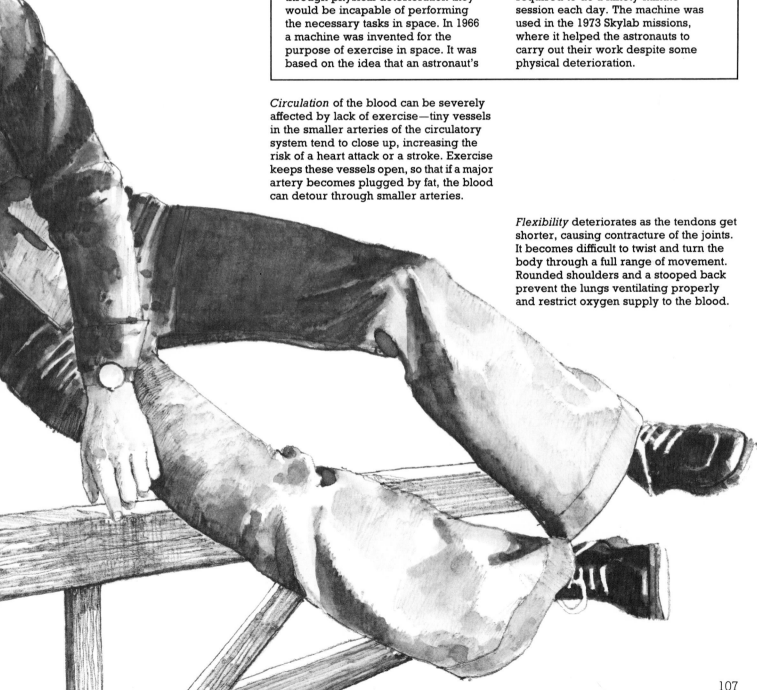

The heart is a muscle like any other and requires exercise to function efficiently. It is a volume organ, which means it has to store blood from the muscles as well as pump blood into the veins. Without the stimulation of physical activity, the heart gets smaller and is put under stress because it is unable to store sufficient blood for a strong contraction. As the heart and lungs work together, the less efficient the heart the less efficient the exchange of oxygen in the lungs.

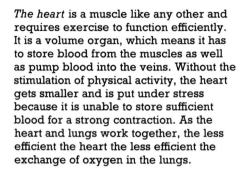

Astronauts—inactive space captives

The effects of lack of exercise were quite spectacular in astronauts during early space voyages in the 1960s. In week-long trips they lost nearly ten per cent of their bone mass. During the course of a fourteen-day flight they lost up to fifteen per cent. Not only were they missing normal exercise but they lacked the gravitational force that our muscles must automatically push against when we move. This meant that they were deprived of any postural exercise. It was feared that through physical deterioration they would be incapable of performing the necessary tasks in space. In 1966 a machine was invented for the purpose of exercise in space. It was based on the idea that an astronaut's heart rate while exercising would give an indication of how hard his system was working in weightless conditions. A low heart rate would show that he needed more work. The resistance of the machine—a sophisticated stationary bicycle—was automatically adjusted in response to heart rate. If actual heart rate was lower than desired heart rate then more resistance was put on the pedals and heart rate would increase. Astronauts can now exercise at a prescribed heart rate and on prolonged flights are required to do a ninety-minute session each day. The machine was used in the 1973 Skylab missions, where it helped the astronauts to carry out their work despite some physical deterioration.

Circulation of the blood can be severely affected by lack of exercise—tiny vessels in the smaller arteries of the circulatory system tend to close up, increasing the risk of a heart attack or a stroke. Exercise keeps these vessels open, so that if a major artery becomes plugged by fat, the blood can detour through smaller arteries.

Flexibility deteriorates as the tendons get shorter, causing contracture of the joints. It becomes difficult to twist and turn the body through a full range of movement. Rounded shoulders and a stooped back prevent the lungs ventilating properly and restrict oxygen supply to the blood.

The myths and misconceptions of exercise

Some people still believe that exercise, like medicine, does you good only when it is unpleasant. This view is mistaken—even risky.

Misconceptions about keeping fit are perpetuated because the image of physical fitness has been dominated for years by puritan masochists—the kind of people who enjoy an ice-cold shower, set out to train to the limit of their endurance and believe that everyone else should do the same. It was only when a few individuals began to explore how little you need do to keep fit, rather than how much, that it was appreciated just how much cant, nonsense and myth surrounded the whole subject of exercise.

Much of the antagonism to the idea of exercise comes from the kind of misleading advice that follows:

"So you want to get fit? Right, the first thing you have to accept is that it is going to hurt. If you aren't as stiff as a board the day after you start exercising then you can be sure it is doing you no good at all. There's only one way to get rid of stiffness—go out for a run and keep running until you feel you can't go any farther. Then make yourself keep going.

"What I would recommend is a cold bath every morning. Take some sugar or glucose tablets to give yourself extra energy and then go for your run. Running is the best exercise you can get, but it is

essential to work up a good sweat—so wear a track suit, or if you can get a rubberized outfit that will be even better. You should run—or do some kind of hard physical exercise—for at least an hour every day. Any less, and you are wasting your time.

"When you finish, put on a sweater straight away to keep warm and avoid catching a cold. Then it's a good idea to take a hot shower, followed immediately by a cold one to tone up your system.

"Now, as far as diet is concerned; make sure you eat plenty of protein because you will need the extra energy it gives you to sustain the exercise. If you find you are getting overtired it could be for two reasons—you are losing too much salt or not getting enough sleep.

"Try taking salt tablets before exercise every morning and go to bed earlier. If you only get six hours' sleep one night make sure you have ten hours next night to catch up.

"Follow this regime and you'll be fit for anything in a couple of months. Oh, one final word—no matter how thirsty you are, never drink while you are exercising."

This advice sounds convincing enough, if somewhat spartan. It probably reflects, to

Athletes may eat T-bone steaks at every meal in the belief that they are building themselves up, but in fact protein cannot be stored in the body as an energy source. Proteins build new tissues, enzymes and hormones and are essential because their component amino acids cannot be manufactured in the body. But they are not significant as a source of Calories and once you have taken in enough for your body's requirements, further supplies are unnecessary.

Working up a sweat is unhealthy and possibly dangerous. As you get hotter a large volume of blood moves out towards your skin (that's why you go red in the face) and deprives your muscles of the volume of blood they need to function well. Your heart may be strained pumping to keep up supply.

a greater or lesser extent, what many people imagine they would have to put themselves through to become really fit.

Fortunately, all the above is rubbish from beginning to end. It is based entirely on myths, rather than on sound physiological principles.

Such a regime will not produce all-round fitness; and what is more it can be downright dangerous to your health.

The suggestions put forward in the "advice" above can all be refuted.

First, the idea that exercising only does you good "when it hurts" fundamentally contradicts the philosophy of physical training today. Now it is agreed that the right way to start is with a series of gentle exercises in a balanced programme designed slowly to improve the condition of your body. Thus you should never suffer from stiff muscles and you should certainly never approach the point of exhaustion. Fitness does not have to be achieved at the cost of bodily discomfort.

It is a popular fallacy that the more protein you eat, the more energy you will have. Sugar (or glucose) does not create extra energy, either. Taken in quantity before exercise it could stimulate an undesirable insulin reaction. Only after a strenuous physical work-out lasting more than an hour is it necessary to replace lost body sugar artificially.

Extra salt can do more harm than good and will not stop you getting overtired. When you perspire you lose salt, which should be replaced, but a tiny amount with food after exercise will adjust the balance. Salt tablets taken before exercise can dry out your body cells and cause nausea and muscular cramp.

It is best to exercise in as little clothing as possible in order to stay cool. You cannot catch a cold because of a change in temperature. It is healthier to leave your sweater off until you cool down.

A cold shower following immediately after a hot one will do you as much good as a cold bath—that is, no good at all.

Running is not the best exercise you can get. It is a good exercise for your heart and lungs, but it cannot of itself produce all-round fitness.

It is not vital to exercise every day; neither is it necessary to spend hours at it— you can get just as fit by exercising for minutes. The Canadian BX exercises are rigorous, yet occupy a maximum of eleven minutes a day for men and twelve minutes a day for women. In Britain, Alistair Murray's fitness course takes up no more than forty minutes a week and in America Dr Laurence Morehouse has devised a thirty-minute-a-week comprehensive exercise programme.

Even the idea that you will be fitter if you get more sleep is usually wrong. Sleep cannot be stored. If you get only a few hours' sleep one night, there is no benefit to be gained by sleeping longer the next night. For adults, sleeping beyond about nine hours can actually have a detrimental effect on energy because the body begins to run down—heart beat slows, metabolism lowers, circulation gets sluggish. Thus when you get up, you will be weaker than you would have been if you had risen earlier. What happens is that you "charge your batteries" during the first six hours of sleep, but the "charge" starts slipping away after eight or nine hours.

Myths die hard, particularly for generations with youthful memories of gasping for breath, spots before their eyes, in some never-forgotten gymnasium while a barrel-chested instructor urged greater effort in painful pursuit of fitness. Small wonder so many were left with the distinct impression that "it only does you good when it hurts".

Running or cycling until you can go no farther could be fatal for a normally inactive person because of the sudden strain placed on the heart.

If you are thirsty, drink—especially while you are exercising. Fluid lost through physical activity has to be replaced, otherwise the body becomes dehydrated and additional strain is placed on the heart. The old idea that drinking during exercise leads to cramp has no foundation in fact.

Cold showers are fine for masochists, but useless for keeping fit. Sudden immersion in cold water can constrict the blood vessels of the heart and aggravate problems such as angina.

The revolution in fitness thinking

Exercise has swung from too little to too much. Now the right balance can be established.

Fitness for its own sake was an idea that had little currency 150 years ago. Writers of the 19th century extolled climbing or walking because they were pleasurable pastimes that put man in touch with nature rather than because they might forestall bodily ills. Exercise was also largely military—riding, shooting and fencing were all useful skills, and even swimming and rowing could come in handy.

Women might play tennis—a very slow game by comparison with the one we now know—or croquet, and they might take fairly short walks. Only gentle exercise was thought suitable for them, and the idea of exercising for fitness would have been mildly distasteful. When young women took to bicycles in the 1890s they were told they were risking their femininity for a fad.

In boys' private schools organized games made an appearance early in the 19th century, but more as a means of recreation than of keeping fit. The revival of the Greek ethic of "a healthy mind in a healthy body" gave athleticism a moral purpose, but still not a medical one. While privileged schoolboys enjoyed those sports they thought to be gentlemanly, physical education was introduced into ordinary or elementary boys' schools in the form of military drill and gymnastics. Girls' schools were slower to introduce physical education, but towards the end of the century Roedean, one of Britain's top girls' schools, made physical exercise—in dress that did not "excite attention by eccentricity"—compulsory for its pupils.

Although advertisements for an array of eccentric-looking exercise machines began appearing in Britain well before the end of the century, most adult Victorians saw no need to take special measures to keep fit. Physical education and team games were seen primarily as "character building". More practical considerations prompted Swedish landowners to keep their peasants in good physical condition by instituting a programme of regular exercise based on callisthenic principles. Germany similarly used callisthenics to improve the well-being (and work capacity) of the working population.

But America was the first country really to seize on the idea of "the body beautiful". At the turn of the century, a Dr Dudley Sargent of Harvard University put forward his plans for creating the ideal physique— a complex and detailed programme of exercises aimed at building the body to conform to an "ideal" standard of measurements. In truth, it did not do much to improve overall fitness, but no matter:

Grace, not muscles

In this "gymnastics" class (*below*) at a girls' school in 1888 the young pupils are in fact exercising more for poise than fitness. At the London College of Women in 1880 the only exercise was "a daily walk two by two along the same road preceded by two or three governesses, all primly dressed."

The iron horse

Exercising was approved in the late 19th century if it was for medical purposes on patent machines (*left*). The belief in the health-giving properties of horse-riding was such that horse machines were as popular then as rowing and cycling machines are now. Most devices were of dubious benefit.

The vaulting horse

Gymnastics often had a military flavour in the late 19th century. They also aided the well-muscled physique that was held desirable in a gentleman. The exercises embodied the purity of form— which, the theory went, was allied with a Grecian purity of mind.

it was a first step towards recognizing that fitness was desirable for its own sake. Soon Americans were puffing and panting every morning with Walter Camp's Daily Dozen. Then Charles Atlas, the "world's most perfectly developed man", in 1921 introduced his "dynamic tension" exercises (see pages 144–7).

Over the next three decades it was firmly established in America and elsewhere that the advantages of keeping fit, for both men and women, were many and indisputable. Yet it was clear that too few people were getting the message.

By the 1950s deaths from heart disease in both America and Europe were reaching epidemic proportions. Doctors knew that a combination of overeating and inactivity was largely to blame. But why were so many people ignoring advice that they should take more exercise? Research into public attitudes towards fitness slowly began to uncover the answers—and a picture of total confusion about the requirements for fitness. Physical training instructors dedicated to hours of "knees

bend, arms stretch" exercises (sometimes as a punishment) and the introduction of gruelling training schedules for athletes had left their mark: an impression that keeping fit was difficult and unpleasant.

Clearly, a new approach was needed. Doctors and other experts began to look at the problem from the other direction, to find out just how little an individual needed to do in order to keep fit. Not fit to run a four-minute mile or climb Everest, but simply fit enough to cope with the stress of everyday life and lessen the risk of cardiovascular disease.

What emerged led to a revolution in thinking about physical fitness, because it was shown that you need to do very little indeed to get fit and stay fit. The breakthrough came with the publication in 1958 of the Royal Canadian Air Force BX exercises, a regime that was designed to improve muscular strength, bodily flexibility and the efficiency of the heart and lungs. Anyone could do them and they occupied only a few minutes a day.

The only weakness of the BX system was

that it was geared to age rather than individual condition. Obviously the level laid down for any age would be too strenuous for some but not demanding enough for others. A more accurate measure was needed.

In the early sixties researchers in America and Britain came up with the answer—a progressive series of exercises monitored by the pulse rate. Your own pulse indicates how hard your body is working, so if you are provided with a set of guidelines you can not only keep a check on your progress but you can also ensure that you are exercising at a level that is adequate but does not cause excessive strain. It is knowing how to interpret that throbbing vein in your wrist that now provides the key to achieving physical fitness with a minimum of wasted effort and in a minimum of time.

Fitness for all
Increased awareness of the need for fitness was shown in Auckland, New Zealand, when, in March, 1976, 12,000 citizens set out on a mass jog.

How fit are you— really?

The answer may be revealing. We all tend to think of ourselves as being fitter than we actually are.

Athletes need to train for many hours to achieve the extra margin of performance that wins competitions. They push themselves to limits far beyond the boundaries of ordinary physical fitness. For most people, however, this is unnecessary, for fitness and performance are separate phenomena. The object of getting fit is to be able to run for a bus, not run a four-minute mile; to be able to carry home a heavy bag of shopping, not an Olympic gold medal; to enjoy an occasional game of tennis, not win Wimbledon.

If you embark on any course of physical exercise with a picture in your mind's eye of emerging as superman or superwoman, the result is inevitable: disappointment.

Becoming physically fit simply means improving the condition of your body so that you can easily meet the demands of everyday life and still have something in reserve to cope with unexpected or sudden stress. The object, in essence, is to recapture some of the health, strength and vitality of youth. Most people find as they get older that their physical condition deteriorates. However, much of this deterioration is caused not by the ageing process itself but by neglect of your body.

If you are strictly honest with yourself, you will probably have a reasonably clear idea of just how fit or unfit you are. Can you feel your heart thumping after climbing a few flights of stairs? Are you left gasping for breath if you have to run a short distance? Is it a terrible effort to bend and tie your shoe-lace? Do you ache after digging a small patch of the garden? Are you overweight or a heavy smoker or both? Do you, even subconsciously, tend to avoid physical effort if you can?

Perhaps you feel that none of the above applies to you. If you think you are reasonably fit and healthy, try this simple "How

An all-round test

These simple exercises will give you an indication of your state of fitness. However, they should not be attempted without a doctor's advice if you are undergoing medical treatment or have a history of heart disease. Stop if you begin to feel overstressed.

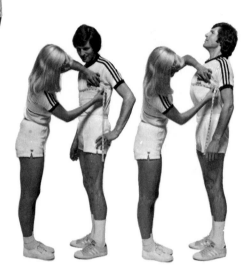

Weight: Pinch your body at the waist. Is the skin-fold less than 2.5 cm (1 in)? (Every 0.6 cm [0.25 in] in excess equals 4.5 kg [10 lb] of body fat.)

Lung efficiency: Take a deep breath. Can you hold it for at least 45 seconds?

Chest expansion: Let all the air out of your lungs and measure your chest. Then inhale as deeply as you can and measure again. Is the difference at least 9 cm (3.5 in)—6 cm (2.5 in) for women?

Strength: Lying flat, hook your feet under an immovable object such as a bed or heavy chair. Sit up slowly, with your arms held out in front of you. Can you repeat this exercise ten times?

Press-ups: Lie face downwards, palms on the floor under your shoulders. Keep the body rigid.

Can you straighten both arms, then lower to the original position at least five times without undue effort?

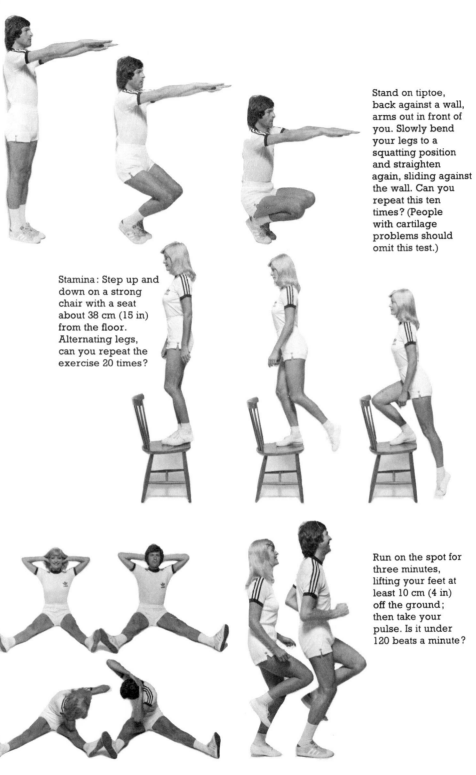

Stand on tiptoe, back against a wall, arms out in front of you. Slowly bend your legs to a squatting position and straighten again, sliding against the wall. Can you repeat this ten times? (People with cartilage problems should omit this test.)

Stamina: Step up and down on a strong chair with a seat about 38 cm (15 in) from the floor. Alternating legs, can you repeat the exercise 20 times?

Run on the spot for three minutes, lifting your feet at least 10 cm (4 in) off the ground; then take your pulse. Is it under 120 beats a minute?

Suppleness: Sit on the floor, legs wide apart, hands clasped behind your head. Can you, without undue straining, lean forwards and touch each elbow to the opposite knee?

If the answer to any of these questions is "No", or if any of the exercises involved particular effort, then you are not as fit as you should be and it is evidence of your need to take more exercise.

fit am I?" test. Dr Laurence Morehouse, professor of exercise physiology at the University of California at Los Angeles in America, lists five basic requirements for the minimum maintenance of the average human body.

1. Twist and turn the major joints through a full range of movement to keep the body supple.

2. Stand for a total of two hours a day (not necessarily at one stretch) to help the circulation of the blood and put stress on the bones to maintain their structure.

3. Lift an unusually heavy load for at least five seconds to maintain muscular strength.

4. Raise the heart rate to 120 beats a minute for at least three minutes every day, thus exercising that vital organ.

5. Burn up 300 Calories a day in physical activity to prevent becoming overweight.

All of these requirements can be fulfilled during the course of an ordinary working day without formal exercise. For example, a housewife who walks briskly to the shops, never hesitates to bend down to the lowest shelf or stretch to the top shelf, carries her bags home herself and then vacuums through the house, has probably completed the minimum maintenance schedule.

Similarly, an office worker who climbs the stairs instead of taking the elevator, resists opportunities to sit down, gets off the bus one stop early and does not ask a secretary to fetch and carry for him, is also going a long way towards fulfilling basic maintenance requirements.

The flaw in the idea of staying fit without exercise is that it requires you to *think* fit and resist the very natural inclination to take the easy road. Dr Morehouse suggests as a general principle that you should not lie down when you can sit, not sit when you can stand and not stand when you can move. Unfortunately, human nature inclines us to reverse this order. How many people walk between bus stops instead of standing and waiting?

Another problem is that you have no way of ensuring you have covered all five requirements, short of keeping a detailed log of your day's activities, and no way of accurately measuring your effort. For most people a balanced programme of exercises is probably more efficient.

On the following pages you can learn how to get fit with a simple course of exercises that takes up no more than forty minutes a week. The object is not to achieve a peak of fitness, like an athlete, but a level at which your body is functioning efficiently in all major areas and thus better able to cope with sudden stress. Your own individual level is determined by your pulse rate (see pages 120–1). The course will, in fact, get you as fit as you need to be.

The quick way to keep your body supple

Seizing up at the joints is not "natural" even in old age. Muscles and tendons simply need to be exercised.

Someone once described modern man as a "constipated biped with a bad back". The implication is that the human body has not adapted too well to the problem of standing up on two legs. Sagging postures and nagging backaches that often accompany middle age appear to support the theory of adaptive failure. But in fact evolution has equipped man perfectly well to stand upright—if only he would.

What happens on the "use it or lose it" principle is that, without adequate exercise, tendons and muscles shorten as we get older. This causes contracture of the joints, making it more difficult to twist, bend and turn. Because it is more difficult, we subconsciously employ tricks to avoid making the effort, thus aggravating the problem. For example, if you want to tie your shoe-lace and you find difficulty in bending, you will probably put your foot on the chair. Of if you are reversing in a car you may turn your legs and pelvis as well as your shoulders to avoid twisting at the waist.

The stance of many elderly people—back hunched, elbows and knees bent, feet apart to maintain balance—shows the effect of increasing immobility. It is thought of as the typical posture of old age. In reality it is the typical posture of a body that has been allowed to seize up at the joints. It is often avoidable, except in the various forms of rheumatism where, through some body malfunction, the joints become inflamed, stiff, and ultimately non-functional.

Postural laziness is not confined to the old. Round shoulders are a posture defect found in all ages. Over the years the horizontal muscles across the upper back lengthen and the chest muscles contract, making it more difficult to straighten the

shoulders. The stretching of one set of muscles at the cost of allowing an opposing set of muscles to contract is often the first symptom of the body stiffening up. In an extreme case even the bones can change shape because they begin to articulate in the wrong position. In the spine the vertebrae may begin to move against each other on the rims rather than flat on top; the edges of the bones wear away and discs may be displaced or "slipped".

Most of these problems can be avoided by five simple exercises that occupy no more than two and a half minutes a day. Physiotherapists call them "mobility" exercises, meaning the mobility of the joints. Their object is to stretch the muscles, tendons and ligaments of the body in order to achieve a full range of unrestricted movement at all major joints.

Mobility exercises do not make you fit, but are designed to keep your frame in shape. There is no real physiological connection between suppleness and physical fitness. For this reason, no benefit can be gained by working at mobility exercises longer than the recommended time. Two and a half minutes a day will give you the full range of movement; only a contortionist would want more.

Holding yourself straight and being able to bend and twist and turn without difficulty also helps your lungs to ventilate more efficiently. Prove it to yourself with this simple experiment. Sit down, lean forwards and hunch your shoulders. Let out all your breath and then try to take as deep a breath as you can. Now sit up straight and try the same thing again—you should be able to feel how much more air you can take in. Leaning forwards hunched up it is impossible to take a really deep breath—and therefore the vital supply of oxygen to your blood and brain is restricted. Once you sit up with your shoulders back your lungs can really expand again.

It is worth repeating that two and a half minutes of exercise a day can mean the difference between suppleness and stiffness, between a sagging shape and an upright, healthy body.

Five for flexibility

The five mobility exercises shown on these pages will make your body more supple and help prepare it for other exercises. Move smoothly, do not rush and repeat each one ten to 12 times.

Arm-circling mobilizes the shoulder joints and chest muscles and helps improve your posture. Stand erect with your feet wide apart and arms by your sides. Moving fluidly, raise both arms forwards and up and try to brush your ears. Then circle back. Breathe in on the upwards movement and out on return.

Side-bending improves the flexibility of the spine. Stand with feet wide apart, hands on hips. Keeping your head square with your shoulders, bend first to one side then the other. Move freely without jerking.

Trunk-, hip- and knee-bending mobilizes hip and spinal joints. Stand up with hands by your sides. Raise one knee and bend over as if to touch your forehead on your knee. Bend the supporting leg slightly to reduce pull on the lower back. Breathe out as you lean forwards and in as you straighten up. For support, rest hands on a chair back.

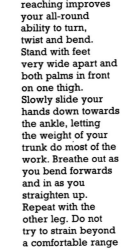

Head-, arm- and trunk-rotating helps you twist your body without undue effort. Stand with your feet very wide apart and arms out straight in front. Keeping your thighs and pelvis straight, swing head, shoulders and arms to the left, bending the right arm at the elbow as you move round. Repeat in the other direction.

Opposite ankle-reaching improves your all-round ability to turn, twist and bend. Stand with feet very wide apart and both palms in front on one thigh. Slowly slide your hands down towards the ankle, letting the weight of your trunk do most of the work. Breathe out as you bend forwards and in as you straighten up. Repeat with the other leg. Do not try to strain beyond a comfortable range of movement.

How to pull your weight properly

Apart from making you a better beast of burden, good muscles can directly help both your heart and your figure.

Most people cut out strenuous physical activity as they get older. Consequently their muscles become weaker and they get trapped in a *Catch 22* situation: the weaker they are, the less they exercise their muscles; and the less they exercise their muscles, the weaker they become.

Some obvious benefits of keeping muscles in good condition are that you will be able to carry heavy shopping or baggage for longer distances and with less effort, and be less tired after everyday activities such as gardening.

But there are hidden benefits, which are far more important. Strong muscles work in support of the heart. When your muscles relax, they fill with blood and when they contract, that blood is pumped towards the heart. Regular exercise of the major muscle groups actually increases the size of the muscle fibre and therefore enables the muscle to pump more blood to the heart. Thus it is that sudden muscular effort is less likely to strain the heart if you make sure that you do not allow your

muscular strength to deteriorate—Sir Winston Churchill suffered his first heart attack while struggling to open a jammed window.

Recent research has uncovered another distinct advantage of maintaining muscular strength. Large muscles use more Calories, even at rest, than small muscles. So if you allow your muscle mass to decrease as you get older, it means you have to do more and more exercise to burn up the Calories. Taken to an extreme, a man in his sixties would have to run six miles every day in order to use the same number of Calories he used while sitting still as a young man, when his muscles were well developed.

The problem can be particularly acute for small-bodied women in middle age, who find that although they eat sensibly they still put on weight. The trouble is that they are using very little energy at rest,

Stage 1 Exercise 1 : **Arm, shoulder, chest muscles. Stand with arms straight in front, hands against a wall 30 cm (12 in) apart. Lift on to your toes, then bend arms to touch your chin against the wall. Straighten arms to original position.**

Stage 1 Exercise 2 : **Abdominals. Sit on the edge of a chair, lean back, legs straight. Grip the sides of the chair for support and bend the knees to almost touch the thighs against the body.**

Stage 1 Exercise 3 : **Legs. Stand 46 cm (18 in) behind a chair, hands resting lightly on its back. Bend knees to squatting position, straighten up on to toes, recover original position. In *Stage 2* dispense with the chair, in *Stage 3* jump as you rise from the squat and in *Stage 4* jump with feet astride and arms wide. Give at the knees as you land.**

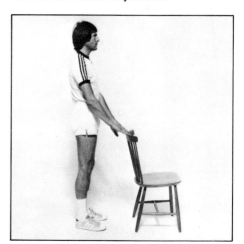

and the answer is to increase the muscle mass in order to burn up more Calories.

Exercises designed to increase muscular strength are based on the overload principle, which simply means that your muscles will grow in response to the daily demands you make on them.

This strength exercise programme, devised by Alistair Murray, does not aim to build you up until you are able to bend iron bars or tear telephone directories in half, but merely to create and maintain sufficient strength for you to be physically fit and able to manage any extra exertion.

The exercises are carefully planned so that the resistance against the muscles is slowly increased. Endurance is built up at the same time by increasing the number of repetitions for each exercise over a period of weeks, as shown in the four-stage programme explained on pages 122–3.

Stage 2 Exercise 1: Press-ups as shown to touch the back of the chair with the chest, making sure that the body is always straight. Breathe out as you go down, in as you rise. In *Stage 3* use the seat of the chair for support and in *Stage 4* go on to press-ups flat on the floor. Women need not attempt *Stages 3* and *4* press-ups but can repeat *Stage 2.*

Stage 2 Exercise 2: Sit close to the edge of a chair as in *Stage 1 Exercise 2*, lean back with legs straight. Keeping the legs straight slowly lift them to above the level of your waist, then lower slowly. Breathe in as you raise the legs.

Stage 3 Exercise 2: Tuck both your feet under a heavy chest, then lie back and stretch your arms behind your head. Swing up and forwards to touch your ankles with both hands; lower slowly. Breathe out as you rise, in as you lower.

Stage 4 Exercise 2: This exercise is like the second one of *Stage 3* in purpose but is appropriately more difficult. Put your heels on the edge of the seat of a chair (or on a low table or chest) and stretch your arms behind you. Swing up to a sitting position and touch the ankles. Breathe out as you rise, in as you lower.

117

The heart: man's miracle muscle

As with all muscles, the heart needs exercising. However, there is a right and a wrong way of doing this.

The heart is a curiously misunderstood organ. In verse, song and fiction its function is a purely romantic one as the source of love and emotion. To be described as "big hearted" is to be thought a warm, loving and generous person.

When Dr Christiaan Barnard replaced a man's heart for the first time it made headlines throughout the world, not so much because of the medical achievement but because it seemed more significant than just transplanting an organ. Could you be the same person with another man's *heart* beating inside your chest?

Yet despite the singers, lovesick poets and romantic novelists, doctors know that the heart is basically a muscle, although a remarkable one, that needs exercise to function efficiently. The bigger it is, the better it works. A big heart will not make you more kind or generous—but it will pump more blood from the venous system into the arterial system. That is its job.

During each beat, the heart fills with blood pumped to it from the muscles and then squeezes that blood out into the veins. So the way to reach the heart, for exercise purposes, is through the muscles. By exercising the large muscle groups you pump more blood to the heart and force it to push harder to squeeze out the extra load. This is the best exercise it can get.

Simply raising the heart beat rate without muscle involvement does not do the job. For example, your heart will beat faster during moments of emotional stress, but it is not being exercised because it is not receiving extra blood from the muscles. Therefore it has nothing to push against and is more likely to be strained than healthily exercised.

Athletes, particularly long-distance runners, tend to develop big hearts with exceptionally slow beats at rest. When Dr

Roger Bannister began training for his attempt to break the four-minute mile, his resting heart rate was in the middle seventies. After he had broken the record his resting heart rate was measured at between only thirty-six and thirty-eight beats a minute.

The dilated heart of the athlete, with its strong, slow contractions, also helps the exchange of gases in the lungs to become vastly more efficient. The lungs of an average adult man contain about six litres of air, only a fraction of which is exchanged with each breath. About half a litre of air is breathed in and out at rest, but this increases significantly during exercise. The "vital capacity" of the lungs is the amount of air you can exhale after taking as deep a breath as possible. It is normally between four and five litres, but decreases with age and inactivity. Exercise maintains the "vital capacity" of the lungs at a high level and improves the essential supply of oxygen to the heart.

Exercise strengthens the heart in three main ways. First, it improves the actual quality of the myocardium (the heart muscle). Secondly, it increases capillarization—that is, it keeps blood vessels open and helps circulation. Thirdly, it improves the co-ordination of the fibres of the heart as they pump out the blood.

Research at the City Gymnasium in London has proved that it is not the intensity of effort so much as the duration that is significant in improving the efficiency of the heart and lungs. As a rough guide, you need to exercise continuously for at least two minutes before you will even begin to achieve any worthwhile benefit to your cardiovascular condition.

Heart and lung exercises only need to be of sufficient intensity to raise your heart beat rate to between 110 and 120 beats a minute, but they must be sustained past the two-minute barrier. In unfit people after around 120 beats a minute the heart is beating too fast to fill to any great volume. Consequently it is not receiving the right kind of exercise.

Although normal heart rates at rest can vary between fifty and 100 beats a minute, men usually average between seventy-two and seventy-six beats a minute and women average between seventy-five and eighty beats a minute. (Why women have slightly higher heart rates than men is not yet understood.)

A resting heart rate of more than 100 beats a minute means in effect that although you are sitting down your heart is working at the rate it should be if you were walking. Without the benefit of extra blood circulation generated by your leg muscles, it is under constant strain.

The most practical way to lower your resting heart rate, thereby improving its

strength and efficiency, is with exercise. However, it is important not to overdo it. The effort you need to exert in order to start improving your cardiovascular condition will largely depend on your age and your present level of fitness.

There is, however, a safe and sure method of precisely determining how much you should do—and that is by counting your pulse (see pages 120–1). It is the magic monitor, which should guide your fitness programme.

Endurance exercises for heart and lungs

First stage—running on the spot. This is as beneficial to your heart and lungs as going for a run and for most people it is much more convenient. If you are unfit, start very gently without lifting your knees too high. You may only be able to cope with 30 seconds or so at the start of exercising, but you will be able to build up your endurance week by week. Remember, until you can keep it up for more than two minutes you will not be making any significant improvement to your cardiovascular condition. Keep checking your pulse to ensure you are not exceeding the maximum pulse rate for your age and physical condition (see pages 120–1). As you become fitter, raise your knees higher and progress at your own pace until you are able to run on the spot for between eight and ten minutes.

Second stage—bench stepping. Take a low stool and stand about 30 cm (12 in) away from it, hands on hips. Step on to it 15 times with the left foot leading and 15 times with the right foot. Slowly increase the number of steps to a maximum of 30 with each foot; then gradually increase the height of the stool to a maximum of 46 cm (18 in). When you can do this easily, work on a time basis, aiming for up to six minutes' exercise without exceeding your pulse rating.

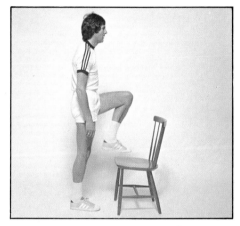

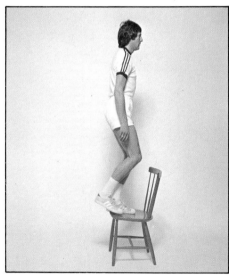

Third stage—You are now fitter and can combine both exercises if you wish, or add outdoor activity. Your fitness handicap on your pulse rating will now be smaller, and you will find you have to work harder to reach the pulse level needed to exercise your heart.

Fourth stage—You should now aim to cut your handicap back to the lowest figure recommended for your age group (see pages 120–1). You can use any combination of indoor or outdoor endurance exercises. You should be quite fit enough to take up jogging at a moderate pace, swimming or cycling.

The pulse: your guide to fitness

Because the pulse tells you exactly how hard the heart is working it is the best yardstick of improving fitness in an exercise programme.

Pulse measurement during exercise is an invaluable safety indicator. Your pulse rate not only tells you whether your body is working hard enough to improve its fitness, but also warns you if you are overdoing it.

The pulse is a wave of blood pushed around the arteries each time the heart contracts. The wave moves at between 3.7 and 5.5 m (12 to 18 ft) a second and can be felt wherever a large artery runs close to the skin, as at the wrist, throat and forehead. If you feel your heart and your pulse at the same time you will notice the time-lag as the blood is pumped. There is considerable individual variation, but a normal resting pulse rate (the pulse rate when the body is not undergoing any exertion) is

between seventy and eighty to the minute.

Your pulse is slowest after you have been asleep for six hours. Any activity, even eating, will increase it. When you get up in the morning it will rise by between five and ten beats a minute and continue to increase very slowly during the day. Any prolonged period of hard physical labour will keep the pulse rate high for some hours after you have finished.

Measuring the pulse rate during and after exercise is important because it provides an accurate index of how hard the heart is working. Without monitoring the pulse you can actually become less and less fit even though you are exercising every day. What happens is that the exercises become physically easier; so easy,

in fact, that you are no longer making sufficient demands on your heart to increase your level of fitness. Thus you gradually begin to "decondition".

Research into using pulse rate to monitor fitness started at the City Gymnasium in London in 1964 with a special study sponsored by the Medical Research Council of Britain. The object was to find a safe way to use exercise as a means of treating cardiac patients. It was known that exercise improved the condition of the heart, but how could a man with a cardiac condition start exercising at exactly the right level of effort—hard enough to do some good, yet not so hard as to be dangerous? Once started, how could he progress without constant risk of overstressing his heart?

Previously the method of gauging cardiovascular effort was by measuring oxygen consumption. It involved cumbersome apparatus and was an unpleasant experience for the individual. Clearly, an entirely new approach was needed. Researchers began studying the relationship between the response to exercise and the pulse rate.

After years of tests involving thousands of volunteer "guinea pigs" a simple yardstick was devised, which would enable anyone—regardless of age or physical condition—to calculate for himself the correct level at which he should exercise to improve the efficiency of his heart and blood system without risk.

An exercise programme developed by Alistair Murray at the City Gymnasium works like this. A pulse rate of 200 a minute is considered the absolute maximum for a man aged twenty in good physical condition. This is the basic figure from which all individual calculations are made on a descending scale.

Before beginning an exercise programme you add to your age a handicap of

The pulse at peak fitness

Olympic 1,500-metre gold medallist of 1976 and world mile record holder, John Walker of New Zealand has a remarkably low resting pulse rate of under 40 a minute, compared with the average male resting pulse rate of 72. Walker's pulse illustrates the apparant paradox that physical training, which makes the heart work harder and beat faster, results in a lowering of the heart rate when the body is at rest. In training the heart enlarges, enabling it to rest longer between beats as it refills. A heart beating at 60 a minute, for example, takes twice as long to fill as one beating at 90 a minute. Other physical attributes that help make Walker a champion include low body fat (three percent of his body weight) and a lung capacity that is 20 per cent above average.

forty (for being unfit) and then subtract the total from 200. The result is a safe pulse rate, which you should not exceed during the first few weeks. Thus a man aged forty-five adds a forty handicap to make eighty-five. Eighty-five from 200 gives 115. This is the pulse rate he should achieve by physical exercise at the start of the programme. If his pulse rate shoots above this limit then he must reduce the intensity of his exercising. If his pulse rate does not reach 115 then the intensity of exercising must be stepped up until it does.

Controlling pulse rate is particularly important when people start exercising after a long period of physical inactivity, because very often their muscular strength is greater than the efficiency of their heart and lungs. They feel they can undertake quite rigorous exercise, but their heart and lungs may be taking a terrible strain. Only by monitoring the pulse can this be avoided and a safe period allowed for the heart and lungs to "catch up" with the condition of the muscles. Tests at the City Gymnasium showed that the resting pulse rate decreases significantly after every month of exercise. As it is such a useful measure of progress, a note of resting pulse rate should be made right at the start of the programme. Despite the relative safety of pulse-rated exercise obviously nobody with a real or suspected heart condition should undertake the exercises without a doctor's advice.

Very unfit people may find their pulse rate rockets above the limit almost as soon as they start exercising. In this case they should rest between exercises to keep it down. Within a few weeks they will be able to reduce the rest pauses and finally eliminate them altogether.

As you become fitter you should start to reduce your handicap and thus increase your optimum pulse rate. The exercise programme recommends that the handicap should be slowly cut back from forty to thirty-nine to thirty-eight and so on. Most people under the age of thirty should eventually be able to eliminate their handicap altogether. Over thirty you should be content to end up with a residual handicap that will depend on your age. As a rough guide, between thirty to forty you should aim to reduce your handicap to under five; between forty-five and fifty do not go under fifteen; and people above the age of fifty should probably not go below twenty.

Cutting your handicap to its absolute minimum is not important because you will have received the greatest benefit to your heart and circulation during the early stages. For example, reaching a state of fitness at which you can safely exercise at 120 pulse beats a minute rather than at 110, is more advantageous than being able to raise your safety limit from 150 to 160.

How to take your pulse

Taking your own pulse will quickly become a routine part of your exercise programme. If you wear a watch on your left hand, take the fingers of that hand and put them on the inside of your right wrist near the base of the thumb where you will feel the pulse. Count the beat for ten seconds on your watch and multiply by six for the rate per minute.

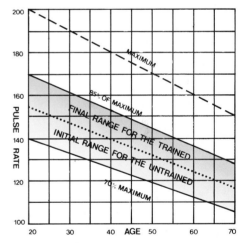

The safe pulse rate

The pulse rate is the best guide to the efficiency and safety of a physical training programme. The graph shows a range of safe pulse rates reached during gymnasium training by a study group of 302 men ranging in age from 26 to 57, none of whom had a history of heart disease. Working on the basis of the maximum possible rate at which the heart can beat (top line), the safe rate to which the pulse was allowed to rise in the untrained was taken as 70 per cent of that maximum. By the end of the training programme the safe rate was allowed to rise to 85 per cent of the maximum. The restriction on the amount the pulse rate was allowed to rise ensured that the trainees did not put too much stress on their hearts and lungs.

How to get fit in forty minutes a week

A fitness programme need not be time consuming. For just a little effort each week you can get fit and stay fit for life.

All it takes to get fit are two twenty-minute sessions of exercise every week. You can do more if you feel like it, but there is no need to do so.

You do not have to punish yourself to get fit. The process should be easy, enjoyable, painless and free from guilt or worry. If you find the exercises too difficult at the beginning or you cannot complete the suggested number of repetitions, do not worry—just do what you can. If you keep plugging away steadily you will eventually be able to complete the schedule without resting between exercises and without strain. It may take months to achieve, but that does not matter: there is no hurry and you are not competing with anyone.

The exercise programme described here combines three basic factors: time, repetition and pulse rate. The schedules contain exercises for strength and endurance and are designed to accommodate differences in age, sex and physical condition. Your pulse rate will tell you how you are progressing and when you are over-exerting yourself. So be guided by common sense.

Before launching yourself into any physical exercise programme be sure that you

are physically able to cope with it. Although the forty-minute schedule of exercises is very gentle, if you are over fifty check with your doctor, for safety's sake, before starting. Anyone who suffers from chest pains, severe shortage of breath, backache or joint trouble after physical exertion should also consult a doctor before embarking on exercise. If you are grossly overweight—by more than 19 kg (42 lb)—you should diet to lose the excess before beginning physical exercise. If these warnings do not apply to you, there is no reason why you should not start the programme today.

Although there is no scientific evidence to prove the theory, many people still feel that the best time to exercise is at crack of dawn. In fact this may be the worst time if you are the kind of person who needs to summon every bit of will power to get out of bed in the morning, whose joints feel stiff at that hour of the day and who feels lethargic until the body has had time to pump energizing fat and sugar into the blood stream.

Mid-morning or early evening are preferable times for exercise if you are a slow starter. But never exercise after a heavy

Plotting your progress

On the charts below one vertical column represents a complete exercise session. First record your pulse, then warm up with ten to 12 repeats of the five mobility exercises described on pages 114-15—arm-circling; side-bends; trunk-, hip- and knee-bending; head-, arm- and trunk-rotating; and alternate ankle-reaching. Next do the three strength exercises (see pages 116-17), then the endurance exercises (pages 118-19). On completing each part of the programme, check your pulse and tick the box if this is satisfactory. When you have completed all four exercise sessions in stage one move on to stage two and cut back your handicap to 35. In stages three and four choose the endurance exercises you enjoy most. Never exceed the safe maximum pulse rate. The optimum pulse rate in stage four is the rate you can maintain for ten minutes without overexertion.

Warming up

STAGE ONE Maximum safe pulse rate = 200 minus (age + 40)				
Date	Aug. 12			
Pulse before warm-up	80			
Strength exercises (*below*)	do 10 to 15 times	15 to 20	20 to 25	25 to 30
Wall press-ups				
Abdominal exercises				
Leg exercises				
Minutes spent on endurance exercises (running on the spot)	1	3	5	8
Pulse after exercise	120			

STAGE TWO Maximum safe pulse rate = 200 minus (age + 35)				
Date				
Pulse before warm-up				
Strength exercise repetitions	10 to 15	15 to 20	20 to 25	25 to 30
Table press-ups				
Abdominal exercises				
Leg exercises				
Endurance exercise repetitions (bench-stepping)	15 to 20	20 to 25	25 to 30	repeat for more than 3 minutes
Pulse after exercise				

meal because so much blood becomes pooled in the stomach and intestines after eating that there is. insufficient supply for the muscles and cramp can very often be the result.

Wear loose, comfortable clothes, or just your underwear to exercise in and find a place that will allow you enough room to lie flat on the floor and swing your arms and legs without bumping into any furniture or other obstacles.

The week's forty minutes' exercise can be divided into two twenty-minute periods or three shorter sessions and fitted into the week at the most convenient time. (As you get fitter you may not even need the full forty minutes to complete the schedule.) Some people prefer the discipline of fixed times so that they get into a routine. As long as you do not leave more than about four days between sessions and exercise for forty minutes a week it is not important which days you choose. The reason for this is that the benefits of physical activity, such as the burning up of surplus body fat, are not confined to the time you are exercising but continue for several days.

You will probably start to feel better after the first week of exercise, but this will be a figment of your imagination because after only a week improvement in physical condition is so small that it is barely measurable. But if you are feeling better then you have taken the first step towards fitness and after three or four weeks you will begin to notice real improvement, which will steadily increase over the following months.

The first sign of progress will be an easing of effort when you turn, twist and bend in the mobility exercises. Your muscles will be bigger and stronger and thus you will be able to do more repetitions of the strength exercises. Because your heart and lungs are working more efficiently you will be able to do more without exceeding your pulse rate level.

For a more accurate measure of progress, take your pulse immediately before and after exercise, add the two together and make a note of the total using the charts below. Week by week the total figure will drop, showing that your heart is beating more slowly both at rest and during activity.

No matter how well you progress, resist at all costs the temptation to speed things up by attempting too much or increasing the number of repetitions beyond those recommended in the schedule. You get most benefit from the first minutes of exercise and least from the last. Just as there is a level of effort that you have to reach before your physical condition will improve there is an upper limit beyond which there is not only no advantage to be gained and indeed a risk of doing more harm than good.

It takes about three months, on average, to get fit. If you then stop exercising it will take about the same time to return to your original physical condition. So if you want to stay fit, exercise must become part of your way of life. Nothing is to be gained from a brief flirtation with exercise. If you are going to decide to start this programme then you should also make up your mind to continue exercising indefinitely.

This re-education of your physical activity is not as daunting as it sounds. Most people find that the investment in effort to stay fit is richly rewarded because they get so much more out of life. Once you are fit, it is easy to stay that way by "topping up" your condition with a minimum of exercise.

Strength

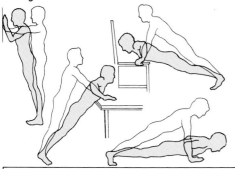

Strength

Endurance

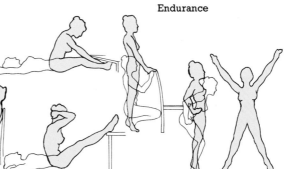

STAGE THREE Maximum safe pulse rate = 200 minus (age + 30)				
Date				
Pulse before warm-up				
Strength exercise repetitions	10 to 15	15 to 20	20 to 25	25 to 30
Chair press-ups				
Abdominal press-ups				
Leg exercises				
Minutes spent on endurance exercises	5	6	7	8+
Pulse after exercise				

STAGE FOUR Maximum safe pulse rate = 200 minus (age + min. handicap)				
Date				
Pulse before warm-up				
Strength exercise repetitions	10 to 15	15 to 20	20 to 25	25 to 30
Floor press-ups				
Abdominal exercises				
Leg exercises				
Minutes spent on endurance exercises	7	8	9	10+
Pulse after exercise				

Sport: the preparation you need

Warming up before any kind of exercise may lead to better performance and will certainly reduce the risk of heart or muscle damage.

No matter how fit and well trained you are for a particular sport, you risk injury if you do not take the time to warm up before playing. In the next few pages specific exercises are given to prepare you for some of the major sports; they are also in themselves useful for warming up.

Warming up prepares the body for physical activity in three ways. Firstly, circulation in the coronary system is stimulated so that sufficient blood and oxygen can be pumped to the heart when the real effort begins. Secondly, the cartilages in the major joints thicken perceptibly, thus improving the strength of the joints and making them less liable to injury. Thirdly, the muscles themselves actually get warmer and increase in elasticity as well as power.

There are inherent dangers in rushing into strenuous physical activity without a warm-up: your body is just not ready to meet the demands you are making on it. At best you are risking a severe cramp; at very worst you might have a heart attack from a condition called myocardial ischemia (inadequate circulation). It is true that there are not many people who warm up before running for a bus, so you can often get away with no preparation, but it is not the best approach.

Nobody knows precisely what causes cramp: it can affect an athlete just as severely as someone who never takes exercise. Cramp—and stitch—are involuntary contractions of a "flexer" muscle, far beyond that caused by normal movement. There are countless pet remedies for cramp but no scientifically proved cures. Russian athletes, for example, put paper bags over their faces and breathe in their own used air to cure cramp. Unfortunately, this does not always work. The calf muscles are most commonly affected, and one well-tried remedy for cramp in them is to lean with both hands against a wall and edge backwards, keeping the heels flat on the ground.

Each of the major joints is cushioned by cartilage plates between the bones. When you start to bend and stretch and twist in the mobility exercises the cartilage plates absorb a body lubricant known as synovial fluid and get thicker (by as much as fifty per cent). This makes for a better fit between the bones as well as a firmer, stronger joint.

Meanwhile, the temperature of your muscles quickly increases as sixty per cent of the Calories used by them is converted into heat. This happens long before you actually begin to feel warmer from physical exertion—only when the muscles have warmed the blood stream does your body temperature start to rise.

When you start to exercise, every gramme of glucose fuel demanded by the muscles releases about four Calories of energy. Of these energy units, only 1.4 are actually used for the working of the muscle; the remaining 2.6 generate heat. For each one degree centigrade rise in the temperature of the muscle, the metabolic rate of the muscle cell (that is, the speed with which energy can be produced) increases by fourteen per cent. After a ten-minute work-out, cell metabolism increases by about one-third, and in consequence the muscle has thirty per cent more energy to call on.

The most common misconception about warming up is that you need to work up a sweat by wearing a track suit and by really strenuous preliminary activity. In fact, if you limber up to the point of perspiration, you have expended far too much energy and probably will not have your full strength for whatever it is you want to do.

In warming up for any sport all you need do is gently raise your pulse rate to between 100 and 110 beats a minute. It need take no more than a couple of minutes. If you go at it too violently or for too long you could do yourself more harm than good by overstretching ligaments and thus risking injury.

Curiously, there is considerable disagreement among athletes about the degree of warming up that is necessary. Some runners go through a limbering-up routine lasting as much as three-quarters of an hour before a race, while others prefer to walk straight out on to the track for the start with almost no preliminaries. Research has been frustratingly inconclusive—sometimes performances are better, sometimes worse. In one experiment in America a group of schoolboy athletes was asked to stand under cold showers for ten minutes immediately before a race. All of them either surpassed their previous best time for the distance or at least matched it.

Some people believe there is advantage to be gained in limbering up with heavier equipment than they normally use. Practising golf swings with a weighted club, for example, is supposed to improve your strength. As a training device it may have value, but used in warming up it is much more likely to upset your sense of balance and adversely affect performance.

After exercise you should "warm down" slowly. This apparent contradiction can be simply explained. When you are active, all the blood vessels of the body open up to help circulation to the muscles, which squeeze blood to the heart. If you stop suddenly and just stand still with vessels still dilated, the heart has difficulty keeping up supply to some areas without the help of the muscles: gravity drains the blood away from the brain and you are liable to faint. You can observe this draining process in action if your ankles swell after a game of tennis or during a half-time break in a football match.

The best way to warm up for a sport is to practise non-competitively for five or six minutes. This will adequately exercise the muscles you will use in the game.

Exercises for racket games

Tennis, like all racket games, should be approached with caution if you are very unfit. It is a game that demands occasional explosive effort and without adequate preparation can result in strained muscles or joints. What starts out as a friendly knockabout on the tennis court can often develop into a fierce competition, so it is not difficult to over-exert yourself.

The secret of tailoring exercises for different sports is to achieve duplication of the effort and movement involved in the sport. Racket games require strength in the racket hand and arm, with supporting mobility of the shoulder, good flexibility in the trunk, muscular strength in the legs and cardiovascular efficiency to withstand the strain of sudden intense spurts across the court.

Specific exercises for tennis should prepare the body for these demands. "Tennis elbow", for example, can be avoided by building up muscles and ligaments in the elbow region.

Racket games do not necessarily keep you fit. Too many people think that an occasional game of tennis, squash or badminton is all that is required, but you need to look at the frequency, duration and intensity of effort. If, for example, you are an exceptionally good player, you may find that you actually do very little running around on court. If you play only once every couple of weeks, regardless of your standard, you are certainly not getting enough exercise to keep yourself fit.

EXERCISES FOR TENNIS

Spurt jogging

After reaching the jogging stage of the 40-minute fitness programme (pages 122-3), gradually introduce spurts of fast running, each of no more than 60 seconds. Start with straight-line spurts, then zigzag across a field or park. Try to imagine yourself in the centre of a box about the size of half the court. Dash to all four sides and corners as quickly as possible, returning to the centre each time.

Side-stretching

This is for mobility of back, waist and hips. Stand with feet apart and a broom handle held above your head. Keeping both arms and legs straight, bend and press first left and then right. Repeat the exercise 20 to 40 times.

Sit-ups

Sit-ups strengthen abdominal muscles. Lie down, holding a broom handle over your head with both hands. Slowly curl the upper body and try to touch the toes with the broom handle. Do not strain. Start with 15 repetitions and progress to 40.

Isometric exercises

Face a wall and slowly bring an old racket into contact with the wall by simulating different strokes. At the point of contact, press gently against the wall with an isometric contraction of six to 12 seconds.

Stroke exercise

Practise the strokes—forehand, backhand, smash and serve—with a racket in each hand, leading with your normal racket hand. This increases mobility of the non-striking arm and shoulder and helps improve balance.

Grip exercise

Strength in the hand and wrist is essential for all racket games. You can improve the power of your grip by squeezing an old tennis ball (two together if you have big hands). Squeeze as hard as you can for about ten seconds. Repeat five to ten times.

Elbow strength

Power in your elbow is best improved by simple press-ups. If you are already including press-ups in a general fitness programme you can either increase the repetitions or concentrate on improving technique, with the body raised and lowered perfectly straight.

Heel-touching

To strengthen legs and safeguard against sprains and pulled muscles: stand feet astride, with a weight in each hand of no more than 4.5 kg (10 lb). Keeping the back straight, bend at the knees to a half-squat. Lift up on your toes and try to touch the backs of your heels with the weights. Repeat ten to 30 times, then sit.

The quick and the slow: skiing and golf

Skiing is strenuous exercise, making demands on little-used muscles, but the benefits of golf are little more than those of a walk.

The average golfer walks about four miles during an eighteen-hole round, and it is this walking that provides the sport's main physical benefit. The twisting movement while you are driving the ball can be good for the waistline, but otherwise the exercise value of golf is rather limited. Certainly, if you stroll about slowly and use a golf cart, you should not delude yourself that golf will keep you fit—no matter how many rounds you play.

One of the problems of golf is, paradoxically, the obsessive enthusiasm it engenders. The sport should provide mental recreation and relaxation, an opportunity to take a break from work and worry. But if your sense of competition is such that a bad score or half a dozen balls sliced into the rough make you irritable and angry with yourself, the tension and consequent raising of blood pressure can actually result in more harm than good. You should get enjoyment from golf, not a bad temper.

To improve your golf, you need first of all to be able to walk the course without fatigue or loss of concentration. You then need to be able to get a good, powerful swing. If you complete the forty-minute fitness programme on pages 122–3 to your own particular fitness level, a round of golf will not tire you. Specific exercises concentrate on strengthening the hands, wrists and arms and improving the flexibility of the shoulders and trunk. Do not do the exercises on the days you play golf—keep them for between match days.

EXERCISES FOR GOLF

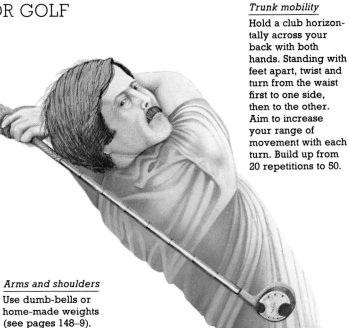

Golf swing mobility
Hold a weight in each hand (a can of food will do) and simulate a golf swing, making sure you twist waist and shoulders to the fullest extent. Start at 20 repetitions and work up to 40.

Overhead roll
Lie on your back with feet together, arms out at an angle of 45 degrees. Pressing down on the floor raise legs together, keeping them straight. Do this 15 times and slowly try to get your legs farther back over your head.

Wrist-strengthening
You need a rolling pin, about 1.2 m (4 ft) of string and a weight of around 2 kg (5 lb) to tie on to the string. Attach the other end of the string to the rolling pin. Standing with arms outstretched raise the weight as far as possible by turning the pin. Do five to 15 times.

Arm-circling
Hold two golf balls tightly in each hand; stand with feet apart and circle both arms together, first in one direction, then the other. As the arms come back, try to get the hands as far behind as possible. Do 20 to 50 times.

Arms and shoulders
Use dumb-bells or home-made weights (see pages 148–9). Stand with feet slightly apart; hold one weight straight up, the other straight forwards. Raise one arm as you lower the other. Do ten to 20 times.

Leg-raising
Stand about 0.6 m (2 ft) behind a strong chair and rest both hands on its back. Lean forwards at the waist and press the head back. Alternately raise legs backwards, keep them straight and press as high as you can, five times with each leg at first progressing to 20.

Trunk mobility
Hold a club horizontally across your back with both hands. Standing with feet apart, twist and turn from the waist first to one side, then to the other. Aim to increase your range of movement with each turn. Build up from 20 repetitions to 50.

Skiing has a high accident rate—not so much because of inherent dangers, but because many people come to skiing totally unprepared for it physically. The exhilaration of being on a mountainside tempts them to try too much, too soon. Altitude increases fatigue. Their skill diminishes along with their strength and they become prime candidates for falls and often serious injuries.

More perhaps than any other sport, skiing requires deliberate preparation. It is a physically demanding activity, even under ideal snow conditions; a learner has to exert constant muscular effort to maintain the correct body position and execute different movements. Because many people ski only once a year, they find themselves using muscles that have been more or less dormant for fifty weeks.

When skiing first became popular as a sport there were fewer injuries. This was in part because you had to climb uphill in order to ski down and this provided inbuilt physical conditioning for the skier. Today you ride to the top of the slope—and gravity, which brings you down, may exert more force than you are able to handle if you are unprepared.

Pre-ski training is advisable even for a fit person, because skiing requires the use of a unique combination of muscles. The correct stance for traversing a slope, for example, sets the feet, legs, hips and shoulders at angles unlike those demanded by any other sport. So exercises can prepare you for skiing and significantly reduce the dangers of injury or excessive muscle soreness.

EXERCISES FOR SKIING

Squat-rolling

Sit with knees apart and the soles of your feet held together with both hands. Keeping the back rounded, roll back and over so that your toes touch the ground behind your head. Use hands and arms to pull on the feet. Repeat full sequence from 15 to 30 times.

Side jumps

Stand with feet together as if tied. Jump sideways over an imaginary barrier, first left then right. Try to jump higher each time. Do 20 to 40 times.

Ankle strength

Ankle strength is of primary importance in skiing. Stand on the balls of the feet on a shallow step so that the heels protrude over the edge. Keeping a rhythm, raise up on to your toes and lower until your heels touch the ground. The height of the step should be sufficient to permit full flexure of the ankles. Do 20 to 40 times.

Wall-sliding

Lean with your back against a wall, hands by your sides, feet about 45 cm (18 in) from the wall. Slowly slide down to a sitting position, hold it 30 seconds and straighten up. Gradually increase sitting time to 60 seconds, then try the same exercise on one leg. Do three to five times.

Knee flexibility

Stand upright with feet and legs together. Keeping your feet flat, bend at the knees and at the same time twist them to one side. Straighten up, bend knees again and turn to the other side. Keep chest facing forwards and try to press farther down and farther sideways each time you bend. Do 20 to 40 times.

Press-up straddle

From a raised press-up position, jump the legs forwards and outwards so that the feet are as wide apart as possible. Try to get the feet in line with the shoulders. Do ten to 15 times.

Team games and the value of sport

Team games make all sorts of physical demands on players, which is why the more energetic games are excellent for all-round fitness.

Team games demand more than just a high level of individual fitness: they require interdependence by a group of people working together with a single aim. Thus preparation for football, hockey, basketball, baseball and so on, inevitably means training as a team to design strategies, understand other players and develop a sense of mutual responsibility.

But there are a number of exercises that players can do as individuals to prepare for team sports. These exercises concentrate on further developing certain muscles for kicking, catching, throwing, controlling a ball and tackling an opponent, as well as improving mobility with particular games in view.

Most ball games involve sporadic bursts of intense exertion interspersed with periods of relative inactivity. Sudden effort of this kind makes great demands on the body, particularly the heart and lungs, and therefore it is essential for players to maintain a reasonable level of fitness throughout the year. This is the first priority—specific exercising for particular sports should come later.

When considering an exercise programme for sport, two elements have to be taken into consideration: first, your own requirements to build up areas of weakness so that you become generally fit and, second, the requirements of the game.

You may need more muscular strength for kicking and throwing, or more stamina, or more suppleness to twist and turn and weave round other players. By breaking down typical movements in play it is not difficult to work out which muscles are used most and consequently need to be developed. You may well have vivid memories of what hurt most at the beginning of last season—they are an excellent guide on which to base exercises.

These advanced exercises for specific muscular improvement, stamina building, balance and mobility are designed for people involved in all team games.

Strength and mobility exercises for team games

Abdomen

Lie on your back on a bench, with legs over the edge and a football (or any large ball) held between your ankles. Slowly raise and lower the legs, keeping them straight. Do 15 to 30 repeats.

With a football under your abdomen in the raised press-up position, take away your hands so your weight is supported on toes and abdomen. Do ten to 20 repeats.

Back and shoulders

Stand up, feet astride, with a 4.5 kg (10 lb) weight in each hand. Breathe in deeply, then bend forwards at the waist, pushing your arms backwards and as high as you can. Breathe out as you return to normal position. Repeat ten to 15 times. Very good for basketball and cricket bowling.

Chest and shoulders

Holding a chair with arms straight, swing it up and in a full circle over your head. Repeat ten times.

Stamina

Stand with arms folded across chest, then jump into a forward stride with the front leg bent and the rear leg stretched out straight behind you. Reverse the legs with each jump. Repetition: ten to 20 for each leg. This exercise is very good for building take-off power in the leg muscles.

Attach equal weights—start with 2.3-4.5 kg (5-10 lb)—to each end of a broom handle and hold it across the back of your shoulders. Climb up and down any convenient flight of stairs for 60 seconds. Slowly progress by increasing duration and weight.

Stand with one foot on the floor, the other on a bench between 30 and 40 cm (12 and 16 in) high. Jump up and reverse the position of the legs. Do 15 to 30 repeats.

BENEFIT CHECK-UP

Balance and agility

Stand on one foot, with the other leg tucked up behind you. Jump up as high as possible. Land on the ball of the foot, take the shock with a small spring hop, then jump up again. Keep the upper leg tucked in tight throughout. Repeat 15 to 25 times with each leg.

Holding a broom handle across the back of your shoulders with both hands assume a squatting position, then twist to touch the floor each side with the end of the broom handle. Repeat ten to 20 times.

Stand with a large ball held as high as possible with both hands above your head. Drop to a full squatting position, hold it for the count of five, then slowly stand up. Keep your arms up throughout. Do ten to 20 repeats.

Stand, feet together, in the centre of an imaginary clock. Jump out to the one o'clock position, then back to the centre and continue round the clock, keeping your feet together throughout.

Arms and shoulders

From a raised press-up position, arch the body as high as possible, then sink to the floor, bending backwards at the waist but keeping the arms and legs straight. Repeat ten to 15 times.

Legs and feet

Sit with the heels of both feet resting on a brick. Place a heavy object such as a bar or a large book over your feet. Pivoting at the heels, lift the toes as high as possible. Repeat 15 to 30 times.

What you get out of golf

General: golf should provide you with mental relaxation; a round of it should leave you refreshed.

Shoulders: the golf swing improves the mobility of the shoulder muscles, particularly the deltoid and major pectorals.
Arms: some value for strengthening the arms generally, but wrists should particularly benefit from increasing power.
Heart and lungs: minimal value. Only what you would get from a brisk walk in the country.
Trunk: the swing helps mobility, but not the strength of the abdominal muscles. Golf will not make much impression on a large stomach.
Legs: minimal value. Golfers need to walk at a sharp pace between holes to make much improvement.

What you get out of skiing

Skiing is one of the best sports for all-round fitness. Few forms of exercise are so exhilarating. But except in some countries with suitable conditions, most people cannot get to a ski-slope as often as they wish.

Shoulders: very good for mobility and for strength.
Arms: good for strength. Heart and lungs: very good for cardiovascular efficiency.
Trunk and hips: excellent for increasing mobility.
Legs and ankles: excellent for both strength and mobility.

What you get out of racket games

Squash is the most physically demanding of the racket games and is thus likely to make most improvement in cardiovascular efficiency. Tennis comes second, with badminton close behind, in terms of overall benefit.

Shoulders: increased strength and mobility. Arms: greatly increased strength in the racket arm, but only improved mobility in the non-playing arm. Heart and lungs: cardiovascular efficiency will improve in direct relation to the frequency, duration and intensity of your game. Your opponent's skill is therefore important.
Trunk: mobility increases in relation to intensity of game.
Legs: muscular strength increases according to the game's intensity.

	Mobility	Strength	Endurance	Social
Football (US)	***	***	***	***
Soccer	**	*	***	***
Rugby	***	***	***	****
Cricket	*	*	*	****
Baseball	**	**	***	***
Basketball	***	*	***	***
Hockey	**	**	***	***
Skiing	***	**	***	****
Water-skiing	*	*	*	**
Rowing	***	***	***	**
Canoeing	**	***	***	*
Skating	**	*	**	***
Bowling	*	*	*	****
Volleyball	***	**	**	**
Karate	****	***	**	*
Tennis	**	**	**	****
Squash	**	**	***	**
Badminton	**	**	**	***
Golf	*	*	*	****
Jogging	*	**	****	*
Cycling	*	**	***	**
Swimming	***	***	****	***

The more asterisks in each category the better the sport for that purpose. "Endurance" is short for cardiovascular endurance.

Jogging and cycling to aerobic rules

Dedicated followers of these two popular recreations can find guidelines in the aerobic system.

Jogging was launched on a receptive public in the early 1960s. It was about the time when the dangers of heart disease were beginning to be acknowledged; when we became aware that the comforts of modern life were killing us.

With an affluent society and an efficient transport system, physical exercise became restricted. At the same time, with increasing competition and consequent emotional and social pressures, stress became part of our lives. All medical evidence strongly suggested the need for some form of voluntary exercise suitable for urban dwellers who might not have easy access to sports areas.

Jogging, it seemed, was the answer. It was promoted as a panacea for all ills. First, it was easy—anyone can jog. Secondly, it was fun. And thirdly, above all, it was fashionable. Film stars, politicians and tycoons were photographed jogging. In the United States tee-shirts were emblazoned with the accusing question: "Do *you* jog?"

Then some joggers began dropping dead, thus making more headlines. The trouble was that some people who had not taken exercise for years had bought themselves training shoes and gone straight out jogging. Nobody had warned them that their hearts might not be able to take the strain.

Meanwhile, Kenneth Cooper, formerly a doctor in the United States Air Force, was working on a concept of exercise he called aerobics. It was eventually to provide safeguards for the incautious.

Dr Cooper's idea was to slot the physical activities that people enjoyed most into a realistic fitness programme. An individual could measure and control progress, thus avoiding the dangers of overstress while at the same time ensuring that the level of exercise was sufficient to show worthwhile improvement in physical condition. Aerobic exercise (the name is taken from aerobic capacity—the maximum amount of oxygen the body can process) is any activity that improves the efficiency of the heart and lungs.

Using complicated laboratory equipment, Dr Cooper measured the aerobic capacity of thousands of volunteers and produced an index of fitness based on the amount of oxygen processed in a minute. He discovered, for example, that an unfit man in his forties could process only about 25 millilitres of oxygen per kilogramme of body weight, while a fit man of that age would process almost twice as much.

After further extensive field research, he worked out a correlation between effort exerted during different aerobic activities and oxygen consumption. In this way he was able to devise a system of points based on age, distance covered, time taken and frequency. To achieve aerobic fitness, a score of thirty points a week was required. Scoring is precise. For example, at the start of training a man over fifty would, by jogging one mile in about eighteen minutes five times a week, earn a total of five points towards the thirty he needs ultimately to attain every week. By the sixth week, jogging one mile in just under fourteen minutes five times a week, he would earn ten points. At the sixteenth week, with increased distance and reduced time, his total marks would be thirty-four.

The result was a tailor-made programme for the jogger, runner, cyclist, swimmer and amateur sportsman. Dr Cooper published his findings in his book *Aerobics*. A second volume, *The New Aerobics*, went into twenty printings in less than five years.

Used in combination with the pulse-rated exercise programme (see pages 120–1), aerobics is ideal when you have reached the point at which you want to exercise outdoors. Apart from jogging, the most popular aerobic sports are swimming (see pages 132–3) and cycling.

Cycling is an excellent way of keeping fit because it requires regular, rhythmic effort of variable intensity according to the gradient and wind conditions. It is also one of the few exercises that can be incorporated into day-to-day life without any disruption: you do not need to change your clothes and the bicycle offers a cheap alternative to other forms of transport.

As with most other single activities, however, cycling alone is not the passport to all-round fitness. It needs to be incorporated into an exercise programme, for while it is good for the heart, lungs and leg muscles, it makes little contribution either to muscular strength or to mobility.

Cycling can, however, replace other cardiovascular exercises such as running on the spot or jogging. The same rules apply: slowly increase speed and distance until you reach an optimum level for your age, then maintain your condition with regular exercise.

Rules for jogging

1. If you are more than 40 years old and have not exercised for some time, have a check-up with a doctor before you start a programme of jogging.
2. Wear warm, loose, comfortable clothes, preferably shorts. Never jog in rubberized "sweat suits" or too many sweaters.
3. Jog on soft surfaces if you can. If hard surfaces are unavoidable, jog flat-footed—not on your toes.
4. Do not go out if you feel off-colour or have recently been ill.
5. Do not overdo it. A useful rule is never to jog at a pace that would make it difficult for you to chat with a friend.
6. Taper off slowly and avoid a hot bath or shower immediately after exercise. Wait until you have cooled down.

As an indication of how fast you should progress, the aerobic running programme for people between 40 and 49 years of age covers a period of 16 weeks before the 30-point fitness level is achieved. For the first six weeks, the maximum distance recommended is only one mile, with the time taken progressively cut down from 18 minutes to about 13 minutes. This is based on going out for a run five times a week. During the final weeks, you should be covering one mile in about 9 minutes, $1^1/_2$ miles in 14 minutes and 2 miles in 20 minutes. When you are really fit you can attain your minimum 30 points by running $1^1/_2$ miles, four times a week, in about 12 minutes. Younger people have less time to complete the required distance, older people more.

Aerobic cycling

For people between 40 and 49 years of age, the aerobic cycling programme starts with two miles a day, five days a week, to be covered in 11 minutes. This increases during the next seven weeks to four miles covered in about 16 minutes and slowly progresses to six miles in 23 minutes. This is the level at which you achieve 30-point fitness. Times are adjusted for older and younger people.

All these times are based on continuous exercise and are clearly difficult to attain for urban cyclists coping with traffic jams. They are shown as guides only: the more delays you encounter the greater distance you will have to cover in order to get cardiovascular benefit.

Drawbacks of cycling in cities include the risks of injury in an accident and the disadvantage of exercising in clouds of exhaust fumes. Unfortunately, few modern cities have proper facilities for cyclists, but pressure is growing from an ever-increasing lobby for bicycle paths. As for pollution, there is no scientific evidence to show that cyclists suffer any more than pedestrians.

Swimming: a good all-round exercise

Ten minutes' non-stop swimming each day, if done properly, is all the exercise you need for all-round fitness.

If you were to swim without a pause for ten minutes every day, dividing the time equally between breaststroke, crawl and backstroke, you would need to take no other exercise. Swimming is excellent for the heart and lungs, for mobility of major joints and for muscular strength. In addition, it is one of the few sports in which being overweight is not a disadvantage and may in fact be a practical help: if you have too much body fat you float higher in the water and are better insulated against the cold.

The trouble is that swimming, unless taken seriously, can become a social sport and you can easily be lulled into a false sense of security about your physical condition if you just splash about once or twice a week. You may think you are getting enough exercise, but what do you actually *do*?

It can be difficult in a crowded public pool to swim without interruption for ten minutes—which you must do to get full benefit from the exercise. In addition most people, if they are honest with themselves, will admit that much of the time at the pool they are talking to friends, treading water, or hanging on to the side and watching others. You can in fact get the benefits of swimming, if not the pleasure, in a small private pool by making a simple harness and attaching it by a rope to the side of the pool. You can then exercise vigorously in a fixed position.

If you dive in at one end, swim a furious length, then sit on the side and rest for five minutes, you are barely exercising at all (to improve the condition of your heart and lungs you have not only to raise your pulse rate to above 120 beats a minute but to keep it there for about ten minutes).

BREASTSTROKE
Breaststroke is not as demanding as the crawl or backstroke unless swum very fast. But it is excellent for all-round exercise—and is ideal in public pools because forward visibility is good.

BACKSTROKE
The powerful circling motion of the arms in the backstroke is especially good for the heart and lungs. You can get slightly more bite in the water by rolling the body a little with each stroke.

Exercises for swimmers

Cardiovascular endurance can be improved just as efficiently by swimming as by jogging. But swimmers can build strength and improve the mobility of their bodies quicker if they combine their swimming with a programme of exercise on dry land. The following exercises are particularly beneficial for swimmers because they concentrate on muscles and major joints used in the crawl, breaststroke and backstroke. They should not be started until an all-round physical fitness programme has been completed. Once you are sure that you are fully fit you can concentrate on the specific exercises that improve the efficiency of the swimming muscles.

Strength
Press-ups develop the arm and shoulder muscles that provide the prime power for all swimming strokes. If you can do press-ups with just your fingertips on the ground the exercise is even more effective. Aim at 25 repetitions.

Squat press-ups
Stand with arms by sides, bend knees to reach squatting position with palms flat on the floor. Kick your feet back so that your weight is on toes and hands. Jump back to the squat position and stand up. Ten to 25 repetitions.

Prolonged effort is difficult for many ordinary swimmers because they find themselves out of breath after a few strokes and tend to float on their backs while they recover. Efficient breathing, which is the essence of good swimming, cannot be learned from physical exercises. (Fresh-air fiends who stand in front of the window every morning, beating their chests and taking in great gulps of air, are achieving very little apart from mobilizing their lungs. Only by exercise, when the muscles create a demand for oxygen and you consequently breathe deeper and faster to meet that demand, is the efficiency of the heart and lungs being improved.)

A swimming programme that focuses on breathing and thereby on strengthening heart and lungs is Dr Kenneth Cooper's aerobic scheme (see pages 130–1). It is based entirely on the crawl, because breaststroke and backstroke make fewer physical demands. But, if you use all three strokes during a swimming session, what you lose in cardiovascular effort with the easier strokes you gain in mobility and strength by using more muscles through a greater range of movement.

The aerobic programme for the forties age group requires five sessions a week, starting with a 100-metre swim in 2.7 minutes (or 100 yards in 2.5 minutes). During the first six weeks the distance is gradually built up to 250 metres, which has to be completed in 6 minutes (250 yards in 5.5 minutes). Then the length increases in 100-metre or 100-yard steps and the permitted time decreases until by the end of the sixteenth week you should be able to swim 800 metres in 17.8 minutes (800 yards in 16.5 minutes). Overall fitness can be maintained thereafter by swimming four sessions of 800 metres or 800 yards a week.

A rather curious swimming myth is that swimming in freezing water is especially good for you. Nobody has yet produced any scientific evidence to support the idea. At best, a cold water plunge probably generates a shot of noradrenaline and accounts for the kick the participants get out of it. At worst, it could cause a sufficient shock to the system to induce a heart attack. So use a heated pool in winter.

Because swimming is an all-round physical activity, the best way to get fit for it is by all-round physical exercise, as detailed in the forty-minute fitness programme (see pages 122–3). There are no special exercises that will increase your swimming ability: the only way to improve your swimming is to swim. If you have trouble with your breathing or style you need a swimming instructor.

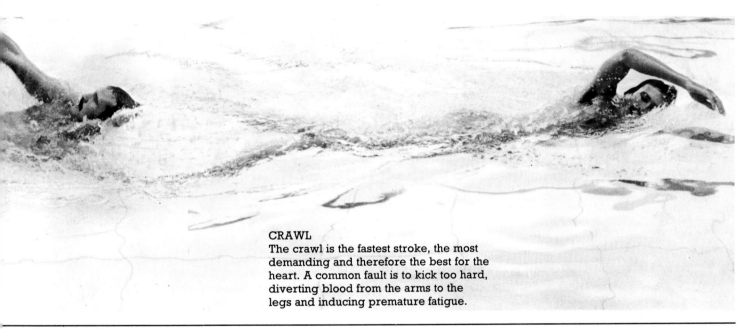

CRAWL
The crawl is the fastest stroke, the most demanding and therefore the best for the heart. A common fault is to kick too hard, diverting blood from the arms to the legs and inducing premature fatigue.

Jumping squats
Good for the action of the legs in the breaststroke. Stand with arms by your sides and bend knees to a half-squat position. Jump as high as you can, throwing your arms into the air at the same time. Start with ten repetitions, build up to 25. Then do the same exercise, but dropping into the full-squat position.

Sit-ups
Lie on your back with knees slightly bent and fingers interlaced behind neck. Sit up and bend forwards, pressing your forehead close to your knees. Ten repetitions, progressing to 30.

Ankle-stretching
Kneel down and sit back on the soles of the feet. Rock backwards to put the weight on the feet. Ten to 20 repetitions.

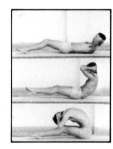

Shoulder-stretching
Top: stand with arms out at shoulder height in front of you, palms facing. Swing them back in a horizontal plane and push hard. Repeat with elbows bent at 90 degrees. Start with 15 alternate repetitions progressing to 30. Bottom: raise arms in front then swing them back in as wide a circle as you can. Repeat 20 times forwards, 20 backwards.

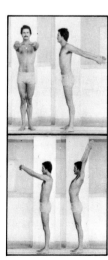

The 5BX plan: an alternative regime for men

The BX fitness plan, devised by the Royal Canadian Air Force, helps people in all walks of life attain peak fitness.

It is rare that training booklets written for air force personnel make the best-selling list, but this is what happened in the late 1950s and early 1960s following the publication of the BX exercise programme by the Royal Canadian Air Force. The exercises, which remain very popular, but which are more rigorous and designed to achieve a greater level of fitness than those described elsewhere in this chapter, were originally planned to keep the airmen—and women—at a peak of physical fitness, regardless of their jobs.

The great attraction of the BX exercise programme is that it is a progressive and daily routine. Even someone who is supremely unfit should find that the first day of exercise does not require any undue effort. Thereafter, each individual can progress at his or her own pace.

The fundamental feature of the exercise system is a daily routine of simple exercises, which progress in difficulty in easy stages. As fitness improves the workload on the body is increased until an optimum level of fitness is reached, which varies according to age. The exercise routines themselves—five for men and ten for women—are carefully balanced to make sure that muscles in all important parts of the body are used, particularly those of the arms, legs, shoulders, abdomen, back and heart, as well as the lungs.

You need no special equipment, very little space and no more time than a few minutes a day to complete and keep up the BX programme. But you do need the motivation to start and the strength of will to carry out the exercises every day without fail. If you miss out more than a day you cannot restart where you left off but must fall back to a lower level. If you stop the exercise programme for more than a month then you must start at the beginning again.

To help make the exercises as much part of your daily routine as eating and sleeping, try to set aside some time of day that can be maintained without difficulty as an exercise period. This should not be immediately after eating. The best times for exercise are before breakfast, lunch or dinner.

The BX system is in no way a magic formula for overnight fitness. It is a well-designed programme with physical fitness as its goal. A man aged between forty and forty-four, for example, will need about 203 days (or six and a half months) to reach his peak fitness level. But once he has reached that level he can sustain it with only three periods of exercise each week.

The exercise plan for men is known as the 5BX and comprises five daily exercises to be completed within a period of eleven minutes. (The companion XBX programme for women is described fully on pages 138–41.) No warming up is required for either programme because the first exercise, which strengthens and loosens the large muscles of the body, is sufficient warm-up in itself.

The programme for men is divided into five phases. Each of these separate phases has five exercises that must be repeated an increasing number of times as you progress through the phase. The time allowed for each exercise routine is the same for all of the phases. You will probably find that you can complete some exercises in less than the time allotted while others take longer. This is not important as long as you finish the day's programme within eleven minutes.

However fit you think you are, resist the temptation to rush the exercise programme. Start at the initial level of the first phase and do not move on to the next level until you have completed the number of days recommended for your age group (shown at the side of each phase). If the exercises start causing stiffness or soreness of your muscles then you are trying to get fit too fast. Do not stop exercising but drop back to a level that you find you can complete without undue effort.

It is certainly unwise to proceed past the optimum level for your age group as indicated opposite. By the time you reach that level you will have achieved the correct degree of all-round physical fitness for your age. If you have any doubts at all about starting the programme, or about your physical condition during its course, do not exercise until you have sought medical advice.

As you progress through the programme you will gradually feel the benefits of increased fitness because your body will be working more efficiently. As a result you will find that simple physical tasks such as climbing stairs demand much less physical effort. If you wish to keep a record of your progress, a publication on the BX system, such as *Physical Fitness* (Penguin Books) will give details.

PHASE 1 EXERCISES
As in all the phases, two minutes should be spent on repetitions of exercise 1, one minute each on exercises 2, 3 and 4 and six minutes on exercise 5 (run on the spot for 100 steps at first and lift this to 400 gradually during the next three weeks if you are under 30). If aged over 40, take six weeks to reach this level and 12 weeks if you are over 50. Start with a few repeats of the other exercises and build up to 15–20 over the period suggested for your age.

PHASE 2 EXERCISES
Build up from about 300 steps to 500 in exercise 5 during this phase, following the same time schedule outlined above for different age groups. Start with ten repetitions of the other exercises and build up to 20–30. But if you are aged over 50 do not try to progress beyond 400 steps running on the spot and 15–20 repeats of the other exercises. Men aged 45–50 reach their optimum at the end of this phase.

PHASE 3 EXERCISES
Still following the same time span for this phase according to your age, build up from about 20 to 30 repetitions of exercises 1 and 2, from 30 to 40 of exercise 3 and from 15 to 20 of exercise 4. Progress from 400 to about 550 steps in exercise 5. But men aged 35–45 should stop trying to increase their repetitions about half way through this phase and regard that level as their optimum.

PHASE 4 EXERCISES
Men aged 30–35 should reach their optimum level about half-way through this phase and those 25–30 should not progress beyond the end of the phase. The phase builds up from 20 to 30 repetitions of exercise 1, 18 to 22 of exercise 2, about 40 to 50 of exercise 3 and 20 to 40 of exercise 4. The modified running on the spot exercise starts at 300 steps and builds up to a peak of 400 steps.

PHASE 5 EXERCISES
The programme becomes quite gruelling in this phase, which should be attempted only by men aged 18–24 years who have spent about three months working up to it. Do about 25 repetitions of exercise 1, 25–30 of exercise 2, 40 of exercise 3 and 30–35 of exercise 4. Start with 375 steps in exercise 5 and build up in two-day stages to a peak of 420. At this optimum level, the whole exercise session should still take only 11 minutes.

The five phases of the 5BX programme, each containing five exercises, are arranged horizontally across this and the following two pages. Start with exercise 1, phase 1 (*right*), then turn the page to complete the phase.

EXERCISE 1
Phase 1

Bend and stretch with feet astride, arms up. Bend forwards to touch the floor, then stretch up and bend backwards.

Phase 1 continued over the page.

Phase 2

Bend and stretch as in phase 1 but bob and press with each forward bend.

Phase 2 continued over the page.

Phase 3

Stand with feet astride and arms up. Bend to touch the floor outside the left foot, then between the feet and press once, then outside the right foot. Bend backwards and stretch.

Phase 3 continued over the page.

Phase 4

Repeat phase 3 but when stretching backwards describe a full circle with your hands, bending from the waist.

Phase 4 continued over the page.

Phase 5

Bend and stretch as in phase 4. Always remember to change direction half-way through the exercise repeats.

Phase 5 continued over the page.

5BX/2

EXERCISE 2
Phase 1

Lie on back with feet 15 cm (6 in) apart, arms by sides. Lean forwards to look at your heels so that head and shoulders are off the floor. Keep legs straight.

Phase 2

As phase 1 but sit up into a vertical position, keeping feet on the floor. If necessary hook ankles under some heavy furniture.

Phase 3

Lie on back with hands clasped behind head. Sit up to a vertical position. Try not to hook feet under anything.

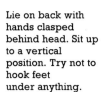

Phase 4

Lie on back with arms outstretched behind head. Lean forwards to touch toes keeping arms and legs straight.

Phase 5

Lie on back with feet together and arms linked behind head. Sit up, bend knees with feet off the floor and twist to touch left knee with right elbow. Repeat in the reverse direction.

EXERCISE 3
Phase 1

Lie on front with palms under thighs. Raise head and one leg alternately (count one each time second leg touches the floor). Keep legs straight.

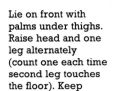

Phase 2

Repeat as in phase 1 but lift both legs, head and shoulders.

Phase 3

Lie on front with hands linked behind back. Arch body to lift chest and straight legs as far from the floor as you possibly can.

Phase 4

Repeat phase 3 but with arms stretched out sideways.

Phase 5

Repeat phase 3 but with arms stretched forwards and upwards.

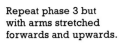

EXERCISE 4
Phase 1

Lie on your front with palms flat on the floor under your shoulders. Press up, keeping body straight from the knees, then lower until chest touches the floor.

Phase 2

Press up as in phase 1 but lift the whole body so that only hands and toes touch the floor. Keep the body straight.

Phase 3

Lie in the press-up position with chin touching floor in front of hands. Touch forehead on floor behind hands, straighten arms and body, then lower.

Phase 4

Lie on front with palms on floor 30 cm (12 in) from ears. Press up as high as possible, keeping your body straight.

Phase 5

Press up with body straight. Push off the ground, clap hands then return to original position.

EXERCISE 5
Phase 1

Run on the spot with feet at least 10 cm (4 in) off the floor, counting steps with one foot. Every 75 steps do ten scissor jumps: start with opposite arms and legs extended, jump and change positions of arms and legs before landing.

Phase 2

Repeat phase 1 but do astride jumps instead of scissors: stand with feet together, arms at sides. Jump and land with feet astride, arms up; jump and return to your original position.

Phase 3

Repeat phase 2 but do half-knee bends: put feet together and hands on hips. Bend knees to make an angle of 110°, keep back straight and stretch upright on your toes.

Phase 4

Repeat as phase 3 but do semi-squat jumps: drop to a half-crouch, back straight and one foot just behind the other. Jump into upright pose, reverse feet before landing; return to half-crouch.

Phase 5

Repeat as phase 4 but do semi-spread eagle jumps: with feet together drop to a half-crouch, jump up to feet astride, arms-up position then return to half-crouch, feet together.

The XBX plan: ten exercises for the woman

Domestic chores make a woman tired but not fit. The XBX exercise plan is designed to produce all-round fitness.

None of the daily activities undertaken by the average woman provides the balanced exercise she needs for all-round physical fitness. The XBX plan for women, originated by the Royal Canadian Air Force, is designed to solve this problem. It comprises a daily programme of ten exercises in three progressively more demanding phases, illustrated here and overleaf, and takes no more than twelve minutes a day.

The first four exercises in the programme last a total of two minutes and are planned primarily as a warm-up and to improve those areas of the body neglected in everyday activity. The remaining six exercises all have a specific intention. Exercise 5 strengthens the abdominal region and the muscles at the front of the thighs. Exercise 6 exercises the long back muscles, the buttocks and backs of the thighs. Exercise 7 tones up the muscles at the sides of the thighs. Exercise 8 is mainly for the arms, shoulders and chest. Exercise 9 is for flexibility in the waist and strengthens the hip muscles. Exercise 10, by exercising the legs, conditions the heart and the lungs.

Exactly the same principles apply to the XBX system as to its male counterpart, the 5BX, described on pages 134–7. Always start at the initial level, do not progress faster than the recommended rate, slow down if you find you are becoming stiff and sore and fall back to a lower level if you stop the programme for any reason.

The number of repeats and the time allowed are shown in the right-hand column over the page, but the age levels need not be so rigidly applied as in the male plan. Some women will have difficulty in reaching the level for their age while others will surpass it easily. The time to stop is when you cannot move on with ease after about a week at one level. Accept this as your peak and maintain it with three exercise periods a week.

If you plan to use the XBX system as a slimming aid remember that exercise is effective for losing weight only if combined with a Calorie-controlled diet.

EXERCISE 1

Phase 1
Stand with your feet 30 cm (12 in) apart and arms up in the air. Then bend to touch the floor, but do not strain to keep your knees straight. Return to the original position.

Phase 2
Repeat the floor-touching as in phase 1 but on each bend bob and touch the floor a second time.

Phase 3
Repeat the floor-touching as in phase 2 but bob and touch the floor three times, first outside one foot, then between the feet and then outside the other foot before returning to the starting position.

EXERCISE 2

Phase 1
Stand with your hands at your sides and with feet together. Raise one knee as high as possible, grasp it and pull in for a count of one, keeping your back straight. Repeat with the other knee.

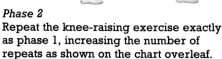

Phase 2
Repeat the knee-raising exercise exactly as phase 1, increasing the number of repeats as shown on the chart overleaf.

Phase 3
Repeat the knee-raising exercise as in phase 1 for the appropriate number of repeats.

EXERCISE 3

Phase 1
Stand with your feet 30 cm (12 in) apart and hands at your sides. Keeping your back straight, bend sideways and slide your left hand down your left leg for a count of one. Repeat for the right.

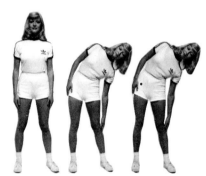

Phase 2
Repeat the lateral bending as in phase 1 but bob and press down a second time on each bend.

Phase 3
Stand with your feet apart and with one arm bent over your head from the elbow. Slide the straight arm as far down your leg as possible, pressing in the same direction with the raised arm. Repeat in the opposite direction. Count one for left and right bends.

EXERCISE 4

Phase 1
Stand with your feet 30 cm (12 in) apart and hands at your sides. Trace out large circles with one arm then the other. Count one for each full arm circle, forwards and backwards alternately.

Phase 2
Repeat the arm-circling as in phase 1 but with both arms at once. Reverse direction half-way through the required number of repeats.

Phase 3
Repeat the arm-circling as in phase 1 but circle the arms in a windmill action—both moving at the same time but one following the other. Reverse the direction half-way through and count one for each full circle.

EXERCISE 5

Phase 1 continued over the page.

Phase 1
Lie on your back with feet together and arms at your sides. Lift your head and shoulders until you can see your heels, then lower to the starting position.

Phase 2 continued over the page.

Phase 2
Lie on your back with knees bent and arms overhead. Swing arms and feet forwards to a straight-legged sitting position and try to touch your toes.

Phase 3 continued over the page.

Phase 3
Lie on your back with legs straight and arms at your sides. Rise to a sitting position, sliding hands along your legs to try to touch toes. Return to original position.

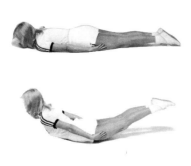

Phase 1
Lie on your front with hands under your thighs. Raise your head, shoulders and alternate legs as high as possible, then lower. Each leg-raise counts one.

Phase 1
Lie on your side with the lower arm stretched out under your head. Using your upper arm for balance, raise your upper leg, then lower. Do half the number of repeats, then roll over to exercise with the other leg.

Phase 1
Lie on your front with hands under your shoulders. Press up, keeping your knees on the floor. Sit back on your heels, then return to the starting position.

Phase 2
Lie on your front with feet together and palms under your thighs. Raise your head, shoulders and both straight legs as high as possible, then lower.

Phase 2
Repeat the exercises as in phase 1 but raise your leg as near to the perpendicular as possible.

Phase 2
Lie on your front with hands under your shoulders. Press up to straighten your arms, keeping your knees on the floor and your body straight.

Phase 3
Lie on your front with legs together and arms outstretched. Raise the upper body and both legs as high as possible, keeping your legs straight.

Phase 3
Repeat the leg-raising exercise as in phase 2.

Phase 3
Lie on your front with legs together. Rest on elbows placed under your shoulders and clasp your hands. Raise the body by making it straight from head to heels. Keep your head up and leave only forearms, elbows and toes in contact with the floor.

EXERCISE 9

Phase 1
Lie on your back with legs together, arms at sides and palms down. Raise one leg to make a right angle with the body, then lower. Repeat with the other leg. Count one for both leg-raises.

Phase 2
Lie on your back with feet together and arms outstretched. Raise one leg to the perpendicular then swing it over to try touching opposite hand with toes. Return to starting position and switch legs. Keep body straight and shoulders flat on the floor. Each leg-raise counts one.

Phase 3
Lie on your back with legs together, arms outstretched with palms down. Draw up both legs, bending at hips and knees to tuck position. Swing to left and right to touch floor on each side with knees, keeping shoulders flat on floor, then return to original position.

EXERCISE 10

Phase 1
Run on the spot with your knees up and feet at least 10 cm (4 in) off the floor. Count one each time the left foot touches the floor. After 50, do ten hops with your feet together.

Phase 2
Run on the spot as in phase 1 but after 50 do ten astride jumps—stand with feet together and arms at sides then jump to astride position with arms up before returning to starting position.

Phase 3
Run on the spot raising each foot at least 15 cm (6 in) off the floor. After 50 do ten half-knee bends—start with your feet together and hands on hips, then bend at the knees, lowering your body until legs are at an angle of about 110°, keeping your back straight. Return to starting position.

PHASE 1 EXERCISES

In all the phases, two minutes should be spent on the first four exercises; two minutes each on exercises 5 and 8; one minute each on exercises 6, 7 and 9 and three minutes on exercise 10 (run on the spot for 50 steps at first and gradually raise this to 70). Take 12 days to reach this level if you are under 25, three weeks on this phase if you are under 35, six weeks if you are 35–40, two and a half months if you are 40–45, three months if you are 45–50 and three and a half months if you are over 50. Start with four repetitions of exercises 1, 2 and 3, building up to ten; begin exercise 4 with 20 repetitions, building to 40; exercises 5, 6 and 7 with four repetitions, building to 25; exercises 8 and 9 with three repetitions building to 15. Women who are 50 and over will then have reached the optimum level for their age.

PHASE 2 EXERCISES

Build up from about 120 steps to 200 in exercise 10 during this phase. Start with ten repetitions of exercises 1, 2, 3, 5, 6, 8 and 9, building up without undue strain to between 15 and 25. Start exercise 4 with 20 repetitions, building up to 30 and start exercise 7 with 30 repetitions, building up to 50. Phase 2 should be completed in three weeks by women under 25, five weeks by those aged 25–30, and two months by those aged 30–35. Those aged 35–40 should complete three-quarters of phase 2 in 40 days and then stay at that level; women of 40–45 should complete half the phase in six weeks and those aged 45–50 one-quarter of the phase in four weeks. These three age groups should regard those as their optimum levels. Always drop back to a lower level if, for any reason, your exercise programme is interrupted.

PHASE 3 EXERCISES

Women under 25 should spend five weeks on this phase. Build up from 150 steps to 250 in exercise 10. Start with 15 repetitions of exercises 1, 2 and 3, building up to 20; with 25 repetitions of exercises 5, 6 and 8, building up to 40; 50 repetitions of exercise 7, building to 60, and with ten repetitions of exercise 9 building to 20. Women aged 25–30 should aim at only half the final level of repeats and take four weeks to reach it. Those aged 30–35 should regard the initial number of repeats as their peak. At these levels all age groups will have reached the optimum physical fitness for their age. Precise guidelines to the number of repetitions and progress charts can be found in books on the BX programme. It is unwise, in a search for even greater fitness, to exercise past the optimum level for your age group.

Ways to improve your body shape

Despite the claims of some massage parlours and health farms, there is no quick way to a more beautiful body.

For the chin and neck
Drop your head forwards, then slowly move it in a wide circle, first in one direction, then the other. Repeat five to ten times.

For the breasts
Clasping your raised forearms, push your hands with a jerk towards your elbows and relax. Repeat 20 to 30 times.

"Spot reducing"—that is, taking weight off just one particular area of the body and attempting to do so without exertion, as with the use of vibrator pads—is impossible, despite the fact that there is a small but thriving industry devoted to selling the idea.

It is, of course, perfectly possible to put on muscle bulk in specific areas, for example by isometric exercising (see pages 144–7). Losing weight, however, is a different matter, for it is physically impossible to do so without either exercising in one way or another or reducing food intake, and even then we have limited control over the sequence in which the fat will be shed.

Fat is formed from stored Calories. If every day you take in more Calories than you use up during the course of the day, the excess is stored in your body as fat. An accumulation of about 7,000 Calories over a period of two weeks will add an extra 1 kg (2.2 lb) to your body weight. The only ways to get rid of this fat are either to burn Calories by taking more exercise, consume fewer of them, or to do both these things. Nothing else will work. You can lose weight by massage—but only if you are the masseur. The physical activity of massaging will use up the Calories: being massaged will not.

Massage and similar techniques can only improve muscle tone, which means the muscle is slightly tightened and more "alive". Improvement in muscle tone will not do much to improve your shape. You may feel a little better—but you will look almost exactly the same.

Losing weight and improving your shape is a slow business. It can also be disappointing. You may lose some outer "padding", but your basic body shape is determined by your bone structure and this you can do little about. If you have a slim trunk and wide hips no amount of slimming and exercising will change your basic "pear shape".

Crash diets and intensive exercise programmes can speed up weight loss and shape improvement, but you may not be pleased with the results. If you try to lose weight too quickly your face becomes thin and drawn, and your arms and legs get thinner. The last area to show improvement is often where you most want to lose weight. Sometimes a crash diet can result in a woman improving the shape of her waist, for example, at the expense of her bustline—the breasts become smaller because she is shedding the excess weight too quickly.

The best approach to the problem is a sensible diet and a gentle, progressive exercise routine that does not promise overnight miracles.

Exercise does more than just burn up Calories and get rid of fat—it improves the posture and both strengthens and tightens the muscles. Contrary to popular belief, normal exercise does not build up large, unsightly muscles—it takes a special daily regime to do this.

The business executive's paunch is often caused by slack muscles in the abdomen rather than fat. If the muscles are weak, they stretch and allow the abdominal organs to fall forwards, forming a "pot belly". Layers of fat develop on the outside of the muscles, but never as thickly as the size of the paunch might suggest. So exercise to strengthen the abdominal muscles can dramatically reduce the dimensions of a "pot belly"—even without going on a diet.

Undoubtedly the best way to improve your shape is with the forty-minute fitness programme on pages 122–3, in tandem with a moderate restriction of your Calorie intake. If, having reached your fitness level, you are still bothered by problems with your figure, you can introduce one of the specific exercises on these pages into your exercise routine to tone up specific parts of the body.

Remember, the first priority—for the sake of your health and not your vanity—is to get fit. At the same time, you are likely to find that your figure becomes slimmer, firmer and a better shape. Forty minutes' exercise a week will do more for you than twenty weeks on the massage table. Money cannot buy you a good body: unless you are involved in some kind of physical effort, you cannot improve your shape to any great extent.

For the hips
Lie on one side, resting your head on an elbow, and raise one leg as high as possible, then lower it. Repeat ten times, then change sides and raise the other leg. Progress to lifting both legs and moving them in a scissor pattern parallel to the floor. Do 20 to 30 times.

For neck and shoulders

Sit cross-legged with your back straight and link your hands on your forehead with your elbows held high. Take a deep breath, then press hard against your forehead. Hold for five seconds and repeat the exercise with hands linked behind your head.

For the abdomen

Lie on your back with feet apart and hands linked above your head. Sit up quickly and twist to touch a foot with both hands. Do 15 to 20 times.

For the buttocks

Kneel with both legs together, keeping your back straight and your arms above your head. Facing forwards, slowly lower your body so that you are sitting on the floor, first on one side of your legs and then the other. Repeat ten to 25 times, alternating from side to side.

For the chest

On hands and knees, bend at the elbows to touch your chin on the floor and stretch a leg out behind you alternately.

For the waist

Lie on your back with your arms at right angles. Raise both knees towards your chest. Then keeping your shoulders and back on the floor, roll your knees over to touch the floor, first on one side, then the other. Do 15 to 25 times.

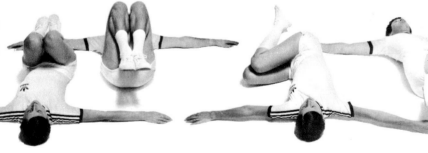

For ankles and calves

Stand with your feet 15 cm (6 in) apart, and toes turned out. Lift up on to your toes as high as you can. Repeat 20 to 30 times. Then do the same exercise but with your toes turned in.

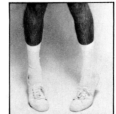

For the abdomen

On your back with arms at 45 degrees, lift your legs and bicycle. Partially sit up and continue with hands off the floor.

143

Isometrics: a quick way to strength

Isometric exercises provide a simple and inexpensive means of building greater muscle power and improving posture and figure. But they are not enough for total fitness.

For most people who take no exercise, the most extreme exertion in a normal day demands only about twenty to thirty per cent of potential muscle strength. An office worker walking for a bus or a housewife lifting a load of washing will use no more than this. As a result of inadequate muscle development their bodies have few reserves of strength and any extra exertion, such as having to push start a car on a cold morning, can strain muscles and ligaments. One method of improving strength quickly, effectively and without too much fatigue is isometric exercising.

Whereas conventional muscle-building calls for muscular effort against objects that can be moved, isometrics call for brief efforts against objects that cannot be moved—for example, a wall or door-frame. During conventional, or isotonic, exercising the muscle fibres lengthen or shorten with movement; during isometric exercising they are in a state of static contraction with no movements at the joints—hence the name of the exercise, which means "same length". Theoretically, the two forms of exercise can be equally beneficial in building muscular strength, as demonstrated by a classic experiment on a frog at the Max Planck Institute in Dortmund. One leg was tied, the other left free. The leg that seemingly got no exercise in fact gained strength faster as a result of tugging against an immovable object—its bond.

This isometric effect can be applied to the human body with a number of advantages. Ordinary muscle activity brings into play only some muscle fibres in any particular set; but when maximum effort is demanded of a muscle all the muscle fibres are exercised. Isometric exercises which involve maximum effort against an immovable object can strengthen muscles by up to 100 per cent.

Charles Atlas, using his so-called

If you are overweight or suffer from any form of cardiovascular disease, these exercises are best avoided. Even for a fitter person, isometrics can be made safer and produce better results if the following simple advice is followed.
1. Before beginning training, carry out the five mobility exercises as described on pages 114–15.
2. Apply mild force for two seconds only at first; then, when strength improves, more and, finally, full force may be used.
3. Even when full force has been achieved, it should be exerted for two seconds only. Then slowly build up to a maximum of six seconds for each exercise.
4. Breathe as freely as possible between exercises and, when you have completed the session, do at least two minutes' running on the spot.

The exercises here and overleaf were devised by Alistair Murray to provide a course of training that will benefit the entire body. All you will need are a strong broom handle and a piece of rope, the length of which can be altered to suit the different exercise positions (see illustration of slip knot, *right*).

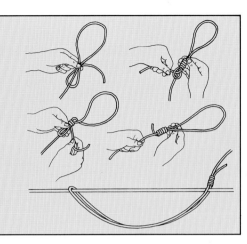

To condition spine and waist, stand with feet wide apart, the rope under both feet, bar across shoulders. Bend trunk to the right by pushing left arm up harder than the right.

Repeat the exercise, but this time bending the trunk to the left while resisting with upward pressure of left arm. As with all these exercises, apply pressure for two seconds only.

Arms and upper back: feet apart, rope under both feet. Legs, back and arms as shown above.

Front view of the same exercise, showing upper arms parallel to the bar. Lift upwards as if trying to raise the bar.

"dynamic tension" isometric method, won the title of the world's most perfectly developed man in 1921 and introduced a period of popularity for isometrics.

Enthusiasts cite many examples of the effectiveness of the isometric method. An American weight-lifting team, when in Kiev for a contest against the USSR, was reported to have pushed down the wall of an hotel during isometric training. A Russian, Alexander Zass, provides another example. As a prisoner in World War I Zass exercised by pulling and pushing against the bars of his cell. When released, he had built up such muscular strength that he toured the world in circuses and music halls, using the stage name of Samson, demonstrating his power by breaking chains and bending iron bars.

The isometric method does have some real advantages. Increase in strength and muscle tone develops rapidly—improvement will be evident within days rather than weeks. Moreover, the exercises are easy to do; each contraction lasts only six seconds and fifteen exercises are sufficient to condition the entire body. A minimum of only ninety seconds' daily exercise will thus ensure comprehensive results. And, since any immovable object will serve (an opposing fist, a wall, chair or table) no expensive equipment is needed. Finally, isometric contraction can be practised anywhere—in an office, in a car, even in bed. For example, when a car is stationary at traffic lights, the driver can condition his arm and chest muscles by holding the steering wheel at either side and pressing his hands inwards as if to make them meet. The sides of a typewriter will serve equally well. A man exercising in an office can develop the broad upper back muscles by sitting about 30 cm (12 in) from his desk or table and, keeping erect and with palms downwards, pressing hard on the desk top.

There are, however, certain things that isometric exercises will not do. Most important, they do hardly anything for the

Isometrics/2

Arms and shoulders: stand with feet slightly apart, rope under feet, the rope tight, as with all exercises in this sequence, and the bar at forehead (*far left*). Apply force as if trying to lift the bar upwards.

Arms: stand with feet slightly apart (*left*), arms bent to right angles, rope under feet. Apply pressure upwards, ensuring that the heels do not leave the floor.

Legs and back: stand with feet slightly apart (*below*), rope tight and under both feet, bar at knee level. The head should be upright, looking ahead, the back and arms straight, the knees slightly bent. Apply force upwards, pulling with legs, arms and back. The front view of the same exercise (*below right*) shows the correct position of the head.

heart and blood system, or for the lungs. Ideally, therefore, they should be combined with some other form of exercise, such as walking, running or cycling, that increases blood flow and oxygen intake. Some isotonic exercise, such as two minutes of "running on the spot" or jumping, should always precede and follow isometric training to prepare and then relax the body.

Although isometrics exercise and develop muscles to the maximum, they do so without sweat and without moving the joints, and are therefore not effective for slimming or for suppleness.

Always approach isometric exercises with caution: in certain circumstances they can be positively harmful. Isometric exercising constricts the muscles for a relatively long time; this compresses arteries and the veins, shuts off oxygen supply to the heart and abruptly pushes up blood pressure. It is unsuitable for anyone with a heart condition.

Many isometric instruction books will tell you to take a deep breath before starting an exercise and hold it during the contraction exercise. If you are reasonably healthy this will certainly do no harm, but it is inadvisable because it may impose an unnecessary extra strain. Each contraction should last for six seconds (no additional benefit comes from holding the position longer). Then relax and breathe normally for a few seconds before repeating or going on to the next exercise.

Isometric exercises can be performed for almost any muscle or set of muscles. The exercises illustrated here form no more than a basic course for everyone, regardless of age or sex. There are many other exercises designed for individual needs—for women, children and the elderly, for athletes and body-builders.

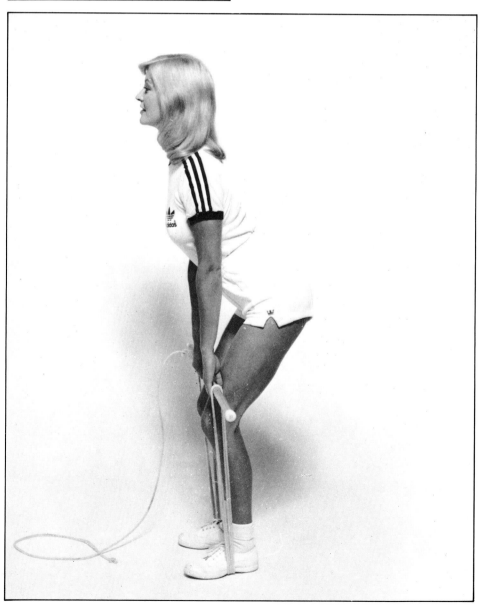

Legs and back: feet slightly apart, rope under feet, bar across shoulders, knees bent as shown. Pull up.

Shoulders: pass rope under the seat of a chair, bar at forehead, arms bent. Apply force upwards.

Arms, shoulders and chest: back lying, shoulders on a cushion, rope under shoulders. Apply force upwards.

Your record of progress

It is a helpful incentive to keep a chart of progress. Measurements can be taken of the upper arm, chest, waist, neck, hips, thigh and calf. Your weight should also be recorded. Thereafter, further entries should be made at four-week intervals.

The muscles should always be measured at the same spots and in the same way.

Biceps: measure around the broadest part; the arm should be flexed for men and relaxed for women.

Chest: standing upright, pass a tape below the armpits and across the nipples.

Waist: measure around the slimmest part.

Neck, hips, thigh and calf: measure around the broadest part.

The chart below is designed so that the exerciser can see his progress at a glance and be able immediately to identify any muscles that may need special attention. After 20 weeks, progress will necessarily be less dramatic, but the chart can, of course, be extended indefinitely.

	Starting date	Weeks				
		4	8	12	16	20
Biceps						
Chest						
Waist						
Neck						
Hips						
Thigh						
Calf						
Weight						

Weights: the advanced way to fitness

Training with light weights three times a week will give you a firm physique and help your all-round health.

Training with weights is not intended to turn you into a rippling-muscled Mr Universe or a woman with bulging biceps. Neither does it have anything to do with competitive weight-lifting. It is designed for ordinary people who have completed the forty-minute fitness programme (see pages 122–3) but would like to continue with more advanced exercises. Its aim is to further improve your all-round condition.

Contrary to popular belief, weight-training is suitable for both men and women. Because the emphasis of these exercises is on fitness rather than physique, there is no danger of a woman developing huge shoulders or bulging muscles in her arms and legs. What she *will* develop is a firm, well-rounded and healthy figure.

There is considerable confusion in the public mind between weight-training, weight-lifting and body-building. In fact they are three separate activities. The weight-lifter is primarily concerned with pure strength and technical skill—his object is to lift above his head the heaviest load that his body is capable of bearing.

Body-builders, however, are interested in the physical perfection of their bodies. They will spend months developing obscure muscles and practising the means of displaying them. Curiously, they need not necessarily be the fittest of men: their huge muscles increase their body weight to such an extent that it can impair movement and performance in exactly the same way as if they were excessively fat.

Weight training is concerned with fitness for everyday life: therein lies the difference. Following a programme, weight training can also improve your general sporting performance.

Once you have achieved a reasonable level of fitness by conventional exercise, training with weights is the easiest and most efficient way to continue making progress. The weights used are comparatively light, because the accent is on increasing repetitions rather than lifting

Chin-high pull

Exercise for legs, back, arms, shoulders. Place feet under bar, 25 cm (10 in) apart. Bend knees, look ahead and keep back straight. Extend body and pull up bar in a straight line close to body until under chin.

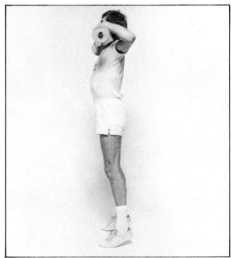

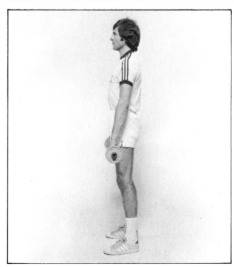

very heavy loads. You should start with only about 0.9 kg (2 lb) and not exceed a maximum total load of 13.6 kg (30 lb).

Obviously, you will need equipment, ideally a bar-bell—a steel bar about 1.5 m (5 ft) long with disc-shaped weights at either end—a selection of disc weights and two dumb-bells (wooden or steel bars supporting balls at each end). This can be expensive, so at the start it is a good idea to make your own weights. Waisted plastic bottles, such as those used for liquid detergent, are perfect. Two of them filled with water and wrapped in bandages to improve the grip make serviceable 0.9 kg (2 lb) weights to start training with. Replacing the water with sand doubles their weight.

Always warm up for a weight-training session with the five mobility exercises on pages 114–15. Although by the time you

start thinking about using weights you probably consider yourself to be reasonably fit, the same safety rules should apply as the day you began to exercise: keep checking your pulse rate (see pages 120–1) to make sure you are not over-exerting yourself; never exercise to the point of exhaustion and progress slowly.

If you are exercising regularly, three times a week, start with fifteen repetitions of each exercise, resting in between if you feel the need or if your pulse rate is shooting up too high. At the end of the second week increase the number of repetitions to twenty and add a further five after the third and fourth weeks. When you can complete thirty repetitions with ease, you can then increase the weight. Your personal pulse rating will determine when you have reached the maximum weight you should lift.

Progress can easily be measured by keeping a record of the number of repetitions completed at each session, the weights used and the time taken to rest between exercises.

Because exercising with weights offers the most complete all-round training programme for physical fitness that it is possible to devise, specific exercises for strength or cardiovascular efficiency become unnecessary. All the requirements of the body are encompassed in this schedule because each of the eight exercises is designed to "work out" particular parts of the body.

Both men and women may worry that training with weights will cause a rupture or heart strain. Providing you are in good health and train sensibly—gradually increasing the exercise time and the weights used—there is no need for any such fear.

Palms forward curl

Exercise for the arms. Stand upright holding bar close to body, arms straight, palms facing forwards. Bend arms to bring bar up to chest; return bar to starting position. Repeat 15 times during each preliminary session.

"Rowing"

Exercise for shoulders and forearms. Feet astride, bend forwards at 45 degrees, the bar-bell, held with knuckles facing forwards, hanging downwards. Raise bar to top of chest, keeping rest of body motionless.

Press behind neck

Exercises for the shoulders, arms and upper back. Stand upright with bar resting across back of neck and shoulders. Extend arms to full length above head; return bar to neck. 15 to 30 repetitions.

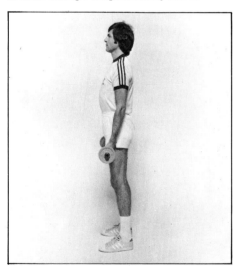

Weights/2

Side bends
To exercise the spine and waist, hold a dumb-bell loosely in one hand with the other hand on your hip and bend from side to side. Change hands and repeat.

Squats (right)
To strengthen legs and back, rest barbell behind neck. With feet about 25 cm (10 in) apart and back straight, squat and come briskly up on tiptoe.

Bench press
For arms, chest and shoulders, lie on a firm bench, rest bar-bell on chest and push it straight up until arms are fully extended. Do 15 times.

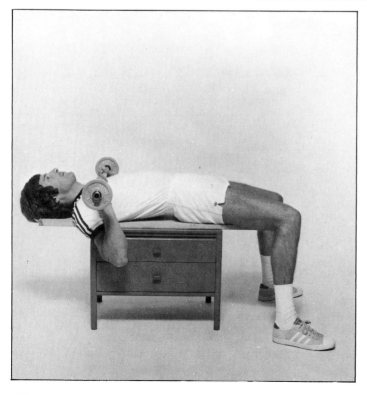

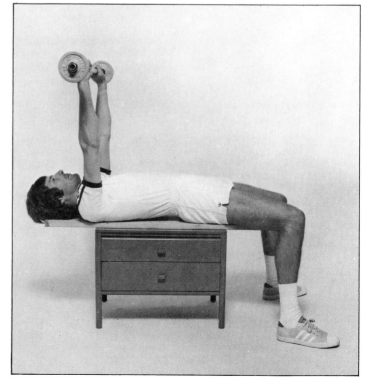

Clean and press

This exercise strengthens the shoulders, arms, back and legs. Place toes under bar 25 cm (10 in) apart. Keeping back straight, bend to grasp bar (knuckles forwards) and lift straight up to top of chest. Then push bar up to arm's length. Lower in stages to floor.

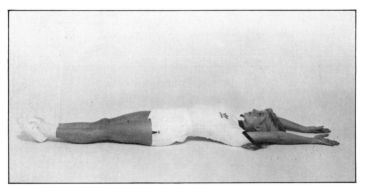

Sit-ups

Although done without weights, this abdominal exercise is useful in weight training. Lift legs and arms from prone position to touch ankles as shown.

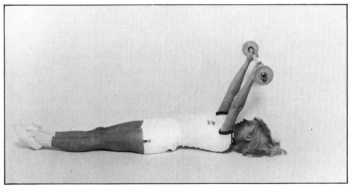

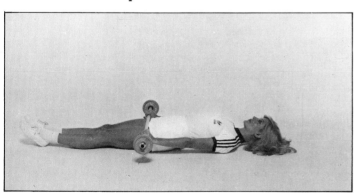

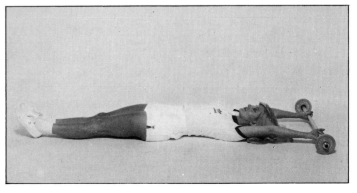

Straight arm pull-over

To strengthen the chest, arms and shoulders, lie flat on floor with bar across thighs and palms on top of bar. Keeping arms straight, lift bar in a wide arc to touch floor behind head. Return bar to thighs and do 15 times, as with all the weight exercises.

What to look for in a health gym

Health gyms exist to help people get fit, but there is great variety in the care they take and the advice they provide.

How the machines work

The ergometer cycling machine exercises leg muscles and stimulates the heart and lungs. Intensity of effort can be increased gradually by adjusting the resistance of the pedals.

More and more people are using professional gyms to help them get fit. Health gyms have been opening up all over Europe and the US to meet the demand, but most fitness experts agree that the standard of instruction they provide—particularly for unfit people—is variable.

How can you tell a good gym from a bad one? First, you need to differentiate between training gyms and health gyms. Training gyms simply provide the premises and facilities for *keeping* fit. They are used mainly by athletes or sportsmen and women who want to maintain their physical condition throughout the year.

Health gyms exist to provide not only facilities but also advice and instruction for ordinary people who want to get fit, lose weight or both. Because they cater for unfit people it is even more important that their standards are impeccable. Health gyms offer a service to both men and women, whatever their age or physical condition. A typical client is a middle-aged executive who prefers to take time off from the office for a regular work-out in a gym rather than exercise at home.

Before joining a health gym you should first establish the qualifications of the staff. Many gyms are run by former athletes or sportsmen with little or no training in the treatment of very unfit people. Instructors in the best gyms are either physiotherapists, remedial gymnasts, academically qualified teachers of physical training or all three. Long experience as a star sportsman is no substitute for any of these skills.

The equipment of a good health gym should include, at minimum: a selection of dumb-bell and bar-bell weights ranging from 2.3 kg (5 lb) and increasing in 2.3 kg (5 lb) stages to around 45.5 kg (100 lb); horizontal benches and sloping benches to alter the angle of exercise; wall pulleys for arm and shoulder strengthening; leg exercising machines; and, most important of all, a pulsometer. This last piece of equipment is an electronic machine that monitors your pulse rate while you are exercising. Every gymnasium should check a new client's pulse rate before prescribing a course of exercises.

The reason for paying such attention to the pulse is simple: no instructor, however experienced or well qualified, is

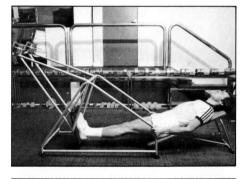

Inclined leg-press machines are used primarily for remedial exercising. The action of pressing down a weighted bar with the feet gently develops leg muscles that have grown weak.

Inclined benches are essential equipment in every gymnasium. The effort demanded in performing sit-ups on them is increased by making the angle of incline of the bench steeper.

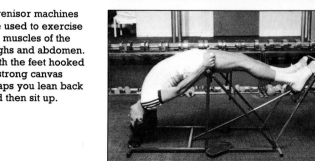

Juvenisor machines are used to exercise the muscles of the thighs and abdomen. With the feet hooked in strong canvas straps you lean back and then sit up.

able to gauge from external indications what is happening to your heart and lungs when you exercise. If you have strong abdominal muscles, for example, you may be able to complete thirty sit-ups from a prone position without showing any signs of stress—yet if your cardiovascular system is weak you could be placing an intolerable strain on your heart and lungs. The only way to safeguard against this is to measure your pulse rate. At the time of joining a gym you should be asked when you last had a medical check-up and if you have any particular problems such as a bad back, asthma or knee trouble. A gym that does not want to know these things should be approached with caution.

Similarly, if you are given the go-ahead to start exercising without first taking a pulse test, you should beware. Most gyms set new clients a gentle exercise test aimed at raising the pulse rate to between 100 and 110 a minute. If this test causes your pulse to shoot up far above this figure, you should be advised to have a medical check-up before starting exercise. This is not necessarily a cause for alarm—very often it simply means that the individual is extremely unfit. But a high pulse rate from gentle exercise is also a warning of problems that may need to be medically diagnosed.

The best health gyms strictly control the individual progress of their clients. They not only demonstrate how the exercises should be done but also draw up a detailed programme for each session, listing exactly which exercises have to be completed, in what order and for how long.

A good instructor curbs overenthusiasm because he knows that getting fit should be a slow and gentle process. It is a bad sign if a gym allows you to choose your own weights or exceed the prescribed number of repetitions of a particular exercise, or if you are allowed to use equipment for as long as you like.

Having made the decision to go to a gym, it is a great temptation to overexert yourself by increasing the weight of a dumbbell or pedalling too long and too hard on a bicycling machine. The same criterion applies to exercising in a gym as exercising at home: if you are stiff after a work-out you are overdoing it.

Health farms should not be confused with health gyms. The collective value of their facilities—massage, sauna, diet, exercise and so on—is of great benefit if you simply want a rest and an opportunity to "recharge your batteries". But most people stay only about two weeks—and you cannot get fit in a fortnight. The only long-term benefit of a trip to a health farm is if it teaches you a healthy way of life so that you continue exercise and a sensible diet after you have left.

This complex arrangement of sliding bars and weights is an exercise machine that can be adapted for a number of different activities designed to improve the strength of the major muscle groups.

Lifting bar-bells alternately from an inclined bench is effective in improving arm and shoulder strength. The weight of the bar-bells is gradually increased under the supervision of the gym staff.

Weighted pulleys are particularly useful for remedial exercising of arms and legs. Exercising with them helps build up muscle fibre that has wasted away after illnesses or long periods of inactivity.

Hanging from the bar of this multi-purpose exercise machine develops strength in the arm and shoulder muscles. Advanced exercises on this machine involve pulling the chin up to touch the bar.

Raising and lowering a weighted bar from a back-lying position greatly increases the strength of the hip and leg muscles. Extra weight is added as strength improves to make you work harder.

This vibrating belt machine is used only to improve the tone of muscles. Although this is beneficial in a general way it does not assist directly in achieving fitness, as it requires no physical effort on the part of the user.

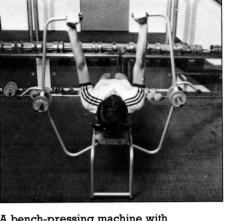

A bench-pressing machine with adjustable pivoted weights can be used for a number of different exercises for strengthening the arms, the shoulders and the chest.

A weighted bar rests across the user's shoulders on this calf-exercising machine. You start with heels on the base of the machine and rise up on the toes, taking the weight of the bar as you rise.

Treadmills improve cardiovascular efficiency by simulating walking, jogging or running conditions. A pulsometer is on the treadmill so that the user's pulse rate can be checked during exercise.

The leg extension machine is used to develop thigh muscles and is of special value to people with cartilage problems. The insteps are hooked under the weighted bar and the legs are then raised and lowered.

Old age can still be a beginning

Age is no barrier to maintaining a good physical condition. By following the exercise plan on these pages the physical process of ageing can be slowed and some of your youthful vitality rediscovered.

It is never too late to start getting fit. Regardless of your age, a balanced programme of exercises will always improve the condition of your body.

Older people who have been inactive for a long time need to approach exercise with caution. The best and most accurate guide to the safety of an exercise programme is your pulse (see pages 120–1) because it signals any overexertion.

Many of the aches and pains associated with advancing years can be avoided by keeping fit and active as you grow older. Backache in particular is often caused by contraction of the spine, a complaint that can easily be prevented by the simplest of bending exercises.

The stooped posture that many older people think is inevitable is in fact usually just the result of inactivity. There is no physiological reason why people in their eighties should not stand as erect or walk as tall as they did in their teens.

There is no reason, either, why actual physical disability should present an in-surmountable obstacle to fitness. Competitors in the Paraplegic Olympics are a heartening and most reassuring example of how disability can be overcome and fitness maintained. Any hospital physiotherapist will confirm that mobility and muscle-contracting exercises performed in bed or while sitting in a chair play a vital role in recovery after illness or surgical operations.

The exercises shown on these pages are designed for older people who have been inactive for some time and are aimed at improving suppleness and posture—but very slowly. They are essentially the same as the mobility exercises (see pages 114–15), except that they are all performed sitting down. None should cause any strain—if they do, you are probably trying too hard. There is no age barrier to continuing with the complete programme of forty-minute fitness (pages 122–3), providing you have a medical check before you start and use your pulse rate to monitor the intensity of exertion.

A mobility routine for the elderly
For mobility of trunk and spine, sit with feet apart and arms outstretched (*above*). Keep thighs and pelvis still and turn head, shoulders and arms to left then right (*below and right*), bending elbow.

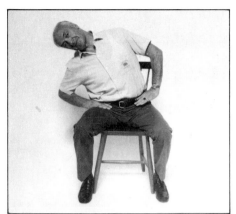

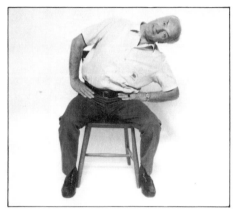

To mobilize hip and spinal joints, sit with legs outstretched and together (*top*). Raise one knee, bringing your head down towards it and bend the other knee for support (*above*). Repeat ten times.

For spinal mobility, sit with legs wide apart and hands on hips (*top*). Keeping the head at right angles to the trunk bend alternately to right and left (*above*) without jerking. Repeat ten times.

To improve turning ability and spinal mobility, sit with feet apart and hands on one thigh. Bend over from the waist

and slide your hands down the leg towards the ankle. Repeat on alternate sides, ten times on each leg.

EXERCISE: UNIVERSAL ELIXIR

Never before has it been more vital for everyone, male and female, of whatever age, to set aside some time every week to take physical exercise. The need has been created by the convenience of modern life: in this age of escalators and elevators, of taxis and television, of two-car families and domestic appliances, fewer and fewer people actually need to do the things that amount to exercise. But the body's needs are still there. The evidence is irrefutable, for heart disease is near epidemic proportions in both Europe and the US, and hospitals are full of people who found too late the truth in the old maxim that fitness is health.

Yet there is more to it than that. Medical research has proved that the benefits of being fit extend far beyond physiological improvement. To be fit means to get more out of life in every way. It means being less tired, less prone to worry, less tense. It means having more energy to devote to both your job and your family. It means more fun for you and those around you.

If people could wake up and experience, just for a single day, how it feels to be fit again, there would be no further need to convince them of the value of exercise. Until now one of the problems has been an over-abundance of conflicting advice about what you need to do to get fit—how to exercise, when, where and why. Past images of barrel-chested physical training instructors bellowing orders, of sore muscles, of endless knees-bend, arms-stretch routines—of *pain*, sheer physical pain—have not helped. If there was any agreement at all it was that keeping fit required the daily repetition of boring exercises as physically demanding as they could be in conditions as Spartan as possible—the theory that "it only does you good if it hurts".

Today the advice is both clear and reassuring. Pioneer research over the last two decades has proved that you need not suffer to get fit. You do not have to exercise for very long, but you do have to keep it up. Regular physical activity has to become part of your way of life if you are to reap the real benefits to your health.

Perhaps the thought of lifelong exercise is rather daunting. You may feel that you cannot afford the time or spare the effort. The reality is that you cannot afford *not* to find the time. Relax—getting fit doesn't hurt.

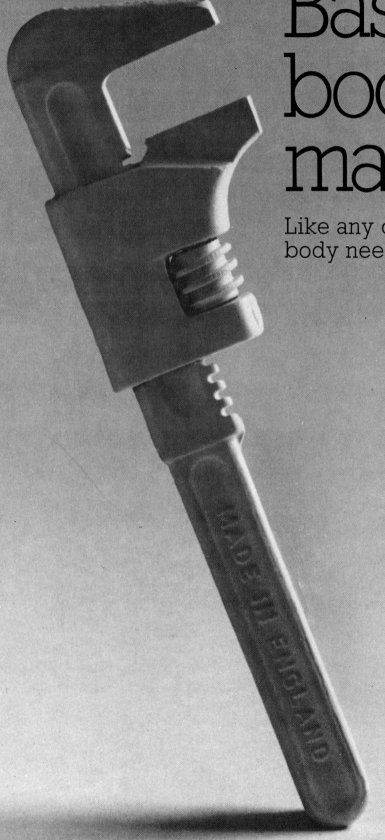

CHAPTER 5

Basic body maintenance

Like any complex machine, the
body needs regular servicing.

Apart from good diet and exercise, there are many ways in which you can keep the body in a basically sound "tick-over" condition. These are the ground rules of general bodily health and fitness which everyone ought to follow, regardless of whether they wish to tune themselves up to an absolute peak of physical perfection. It demands no excess of zeal—just self-respect and an awareness of how the body works, what it needs in day-to-day care and how the stresses and abuses of modern living can be kept under control.

Hygiene: the key to body maintenance

A daily hygiene routine not only wards off infection but is also the first step towards healthy good looks.

Although the body has its own inbuilt hygiene mechanism, like a watch it needs to be kept clean to run smoothly. Attention to hygiene is not only fundamental to good health, but will help improve your appearance—and your social acceptability.

"Automatic" body hygiene goes on all the time without any conscious effort on our part. Old cells, such as red cells in the blood stream, are broken down and the products of this process carried away in the blood. Anything useful is recycled and the waste products passed out in the urine and faeces and through the lungs and skin. Externally, the top layers of the skin consist of dead cells that continually flake off, taking dirt with them.

Contamination of the body is dealt with internally by white blood cells. Externally, every bodily entrance or exit is either able to close (for example the mouth and anus) or is guarded by some mechanism for trapping and expelling foreign particles—tears wash the eyes, fine hairs and wax protect the ears, while hairs and a clear sticky fluid called mucus in the nose and respiratory tubes trap dirt particles and bacteria, which are eventually swallowed or expelled.

The skin is, in fact, covered with many organisms, both harmful and harmless,

and it has its own method of dealing with germs. On a clean and healthy skin, the harmless organisms produce antibiotics against disease-causing bacteria. Sebaceous glands, just under the skin and alongside hairs, secrete an oily substance (sebum) through the pores and on to the skin surface to keep it soft and pliant.

When the skin is dirty and the normal proportion of harmful to harmless bacteria is upset, or when the skin is damaged, it forms a less effective barrier and disorders and infections occur. Without regular washing, the skin can become covered with dirt, bacteria, fungi and flakes of dead skin, trapped in an oily sebum. This layer is potentially dangerous in several ways. It can block skin pores and set up infections such as boils, pimples and "blackheads", and it can harbour bacteria that would be dangerous if they entered the body through a cut. Fungi settling on the body may find the environment just right to cause rashes such as athlete's foot and ringworm.

Some parts of the body need more attention than others—especially the armpits, the genital areas and the cleft between the buttocks. These are regions that contain the richest populations of bacteria and body hair and that also have special sweat glands, called apocrine glands, producing a milky fluid concerned with sexual attraction. Areas such as these, which are poorly ventilated and become moist with sweat, provide fertile breeding grounds for bacteria. The bacteria feed on the oil in the fluid and their metabolic by-products make the sweat, which is normally odourless, become offensive. A similar problem arises if feet producing normal sweat are enclosed in thick socks and shoes. Proper hygiene is particularly necessary in warm or hot weather when the body sweats even more to provide a natural cooling system—by means of evaporation of the perspiration. Failure to wash areas where moisture can become trapped is a common cause

of rashes, especially in babies. There is no automatic way of removing the accumulating "scum" and so it must be deliberately washed off.

Washing too often is preferable to washing too seldom. How often you need to bathe largely depends on your rate of sweating, your level of activity, and the temperature, humidity and "dirtiness" of your environment.

Because of their rich supply of sweat glands, the armpits, pubic areas and feet sometimes need more than simple washing. Deodorants contain an antibiotic that kills the odour-producing bacteria, together with a perfume, and water or propellant for easy application. Antiperspirants are even more effective against body odour because they contain aluminium or zinc salts that block sweat ducts and slow down the rate at which bacteria multiply.

Keeping the hands clean is particularly important since they are the most active parts of the body, coming into contact with millions of germs daily. Hands need to be washed regularly, especially before handling or preparing food and after going to the lavatory.

Although the parts of the body protected by clothing are kept cleaner for a longer time than exposed areas—such as the hands and face—they also include areas that tend to perspire most of all. The perspiration rubs off on clothing—especially those clothes worn next to the skin, such as undergarments, socks and stockings—and it is thus an important part of personal hygiene to wear clean clothes. Clothing next to the skin should be changed daily to minimize unpleasant body odours and avoid fungal or bacterial infections. Not only should ordinary street clothing be kept clean, but it is equally important to change bed sheets and nightclothes regularly. Dirt is dirt and, apart from its hazard to health, it's unpleasant sleeping in it or living with it.

The feet

The average person takes 18,000 steps a day and walks nearly 120,000 km (75,000 miles) in a 70-year life. So care of the feet (pages 164–5) is vital.

The skin

In an adult the total area of skin is 1.7 sq m (18.5 sq ft) and weighs about 2.7 kg (6 lb). It has its own cleaning system but needs back-up (pages 170–1).

The sex organs

Genital areas (pages 168–9) need daily washing to help avoid infections that can start as a result of neglect.

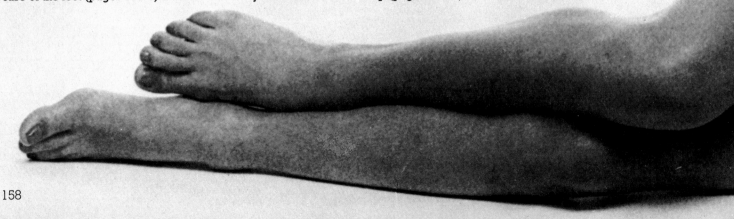

Teeth, eyes and ears

It takes only 20 minutes for plaque to form on the teeth after a meal—and the process of tooth decay can then begin. Inappropriate diet is one major cause of loss of teeth, but another is simply ignorance of teeth and mouth hygiene (pages 160–1). As for the eyes and ears (pages 166–7), they are exposed to more dirt each day than you dust from your furniture.

The breasts

Exclusively female features, among them the breasts, can be the site of problems if not regularly checked (pages 178-9). In pregnancy (pages 176-7) the whole female form needs extra care for the health of both mother and child.

Head and hair

Up to 200,000 hairs grow on the head—and as many as 100 a day fall out. Hygiene plays a key part in stimulating new growth and in keeping the scalp free from infection (pages 162–3).

Posture

Short of suffering a crippling illness, you can keep your body supple as long as you like. Good posture (pages 172–3) extends from head to toe. It not only adds the finishing touch to healthy good looks but also protects the spine from damage.

The hands

Keeping your hands clean is especially important if you are handling food. There are specific ways to look after your nails (pages 164-5).

Retaining your teeth by cleaning them

It is easy to avoid tooth decay by regular brushing and attention to what you eat. It is harder to repair decayed teeth.

Teeth are the hardest parts of your body—and usually the first to decay. They are easy to care for, and yet the most neglected.

Few people have a good set of teeth. In Britain, ninety-eight per cent of people have some decayed teeth, 40,000 children receive treatment involving dentures, and one person in every three has no teeth at all. In America, figures are slightly lower (ninety-five per cent with decay and one in five with no teeth) because there are more dentists available, but the figures are nevertheless astounding. The reasons are quite simple—ignorance and laziness about cleaning teeth (in Britain nearly one-quarter of the population do not even have a toothbrush), fear of the dentist, and above all the ruinous sugary diet.

Fossil remains show that early man had very little tooth decay. While he lived on a natural diet, chewing meat and roots and coarse grain, his teeth probably wore out before they fell out. Similarly, the proportion of decayed teeth among Eskimos living on a primitive diet was less than one per cent until "civilization" brought sugary foods and drinks.

Teeth will decay if you allow food debris to remain on and between the teeth for too long, because bacteria normally present in the mouth convert the food residues into acid. Sticky, processed starchy foods and sugars cling to the teeth and are converted more rapidly than other types. The acid starts to dissolve the hard outer layer of the teeth (the enamel) and eventually eats into the bone-like dentine underneath, producing a cavity, or caries. A survey in Britain in 1969 showed that more than three-quarters of five-year-olds who ate sweets had decayed teeth against half of those who did not. It is vitally important that parents and teachers appreciate the harm caused to teeth by sugar so that they can pass on their knowledge to children. A childhood diet containing plenty of calcium, phosphorus, and vitamins C and D may build strong, healthy teeth, but neglect and poor dental hygiene will nevertheless lead to decay in the end.

Over a period of six months or so a superficial cavity may reach the central, nerve-containing pulp, which will become inflamed and ache. Worse still, the tooth pulp may die and bacteria may enter the tooth root to form an abscess, or gumboil. In some cases the tooth may have to be removed. It is therefore essential to go to a dentist every six months so that caries can be "caught" before too much damage is done. Never put off a visit to the dentist for fear of having a "bad" tooth removed. Today the prime concern is to save teeth, and they will not be removed unless absolutely necessary.

Tooth decay is directly related to the

How to clean your teeth
A good idea is to watch yourself in a mirror and to progress methodically round your mouth, spending at least three minutes on the cleaning routine.

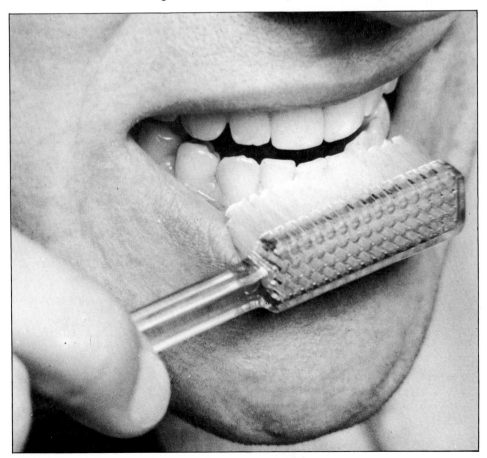

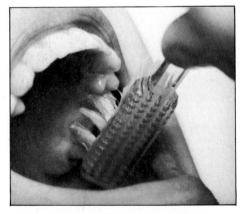

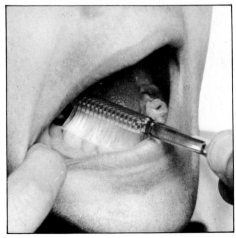

gradual accumulation on the enamel of a sticky substance called plaque, formed when the bacteria on the teeth combine with tiny particles of food residue. It is an invisible film that forms within twenty minutes of eating and which traps the harmful acids, helping them to dissolve the enamel. Uncleaned teeth become heavily coated with plaque within a few days, so much so that a rough layer can be felt with the tongue. More teeth are lost through gum disease than through caries. If you do not clean bacteria off the tooth surface they collect mineral salts from the saliva and form calculus, or tartar, which irritates the gums and makes them bleed. Eventually inflammation makes the gums recede and the teeth loose—sometimes beyond dental help. The advice is to clean your teeth regularly to prevent calculus and to keep the gum margins free from plaque. The tartar can also be removed by your dentist in a routine clean. Regular dental check-ups will also ensure that any gum disorders are treated in the early stages.

To have healthy teeth you should restrict sweet eating (if any) to meal times and replace sweet snacks by cleansing foods such as raw vegetables. You should also clean your teeth at least once a day to remove plaque, ensuring that all sides of the teeth are reached. The brush should be medium hard (a hard brush does no more good, and can be abrasive) with natural or nylon bristles that are all the same length. More important, be sure to replace your toothbrush as soon as the bristles become splayed, or at least every two to three months.

A brush can reach only the front, back and top of the teeth. Areas between the teeth need to be cleaned with toothpicks or a nylon string called dental floss.

When you have finished your cleaning routine, rinse your mouth with warm water or an antiseptic mouthwash to remove any food debris you have dislodged.

The kind of toothpaste and powder you use is not as important as the way in which you brush your teeth. In fact, you could clean your teeth quite adequately without paste. An effective and cheap toothpowder can be made by mixing two parts of sodium bicarbonate with one part of common table salt. The beneficial effects of the various additives in commercial pastes, such as chlorophyll or antiseptics, are doubted by many dentists. But one additive—fluoride—does seem to be useful. Although not conclusive, there is strong evidence that it strengthens the enamel and helps to prevent caries. Most dentists approve the use of fluoride toothpaste, especially for children. There is also some evidence from studies in Britain and the US that painting children's teeth with fluoride solution every few years reduces the number of cavities they could otherwise be expected to develop.

Fluoridation of water supplies has been adopted in many cities and towns in Europe, North and South America, Australia and New Zealand, Russia and Southeast Asia since it was found that in areas where fluoride occurred naturally children had fewer, if any, caries. Studies during the past ten years in Europe and the US have shown that the addition of one part fluoride to one million parts of water halves tooth decay in children who have access to the treated supplies.

If you are unfortunate enough to get toothache it can be temporarily relieved by taking recommended amounts of aspirin, painting the affected tooth with oil of cloves, or placing a warm hot-water bottle against the side of your face. If the pain persists you should see your dentist. The problem is usually decay, which can be treated by removing part of the tooth and filling the cavity with a substance such as amalgam (an alloy containing mercury). These are repair jobs. Dentists are now much more concerned with preventative measures, including teaching people to look after their teeth and adopt the simple daily cleaning routines that can help to prevent decay beginning at all.

Brushing technique

Always brush from the gums to the tooth surface so that you clean the gum margins and massage the gums at the same time. After the outer sides of the teeth do not forget the inner sides and the biting surfaces—which should be brushed backwards and forwards. After normal brushing try using disclosing tablets. Crunched and "swooshed" round your mouth, the tablets will show how well you have cleaned your teeth, as remaining plaque will be stained pink. Then if you want to thoroughly clean your teeth, use an interspace brush, followed by dental floss and wooden sticks.

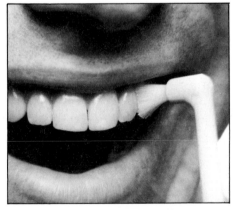

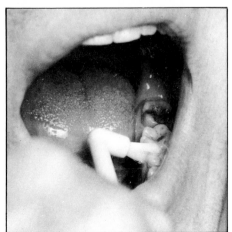

Interspace brushing

The single-tufted brush can be used in a circular motion to clean the gum margins and between the teeth as shown at top and bottom right.

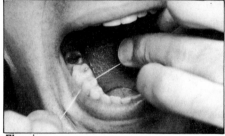

Flossing

However well you brush it is not possible to remove the plaque between the teeth. These surfaces should be gently cleaned with waxed or unwaxed string or floss.

Wooden interspace sticks

Sticks remove plaque and massage the gums, but should not be forced between teeth that are set close together.

Keeping your hair in good condition

Up to 100 hairs fall out of the head each day; if a strong rate of regrowth is to be maintained, it is important to keep the hair and scalp healthy.

Washing your hair
Massage a shampoo into the scalp and hair with your fingertips, then rinse it away with warm water. Use two applications of shampoo and rinse thoroughly after each, making sure that you get rid of all the lather. Washing removes not only grease, dust and dirt from the scalp but also the natural oils. If your hair is naturally dry, massage some pure olive oil into it after washing.
Hair should be dried by gently rubbing it with a soft towel; hard rubbing with a rough towel tends to split the hair ends. The drying should be completed with an electric hair dryer or in sunlight.

The whole surface of the body—except for the lips, palms of the hands, soles of the feet and the external genitalia—is covered with hair, although some of it is so fine that it is virtually invisible. Most of the body hair is on the scalp (between 100,000 and 200,000 hairs grow there) and the condition of this hair often reflects the general state of your health.

Each hair grows from the base of a tiny sheath, the hair follicle. The visible hair is made up of a series of dead, horny cells; the only living part of the hair is its root, which is embedded in the base of the follicle and is supplied with nerves and blood vessels. Each hair grows at an average rate of 1.25 cm (0.5 in) a month and drops out after three years. About 100 hairs a day are normally shed from the scalp and all are normally replaced by new ones. Alongside the hair follicle are sebaceous glands, which secrete an oily substance on to the surface of the skin, and this helps to keep the hair in good condition.

If your general health is good, the best way to maintain a head of healthy hair is to keep it clean. Daily brushing and massage of the scalp with the fingertips not only removes dust and dirt—together with waste materials and dead cells produced by the scalp—but also stimulates the blood supply, which brings with it nutrients that help the hair to grow. However, brushing, especially if over-vigorous, is not good for thinning hair. It can dislodge hairs and leave tiny ridges on the scalp that

may become breeding places for infection.

Hair should be washed every four to ten days; oily or greasy hair needs more frequent washing than dry hair. Use a shampoo rather than a soap, which tends to produce scum. The basis of a good shampoo is a readily soluble detergent with a powerful grease-removing action, but some cheap shampoos contain a mild alkali that may irritate the scalp. Special-purpose shampoos have additional ingredients for treating dry and greasy hair.

Those who live or work in a dusty, dirty or smoky atmosphere will find that their hair quickly becomes dirty and needs frequent washing; this results in increased wear and damage to the outer surface of the hair. Conditioners, which coat the hair with a layer of wax, can be used after shampooing to offset dryness. Best results will be achieved by using first a shampoo and then a conditioner, rather than products that are a combination of the two.

Always clean your brush and comb when you wash your hair: much of the benefit of washing will be lost if they are allowed to get dirty.

Many people suffer from dandruff—flakes of dead skin which often become very greasy. This type of dandruff is caused by overactivity of the oil-producing (sebaceous) glands in the scalp. It can usually be treated successfully by washing the hair several times a week with a medicated shampoo for greasy hair until the condition clears up. Dandruff can also be

caused by the production of too little oil by the sebaceous glands, in which case the scalp becomes dry and the hair brittle. Again, a medicated shampoo (for dry hair) can often help.

If the scalp does not respond to this treatment it may be because the dandruff is caused by an infection. In that case a safe and usually effective treatment is to wash the hair every two or three days with a dilute (one per cent) solution of cetrimide, an antiseptic detergent. For other infections and disorders of the scalp you should consult your doctor.

Many people put brilliantines, hair creams and other oily dressings on their hair. These tend to clog the openings of the glands and may encourage dandruff. If you use hair lacquer, do not hold the aerosol spray too close to your hair. Thorough daily brushing of lacquered hair will help prevent it from becoming dull and brittle.

A few simple precautions should be taken if you intend to bleach or dye your hair. Hair rinse is effective for up to about two weeks only, for the rinse comes out with washing. It is therefore possible to experiment until you find the colour you want. Bleaching and dyeing alters hair colour and lasts until the hair grows out, which takes some months. Continual bleaching or dyeing tends to alter the hair's texture and make it brittle. To counteract this, conditioners should be used. The best bleach for home use is a solution of hydrogen peroxide and water to which a few

Hereditary male-pattern baldness

The most common type of baldness is hereditary and irreversible. Whether adults lose hair depends on how their hair follicles respond to testosterone, a male androgen hormone. This response appears to be genetically programmed. The genes for baldness do not act if the level of androgens is low—hence fewer women suffer extensive baldness. (There is some recent evidence that women, having assumed more dominant or "male" roles, are secreting more testosterone and are becoming more prone to baldness.) Men with normal levels of testosterone will go bald if they have a dominant baldness gene, while others with the same amount of testosterone will not. A bald man will, on average, transmit the bald gene to half his sons. The baldness gene can also be transmitted through the female line to grandsons.

Male-pattern baldness can start in a number of ways. An overall thinning may develop (Sean Connery, *above left*), a patch may form at the back of the head like a monk's tonsure (*above centre*), or a receding hairline may spread over the top (British golfer Neil Coles, *above*).

drops of ammonia have been added. It is a wise precaution to make a test on a small section of your hair first to ensure that you are not allergic to a particular product.

A great variety of colour rinses can restore colour to greying or faded hair and can be used successfully at home. But they need to be reapplied about once a month to maintain the colour. It is best to seek professional help from a hairdresser if you are thinking of using a chemical dye or a strong bleach. The hairdresser can advise you about the suitability for your particular type and colour of hair and will also test your scalp for hypersensitivity to the dye.

Many men (and some women) suffer from baldness. There are several causes, including the normal consequences of ageing and a hereditary response to stimulation of the hair follicles by the male sex hormone (testosterone). This last factor has given rise to the myth that bald-headed men are highly sexed, the misconception being that they have more male sex hormones than men who retain their hair. Males castrated before puberty do not lose their hair, but this is because, after the loss of the testicles, they produce no testosterone at all. If an adult male is castrated, any hair loss will similarly cease. In women baldness is most commonly the result of some disease that destroys the hair follicles. It can also be brought about by injury or in consequence of excessive bleaching, pulling the hair into tight pony tails or the use of curlers.

Aids to hair health

Brushes and combs are used to untangle, tidy and style (1, 3) the hair. A brush made from natural bristle (5) is less likely to damage the hair than one made from nylon or plastic but is more expensive; a brush with bristles mounted on rubber (6), excellent in some cases, may not be firm enough for very thick hair. Brushes are made in a variety of shapes (2, 7) to suit every taste, and one (4) is specially designed for massaging the scalp, and is of particular use when washing the hair. The best combs are saw-cut and made from hard materials—ivory, bone or tortoiseshell— but are expensive. A saw-cut, vulcanized rubber comb will do as well and is cheaper. Metal combs (10) have the advantage of durability, while plastic combs (8, 9) are cheaper.

Care should be taken to choose a brush and comb that are suited to the thickness or otherwise of your hair. Excessive brushing or hard combing can cause damage.

Care of the hands, feet and nails

These crucial parts of the body are among those most often treated too harshly.

The human hand is the most versatile of instruments and has to withstand a good deal of rough treatment. Even in today's mechanized world, hands are tools used for hard work—the skin on the palm is especially thickened for this purpose. Similarly, the skin on the soles of the feet is thickened to withstand the weight of the body and the pressure of walking. But both hands and feet need looking after—particularly the feet, for even with the best shoes they are vulnerable.

Many hand complaints start from exposure to harsh washing powders. Detergent is effective in removing grease and grime, but it attacks the skin as well as the plates or clothes that are being washed: stripped of its natural oils, the skin becomes dry, flaky and leathery. Biological detergents can "digest" the surface layers of the skin and they are often a cause of skin rashes and brittle nails.

Wearing rubber gloves when you wash dishes or clothes and when you do other household chores will help protect your hands; a daily application of hand cream and lotion can also help.

The nail is an outgrowth of the skin composed of a protein substance called keratin. Healthy nails are firm yet flexible and pinkish in colour. The average nail grows about 0.3 cm (0.1 in) a month. If you lose a nail by accident or through infection, it will be replaced—provided the actively growing tissue at the root of the nail is still healthy. If the nail bed, the skin on which the nail rests, is cut or damaged the new nail may be misshapen.

The condition of your nails reflects your general state of health and your diet. Brittle nails may mean that you are not getting enough calcium—the mineral essential for nail growth—which is found in milk, cheese and cream.

Careless filing and excessive use of nail-polish remover and strong soaps and detergents will make matters worse because they dry out the nail and cause its layers to separate. There are several products on the market that can be applied to seal the nail.

Biting the nails is a common, disfiguring habit. You can help yourself or your children to break the habit by painting the nails twice daily with white iodine. This colourless liquid hardens the nails, making it unrewarding to bite them.

Because the feet are usually enclosed in socks or stockings and shoes all day long, they sweat. Stale sweat not only smells unpleasant but creates a fertile environment for the development of infections. It is therefore important to wash your feet at least once a day and to dry them thoroughly between the toes. Talcum powder helps to absorb sweat. (Deodorant sprays are relatively ineffective on the feet.)

Dampness between the toes can provide a starting place for athlete's foot—a type of ringworm infection that manifests itself as soft white itching blisters between the toes that may spread over the sole of the foot. Once acquired, this infection tends to recur. Fungicidal powders can provide temporary relief, but soaking the feet daily for ten minutes with just enough potassium permanganate to colour the water should clear up the infection for good.

A daily change of footwear also helps keep the feet healthy. When choosing

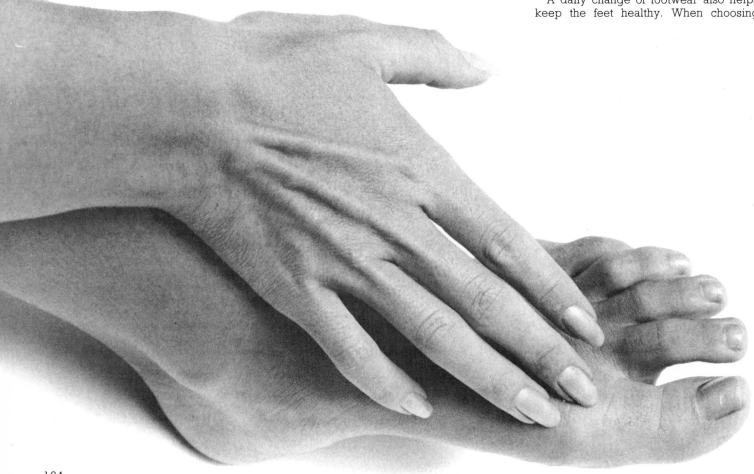

socks remember that cotton and other natural fibres are absorbent and can help to avoid problems like athlete's foot.

Corns and callouses are hard areas of skin at pressure points on the feet—including the ball of the foot—and can be caused by excess weight, poor posture or badly fitting shoes. Do not be tempted to try to deal with corns yourself—they should be treated by a chiropodist. Infections such as verrucae also need expert attention.

Obesity accounts for much unnecessary stress on the feet and can give rise to several complaints apart from corns and callouses—such as swollen feet and ankles, and fallen arches (flat feet). In the last of these conditions the instep arch falls and the entire sole rests on the ground. People who spend a lot of time on their feet are particularly prone to flat feet. There is no specific cure, but choosing good shoes with adequate support on the instep can greatly lessen the discomfort.

Nearly all foot complaints arise from wearing ill-fitting shoes, particularly in childhood. Once the damage has been done it is extremely difficult, if not impossible, to rectify. Children's feet ideally should be measured for length and width at least every two months. Good shoes provide adequate support under the instep and heel and room for the feet to spread inside the shoes. Reputable shoe shops will always measure children's feet, both for length and width, and will help with expert advice.

Shoes should be discarded as soon as they become too small—that is, when the big toe becomes pressed against the top of the shoe. Cramped shoes cause many deformities, including ingrowing toe-nails, splayed toes and inverted big toes, which can lead to bunions.

It is also unwise for one child to be given the shoes of another to wear; the inside of a shoe gradually becomes individually shaped and, in effect, contains the personalized footprint of the original wearer. So passing on shoes is a false economy.

Many problems are caused by trying to get children to wear shoes at too early an age. They should be allowed to run around barefoot as much as possible, as long as there is no danger of them stepping on sharp objects.

The choice of materials for shoes is important. Leather and suede are warm, wear well and are fairly waterproof. Both materials allow the feet to "breathe", because they absorb sweat. Plastic, although cheaper than leather, does not do this, is cold in winter and hot in summer and can thus contribute to foot problems. Fashionable shoes, such as stiletto heels or platform soles, can be injurious, for they tilt the body to an unnatural angle. "Earth" shoes, which have heels lower than the front of the shoes, may create problems too.

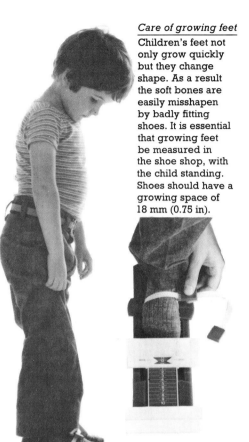

Care of growing feet
Children's feet not only grow quickly but they change shape. As a result the soft bones are easily misshapen by badly fitting shoes. It is essential that growing feet be measured in the shoe shop, with the child standing. Shoes should have a growing space of 18 mm (0.75 in).

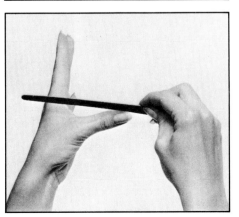

Care of fingernails

After cutting your nails shape them with an emery board, filing in one direction only to prevent splitting and to give an even finish. Cuticles can be easily damaged and future growth may be thicker and extend up the nail. Soften with cuticle cream and then warm water, and very gently push back.

Care of toe-nails

After soaking your feet in warm water, remove any dirt under the nails with an orange stick. Keep the nails short and file them straight across, in one direction only. Really tough nails can be cut straight across with scissors. Never cut down into the sides of the nails as this, like shaping the nails, can cause ingrowing toe-nails.

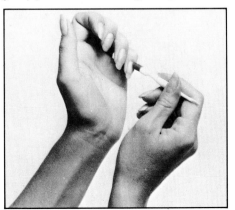

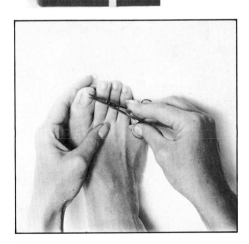

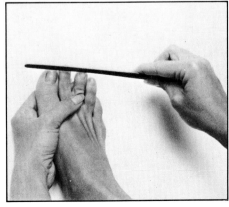

Eyes and ears: versatile and vital senses

The marvel of eyes and ears is that despite their apparent fragility they should stand up to such hard wear for so long and fail so rarely.

Eyesight and hearing are two of the delicate senses on which we rely most for receiving information about our surroundings. It is perhaps because they are so essential that eyes and ears are designed to need little maintenance apart from that of general good health.

Many myths exist about eye care. For example, there is no such thing as "eye-strain"—you cannot strain your eyes by seeing too much any more than you can strain your ears by hearing too much. The eye muscles, which contract to bring near objects into focus do get tired, however, particularly after prolonged use in poor light. If you also get a headache you are actually suffering "brainstrain"—the brain is protesting at the effort of sorting out optical data that is insufficiently clear. The best way to avoid eye fatigue and headaches is to make sure that the light source is adequate for the purpose. If you do suffer persistent eye fatigue, bathe the eyes night and morning with a warm solution of one teaspoonful of salt in a pint of boiled water.

Always work in daylight if you can. For close work the best source of artificial light is a lamp placed above and behind the left shoulder (if you are right-handed) so that the light falls on the working or reading area without creating shadows. The strength of the bulb should be such that it does not create glare.

To remove an irritating particle lift the eyelid gently by the lashes until the particle can be seen and remove it with the corner of a clean handkerchief. Do not try to remove a particle that lies over the pupil (the central part of the eye), but blink until it moves elsewhere on the eyeball or inner surface of the eyelid.

The parts of the eye most likely to become infected are the eyelid and the membrane that covers the eyeball and inner surface of the eyelid. Inflammation of the eyelids may be associated with a stye or crusty scales on the lids. If there is an eyelash at the centre of a stye, its removal can often relieve the stye. Alternatively, frequent applications of a warm, moist compress will bring the stye to a head so that it can open and drain. Mild inflammations can be treated effectively by bathing the eyelids with a warm, weak solution of sodium bicarbonate, but consult your doctor if the problem does not clear up within a few days.

A fairly common—and contagious—eye infection is conjunctivitis, which results in reddening and soreness of the eyeball, swelling of the eyelids and sometimes watering of the eyes and a discharge. If bathing with warm, previously boiled water does not help, consult your doctor.

Two-thirds of us have "defective" eyesight, just as two-thirds of us are either shorter or taller than the average. Either side of the middle third of the population people are progressively more short- or long-sighted. There is, therefore, nothing unusual about needing to wear spectacles.

It is part of the mythology of spectacles that you can harm your eyes by not wearing your own spectacles, by wearing someone else's or by wearing cheap dark glasses (without corrective lenses). Spectacles do not affect your eyes, only how much you see. They will not therefore harm your eyes unless you consistently wear spectacles that are drastically wrong.

The eyes are adequately constructed to deal with all ordinary light conditions; it is only intense light or heat that harms them. Medically, dark glasses are therefore largely redundant, though protection is essential if you wish to look straight into a furnace, for instance. On bright days both the sea and snow can reflect a painful amount of light, so it makes sense to wear

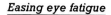

It is always better to pat eyes dry with a soft towel than to rub them. Rubbing may feel better at first but is likely to act as an irritant.

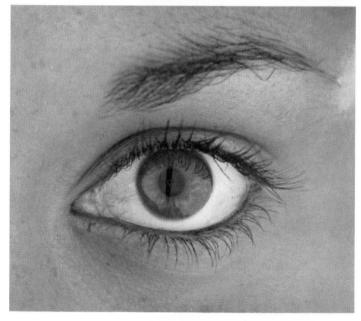

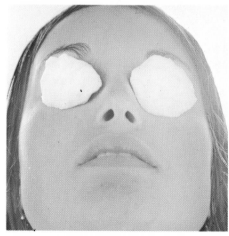

You can ease tired eyes by lying down for a few minutes with pads over them to act as blackouts.

Noise and pain

A noisy jet taking off produces a sound level of more than 100 decibels (dB). For the human ear, discomfort comes at about 120 dB and pain at about 140. Normal conversation, by comparison, is about 60 dB and a whisper is 30 dB.

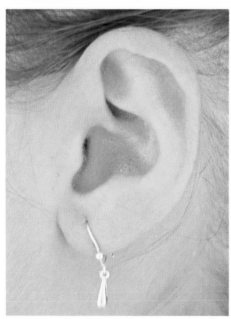

Even the quieter rock groups can produce sound levels well in excess of 100 dB in concert. A noisy band can reach an output of 140, so it is not surprising that both musicians and their regular audiences often suffer partial hearing loss.

polarized sunglasses, which, by cutting down glare, allow you to see much more comfortably.

Contact lenses are a cosmetic alternative to spectacles. In a few cases (but only a few) they function better than spectacles. Some people can wear them in comfort all day long, others have to take them out after eight or ten hours.

If you suspect you need spectacles go to your family doctor first. If you already wear spectacles or contact lenses have your eyes checked every eighteen months or so. If you are elderly, even if you don't wear spectacles, make sure you get your eyes tested every second year—the eye muscles age just like other muscles and become less flexible. Children, whose sight may change as they grow, should have their eyes examined with at least the same frequency.

The noise of heavy urban traffic is about 80 dB, a level that is much too high for selective hearing to operate successfully.

Most of the ear lies within the skull. The part that is visible is the outer or external ear, which receives and channels sound waves through the ear canal and on to the eardrum. But the ear has a second function in that it contains the extremely delicate organs of balance; this explains why some ear infections can make you feel giddy.

Small glands in the ear canal secrete wax (cerumen), which traps particles of dust and dirt entering the ear and prevents them from reaching the eardrum, which they might irritate. Normally, the wax flakes off and is washed out of the ear, carrying with it any foreign particles it has picked up. To keep the ears in a healthy condition all that is normally needed is daily washing of the outer ear with soap and warm water. While cleaning the ear make sure that you do not insert any

pointed object into the ear canal as it may damage the eardrum.

Some people secrete more earwax than is necessary. It tends to accumulate and harden in the canal and may interfere with hearing. Many people with excess earwax worry needlessly that they are becoming permanently deaf, but the treatment is simple and totally effective. Your doctor will prescribe ear drops to soften the wax, which he can then easily remove with a special syringe.

Excessive wax is one cause of earache; the other common causes are germs spreading from throat infections such as tonsillitis or laryngitis and inflammation of the middle ear during or after head colds and flu, when fluid pressures within the skull are temporarily unbalanced. Minor pain can usually be relieved by aspirin or by placing a warm damp cloth over the ear. Persistent pain in the ears needs a doctor's attention.

The normal human ear can apprehend a very wide range of sound waves, from about 20 cycles per second (cps) to 20,000; (middle C on the piano is 256 cps, top C 4,096; the male speaking voice operates at about 100 cps, the female at about 150). The capacity of the ear to withstand varying intensities of noise is more limited. Whereas deafness means a limiting of the range of frequencies you can hear, and the clarity with which you hear them, it can be caused by excessive noise intensity. There is no doubt that frequent exposure to very high noise levels can cause irreparable damage to the hearing apparatus.

Probably one person in twenty-five suffers from some significant loss of hearing in one or both ears. There are two main kinds of deafness: conductive and perceptive. In conductive deafness the apparatus and channels that conduct sound from the outer ear to the membrane in the inner ear are defective or blocked. Perceptive deafness involves damage to the inner ear, to the brain or to the brain centre which translates impulses from the ear into recognizable "sounds".

Conductive deafness can usually be helped by a hearing aid, which amplifies sounds to a level at which the defective ear can make sense of them. Perceptive deafness is much harder to overcome.

With advancing years hearing becomes less acute because there is a gradual degeneration of the nerve connecting the inner ear and brain. This is quite normal. Defective hearing in children, however, is not. Since a child's ability to learn to speak depends on how well he hears, it is always worth having a child's hearing tested at the age of a few months so that remedial work, should it be necessary, can start at once.

Maintaining a healthy sex life

Anxieties often start from inadequate knowledge of the sex organs and how they work.

From a purely physiological point of view, the best way to maintain a long, satisfying and active sex life is to keep in practice. Sex is, for most people, an essential and natural part of a loving relationship and it is far more likely to be jeopardized by psychological tensions than by any kind of physical process.

Because individual needs vary, there is no "correct" frequency for sexual intercourse. There is also no evidence that sexual appetite disappears with age, although the rhythm and expression of sex may change. The intimate sharing between two people, the release of tension and the physical exercise that sex provides are as beneficial to your health at the age of eighty as at twenty.

Understanding and proper care of the sex organs are important in maintaining a healthy sex life and avoiding disease. The mystique of the genitalia built up by centuries of inhibitions has led to a good deal of plain ignorance about these parts of the body.

A man's genitals are comprised of the testicles (or testes) and penis. The testes are suspended in a bag of skin, the scrotum, outside the body; this is because the male sex cells, or sperm, need a lower temperature for development than would be possible inside the body. The testes are very sensitive to touch, so for comfort and protection should be shielded or supported when playing games such as football or cricket.

The tip of the penis is covered with a fold of skin called the foreskin. If this has not been removed by circumcision it should be retracted for washing each day. Sometimes, especially in children, the foreskin is too tight to be fully retracted; a simple operation—not necessarily circumcision—will correct this.

Circumcision is a minor surgical procedure performed for social and religious as well as medical reasons. Its necessity is much debated by doctors, but it is almost certainly advisable if the foreskin covers the end of the penis so that urination is difficult, or is so tight that sexual intercourse is painful. One of the main reasons advanced in favour of circumcision is that it is believed to reduce the risk of cancer of the penis in men or of the cervix in their female partners. However, scrupulous attention to hygiene—a thorough daily washing with soap and water—should achieve the same effect.

A woman's external genitalia comprise the vulva (the external vaginal opening) and the surrounding inner and outer folds of skin, the labia. The inner labia meet in front of the vaginal opening at the clitoris: a small, rod-like and highly sensitive organ—the female equivalent of the penis, becoming enlarged and erect during sexual excitement.

Daily washing with soap and water is the best way of keeping the vulva clean. Vaginal douches should not be necessary: they can interfere with the secretions of the vagina, which are themselves naturally cleansing. Vaginal deodorants are not really necessary either, and in any event you should make sure that any deodorant used does not irritate the sensitive skin of the genital area or upset vaginal secretions. Any white, yellow or irritating vaginal discharge indicates an infection and requires immediate medical attention (see pages 178–9).

Stimulation of the sex organs produces pleasurable sensations regardless of age, but orgasm—the release of sperm in the male and the culmination of sexual excitement for both partners—does not come until puberty. Mutually successful sex is not always easily achieved, often because the male partner is more quickly and easily aroused and is therefore capable of reaching orgasm earlier than the woman. Communication and consideration between partners, and an understanding of each other's responses, are the best ways to start tackling sexual problems of this kind—and expert counselling is usually readily available.

Sometimes intercourse becomes inadvisable for medical reasons. If you have just suffered a heart attack, for example, or are recovering from a hernia operation, the doctor will probably recommend a temporary abstinence. During this time, physical closeness and contact between a couple can still be intense and rewarding, as well as being much needed by both the man and the woman.

Many men and women have groundless worries about the size of their genitals, particularly the penis. In fact, size bears little relationship to sexual satisfaction or effectiveness: a woman can obtain the same pleasure from a "small" penis as from a larger one. Equally, the size of an erect penis is not determined by its size at rest. Women may worry, too, that the vagina is too small or too tight to accommodate a penis. But the vagina not only increases in length and diameter during sexual arousal, but can stretch considerably—as is dramatically demonstrated by the fact that a full-term baby can pass through it.

For many people, reproduction has become a secondary function of the sex organs: indeed, sexual activity has several demonstrable functions and it could be argued that reproduction is the minority one. Given that the egg cell released from the female remains fertile for, at most, only forty-eight hours, it is perhaps surprising that only about one in ten of all marriages is childless. During the male's ejaculation, approximately 400 million sperms are discharged into the vagina; even so, considering the woman's monthly cycle of fertility, the actual chance that one of them will swim up the Fallopian tubes to fertilize an egg cell is low.

If you do want children, the most propitious time for conceiving is in the middle of the menstrual cycle, when an egg is most likely to have been released. If you have had no success after six months, seek medical guidance—the reason may be easily diagnosed and corrected, and may be psychological rather than physical, at least in part. (It is an enlightening fact that many people who adopt children after years of barrenness straightaway have their own, as though some psychological release mechanism has come into play.) In any event, it is important to be as relaxed in mind and body as is possible.

For those who do not wish to conceive, it is wise—subject to any religious

Love and sex are for the whole of life

"Ageing induces some changes in human sexual performance . . . however, compared with, say, running ability, these changes are functionally minimal and actually tend in the direction of 'more miles per gallon' and greater, if less acute, satisfaction for both partners. In the absence of two disabilities— actual disease and the belief that 'the old' are or should be asexual—sexual requirement and sexual capacity are lifelong. Even if and when sexual intercourse is impaired by infirmity, other sexual needs persist, including closeness, sensuality and being valued as a man or as a woman."— Dr Alex Comfort in *A Good Age*.

scruples—to take contraceptive precautions. Today's range of contraception methods (see chart) is such that every couple should be able to find a technique that suits them physically and emotionally.

But the effectiveness of any method is reduced if it is incorrectly applied. Fitting a condom or a cap carelessly, or forgetting to take the contraceptive pill, often results in an unwanted pregnancy.

All young people approaching puberty should be taught about contraception and also about the risks of venereal disease.

Many factors—among them changing methods of contraception, and evolution in the codes of sexual behaviour—have led to an increase in venereal disease in many countries. There is evidence that the decline in the use of the condom, which provides a physical barrier against infection, along with the wide use of the contraceptive pill and the rise in promiscuity, are all significant in the spread of venereal disease.

Sexual intercourse is almost the only way that venereal disease can be transmitted.

If you think you might have it, do not delay in seeking medical attention. The usual warning signs are the appearance of a single, painless sore on the penis or inside the vagina (or possibly on the lip or nipple), or the discharge of pus from the vagina or penis, accompanied and usually preceded by a scalding sensation when urinating. However, *any* rash or abnormal discharge should be treated seriously. The chances are that you have a mild infection of some other kind, but even this should never be neglected.

CONTRACEPTION METHODS

Failure rate is expressed as the number of women becoming pregnant per 100 using the method for a full year. The figures are based on British Economic Intelligence Unit statistics and show the effectiveness of each method when used with maximum care (lower figure) and at worst (higher figure).

METHOD	WHAT IT IS AND HOW IT WORKS	ADVANTAGES	DISADVANTAGES	FAILURE RATE
Oral contraceptive (the Pill)	Contains the hormones oestrogen and progesterone, which suppress ovulation and menstruation. Women should take the Pill every day for 21 days, then stop taking it for the next 7 days, during which a reduced form of menstruation occurs.	Very simple to use and nearly 100 per cent reliable if schedule is rigidly followed.	Not recommended for diabetics or those with liver disease or high blood pressure. May increase risk of thrombosis in a few women.	0–2
Sterilization	A surgical operation to cut or tie the tubes carrying sex cells from the sex glands (in men the operation is called vasectomy). It does not interfere with production of sex hormones by the testes or ovaries and therefore does not affect sex life.	A single operation: no further contraception is necessary. The most effective contraception method.	With present techniques, almost always irreversible; people can't change their minds about not having children.	Almost nil
Intra-uterine device (IUD)	A coil or loop (usually of plastic) inserted into the womb prevents the fertilized egg embedding itself in the lining of the womb.	Once fitted and inserted (by a doctor) it can be forgotten, apart from annual check-ups.	May cause discomfort and bleeding when first inserted. May be spontaneously expelled.	2–4
Diaphragm (cap)	A thin rubber cap inserted into the vagina before intercourse to cover the neck of the womb, so preventing the entry of sperm. Women should be fitted for a diaphragm, which is best used with a spermicidal jelly (see below). It should be removed and washed about six hours after intercourse.	Produces no side effects.	Time required for its insertion and removal may disrupt spontaneity of love-making.	3–12
Condom (sheath)	A thin rubber sheath placed over the erect penis, preventing sperm entering vagina during ejaculation. Should ideally be used with a spermicidal cream and should contain space for ejaculated semen.	Easily available without prescription. Reliable if used correctly. Protects against venereal disease.	May tear or slip off. Reduces sensation.	3–6
Rhythm method (safe period)	The couple abstain from intercourse during the 10-day ovulation period of the woman's menstrual cycle (that is, days 10–21 after the start of the last menstrual period). Date of ovulation should be checked with use of thermometer as it usually coincides with a rise in body temperature.	Approved by the Roman Catholic Church.	Unreliable, even with meticulous calculation, as monthly cycles are often variable.	10–40
Coitus interruptus	Man withdraws penis before ejaculation.		Unreliable; risk of leakage of semen. Also causes tension.	10–40
Spermicides	Foams, jellies, or creams that kill sperm. They are introduced into the vagina before intercourse and should be used only to increase the efficiency of the condom and diaphragm.		Messy to use. Unreliable if used as sole contraceptive method.	10–14

The skin: a reflector of good health

Keeping your skin clear and supple depends on diet as well as on knowing when and how to take protective measures.

Skin, the largest body organ, covers the entire outer surface of the body and accounts for one-sixth of its total weight. This supple, resilient layer has many important functions. It protects the delicate internal organs and tissues, acts as a barrier against external injury and blocks the entry of germs that cause infection. It also prevents the evaporation of body fluids. A serious burn affecting a large percentage of the body surface can prove fatal both because of the loss of body fluids and through exposure of the tissues to bacterial infection.

The skin contains special cells that are sensitive to pain, heat, cold and touch—thereby providing important information about both the internal condition of the body and the external environment.

One important function of the skin is to help control the body temperature. Glands in the skin secrete sweat on to the body surface: on a hot day more sweat is produced than on a cold day; in evaporating it draws heat from the body and makes you feel cooler. Other glands secrete an

oily substance called sebum, which keeps the skin in a pliant and healthy condition. It also helps to lubricate the hair, which grows on most parts of the skin.

If it is to carry out all of these important functions the skin needs to be properly looked after. If you have good general health and a normally healthy skin, and follow a simple routine of skin care and maintenance, there is no reason at all why your skin should not continue its good work.

Washing the skin correctly and regularly is of prime importance in keeping it healthy. Do not massage soap into the skin, as this can clog the pores and remove the natural oils; and make sure you rinse off the lather thoroughly.

Skin that is abnormally greasy or dry needs extra care. Greasy skin results from overactivity of the oil-producing (sebaceous) glands. The excess oil tends to clog the pores in the skin and may produce blackheads, spots or (in adolescents) acne. If you have an extremely greasy skin it will need more frequent and thorough washing to remove the oil and prevent the develop-

The skin in the sun: how to tan without burning

1. If you have a fair skin take special care. At first, limit exposure to 15 minutes a day and increase it by ten to 15 minutes each day.
2. Parts of the skin seldom exposed to the sun, such as the soles of the feet, will burn most easily.
3. A sunshade will protect you from direct exposure but not from sunlight reflected off the sand.
4. Sunlight reflected from sea water can burn you before you realize it. Children are especially susceptible to such burning and so need careful supervision in the sun.
5. Oils can give some protection, but will not stop burns if you sunbathe too long.
6. After swimming, reapply suntan oil. If a burn develops apply a cold compress or calamine lotion.

ment of blocked pores or blackheads. In adolescents, however, acne accompanied by a greasy skin may be due to hormonal imbalance and in such cases will not respond to washing or astringent lotions.

A very dry skin tends to flake and wrinkle and will benefit from the daily application of an oily lotion. A dry skin may also improve a little if you take capsules of fish liver oils and eat oily fish such as sardines, pilchards and herrings.

The condition of the skin is affected by the type of food we eat. A sensible, balanced diet is as important for a healthy skin as it is for a healthy body in general. The development of rashes, spots, pimples and so on may be an indication that you are not eating the right types of foods in proper amounts. (For advice on diet see pages 36–71 and 196–213.) If your skin tends to be spotty you should try to eat plenty of fresh fruit and vegetables.

Although the skin provides efficient day-to-day protection for the body it can be damaged by harsh chemicals, extreme cold or heat, and excess wear and tear. If you frequently work with chemicals—including detergents and weedkillers—make sure you wear gloves or a good protective cream.

Exposing the skin to sunlight is normally beneficial as it assists in the formation of vitamin D in the body. In response to sunlight, the skin produces the protective dark pigment melanin and becomes tanned, but too much sun on a skin that is not used to such exposure results in sunburn. Constant exposure to the sun dries and wrinkles the skin, while in tropical regions it may even cause skin cancer. It is known that it is the shorter-wave ultraviolet rays that do most damage, penetrating to the deeper layers of the skin to cause sagging and wrinkling, often years later. The higher the sun in the sky, the more burning the rays. So prolonged sunbathing should stop at about 11 am and not start again until 3 pm. Another hazard is altitude. On mountains the thinner atmosphere allows more short waves to get through; snow also reflects light on to the body, so skiers should use maximum protection. Water, like snow, also reflects light and increases the burning hazards of the sun, while wind is deceptive because it cools the skin and cancels out the warning signals of sunburn.

In cold weather, many people with poor circulation suffer from chilblains. The best way to avoid this painful condition is to wear warm clothing, especially woollen gloves and socks (not fitting too tightly), and to take plenty of exercise to improve the circulation. It may also help if you try not to cool down or warm up too quickly. Unusual pressure on the skin, particularly of hands and feet, will cause blisters. So don't expect to be able to suddenly spend a day sawing logs or tramping across country without damaging your skin. If you are planning a walking holiday, practise with your boots on so that you "wear your feet in" gradually. Nightly applications of methylated spirits will also help harden the skin in advance.

A clean, well-cared-for skin improves your health and appearance. Make the best of your skin by regular washing, a balanced diet and adequate exercise.

Posture: how to look after your back

Unlike muscle, your spine does not strengthen with use. The best way to protect it is simply to stand and move properly.

Luggage hazard

Taking luggage from a car boot the wrong way can be dangerous as it puts serious strain on the spine. Most people stoop to pick up the luggage, turn and then bend at the waist to drop it. This strains the back muscles in the same way as incorrect lifting, and then aggravates the harm by also twisting the spine.

Posture at the sink

Don't stoop over the sink. Keep your back straight and bend one knee.

It is hardly surprising that backache is such a common complaint. Not only does the spine have to support most of the body's weight but it sometimes has to bear the abuse imposed by bad posture and the thoughtless body movements that are part of our daily activities.

If you are overweight then excessive stress is put on the spine—especially at its base. Bad posture when sitting, standing, walking or lifting heavy objects contributes even more towards spinal damage, the results of which can be extremely painful and serious.

When viewed from the side, the spinal column, or vertebral column, can be seen to have four natural curves, while from the front it appears to be straight. Between each separate bone (vertebra) is a cushioning pad of cartilage, which is known as a vertebral disc.

These discs—each of which has a soft core—act as shock absorbers when you are walking, running or jumping. Any unusual or sudden strain on the back may cause one of these soft cores to protrude slightly beyond the edges of the vertebrae above and below, resulting in the painful condition called "slipped disc". The pain, in simple terms, is caused by the pressure exerted on nearby nerves by the extruded portion of the disc.

The best way to avoid back problems is never to put any sudden strain on the spine. As the body ages the bones become more brittle and much more susceptible to fractures, and then it becomes even more important to lift heavy objects properly.

Failure to develop a good posture in childhood may result in nothing more serious than an unattractive slumper or sloucher, or a person who shuffles down streets with stooped shoulders. But as well

Wrong way to lift (right)

Bending from the waist as shown is asking for trouble. It puts too much strain on the back muscles and not enough on the stronger leg muscles.

Sitting badly

Although it is tempting to bend over towards your sewing or your book, this posture encourages round shoulders.

Wrong way to scrub

If you scrub the floor too close to your body your back tends to hunch.

How to do it

In lifting anything from a car boot keep your back straight and bend your legs. Then gradually straighten up, turn your whole body 45 degrees, bend your legs again and lower the luggage on to the ground. In this way, by keeping the spine straight, you will avoid straining and twisting the muscles of your back.

Sitting correctly

Bring your needlework or your book towards you so that your back remains straight against the chair.

Correct way to scrub

Rest your knees on a pad and keep your back straight by working farther out.

as the detrimental effects bad posture can have on your appearance, it may put a serious strain on the bones and joints and cause endless problems in later life. Good posture, on the other hand, eventually becomes automatic—and it is just as difficult to break a good habit as it is a bad one.

When you are lying on your back on a relatively firm bed, your body assumes a natural and comfortable position. If that reclining position could be duplicated when standing, it would demonstrate correct upright posture: the body would be extended with the head held upright and thrown slightly backwards, the chest would protrude somewhat and the abdomen would curve inwards a little in relation to the chest—a naturally comfortable position when the shoulders are held properly, or when taking a deep breath. Adopting a good standing posture may feel awkward at first if you have developed bad postural habits, but a little practice should convince you that it not only puts less strain on your back to stand this way: you also look much more alert, confident and relaxed.

An exaggerated form of supposedly correct posture is the military stance—standing at attention, so that the body is rigidly extended, the chest is thrown outwards as far as it can go, and the chin is drawn in to its limit. Such a posture is not only unnatural but actually strains the muscles of the back.

The correct sitting posture is often confounded by the poor design of much modern furniture. The best chair design is one that provides comfortable support for the lower part of the back. In many chairs, especially those with soft cushions, there is a gap where the back is not supported and this quickly leads to the development of a slumping position in which the spine is bent. If the seat or cushions of a chair or

Correct way to lift (left)

Keep your back straight and squat to get under the weight. Lift not with your back but with the muscles of your legs, straightening up gradually.

sofa are too wide, they prevent you from sitting back far enough to give your spine the proper support. Before buying new furniture be sure to test it. It may look beautiful—but be totally inadequate for maintaining a correct sitting posture.

Good bed design is even more vital because we spend about one-third of our lives asleep. A soft mattress is not advisable, as this allows the spine to bend during sleep; a firm mattress is always better, although it may feel slightly uncomfortable for the first night or so. If you already have back trouble, your mattress should be as hard as possible to give maximum support. (A sheet of plasterboard placed under a normal mattress will provide the necessary firmness.) Whatever the expense, it is safer to change a too-soft mattress rather than wait until it wears out.

Carrying shopping

To avoid straining one side of the body try to split a heavy load with two bags.

Beauty care with a natural look

Cosmetics are only skin deep. Beauty comes from proper attention to every detail of your way of life.

The modern trend in fashion and beauty is towards a fresh, natural look—clear skin, shining hair and bright, alert eyes. This appearance, relevant to men as well as women, comes only from basic good health—a sensible, balanced diet containing plenty of vitamins C and D to enhance skin health, together with weight control and plenty of exercise.

A basic fact to remember when buying beauty products is that the cosmetic industry has a habit of profiting from human vanity and insecurity. Expensive products are not always necessarily better than cheaper ones.

Before you buy any product to put on your skin it is wise to determine what skin type you are. If your skin is shiny, with open pores on the chin and sides of the nose, it is probably oily. A good test is to dab your face with tissue paper. If the paper is slightly greasy you have oily skin. On the other hand, if you have dry skin it will be dull-looking and flaky, especially round the eyes and on the cheeks. If you have combination or "dual-type" skin—in which, for example, the nose, chin and centre of the forehead are oily and the rest of the face dry—then treat each part accordingly.

Never persist in using any preparations or cosmetics that produce an allergic reaction, such as a rash, soreness or itchiness. You may be allergic to the perfumes, pigments, preservatives and bacteriocides in the product. Special hypo-allergic cosmetics, without these irritants, are available for those who have particularly sensitive skins.

It is a matter of personal choice as to whether you clean your face with soap and water or use a skin cleanser as well, but if you do use a cleanser make sure it is right for your skin. A watery cleansing milk is best for oily skin and a heavier cleansing cream for dry skin. Astringents, which contain alcohol, oil and perfume, and which cause the skin to contract and the pores to close, can be used after washing to "tone up" the skin. Oily skins can benefit from a fairly strong astringent, but if you have a dry skin it is best to use

This is an exercise that strengthens the throat muscles and the muscles around the mouth. Stand in front of the mirror and say TOO, pronouncing it in the most exaggerated way you can.

Natural face care

You cannot prevent your face from ageing, but you can slow the process. Massaging your face (*right*) will help to avoid furrows and wrinkles by keeping your skin supple. Facial exercises (*left and below*) tone up the muscles and prevent them becoming flabby.

Always apply cream with care, starting at the neck and working the fingers upwards.

Massage the sides of the nose with a circular motion to stimulate circulation and tone up the skin.

Stroke the skin from nose to hairline to smooth out forehead wrinkles and ease tension.

This exercise for jaw and throat muscles involves grinning as widely as you can with your teeth together. It should follow the exercise above and the two can be alternated about 20 times.

To exercise all the muscles of your face and to stimulate the circulation and get rid of the lines of tension, open your eyes and mouth as wide as you can, as if you were shouting silently.

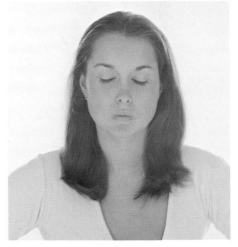

This exercise, which should follow the open mouth one (*left*), also uses all your facial muscles. Close your eyes and mouth and tighten your muscles as much as possible. Repeat three times.

174

skin toner or freshener, which are milder types of astringent. After-shave lotions and eau-de-cologne are also astringents and have the same effects.

To keep your skin smooth and supple you need to prevent it losing too much water. Moisturizers, which are similar to cleansing creams but contain less emulsion, form a waterproof barrier and also supply extra moisture at the same time. Night creams are thicker and creamier because they contain more oil. It is advisable not to apply too thick a layer of cream as the skin will absorb only a small amount and the rest will stay on the surface, block the pores and encourage the growth of spot-producing bacteria. Remove any excess cream with a tissue or cotton wool before you go to sleep.

For a really thorough facial treatment you can use a face pack. Made from a variety of ingredients ranging from oatmeal, yeast and fullers earth (an absorbent clay used for removing grease and as a dusting powder), to eggs, strawberries, honey and yoghurt, such packs work to cleanse, tighten and soften the face as well as relaxing facial muscles.

Beauty care need not be expensive, especially if you use some of the many "home-made" recipes. Once you have made an initial outlay on ingredients—some of which you will have in the store cupboard anyway—you can have beauty treatment for a fraction of the shop price. Home "recipes" make use of natural and inexpensive astringents, such as cucumber, rosewater and lemons, rather than alcohol, natural cleansers such as milk, and natural skin softeners such as avocado pears and honey.

Beauty problems usually can be solved in the home but sometimes need professional treatment. Unwanted facial hair as well as hair on the breasts, lower abdomen and thighs can be permanently removed only by means of a prolonged course of treatment by electrolysis, which must be done by a properly qualified person. A small needle, carrying a small electric current, is inserted into the hair follicle to destroy the root of the hair. Alternatively, bleaching the hairs with a solution of equal parts of liquid ammonia and hydrogen peroxide in water makes them less visible. Hair on the legs can be removed professionally with hot waxes or newly developed cold waxes. Creams for home use are usually only a temporary measure.

Moles and warts are best left alone unless they are causing serious cosmetic problems, and you should report any spontaneous change in a mole to your doctor without delay. Warts, which are generally caused by a viral infection of the skin, often disappear as quickly as they came. Self-treatment of moles can be very dangerous as there is a possibility of melanoma—a tumour of the skin's pigment-producing cells. It is worth recalling that during the 18th century moles were emphasized as "beauty spots".

The skilful use of makeup can disguise almost any facial defect or blemish, but good beauty care does not mean concentrating on the face to the exclusion of other parts of the body. Try to think of yourself as a whole.

Relieve tension, especially between the eyebrows, by gently massaging in a circle round the top of the eyes.

Interlock two fingers of each hand and draw outwards across the forehead to "iron out" lines.

Pinch eyebrows to relieve facial tension and headaches, and draw out lines in forehead.

Using both hands, rigorously pat unsightly flesh under the chin.

Tighten up loose skin on the cheeks by kneading upwards with the backs of the hands.

To tone up the skin of the chin and jawline, pinch the flesh between the thumb and forefinger.

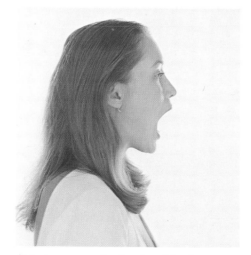

This is an exercise for the chin, throat and jaw muscles. Open your mouth as wide as you can, drop your head backwards; then, for a count of five, try to reach your nose with your lower lip.

This exercise tones up jaw muscles and strengthens the muscles at the front of the neck. Make a face as if you had eaten something bitter and stretch your mouth down. Repeat 20 times.

To firm the cheeks and help prevent creases around the mouth puff out your cheeks and tap them lightly about ten times with your fingertips. Relax and repeat three or four times.

The special demands of pregnancy

During the nine months of pregnancy the mother-to-be needs to safeguard her health—for her baby's sake as well as her own.

Pregnancy is a testing time for any woman and routine body maintenance therefore needs to be supplemented. Regular health checks should be made at monthly intervals to start with, increasing to fortnightly after the thirtieth week of pregnancy and weekly in the last month. After pregnancy has been confirmed, and at every visit to the doctor or antenatal clinic, weight, blood pressure and urine are checked for any signs of setback or complications. Early in pregnancy a blood sample is taken and analysed to determine the blood group (which could warn of the presence of potentially destructive antibodies), and to discover whether you have anaemia, are suffering from venereal disease or have had German measles.

During the first few months of pregnancy, before the fact is noticeable to anyone but yourself, many physiological changes take place. The breasts increase in size and begin to feel more tender than usual and the pigmented area around the nipple (areola) usually becomes darker in colour. It is also normal to pass urine much more often—up to six times during the day and at least twice at night, particularly during the early and later months of pregnancy. Always consult your doctor if urination is painful or difficult.

Nausea and vomiting are common in the early stages of pregnancy but certainly do not affect everyone and rarely persist beyond about fourteen weeks. Early mornings are usually the worst time—hence "morning sickness".

Smokers should make a determined effort to give up cigarettes as soon as they know they are pregnant. Smoking can seriously affect the health of the growing foetus because it drastically reduces the oxygen supply to the placenta and foetus, with the result that the baby may be smaller at birth and generally underdeveloped.

Babies born to mothers who smoke more than ten cigarettes a day during pregnancy often develop more slowly after birth and may experience some form of mental retardation. These risks increase considerably if smoking continues after about the sixteenth week of pregnancy.

Alcohol in moderation will do no harm, but taken in excess throughout pregnancy can cause defects in development. It is good advice to avoid all drugs during pregnancy if you possibly can.

A well-balanced diet is always important for health, but during pregnancy, when you are sharing nutrients with your developing baby, it is essential to pay special attention to the type and amount of food you eat. High-protein food such as meat, fish, eggs, cheese and liver—a rich source of iron—are beneficial. If possible, drink a large glass of milk a day because it contains the calcium needed for bone formation. Make an effort to eat some fresh food (including something green) every day, for fresh fruit and vegetables are important sources of vitamins and minerals. Orange juice (especially from freshly squeezed oranges) is an excellent source of vitamin C; a large glass once or twice a day is both healthful and refreshing.

Even on the best diet you may need extra iron and vitamins because of the needs of the growing baby, but never take these unless your doctor prescribes them.

Although it is normal for weight to be lost during the first three months of pregnancy—as much as 3.6 kg (8 lb) or even slightly more—weight gain should be carefully checked after that time. Throughout the whole pregnancy an ideal weight gain is around 10 kg (22 lb). But you should try not to exceed about 11 kg (24 lb), unless you are expecting twins.

Controlling your weight gain by cutting down on carbohydrates, especially cakes and sweets, gives you more chance of staying completely healthy during pregnancy and remaining that way—and regaining your old shape quickly—after your baby has been born. Excess weight can also be a factor in high blood pressure and if not controlled may lead to complications such as toxaemia.

Stretch marks on and under the breasts and on the thighs and abdomen are likely to occur if too much weight is gained. Although stretch marks will never disappear entirely after the birth, they will become less noticeable.

During pregnancy it is natural that you should feel the need for plenty of rest, even in the early stages when you are carrying little or no extra weight. Don't stand too long in one position, as this impedes the blood circulation and can cause faintness or dizziness. Throughout pregnancy normal exercise is beneficial, par-

ticularly walking and swimming, but avoid strenuous sports such as squash. At no time should you attempt to lift, push or pull anything heavy (though mothers of toddlers may find this difficult to avoid).

Pregnancy is a time when many women feel fitter and happier than at any time in their lives, especially after the first three months. Others find themselves uncharacteristically moody and irritable—try not to get too depressed about this, and discuss the problem with your husband so that he can give you the help and understanding you need. Many women find that they lose interest in sex to begin with, but regain interest later in pregnancy.

Sexual intercourse can continue for the

Total, purposeful relaxation
Relaxation is helpful in pregnancy and will enable you to conserve energy during labour. Lie as shown so that no one part of your body rests on any other.

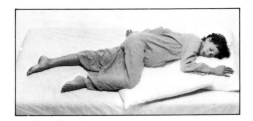

Preparing for labour: breath control
Slow, deep breathing, in which you "sigh" each time you breathe out, will help relieve pain in labour and is well worth practising during pregnancy.

Preparing for labour: panting breathing
Shallow breathing from the top of the chest helps stop you from pushing too early in labour and so wasting energy. Practise this for 30 seconds at a time.

entire nine months as long as the pregnancy is normal and uncomplicated. However, a doctor will usually advise a woman who has a history of miscarriage (or who is likely to miscarry) to avoid intercourse, especially in the first three months. A side-by-side position may be found to be best later on in pregnancy, as this puts the least pressure on the womb. Alternatives to sexual intercourse, such as mutual masturbation, are frequently more satisfactory for both partners at this time. The most important factor, however, is for husband and wife to learn to become sensitive to each other's needs, desires and general feelings, particularly during the later stages of pregnancy.

Exercises for feet and ankles

Aching feet and swollen ankles can be helped by the exercises below. Push your feet up and down as shown, then rotate them from the ankles.

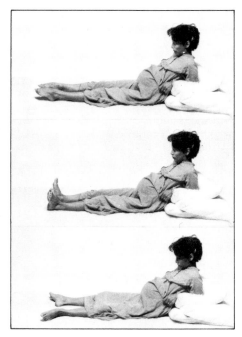

Some problems of pregnancy

Pregnancy puts extra strain on the body and this can result in a variety of discomforts. Although most are not serious, you should tell your doctor if they persist.

Excess weight can make you extra tired and aggravate other problems.

Swollen fingers can be a danger sign that too much fluid is accumulating in the body; it should be reported to your doctor.

Varicose veins and piles both tend to get worse during pregnancy. Keeping your weight under control can help prevent them.

Bending and lifting

To avoid strain on your back and to help prevent backache in pregnancy, always bend from the knees, not from the waist. Mothers with small children often find pregnancy very tiring, but it is still advisable to set aside even a short time each day for total relaxation in the lying position shown on the opposite page.

Morning sickness is common in the early months. To help overcome nausea try eating a dry biscuit before you get up, and avoid fatty foods.

Backache is hard to avoid, especially in the later stages of pregnancy, but you can help by good posture. Try to walk with your back straight, not arched or rounded. For sitting (*below*) choose a chair with an upright back; sit in it with your back straight.

Constipation is a common problem of pregnancy. Drinking four or five glasses of water a day can help avoid it.

Aching legs can be helped by lying down for a period each day and by wearing support stockings. Gaining too much weight tends to make the problem worse.

Fundamental checkpoints for all women

Every woman will benefit from learning as much as possible about her own body, for such knowledge enables her to appreciate the cycles of change that take place within it.

The female body, with its special capacity for childbearing, is a highly complex organism, and an entire branch of medicine—gynaecology—has evolved to deal specifically with all aspects of women's health. The more a woman learns about the bodily changes that occur from month to month and year to year, the more she will be able to accept the landmarks in her reproductive life and to recognize minor troubles at an early stage and help prevent them from turning into major ones.

The first sign that a girl is changing into a woman is usually the start of breast development. This gradual process usually begins before the first dramatic change—the start of menstruation. This is the time when the ovaries start to release eggs and normally takes place at any age from ten to sixteen. The breasts continue to develop after menstruation has begun and body hair, especially under the arms and in the genital area, begins to grow.

A young girl should never be allowed to experience her first period without some prior explanation and understanding of what is going to happen, and of the wider implications of her fertility. A healthy attitude towards menstruation at this early stage will help solve some of the psychological problems of adolescence. During the first year of menstruation the periods are usually somewhat irregular, for this is the time when the body is beginning to adjust to the changes in hormone levels which govern the monthly cycle.

Even after menstruation has settled down into a monthly pattern no woman experiences absolutely regular periods. If your periods are irregular it can be helpful to your doctor if you have kept a personal record of the monthly patterns.

Most women need have little trouble with their periods. The most common difficulties experienced are painful, often heavy periods and premenstrual tension. Period pain is usually most severe during the first day of menstruation, but may last longer. It should not be accepted by any woman as a regular monthly burden to be borne in silence. Tell your doctor about it; he may be able to help. Some women who had not used oral contraceptives were relieved of severe menstrual pains when they started on the contraceptive pill.

The causes of premenstrual tension are not fully understood, but are certainly related to a change in the levels of female sex hormone (oestrogen) in the blood during the reproductive cycle. Typically, tension occurs from about five to ten days before menstruation and is characterized by headache, irritability, depression, a bloated feeling around the abdominal area and a reduced capacity for concentration (making some women accident-prone). Premenstrual tension can be relieved to some extent if you have plenty of rest and reduce your intake of salt and fluids, especially alcohol. The symptoms nearly always disappear with the start of the menstrual flow.

Other problems of menstruation include missed periods, excessive or "heavy" periods, and bleeding or "spotting" that occurs between periods. If any of these persist you should consult your doctor.

Periods can stop for a wide variety of reasons, the most common being pregnancy (see pages 176–7) and the onset of the menopause. Anxiety, excitement or any emotional disturbance can often delay a period or even result in a missed period. Anaemia is sometimes the cause of a missed period, especially if your periods are normally heavy, and if your doctor suspects this he will prescribe extra iron and vitamins.

The start of menstruation is accompanied by the onset of regular secretion of thin clear fluid from the vagina. This is quite normal, but you should consult your doctor if the discharge becomes white, yellow, more copious or thicker than usual, or causes any irritation. Many women find it embarrassing to seek medical help for this problem for they fear being accused of promiscuity. In fact most vaginal infections are not sexually transmitted.

The menopause, which takes about two years to complete, marks the end of the regular menstrual cycle and is the natural culmination of a woman's reproductive life. For women between forty and fifty it does indeed represent the "change of

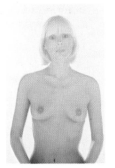

A routine breast examination
To check your breasts, first look at yourself in the mirror (*above*) with arms by your sides, then raised. Note any changes in shape or size. Then lie down with a folded towel under one shoulder (*right*) and hand under your head and examine the breast on that side by moving your hand clockwise and feeling the whole area from nipple to breast perimeter. Repeat on the other side.

life". As hormone levels start to fall and egg production gradually ceases, periods become more widely spaced, then stop altogether. Contraceptive precautions, however, should continue for at least 24 months after the last period.

While some women pass through the menopause with no problems, and welcome with relief the knowledge that they can no longer become pregnant, many find the mental adjustment hard to make, or cannot cope with the unpredictable changes in mood and tempo and increased nervous tension that menopause often brings. They may suffer adverse physical effects, including hot flushes, dizziness, dryness and itching in the vagina with consequently painful sexual intercourse, pains in the joints and dry skin.

Discuss any physical problems with your doctor as frankly as you can. He may recommend hormone replacement therapy, which can do much to relieve the physical discomfort of the menopause. Hormones whose production is diminishing can be supplemented either orally, by injection, or by the implantation of pellets in the body that release hormone gradually for three to six months. Hormone replacement therapy is not a miracle cure, however. It may merely delay the onset of unpleasant symptoms or cause bleeding in the vagina. So be guided by your doctor.

Every woman has the opportunity to obtain advance warning about some kinds of cancer and thus receive treatment before the disease has a chance to take hold and become disfiguring or deadly. This is particularly true in the case of cancer of the neck of the womb (cervix) and the breasts, both of which can be detected early on and for which early detection means, in most cases, early cure.

All women over the age of thirty should make it their business to have a cervical smear taken at least once every two years. This is a simple procedure, performed by your doctor or family planning clinic. It involves the painless collection of a few cells shed from the neck of the womb and nearby areas. After the cells are stained and examined under a microscope, any abnormal changes can be clearly seen. If the test reveals cancer or a precancerous condition, treatment can be started at once.

As well as the normal screenings that doctors perform for the early detection of breast cancer, there is a simple check that every woman, from her twenties onwards, should learn to do for herself, as shown in the illustrations. The best time to do this is immediately after a period, when any breast swelling will have disappeared. If you find a lump, don't panic— most lumps are not serious, but *anything* suspicious should be reported to your doctor without delay.

Exercises for breast support

With hands in the position shown, press them together as hard as possible and breathe out slowly. Repeat five times.

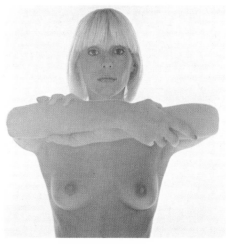

Fold your arms as illustrated, gripping just above the wrists. Sharply move your elbows inwards. Repeat five times.

With fingers on your shoulders as shown, rotate your elbows clockwise, then anti-clockwise. Repeat five times for each pair of rotations.

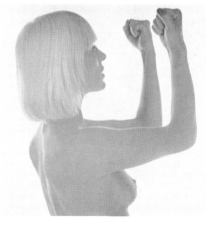

Pretend you are holding a bar with your arms outstretched and elbows bent as shown, then pull your hands slowly towards you, inhaling. Repeat five times.

Lie on the floor with hands under your shoulders and elbows bent. Slowly raise your torso on your hands, then lower it. Repeat five times, but do not overstrain.

Swing your arms over your head and behind your back, then clasp your hands together as illustrated. Count to five, then relax. Repeat five times.

Massage: to tone you up or calm you down

It won't in itself make you fit or slim. But massage can ease aches and make you more interested in fitness.

Massage means, in broad terms, pressing or kneading muscles. Done gently, it is soothing; done more forcefully it has a stimulating effect because it quickens the flow of blood and lymph. Massage is therefore useful to relieve the effects of tension and to tone up muscles that are in poor condition through illness, abuse or simply disuse. Apart from relieving certain kinds of pain, massage can also induce a feeling of well-being that encourages weight control and the pursuit of general fitness.

Physiotherapists often use massage to relieve the pain of rheumatism, sciatica, neuralgia, sprains and stiffness and to maintain muscle tone in cases of muscle wasting and paralysis. This kind of massage should be undertaken only on a doctor's advice and be done only by a trained masseur who understands the physiology of deep massage and the close relationship of some nerves and muscles. But more generally, massage can be used to relieve body tension and there is no reason why you cannot try it at home, using the introductory instructions on these pages.

Since tension involves tautness its effects are often easily recognizable—the flesh is more resistant than it should be to the pressure of the fingers and there may be tiny lumps of knotted tissue below the surface. In addition to relaxing those muscles, massage has distinct psychological effects. The pleasant feeling of warmth and vigour it induces can remind people who are out of condition how much better a fit body can feel. Similarly, if you are overweight, massage can help your posture by firming up muscles and can make you more aware of the benefits of losing weight by exercise and diet control.

All you need for a home massage is a firm surface (a mattress or blanket on the floor will do) and a warm room. A bath first will help you relax. The masseur can use a little light oil on the hands and should try to work with steady, flowing movements in the general direction of the heart. Varicose veins should be avoided, as should any excessive pressure on the spine.

Head and face
Stroke the thumbs up the middle of the brow to the hairline. Lightly roll the temples with the middle fingers. Then starting beside the nose, press the thumbs past the mouth to the jawline.

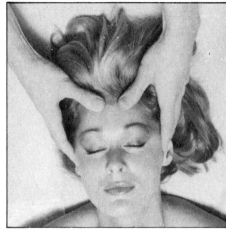

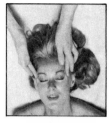

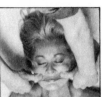

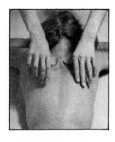

Neck and shoulders
Press the balls of the thumbs down the muscles on either side of the spine from the neck to the lower back.

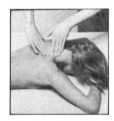

Use the leverage of the fingers to push the thumbs from the collar-bones hard into the muscles along the shoulder blades.

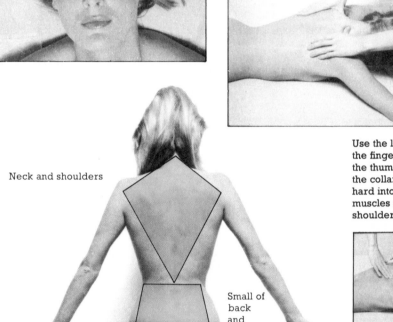

Neck and shoulders

Small of back and buttocks

Insides of thighs

Calves

Points of tension
The calves, insides of the thighs and small of the back are among areas of the body that often become tense (*shaded*). But most tension arises in the shoulders and neck. By easing the pressure of taut muscles on nerves concentrated there, massage can reduce aches in other parts of the body.

Pull the flats of the hands up both sides of the neck towards the spinal column.

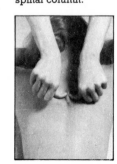

Placing the thumbs one behind the other, run them with light pressure down the spine.

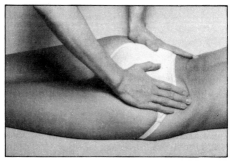

Small of the back

To ease aches in the lower back, put the flats of the hands on the outside of the buttocks and push them down and around in a circular movement completed at the small of the back (*above*). Then press both thumbs, one behind the other, on the coccyx and use small strokes up the lower spine. Next, press down hard on the buttocks with flats of hands. Finally, draw the flats of the hands upwards with pressure on both sides of buttocks.

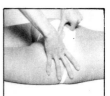

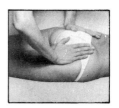

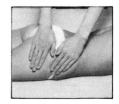

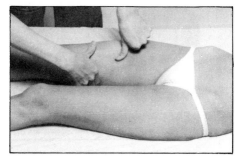

Insides of thighs

Knead both sides of the thighs with the balls of the thumbs from just above the knee to the groin. Then roll the muscles upwards with the flats of the hands.

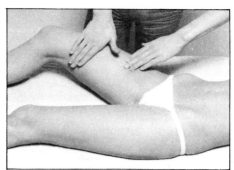

Calf muscles

Massage the calves by pressing upwards with short thumb strokes (*right*) to just below the knee crease. Then slide your crossed hands upwards, using the pressure of the leading knuckle joint (*below*).

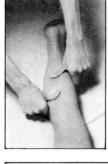

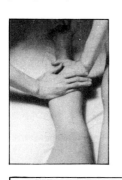

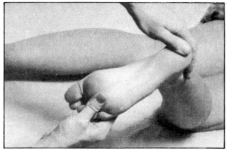

Feet

For tired feet, press thumbs with small strokes from the bottom of the toes up to the ankle bone and round it to the Achilles tendon. Repeat on the sole with increasing pressure around the heel.

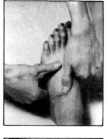

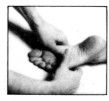

To complete foot massage, stretch the sole by firmly bending back the ball and the heel (*left*).

Pressure massage

This form of relief from tension originated in China and Japan. Instead of piercing certain points of the body, as in acupuncture, pressure is applied with the fingertips, thumbs, elbows and palms of the hands, the pressure lasting between five to ten seconds, depending on the sensitivity of the area being worked. In Japan, Shiatzu, which uses pressure massage, claims to relieve tension, give vitality and sexual energy, and help complaints such as headaches.

The pressure method often brings relief to places other than those being worked. For example if the spine, which protects the spinal cord, becomes even slightly displaced it can cause pain in any of the limbs. By working certain points on the back, therefore, relief can be brought to widespread aches in the arms and legs.

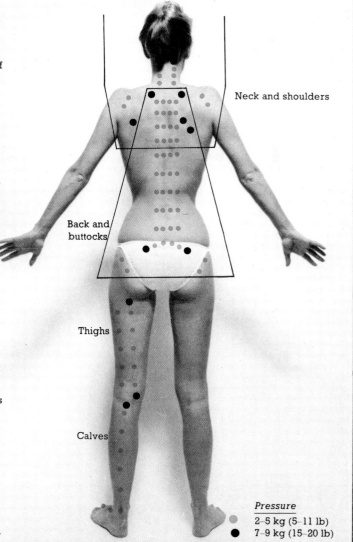

Neck and shoulders

Back and buttocks

Thighs

Calves

Pressure
● 2–5 kg (5–11 lb)
● 7–9 kg (15–20 lb)

Sauna: the dry heat way to cleanliness

Saunas will not bring a long-term feeling of well-being, but they are an ideal means of achieving immediate relief from mental and physical tension.

The simple purpose of the sauna is to sweat grime out of your skin while you relax. The method has been known in Finland for some 2,000 years, but has only become popular worldwide since the 1950s. There are now at least two million saunas in the US, Europe, Japan and Malaysia, many of them in beauty salons or gymnasiums.

The Finnish sauna was originally a simple lakeside log cabin, wood-lined and heated by a special stove overlaid with stones. It is believed to derive from a Scythian custom, dating from the 5th century BC, of inhaling intoxicating vapours from hemp-seed and water thrown on hot stones. The sauna became widely known in Europe in the 18th century when visitors to Finland were amazed to see men and women taking steam baths together, beating themselves with twigs to stimulate blood circulation.

A typical sauna room generates dry heat

Turkish baths

Ingres' painting *The Turkish Bath* has an atmosphere of leisurely self-indulgence somewhat different from the bracing image usually associated with saunas. Modern Turkish baths combine steam and dry heat with a wider range of facilities than the simple sauna.

of up to 120°C (248°F). Four minutes after you enter the room your skin temperature rises to about 40°C (104°F), blood vessels under the skin dilate and body temperature rises by about two degrees centigrade. Your heart beats faster, circulating more blood to the outside of the body to cool and tone up the skin. Skin pores open and sweat flushes out any makeup, dirt, dust and dead skin that may be clogging the pores. After a few more minutes, the loosened debris is washed off in a cold and invigorating shower.

The warmth of a sauna and the rise in body temperature soothes tension by relaxing the muscles. For this reason, and the beneficial effect of increased circulatory rate on inflammation, saunas are increasingly being used in hospitals and clinics to relieve rheumatism and some types of back trouble.

In addition, sweating gets rid of waste

Taking a sauna

Modern professional saunas are usually laid out in a simple sequence. After you have undressed, a warm shower washes away superficial dirt.

products, such as lactic acid, which build up in the muscles during exercise. Saunas attached to gymnasiums are popular ways of easing muscular tension after exercise.

But perhaps the most important benefit is psychological. The sauna is a quiet, simple, soothing environment—a place where you can ease away emotional as well as muscular stresses.

If your health is good there is little circulatory or respiratory risk in taking a sauna. But there are dangers for others. According to a British Medical Journal report in 1972 a normal heart rate almost doubles after only seven minutes in a sauna. The increase in pulse rate is enough to strain a weak heart. In Finland in 1970, sixty-seven people died in saunas, many from heart attacks. (High-fat diets in Finland could have been a contributory factor.)

As a precautionary measure, most saunas display a warning notice to high-

risk groups: expectant mothers, those with high or low blood pressure, with varicose veins, glandular obesity, respiratory or heart conditions, a history of thrombosis or recent major surgery and those on strict diets. Middle-aged and elderly people unused to saunas should use the cooler lower levels and spend not more than five minutes in the hot-room.

In Finland, a sauna building consists fundamentally of a dressing-room, a hot-room and a wash-room, all traditionally walled in pine or spruce because these woods are cheap and freely available there. Other countries have substituted woods such as redwood and hemlock.

In a sauna, you will first be asked to take off your clothes and to have a warm shower to wash off superficial grime before going into the sauna proper. Inside the hot-room you sit or lie on wooden benches while you perspire in the dry heat created by stoves or electric heaters. The stoves warm large stones, which evenly disperse heat around the room. If you wish to step up the effect you can simply move on to a higher bench—for every 30 cm (1 ft) above floor level the temperature increases by 10 degrees centigrade (18 degrees Fahrenheit)—or you can throw a ladle of water on the stones to produce a hot, slightly humid wave of air, which temporarily increases humidity and stimulates perspiration.

After five to ten minutes in the hot-room you may begin to feel uncomfortable and will feel the need to take your first cold shower or dip. (Traditionally, the Finns substituted a roll in the snow or a dip in a lake or river, through a hole cut in the ice, in place of a cold shower.) When alternating periods in the hot-room or shower have left you feeling fully relaxed, you can have a last wash or perhaps a massage, before leaving the sauna clean and relaxed.

The traditional Finnish sauna

The typical old Finnish sauna was a single-room log building. Nowadays a family sauna is often incorporated into the house. In many farms and summer cottages it is, in fact, the only bath available. The smoke sauna (*above*) has a chimneyless oven with smoke circulating around the room. The numerous Finnish lakes provide cold dips between saunas, and the water to create the "loyly"—the steam that rises from cold water on hot stones.

The heat of the hot room is intensified at higher levels. Ladles of cold water thrown on hot stones lower the temperature but increase the humidity. The Finns use birch twigs in their saunas to stimulate circulation.

Cold water washes off sweated-out dirt and tightens up the pores of the skin.

Japanese baths

Unlike the sauna, the Japanese bath is based on the soothing effects of hot water rather than hot air. To most Western people the temperature of the water would be uncomfortable. In the public baths (mixed or single sex) you first wash thoroughly with a low-level shower (*foreground above*) before immersing yourself in very hot water or cooling off by sitting on a shelf around the pool.

Smoking: the indisputable side effects

Smokers run large risks for their pleasure. Equally, they cause offence in large measure to non-smokers.

The body behaves largely in a mechanical way. Put something into it and it will respond in a predictable manner, dictated by its chemistry. But whereas a machine that fails can be quickly repaired, the body cannot. If the lungs are once impaired by smoking the only option is slowly to nurse them back to a healthy state.

Positive methods of improving lung function include taking physical exercise and breathing clean air. It is also important to preserve the body's pumping system. Anything that tends to reduce the internal diameter of the blood pipes throws a strain on the apparatus; nicotine does just that. It also interferes with the secretions and

mobility of the stomach and gut, diminishing the efficiency of the digestive tract.

Smokers medicate themselves with each puff, whether only as far as the air chambers of nose and mouth, the upper bronchial tubes, or down to the smallest components of the bronchial tree. The constituents of tobacco smoke include: carbon monoxide and cyanide, two rapidly acting poisons; benzpyrene and other tar products and a definite carcinogen, all irritants that damage the tissues slowly; and nicotine, which affects the nervous system with widespread results and is addictive. The temperature of smoke increases its irritant properties.

In spite of all this, tobacco has powerful

attractions. Psychologically, it is a social lubricant and breaker of the ice. It provides oral gratification and comfort, such as a baby gets from sucking its thumb, and gives the fidgety something to do with their hands: a fact clearly appreciated by the pipe-smoker or the man who rolls his own. And it is not fattening. For the young, taking up smoking is a gesture meant to convey maturity; for the old it is a kind of companionship; and for the bored it fills the emptiness—this no doubt accounts for the heavy use of tobacco among inmates of long-stay mental hospitals.

In addition, smokers seek the chemical effects provided by the nicotine com-

ponent in tobacco. This immediately releases a small quantity of catecholamines, the nerve transmitters used in every thought and movement—the effect is to reduce feelings of fatigue. After an initial gurgle or two, the stomach and intestines are quietened down and hunger abates.

But if you smoke you cannot sidestep ill-effects. The immediate poisoning effects of the monoxide and cyanide may give you a headache and do something more drastic to your unborn child if you are pregnant. It is noteworthy that the concentration of carbon monoxide in central Tokyo or the mid-city streets of New York is less than it is inside your car when you light up. Also the concentration of this poison in the blood is the same whether or not a smoker inhales.

Nicotine exerts an influence on the relay stations of the autonomic nervous system: that part over which you have no conscious control, but which monitors and makes adjustments to such vital organs as the heart, arterial system, bladder and gastrointestinal tract. In the stomach, increased churning followed by stagnation delays the healing of peptic ulcers. In the blood vessels of the mouth and main airways nicotine paralyses the phagocytes, whose function is to engulf and destroy bacteria and viruses entering the body in the air we breathe. One cigarette puts these first-line defenders out of service for a full fifteen minutes. The effect of nicotine on the heart is to increase its rate, reducing the reserve when physical exertion demands greater output. The blood vessels contract and later relax, causing the blood pressure to fluctuate. In those subject to blood vessel troubles the effect may be serious.

Furred tongue and yellow-stained teeth are unpleasant but no real health hazard; nor is the increased susceptibility to colds, sinusitis and laryngitis that result from the irritant effects of smoke. Acute and chronic bronchitis are definitely life-shortening, as is the greatest danger of all—lung cancer.

Nobody wants to choke to death slowly, from a cancer that is particularly prone to cause secondary deposition in the brain: this can be bewildering, painful and terrifying. But is the causal link between smoking

Venus obscured

If even the gods of the winds took to smoking we would all suffer like Botticelli's Venus in this distortion of his painting. Botticelli lived before tobacco was known in the West. Today, to millions of non-smokers, it must seem as if fresh air has ceased to exist. In choosing to damage their own health, smokers deprive others of a natural right to breathe pure air.

and cancer proven? The facts are these: among regular cigarette smokers lung cancer is the commonest form of cancer, increasing in likelihood the more the person smokes. It has been suggested that the basis is genetic, that some people are born with a constitutional predisposition to the disease and their smoking is irrelevant. Yet since the early 1950s, when a large proportion of British doctors were scared out of smoking by the evidence, there has been a dramatic drop-off in lung cancer in the profession, although there has been no change for the rest of the population. The doctors' genetic loading cannot have changed with their altered habits.

Distillate of cigarette smoke produces cancer in animals wherever it is applied regularly: man applies the same mix to his lungs. It is interesting that those who say that they inhale tend to develop cancers deep in the lung tissue, while those who do not inhale are more likely to have cancers in the bronchial tubes.

The ill-effects of smoking cannot be avoided by not inhaling: this merely moves the risk area higher up. Cigars or pipes are only less dangerous than cigarettes if smoking this way means doing it far less often. Cancer of the tongue occurs in pipe- rather than cigarette-smokers—it may not kill you, but it is still a cancer. On the supposed advantages of mild blends, filters or herbal cigarettes the evidence is insufficient, but in no way reassuring. Cutting down is more difficult than cutting cigarettes right out, and anyway could only delay the ill-effects.

Withdrawal symptoms for an habitual smoker are unpleasant and can last up to six weeks. They include trembling, sweating, anxiety, irritability, insomnia and, of course, craving. There is also a likelihood of wanting to eat more.

If you want to give up smoking, it helps to tell your associates you are doing so: this makes it more difficult for you to let yourself down, and less likely that other people will press you to smoke. It is also sensible to occupy your leisure time fully. Attending a group is helpful to some, just as Alcoholics Anonymous suits some struggling ex-drinkers; most big cities have stop-smoking groups. Medicines have little place in helping you give up, and even nicotine tablets do not replace the cigarette; however, withdrawal effects may be mitigated by a short course of diazepam (Valium). Support from a doctor may be helpful, and from a psychiatrist if the smoking is symptomatic of severe anxiety or depression.

It usually takes several attempts to achieve success in giving up smoking. Nobody should underestimate the difficulty, or despair at initial failure.

Drinking: its pleasures and dangers

Alcohol can be a mixed blessing, for while it may ease tension it is a powerful drug with addictive properties.

Alcohol is one of the oldest drugs known to man and still the most widely used. It is a tribute to alcohol's powerful effects that virtually every society in the world has known how to make it and that its consumption continues to increase.

Most of the alcohol we drink comes from the fermentation of plant sugars by yeast and is relatively weak. Beer, for example, contains on average between three and six per cent alcohol, most wines between ten and twelve per cent. Spirits such as gin and whisky are much stronger, containing thirty-five per cent alcohol or more, and are made by distillation of weaker brews to concentrate the alcohol.

The steady rise of gaiety at a cocktail party might fool you into thinking that alcohol is a stimulant. In fact it has a depressant effect on the central nervous system and loosens the tongue and the inhibitions by numbing the parts of the brain that normally act to restrain our behaviour. This is why drinking is a social lubricant and eases tensions but, at the same time, can lead you to act rashly or

Drinkers in danger

Drivers who drink risk their own lives and those of others because alcohol impairs judgement.

The free-spender who sabotages his family budget to finance his drinking may also ruin his emotional life.

Loneliness, often a problem for harassed housewives, may lead to heavy drinking, while neglected work compounds the misery.

Alcohol can have fatal effects when taken in combination with barbiturates and other medicinal drugs.

make promises regretted (if remembered) in the sober light of dawn. And although drinking may make you feel like a great lover, the Porter in Shakespeare's *Macbeth* rightly said that "it provokes the desire, but it takes away the performance".

The speed at which alcohol takes effect, and the length of time that the effect persists, depend on both how and what you drink. Drinking on an empty stomach makes you feel "weak at the knees" most quickly because the alcohol is absorbed directly into the blood stream from the stomach and very rapidly from the intestine. The presence of a good meal in the

stomach delays this absorption until the alcohol reaches the intestine, so the peak concentration of alcohol in the blood comes later and is not as high.

Oxidation (the process by which alcohol is broken down so that its effects cease) takes place principally in the liver. Only about two per cent of the alcohol consumed escapes oxidation, to be excreted instead in the urine or on the breath. The amount lost on the breath is small but is enough to indicate the total concentration in the entire body. It is for this reason that police in many countries are equipped with breath-test devices to screen out drivers who may be over the legal blood-alcohol level.

Whatever the quantity, the faster you drink the faster you will get drunk. Slow drinking slows absorption and reduces the maximum level that blood alcohol concentration can reach. The strongest drinks, however, do not necessarily have the fastest effects. Research shows that cocktails and fortified wines such as sherry that contain twenty per cent alcohol are more intoxicating in the short term than either wines and beers with up to twelve per cent or neat whisky with an alcohol content as high as fifty-three per cent.

One of the reasons why cocktails have such a powerful effect is that the carbon dioxide gas in mixers such as soda water and ginger ale stimulate the movements of the gut and push the alcohol rapidly from the stomach to the intestine, where absorption is fastest. The same effect is produced by the bubbles in champagne, a drink

Body weight (lb)	Number of drinks											
	1	2	3	4	5	6	7	8	9	10	11	12
100	0.038	0.075	0.113	0.150	0.188	0.225	0.263	0.300	0.338	0.375	0.418	0.450
120	0.031	0.063	0.094	0.125	0.156	0.188	0.219	0.250	0.281	0.313	0.344	0.375
140	0.027	0.054	0.080	0.107	0.134	0.161	0.188	0.214	0.241	0.268	0.285	0.321
160	0.023	0.047	0.070	0.094	0.117	0.141	0.164	0.188	0.211	0.234	0.258	0.281
180	0.021	0.042	0.063	0.083	0.104	0.125	0.146	0.167	0.188	0.208	0.229	0.250
200	0.019	0.038	0.056	0.075	0.094	0.113	0.131	0.150	0.169	0.188	0.206	0.225
220	0.017	0.034	0.051	0.068	0.085	0.102	0.119	0.136	0.153	0.170	0.188	0.205
240	0.016	0.031	0.047	0.063	0.078	0.094	0.109	0.125	0.141	0.156	0.172	0.188
(2.2 lb = 1 kg)	**Under 0.05** Driving not seriously impaired			**0.05 to 0.10** Driving increasingly dangerous			**0.10 to 0.15** Driving dangerous and often illegal			**Over 0.15** Driving very dangerous and usually illegal		

The risky combination

A driver's chance of increasing his blood alcohol above the legal limit depends on both his body weight and his consumption. This chart, based on studies carried out in New Jersey, US, shows levels of blood alcohol. Each drink is taken as being equivalent to one ounce of 100 per cent proof spirit (about the same as a standard single measure in Britain) or 0.6 pint of beer. Legal limits vary between countries.

The steady, heavy drinker, who spends most of his leisure time imbibing, risks alcoholism and declining health.

The total abstainer, unused to alcohol, sometimes becomes a heavy drinker when he abandons his moral scruples.

Many occupations, particularly those of hotelier or publican, can often tempt a person to drink excessively.

Secret drinking from hidden bottles can be a tell-tale sign of addiction—addicts are often ashamed of drinking.

have been drinking, do not drive unless you are still within the safety category shown on the accompanying chart.

In the long term heavy drinking can cause gastritis, an irritation of the stomach lining. This is one of several factors that reduces the drinker's appetite. When drinking comes to take the place of eating then vitamin deficiency and malnutrition can result. Heavy drinking also harms the body by causing cirrhosis of the liver, a disease in which fibrous scar tissue forms in the liver and prevents it from doing its job of metabolizing alcohol.

Alcoholism is not the same as heavy drinking; usually it is a symptom of a deep-seated psychological problem. Alcohol addiction, a costly disease that ensnares new victims at the rate of 100,000 a year in the US alone, is typified by an uncontrollable desire for, and a physiological dependence on alcohol. The reasons why some people become alcoholics while other heavy drinkers do not are unknown, but it seems that in alcoholics social "coping mechanisms" are poorly developed. To begin with, these people use the anaesthetic effects of alcohol to bolster their egos or to drown their problems. But the effect of drinking is to produce more crises, and so the vicious circle continues.

If you feel you are drinking more than is good for you, perhaps as a result of too many business lunches, first try rationing your drinks rather than giving up altogether. Do this by limiting yourself to drinking at particular times and only in certain places, and by cutting down amounts. As you drink less you will find that your capacity for drink will also go down. If you are worried that you have become totally dependent on alcohol, then seek medical guidance.

with traditionally swift alcoholic effects.

For those who love parties but hate getting drunk there are many useful tips—apart from drinking orange squash all evening. Before you start, try to eat meat, cheese or some other protein or drink a glass of milk, for these are the foods that inhibit alcohol uptake most effectively. At the party, drink as slowly as you can and choose drinks that will have the least rapid effects. Mixing your drinks may increase your alcohol uptake as well as presenting the gut with an unacceptable conglomeration of alcohol additives.

If, despite all this, you do get drunk, what are the best remedies? Drinking plenty of water before you go to bed can help stave off some of the worst of a hangover by replacing body water. (Alcohol tends to remove this water because it increases the rate of urine formation.)

The cures for hangovers are legion. Again, liquids help relieve the symptoms of dry mouth and woolly head, and there is some evidence that anything containing vitamin C, such as orange or lemon juice, is beneficial in speeding up the rate of alcohol breakdown in the body. A drink the morning after may stave off withdrawal symptoms after a heavy bout of drinking. But however effective any remedy may seem it always takes about eighteen hours for any alcohol to be eliminated from the blood stream completely.

Alcohol can aid relaxation and sleep and help relieve both mental distress and physical pain but is undoubtedly a mixed blessing. It is Calorie rich (nearly twice as

rich, gramme for gramme, as chocolate) so can add to the problems of people who are overweight. More serious aspects of alcohol are its dangers for drivers, its adverse physical effects and its properties as a drug of addiction.

Drinking and driving are a potentially fatal combination because alcohol reduces reaction times, dulls the sensibilities and clouds the judgement. An intoxicated person is in the worst possible position to assess his own ability to drive. In the US, alcohol is a factor in more than half of all fatal collisions. The only sensible advice to the driver must be don't drink or, if you

Coping with hangovers

A hangover results from the combined effects of impurities in alcohol, dehydration of body cells and a fall in blood sugar levels. As a result, commonsense remedies include drinking plenty of water before you go to bed and eating sugary food the day after. The vitamin C in fruit juice also helps. Aspirin can relieve a headache but may irritate the stomach lining. Milk is more soothing. The "hair of the dog" method (another drink) will perk you up for a while but by adding to your level of blood alcohol simply delays the effect.

Medicines: for emergency use only

Medicines are essential, but many carry risks of side effects that can be worse than the original condition.

The family medicine cabinet

A childproof lock is the first requirement of a family medicine cabinet. Keep inside it the name, address and telephone number of your family doctor, a first aid manual and the following essentials:

In case of illness

Clinical thermometer.
Soluble aspirin.
Kaolin and morphine for diarrhoea.
Senna tablets for severe constipation.
Magnesium trisilicate for indigestion.
Lozenges for sore throats.

For problem skins

Zinc ointment for sore, moist skin.
Soft lanolin cream
for sore, dry skin.
Calamine lotion for itching and sunburn.

In case of accident

Antiseptic cream containing cetrimide.
Waterproof adhesive dressings.
Zinc oxide plaster.
Cotton wool, lint.
Needles and tweezers to remove splinters.
Pins, scissors.
Crêpe, triangular and cotton bandages.

Man has always searched for medicines to cure bodily ills. Leading pharmacopoeias today list more than 25,000 different medicinal drugs, of which some common examples are shown in the chart. They play a critical part in the treatment of disease and the relief of human suffering, both physical and mental, but one of the biggest problems in health care today is their misuse, whether they are bought over the counter (often called patent medicines) or provided on a doctor's prescription.

The much-publicized social abuse of drugs, ranging from marijuana to heroin, is only one aspect of a wider problem. Some drugs commonly taken for medicinal reasons also carry addictive risks. Still more can have serious side effects, not necessarily associated with misuse. Because every drug interferes with the body's working, it is essential to follow guidelines for their medical use.

The simple rules for using medicines are: always follow the instructions to the letter—don't think that you know best; don't leave medicines where children can reach them, and don't call them "sweets" when talking to children; never give medicine prescribed for yourself to somebody else; if side effects occur, contact your doctor immediately.

Of all the drugs available over the chemist's counter, aspirin has by far the largest sale: it is sold in sufficient quantity in the US alone to treat more than 17,000 million headaches a year—that is an aspirin for every man, woman and child about every fourth day. And although aspirin is a cheap and effective pain-killer and temperature-reducer if taken sensibly, it causes more deaths by poisoning in British children than any other chemical. So, like other medicines, it should be treated with respect.

Aspirin is generally safe to use to relieve the many body pains and the symptoms of colds and flu. It is best taken after a meal but should *never* be used to treat stomach upsets and indigestion. Nor should you take aspirin after a bout of heavy drinking, if you have an ulcer, or if you have ever previously had a rash or swelling after taking it. It is always wise to check with your doctor or chemist that it is safe to take aspirin if you are already taking other medicinal drugs.

Paracetamol is thought by many doctors to be preferable to aspirin because it is not only less irritating to the stomach but also has an unpleasant taste that makes it unattractive to children.

The other group of patent medicines most widely bought are those used to treat digestive ills, from diarrhoea to constipation. Medicines to treat constipation are only rarely necessary and most are purchased on the misguided assumption that

the bowels need to be opened every day. These purgatives are likely to do more harm than good because the stimulating action they produce on the muscles of the digestive tract tend to rob the gut of the ability to contract (and so move the contents along) of its own accord. If you or members of your family suffer from constipation it is far better to treat the problem by adding more roughage, especially bran, to your diet. Purgatives should not be taken in cases of severe abdominal pain or during pregnancy except on medical advice.

Antacids are alkaline medicines swallowed by the million to relieve "indigestion" of all kinds. While these generally do no harm if taken occasionally, you should see a doctor if you need to take them every day. Like constipation, acid stomach and dyspepsia are often caused by bad eating habits, particularly the eating of too much rich food, but are also made worse by smoking, drinking and stress.

Infections of the digestive system strike nearly everybody at some time and can cause diarrhoea and vomiting. One of the most effective medicines readily available for treating such infections is a kaolin and morphine mixture, but if the recommended dose produces no improvement in forty-eight hours you should consult a doctor.

The medicines prescribed by doctors are much more varied than those obtainable over the counter, and much more powerful. Often you may feel better before you have finished the course of medicines prescribed. Unused medicines should then be flushed down the lavatory. However, if you are taking antibiotics it is important to finish the course, because a partial treatment tends to encourage the survival of drug-resistant strains of disease-producing bacteria.

The range of tranquillizers and sleeping pills prescribed by doctors continues to increase. These drugs are potentially very dangerous because many of them are drugs of addiction—that is, they can cause a psychological or physiological dependence that seriously impairs the taker's ability to lead a normal life. For this reason alone you should make every effort to cope with your problems without having to take "sleepers" or tranquillizing drugs; or if you do start taking them, try to do without them as soon as possible. Avoid the temptation to seek a repeat prescription from your doctor without going to him for an examination and discussion, and never take it upon yourself to increase the dose.

Medicines often are not the best cures for physical ills—changes in diet and attitude of mind can, for example, be equally if not more effective. So do not feel your doctor is being unhelpful if he does not prescribe medicine for you on every visit you make to him.

GROUP	DRUG TYPE	USES	POSSIBLE SIDE EFFECTS	COMMENTS
Analgesics (pain-killers)	Aspirin	Headache, toothache, rheumatic disorders, menstrual pain, fever reduction	Bleeding from stomach wall, certain allergic reactions, dizziness. Can induce fatal asthmatic attacks; constipation	Soluble form recommended. Should never be used by sufferers from asthma or gastric or duodenal ulcers. Especially toxic to children, more so in presence of fever
	Codeine	Headaches, etc., diarrhoea	Constipation	Less effective than aspirin or paracetamol, and potentially addictive in large quantities
	Paracetamol	As for aspirin	Very mild and rare; blood disorders and skin eruptions	Can damage the liver, but useful to those who cannot take aspirin
	Phenacetin	As for aspirin	As for paracetamol but more common; anaemia, kidney damage	Can affect kidneys adversely
	Mixtures of above	Headaches, etc.	Any of above, depending on contents	Often include aspirin, with possibility of similar side effects
Anti-allergics	Antihistamines	Common allergies such as hay fever, skin rashes, insect bites, colds, conjunctivitis, travel sickness	Most commonly sedation, ranging from drowsiness to deep sleep. Loss of appetite, digestive upset, dry mouth, dizziness, palpitations, blurred vision	Excessive dosage can be fatal, especially in children. Symptoms of overdose include hallucinations, convulsions, coma and heart failure
Anti-bacterial agents	Sulphonamides	Food poisoning, diarrhoea	Skin eruptions, damage to kidneys and urinary tract, blood disorders	Less potent than antibiotics, often used combined with them to overcome drug resistance
Antibiotics	Penicillin	Some bacterial infections, some skin eruptions, syphilis	Main (but rare) danger is allergy producing skin rashes, mouth sores, fever, respiratory and heart failure	Sensitization can accumulate so that second and subsequent doses cause much more severe reactions than the first. People prone to allergies especially at risk
Anti-depressants	Monoamine oxidase inhibitors (MAOIs)	Depression and anxiety states	Skin rashes, headaches, constipation, palpitations, sweating, dizziness, insomnia	Use gradually declining due to adverse reactions when used with many other drugs, alcohol and some foods such as cheese
	Tricyclics	Depression	Headaches, dizziness, fatigue, palpitations, blurred vision, sweating, heart irregularities	Requires 2–3 weeks to take effect therapeutically, but side effects can occur much sooner. Safer than MAOIs
Cold remedies	Atropine (belladonna)	Colds, hay fever, gastro-intestinal spasm, travel sickness	Skin rash, dry mouth, blurred vision, raised blood pressure, fever, nausea, intolerance of light	Can be fatal, especially to children. Poisoning produces excitement and depression, collapse and coma
Sedatives/ hypnotics	Barbiturates	Hypnotics and sedatives mainly distinguished by dose. Sedatives induce tranquillity, hypnotics induce sleep. Barbiturates given for insomnia, anxiety, etc.	Sleepiness, vertigo, mental confusion, slurred speech. Symptoms of intoxication similar to those of alcohol	Drug action exaggerated by alcohol or antihistamines. A third of a lethal dose of barbiturate can kill if taken with alcohol
	Non-barbiturates		Drowsiness, nausea, mental confusion, hangover	
Tranquillizers	Major	Types distinguished by dose. Prescribed in small doses for anxiety and tension	Lack of muscular co-ordination, mental sluggishness, slowed reflexes	Effects of many tranquillizers may be dramatically increased with alcohol. Otherwise the most insidious risk is that, to quote one authority, "They depress the emotional responses concerned with self-preservation"
	Minor	Common nervous disorders complicated by anxiety or tension	Drowsiness, blurred vision, slurred speech, sensitivity to glare, mental confusion	

Folklore of fitness—and the facts

Are traditional folk-cures the distillate of human knowledge and experience about health—or just superstitious nonsense?

Medicine and magic have never been completely separated: in Africa still, the witch doctor with his weird rites and charms works side by side with the orthodox medical practitioner. The ancient wonders of sex and childbirth, of food transformed into human flesh, and of what happens in those recurrent periods of unconsciousness called sleep remain largely mysterious. In disease we are searching still for a cure for the scourge of cancer—and for the common cold. It is not surprising that in these great areas fact and folklore intermingle. We know so much more than we did, yet we know so little. Some of the sayings of our grandparents are applicable today; some are clearly absurd. Some of the pseudoscience of the sixties and seventies of our own century is equally invalid. Each aphorism needs to be examined carefully and individually.

WARTS

"Urine . . . dandelion juice . . . broad bean pods . . . get rid of warts," or, alternatively, *"warts are psychological"*: Both of these statements hint at the same truth, though neither is accurate. A wart is an overgrowth of the papillae of the skin, in response to irritation by a virus. Warts are commonest in the young with growing tissues, and are to some extent infectious by contact. The simple warts that often appear on the hands may disappear spontaneously at any time—such a "cure" can synchronize with the use of treatment, and so get the credit. But it is not as simple as that. Several carefully controlled medical trials have been made which indicate that the body can be induced to reject warts by psychological means. A well-known dermatologist was able to cause warts to fall off in ninety per cent of cases simply by shining a harmless green light on them: his assistant, who was less impressive, achieved only half the cure rate with the same apparatus. Faith in the juice of the dandelion could presumably also lead to a cure.

COLDS

"Wet feet cause colds" (similarly with sitting in a draught): The truth is that chilling any area of the skin is often accompanied by a reflex reduction in blood flow to the back of the throat. If this happens infection is more likely to get a foothold because the main defences are in the blood.

"Mega-doses of vitamin C prevent colds": Dr Linus Pauling, twice a Nobel Prize winner for peace and for medicine, makes this claim. He wrote a book about it. Nevertheless, the link has yet to be proved; comparative trials on children at different schools were inconclusive. All are agreed that vitamin C cannot be stored in the body, and that supplies are necessary for proper healing, particularly of wounds.

"Blackcurrants are good for colds": They make a pleasant drink, and are rich in vitamin C; but there is no evidence of any particular curative properties.

"Starve a fever, feed a cold": Sound advice; with a high temperature the digestive system cannot cope with too much food, while with a cold, although taste is impaired, it is important to eat to maintain activity and to replace the liquid poured ouf through the nose. If you have either a cold or fever, drinking is vital to make up for fluid loss.

"Sniff up salt water" and *"Gargle with salt water"*: As cold "cures", both these manoeuvres act mechanically by washing away infected material, but do little else. Salt is harmless.

"Onions, or fumes of grated horseradish": These stimulate the nasal mucosa to pour forth a watery secretion and, again, wash away some of the infected material if you have a cold. But there is no lasting benefit.

HAIR

"Shaving makes hair grow stronger": Untrue, but the ends of the hairs feel stiffer when cut short than when the same hairs are allowed to grow longer. Cutting scalp hair relatively short removes the old, worn ends, producing a healthier appearance, and very long hair as in plaits may drag on the top of the scalp, so that the growth is discouraged there but is less affected lower down, at the back.

"Brushing is bad for the hair": What is true is that the hair round the face which is brushed, combed and arranged more often, and may also be subject to more bleaching or waving, may be discouraged from growing. Brushing the robust growth near the neck, etc., will provide a beneficial stimulus to the blood flow of the scalp and distribute the natural hair oils. But vigorous brushing is not advisable for thinning hair.

"Beer or eggs give vitality to the hair": Beer, like a vinegar rinse, tends to remove grease and slightly enrich the colour of the hair. Eggs give a coating to the hairs which makes them seem thicker. Neither beer nor eggs has any effect on the hair

follicles themselves.

"Onions . . . box-leaves . . . and eau-de-Cologne rubbed on the scalp cure baldness": No such luck. Hormone injections locally may stimulate tufts of growth, but hundreds are required. Hereditary factors are responsible for the most common type of baldness and an effective remedy has not been found.

MUSCLES

"Copper bracelets . . . seaweed . . . celery seeds . . . help rheumatism": Much rheumatism is psychosomatic, so any method that the patient believes will help him is worth trying; some specific anti-rheumatic medicines are of proven benefit, however.

"Warm baths soothe sore muscles": Warmth induces muscles to relax and so reduce pain from tension, while the increased blood flow in a warmed area carries away products of metabolism that may cause pain. However, a bruised or torn muscle which is painful because of swelling and inflammation may respond better to a cold compress than a warm bath.

SKIN

"Too many chocolates aggravate acne or oily skin": A controlled trial with two groups of acne sufferers given lots of chocolate or none at all showed no difference, so there is no evidence that this parental warning is true.

"Rubbing in olive oil (or vitamin E oil) prevents stretch marks": Untrue, as stretch marks are caused by the breaking of elastic fibres deep in the skin, where no external applications can penetrate. The mechanism is probably hormonal, not simple stretching.

"Put butter on burns": This used to be considered advisable, to exclude air and alleviate pain. It is now realized that the best way of reducing pain and avoiding infection is to cool the burned part with water and, when the pain has subsided, to cover the area with a dry dressing.

"Soap and water is bad for the complexion": If not rinsed off, soap tends to dry up the oils of the skin excessively. But soap and water are useful as a cleanser and disinfectant on the face, especially if cosmetics are being used. People with eczema or damaged skin, as in sunburn, should stop using soap temporarily. Soap is particularly beneficial for acne.

"Steak soothes a black eye": It acts as a ready-made cold compress, but has no other virtue. It's expensive, too.

ALCOHOL

"A hair of the dog helps a hangover": True. A hangover, or post-alcoholic tremor and nausea, are at least partly due to

withdrawal effects from the night before. Withdrawal symptoms from any drug are lessened temporarily by another dose. The headache and general *malaise* of the morning after are better helped by a cold towel round the neck.

"Alcoholism is a disease": Once developed, it has physical effects on heart, liver, nervous system, etc., and the sufferer cannot control the problem without treat-

ment. However, although several members of a family may be alcoholic, it is not inherited.

"Alcohol makes you impotent": True; in the short-term it makes erection difficult; in the long term it may lead to iron deposits in the testicles. Excessive drinking can result in irreversible impotence.

SEX

"Hot baths can cause sterility": They can cause temporary erection difficulties and also low sperm production. They have no effect on women.

"Tight underpants can make men sterile": Pressure and heating of the testicles may impair their function temporarily.

"You cannot conceive the first time you make love": Not true, but usually it takes several months of love-making for a woman's sexual organs to mature fully, and for conception to take place.

"The Pill increases/decreases libido": In general, women on the Pill are less active in all ways, including sexually; some however, are released from inhibiting anxiety and for them the net result is increased libido.

"Sex is necessary; celibacy causes physical/emotional problems": It would be more accurate to say that sex is desirable and its absence may cause frustration unless other outlets are found for libido.

"Men have a menopause, too": There is a fall-off in male sexuality, but it is less sharply marked than in women and comes later, often when the man is about to retire — a crisis that is sometimes equivalent to the woman's loss of role when the children leave home.

"A man's abdomen can swell when his wife is pregnant": This type of phenomenon, called couvade, occurs in psychological states in which a man is unduly anxious about his wife's pregnancy, and disappears when the child is born. The swelling of the abdomen, when it occurs, is due to the relaxation of the intestinal

musculature, so that the contents of the abdomen take up more room.

"Vinegar swabs make contraceptives": This method has been employed—without much success—since the 17th century.

"Masturbation makes you blind, mad, etc.": An almost universal practice, masturbation helps to assuage tension and is totally harmless in itself. Guilt associated with it may lead to anxiety in people brought up prudishly.

"Have a child, lose a tooth": For a variety of reasons, dental decay tends to increase during pregnancy unless special care is taken with diet. But it is a misconception that the baby is taking calcium from the mother's teeth.

"Jumping up and down prevents conception": Vigorous physical exercise immediately after intercourse makes conception a little less likely: this is one reason why conception occurs most often during holidays, when the woman relaxes in the morning. But this is poor contraceptive advice.

SLEEP

"Don't keep plants in the room at night; they use up oxygen": This precaution is followed in some hospitals because in the daytime green plants take in carbon di-

oxide and give out oxygen; at night they do the reverse. But if a room is well ventilated, the effect on the air is marginal. Plants are nice to wake up to.

"Sleep with a window open": Not beneficial if the weather is foggy, or if you have a cough which may be set off by changes in air temperature. In the latter case open the bedroom door for circulation of air without undue cooling.

"Sleeping on your back makes you dream": We normally dream for several periods of about twenty minutes each during the night. We remember our dreams if we wake up during a period of dream sleep, not otherwise. The sleeping position makes no difference.

Heart disease: avoidable and often curable

Care of the heart is the most crucial element in body maintenance— yet one that is too often ignored in the West.

In the advanced, industrialized countries more than half the deaths recorded each year are the result of diseases of the heart and blood vessels—the cardiovascular diseases. More than 1,500 people in the US die of heart disease every day.

Diseases of the cardiovascular system are largely diseases of old age. In the US, for example, two-thirds of all deaths among those over the age of seventy-five are from cardiovascular disease, compared with about seventy out of every 1,000 in the forty-five to fifty-five age group. But diseases of heart and arteries are striking more and more at people who are in the prime of life, especially men aged from

forty to fifty and women just past the menopause. Indeed, by the time they are forty most men in the Western world, and most of them unknowingly, will have suffered some minor form of heart disease.

The exact reasons for this trend are difficult to pin down, but some factors are clearly implicated. Practically all of them arise only in wealthy, developed countries where food is richer and the physical demands on the average person less than in relatively primitive countries. The most significant are obesity, lack of exercise, a diet high in animal fats and hence in cholesterol, cigarette smoking, high blood pressure (itself a sign of some disorder), an ambitious, aggressive and restless personality and a stressful life-style that allows little time for relaxation. Genetic makeup is also implicated: the family history is often significant.

No absolutely reliable evidence exists that any one of these factors or any particular combination actually causes heart disease. But the circumstantial evidence implicating obesity, smoking and stress is very strong. The eating of animal fats (which are rich in cholesterol) is suspect mainly because societies that eat little or no meat also have very little heart disease. Other circumstantial evidence is that the fatty deposits that form on the inner surface of diseased arteries contain cholesterol, although cholesterol does not necessarily help them to form.

Inconclusive though the evidence may be, it is wise to take precautions against

heart disease by cutting down on animal fats, keeping your weight under control, taking more exercise, not smoking and "calming down" generally. This is because heart attacks usually occur as bolts from the blue with few if any warning signs. It is particularly important to observe these cautions as you get older and so possibly less active—or earlier if you notice any increase in weight.

There are several kinds of cardiovascular disease. The most common is associated with failure of the vital supply of oxygen-rich blood to the heart muscle—a condition known as ischaemic heart disease. If the coronary arteries supplying blood to the heart become gradually narrowed and inelastic (arteriosclerosis) or partially obstructed with fatty deposits (atherosclerosis), any sudden burst of physical activity that demands more pumping from the heart may cause the heart muscle to go into a spasm, caused by the muscle trying to work with insufficient oxygen. The result is a gripping pain in the chest that may radiate up the neck and down the left arm—angina pectoris, the most common form of ischaemic disease. Characteristically the pain lasts less than fifteen minutes and is relieved by resting.

For some—the lucky ones—angina is a warning sign. For many more, a heart attack occurs when the heart is suddenly deprived of blood because a coronary artery is blocked. A crushing pain develops in the centre of the chest and possibly radiates into the neck and arms,

The cycling machine
The first exercise in the 20-minute session, like the others, is precisely timed. The resistance of the machine is gradually raised to increase effort.

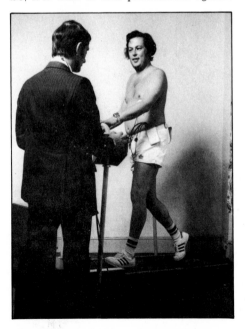

The treadmill
Treadmill speed is gradually increased to work this patient's heart towards the final target of 158. Treatment started, on a resting heart rate of 95.

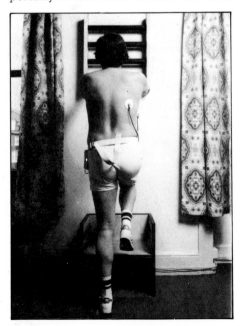

Stepping
Stepping on and off a box is the most demanding exercise in the programme. It is timed to ensure even pace. The box height can be adjusted for effort.

breathing is difficult and sufferers quite frequently feel they are about to die.

Such heart attacks have different names depending on exactly what happens. A coronary thrombosis describes the obstruction of the coronary artery with a clot (or thrombus). If the artery is narrowed by severe spasm the condition is known as coronary occlusion. If the blood supply to the heart is so deficient that part of the heart muscle dies, the condition is myocardial infarction.

Within three months of suffering a heart attack fifty per cent of men are dead, but those who manage to weather these first critical weeks successfully do have a chance not only of returning to a normal life but of living out an average span. To make the most of this chance the patient will have to follow a sensible daily routine, worked out with his doctor, usually involving a diet low in animal fats, plenty of unhurried exercise, the cessation of smoking and avoidance of stress.

Immediately following a heart attack, rest is a vital part of successful recuperation because it prevents overloading of the heart. It was once accepted medical practice, however, to forbid those who survived beyond the critical three-month period to do anything physically demanding, on the logical basis that physical stress could precipitate another heart attack. For some this is still the best advice, but the results of extensive tests have shown that, within limits, the heart often benefits from controlled physical activity.

Research has also shown that people who lead sedentary lives are much more prone to develop some form of ischaemic heart disease than those who take some kind of vigorous exercise on one day or more each week. The best known and most extensive of such studies is that at Framingham, Massachusetts. In a continuing programme, doctors are measuring nearly everything that is measurable in hundreds of apparently healthy people, from the cradle to the grave. Although no causative connection can be established, the Framingham evidence strongly supports the apparent relationship discovered elsewhere between a sedentary life and heart disease. The particular value of this evidence is that it is taken from an ordinary community, not from a selected group, and is therefore likely to be less subject to statistical error because it contains all variables rather than trying to eliminate them. Those most at risk are people who combine lack of exercise with stressful occupations—in particular, bus drivers, doctors and journalists.

Studies in both Britain and the US suggest that a formal course of graduated exercise can produce remarkable results in patients who have suffered some form of ischaemic heart disease. This is due to the heart's remarkable adaptability—for example, it is capable of pumping 400 per cent more blood every minute than the body normally needs, and if heart disease reduces this reserve capacity to 100 per cent, the body is still capable of a restful life. If a coronary artery is blocked, other smaller vessels can gradually enlarge to assist those that remain.

Apart from renewed ability to play a more active role in life, people in cardiac rehabilitation programmes gain enormous psychological benefit. Instead of feeling like cardiac cripples, worried about the move of every muscle, they can take a positive attitude to their condition. Wives of men taking part in such rehabilitation programmes are often asked along to exercise sessions so that they can appreciate the full extent of the change.

Rehabilitation through exercise

A programme of exercise rehabilitation for sufferers from ischaemic heart disease is carried out under the careful supervision of a doctor at a London clinic. He starts treatment four to six weeks after the attack and continues it for ten weeks. His initial aim is to restore patients' confidence in their physical potential and then to exercise the heart back to health. The patient in these photographs is a 32-year-old director of a large company who is subject to a great deal of stress in his work, smoked forty cigarettes a day before his attack and was distinctly overweight. The average age of patients taking part in the programme is forty-five, with a range between twenty-seven and sixty.

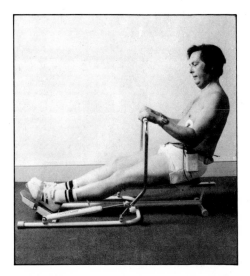

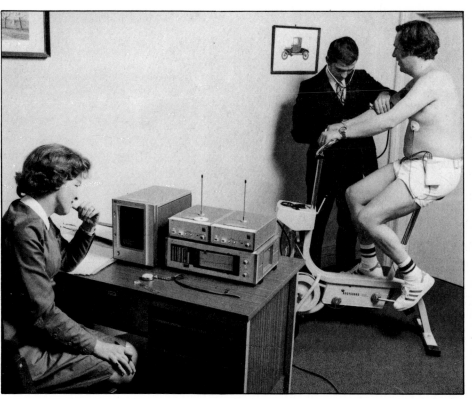

The rowing machine

On the rowing machine, as in all the exercises, the patient is connected to an electrocardiograph to check his heart performance.

End of the session

On a final spell of cycling, the patient's blood pressure is recorded—a pulse meter is used as well. The electrocardiograph is in the foreground.

Appendix

The facts and figures you need
in planning a balanced diet

Health, fitness and diet are an inseparable
trinity: if you overeat, you cannot be healthy;
if you are seriously overweight—as are
about half the people who live in the world's
developed countries—you cannot possibly be
fit, either. The charts on the following pages
will help take the guesswork out of seeking
a balance between food intake, energy output
and the individual's bodily needs. They show
the nutritional and calorific values of more
than 450 foods, introduced by guidelines to
the amount of food you probably need.

How to plan your diet: the food you need

A healthy diet should contain a good balance of essential nutrients and an adequate supply of energy. But the amounts needed vary from person to person.

People vary greatly in their needs for energy and nutrients. Individual requirements depend on such factors as body size, age, sex, occupation and health. The tables on these pages show what is generally recommended in the way of nutrients each day for adults and children of different ages and for pregnant and nursing mothers. Slightly different figures are recommended by authorities in different countries of the world, but all are set high enough to cover the needs of those with even above-average requirements.

Do not worry too much about planning your diet precisely: in any event, the elements shown here in milli- and microgrammes are too small for most people to measure. If you eat a wide variety of foods you are certain to get all the protein, minerals, vitamins and other nutrients you need—and probably too many Calories.

Although recommended intakes in these tables are expressed on a daily basis, this does not mean that every nutrient must be eaten in the stated quantity every day. Except for water, the body can store every nutrient for a few days, which means that it is well able to cope with irregular intakes in particular categories.

Using the tables to suit your needs

The Calorie requirements for adults shown in Tables 2 and 3 are calculated on the basis of a day's activity broken up as follows: sleep, eight hours; washing, dressing and undressing, one hour; sitting or standing, 13 hours; walking slowly, two hours. People such as clerical workers and taxi drivers come into this average category. To adjust your needs to a life-style that is more strenuous than the average (or less so), add or subtract the appropriate figures in the lowermost tables.

Table 1	Age (years)	Body weight (kilogrammes) (1 kg = 2.2 lb)	Calories	Protein (grammes) (10 g = 0.35
INFANTS	¹/₂–1		110–115 per kg of body weight	2.3 g per kg body weight
CHILDREN	1–2 2–3 3–5 5–7 7–9	10–12 13–14 15–17 18–22 23–26	1,100–1,200 1,300–1,400 1,500–1,700 1,800–2,000 2,100–2,200	20–30 30–40 35–45 37–66 37–66
BOYS	9–12 12–15 15–18	27–40 41–50 51–70	2,300–2,500 2,600–2,800 2,900–3,200	37–66 51–87 67–90
GIRLS	9–12 12–15 15–18	28–37 38–49 50–57	2,250–2,300 2,400–2,550 2,200–2,300	36–63 52–75 60–66

*Phosphorus intake should at least equal the calcium intake.

Table 2 MEN*	18–35	55–69 70–84 85–95	2,400–2,650 2,700–3,000 3,050–3,400	66–73 74–78 84–94
	36–55	55–69 70–84 85–95	2,300–2,500 2,600–2,900 3,000–3,200	63–69 72–80 83–88
	56–57	55–69 70–84 85–95	2,200–2,450 2,500–2,800 2,900–3,100	61–67 69–77 80–85

*Iodine 100–150 microgrammes per day.

Table 3 WOMEN*	18–35	40–49 50–64 65–75	1,550–1,750 1,800–2,100 2,200–2,400	43–48 50–58 61–66
	36–55	40–49 50–64 65–75	1,450–1,700 1,800–2,000 2,100–2,300	40–47 49–55 58–63
	56–75	40–49 50–64 65–75	1,400–1,700 1,750–1,950 2,000–2,200	39–47 48–54 55–60
Pregnancy (3–9 months)**		58	2,200	66
Lactation		58	2,700	78

*Iodine 100–150 microgrammes per day.

BODY WEIGHT IN KILOGRAMMES	40–50	51–70	71–95
Maintenance energy requirement for people resting most of the day.	−536	−650	−785
For people with active occupations such as skilled tradesmen or soldiers.	+360	+395	+430

ential y acids (ammes)	*Calcium (milli-grammes)	Iron (milli-grammes)	Vitamin A (micro-grammes)	Vitamin D (micro-grammes)	Thiamin (milli-grammes)	Riboflavin (milli-grammes)	Niacin (milli-grammes)	Vitamin C (milli-grammes)
% of cals. g per kg)	500–700	6–8	450	10.0	0.4	0.6	7.0	25
4.0	400–800	7	350	10.0	0.5	0.8	8	25
4.7		7			0.6	0.9	9	
5.7		10			0.6	1.0	10	
6.7		10		2.5	0.7	1.1	11	30
7.5		12	500	2.5	0.8	1.3	14	30
8.5	600	14	500	2.5	1.0	1.4	16	30–60
9.5	600	15	725		1.2	1.8	20	40–80
10.0	500	15	750		1.4	2.0	22	50–80
7.7	600	14	500	2.5	0.9	1.3	15	30–80
8.5	600	15	725		1.0	1.5	17	40–80
7.7	500	15	750		0.9	1.3	15	50–70
8 10 11	500–800	10	750	2.5	1.2	1.7	19	30–70
8 9 11	500–800	10	750	2.5	1.1	1.6	17	30–70
8 9 10	500–800	10	750	2.5	1.0	1.6	17	30–70
6 7 8	500–800	12	750	2.5	0.9	1.3	15	30–70
6 7 8	500–800	12	750	2.5	0.8	1.3	15	30–70
6 7 8	500–800	10	750	2.5	0.7	1.3	15	30–70
8	900–1,300	15	750	10	1.0	1.6	18	60
10	900–1,300	15	1,200	10	1.1	1.8	21	60

**Phosphorus intake during pregnancy and lactation should equal calcium intake.

BODY WEIGHT IN KILOGRAMMES	40–50	51–70	71–95
Maintenance energy requirement for people with strenuous occupations such as miners or farm labourers.	+810	+885	+960

Food: a guide to contents and Calories

There are hundreds of different foods, each with a specific makeup. The contents of a broad selection of the most common foods are tabulated here.

The tables of foods on these and the following pages have been specially drawn up to help you plan and evaluate your diet as fully as you wish. For this reason single-portion quantities have been chosen for each food (after cooking if appropriate), rather than standard weights of raw food. Only the most important constituents of each have been included.

Because each type of food may vary according to the season, the place it was grown and other such factors the figures are necessarily averages. Some foods are particularly variable—meat, for example, contains both saturated and unsaturated fats, but the exact amount present depends on how fatty the meat is. For each food, cholesterol rating is given in brackets beneath the saturated fat rating.

Variation in fat content affects the Calorie content of food more than any other constituent. The type of fat a particular food contains may depend on cooking methods. So if vegetable oil is used in cake baking the cholesterol and saturated fat content of the final product will be low, but if lard or butter is used then they will be high.

Of all the constituents of food, protein is the least variable, water the most variable. The water content is also reduced by cooking and the other ingredients thus concentrated. This explains why equal weights of rare and well-done steak have such different food values (for example, a rare steak weighing 130 grammes has 440 Calories and 28 grammes of protein compared with 690 Calories and 46.2 grammes of protein for the same weight of well-done steak that has shrunk by cooking). Where headings at the top of the charts are not applicable, or quantities are negligible, boxes are left blank.

Vegetables

Type	Energy (Calories)	Water (grammes)	Protein (grammes)	Fat (grammes)	Carbohydrate (grammes)	Good vitamin source	Good mineral source	Saturated fat	Unsaturated fat
Artichoke Boiled, 60 g (2 oz)	40	48.0	1.0	0	10.0	C, B_1, B_2, Folic acid, A	Calcium, Iron		
Asparagus 3 spears Boiled, 60 g (2 oz)	15	55.0	1.2	0.1	1.2	C, B_1, B_2, Folic acid, A	Calcium, Iron		
Asparagus Canned, 60 g (2 oz)	10	55.0	1.2	0.1	1.1		Calcium, Iron		
Bamboo shoots Boiled, 60 g (2 oz)	15	56.0	1.0	0.2	2.8	C	Calcium, Iron		
Beans, baked Canned, 60 g (2 oz)	65	41.0	3.6	0.3	13.0	B_1, Biotin, Niacin, Pantothenic acid			
Beans, runner Boiled, 60 g (2 oz)	25	54.0	0.6	0.1	6.0	B_1, Biotin, Niacin, Pantothenic acid			
Beans, runner Canned, 60 g (2 oz)	20	56.0	0.6	0.1	3.6	B_1, Biotin, Niacin, Pantothenic acid			
Beans, Lima Boiled, 60 g (2 oz)	55	43.0	3.6	0.4	9.0	B_1, Biotin, Niacin, Pantothenic acid			
Beans, broad Boiled, 60 g (2 oz)	40	50.0	2.5	0.6	6.0	B_1, Biotin, Niacin, Pantothenic acid			
Beans, butter Boiled, 60 g (2 oz)	60	42.0	4.3	0.3	10.0	B_1, Biotin, Niacin, Pantothenic acid			
Beetroot Boiled, 90 g (3.2 oz)	40	80.0	1.5	0.1	9.0	A			
Beetroot Canned, 30 g (1 oz)	10	27.0	0.3	0	2.0				
Broccoli Boiled, 50 g (1.8 oz)	20	45.0	1.6	0.2	3.0	C, Folic acid, A, B_2, K	Iron		
Brussels sprouts Boiled, 70 g (2.5 oz)	30	61.0	2.5	0.2	4.0	C, Folic acid, A, B_2, K	Iron		

Type	Energy (Calories)	Water (grammes)	Protein (grammes)	Fat (grammes)	Carbohydrate (grammes)	Good vitamin source	Good mineral source	Saturated fat	Unsaturated fat
Cabbage Raw, 35 g (1.2 oz)	15	32.0	0.5	0.1	1.9	C, Folic acid, A, B_2, K			
Cabbage Boiled, 60 g (2 oz)	15	56.0	0.7	0.1	2.4	C, Folic acid, A, B_2, K			
Cole-slaw (cabbage and mayonnaise), 60 g (2 oz)	65	49.0	0.7	4.8	4.3	C		Moderate (low cholesterol)	Moderate
Cabbage, Chinese Raw, 35 g (1.2 oz)	5	32.0	0.5	0.1	0.9	B_1, B_2, Folic acid, Pantothenic acid			
Capsicum, (pepper) Raw, 14 g (0.5 oz)	5	14.0	0.2	0	0.6	B_1, B_2, Folic acid Pantothenic acid			
Capsicum Boiled, 60 g (2 oz)	25	42.0	0.6	0.1	4.8	B_1, B_2, Folic acid Pantothenic acid			
Carrot, 1 medium Raw, 60 g (2 oz)	20	54.0	0.7	0.1	4.2	A			
Carrot Boiled, 50 g (1.8 oz)	15	44.0	0.5	0.1	2.5	A			
Carrot Canned, 50 g (1.8 oz)	15	45.0	0.4	0.1	3.0	A			
Cauliflower Raw, 30 g (1 oz)	10	27.0	0.9	0	1.2	K, B_1, B_2, Folic acid, Biotin	Iron		
Cauliflower Boiled, 30 g (1 oz)	10	27.0	0.6	0	1.2	K, B_1, B_2, Folic acid, Biotin			
Celeriac Raw, 30 g (1 oz)	15	26.0	0.5	0.1	2.4	B_1, B_2, Folic acid			
Celery Raw, 30 g (1 oz)	5	29.0	0.3	0	0.6	B_1, B_2, Folic acid			
Celery Boiled, 60 g (2 oz)	5	55.0	0.3	0	1.0	B_1, B_2, Folic acid			
Chick peas Boiled, 60 g (2 oz)	250	6.0	12.0	3.0	37.0	B_1, Niacin, Biotin, E			High
Chicory Raw, 30 g (1 oz)	5	29.0	0.4	0	0.6				
Courgette (zucchini) Raw, 60 g (2 oz)	30	55.0	0.4	0	7.0				
Courgette Baked, 60 g (2 oz)	35	53.0	0.3	1.8	4.2				
Corn (maize) Boiled, 70 g (2.5 oz)	45	53.0	2.5	0.1	8.4	A, E, B_1, Biotin, Niacin			
Corn Canned, 80 g (2.8 oz)	65	64.0	1.6	0.4	14.0	A, E, B_1, Biotin, Niacin			
Cucumber Raw, 30 g (1 oz)	5	29.0	0.2	0.1	0.8	C, B_1, B_2			
Cucumber Pickled, 30 g (1 oz)	5	27.0	0.2	0.1	0.9				
Aubergine (egg plant) Boiled, 60 g (2 oz)	15	56.0	0.6	0	3.0				

Vegetables

Type	Energy (Calories)	Water (grammes)	Protein (grammes)	Fat (grammes)	Carbohydrate (grammes)	Good vitamin source	Good mineral source	Saturated fat	Unsaturated fat
Kale Boiled, 50 g (1.8 oz)	25	44.0	2.0	0.3	3.0	K, B$_1$, B$_2$, Folic acid	Iron		
Kohlrabi Raw, 50 g (1.8 oz)	20	45.0	1.3	0.1	3.0				
Kohlrabi Boiled, 50 g (1.8 oz)	15	46.0	1.4	0	2.5				
Leeks Boiled, 50 g (1.8 oz)	20	45.0	1.0	0	4.0	B$_1$, B$_2$, Folic acid			
Lettuce, 2 small leaves Raw, 20 g (0.7 oz)	5	19.0	0.2	0	0.4	A, C, B$_1$, B$_2$, Folic acid			
Marrow Boiled, 60 g (2 oz)	5	59.0	0.3	0	0.7				
Mung beans (bean sprouts) Cooked, 30 g (1 oz)	15	27.0	1.0	0.1	2.0	C, E			
Mushrooms 6–7 small Raw, 60 g (2 oz)	15	54.0	1.3	0.2	1.2				
Mushrooms Canned, 60 g (2 oz)	10	55.0	1.0	0	1.2				
Mushrooms Fried, 60 g (2 oz)	100	42.0	1.5	9.0	2.5				
Okra (lady's finger) 5–6 pods Steamed, 60 g (2 oz)	20	54.0	0.9	0.1	4.2	B$_1$, Biotin, Niacin, B$_6$			
Olives 3 medium, 20 g (0.7 oz)	30	16.0	0.3	2.6	0.4	E			High
Onions Raw, 30 g (1 oz)	10	27.0	0.5	0	2.4				
Onions Boiled, 30 g (1 oz)	10	27.0	0.4	0	1.8				
Onions Fried, 30 g (1 oz)	95	13.0	0.5	9.0	3.0				
Onions, spring Raw, 15 g (0.5 oz)	5	13.2	0.2	0	1.4				
Parsnip Boiled, 60 g (2 oz)	40	50.0	1.0	0.3	9.0	B$_1$, B$_2$, Folic acid	Iron		
Peas Raw, 60 g (2 oz)	50	48.0	3.6	0.3	9.0	B$_1$, Niacin, Biotin, B$_2$, Pantothenic acid			
Peas Boiled, 60 g (2 oz)	40	49.0	3.0	0.1	7.5				
Peas Canned, 60 g (2 oz)	50	45.0	3.0	0.1	9.0				
Peas Dried, 30 g (1 oz)	100	3.0	6.3	2.0	15.0				
Potato, 1 medium Boiled, 90 g (3.2 oz)	70	72.0	1.8	0.1	16.2	C	Potassium		

Type	Energy (Calories)	Water (grammes)	Protein (grammes)	Fat (grammes)	Carbohydrate (grammes)	Good vitamin source	Good mineral source	Saturated fat	Unsaturated fat
Potato, 17–18 pieces Fried, 90 g (3.2 oz)	295	40.0	3.6	18.0	32.0	C	Potassium		High if fried in vegetable oil
Potato, 1 medium Baked, 90 g (3.2 oz)	80	63.0	1.8	0.1	19.0	C	Potassium		
Potato Mashed with milk 70 g (2.5 oz)	80	56.0	1.4	3.5	13.0	C	Potassium		
Potato, 14–15 pieces Dried crisps, 30 g (1 oz)	165	1.2	1.8	11.4	15.0	C	Potassium		High if fried in vegetable oil
Potato salad 60 g (2 oz)	65	44.0	1.8	5.4	2.4	C	Potassium		
Pumpkin Boiled, 60 g (2 oz)	20	54.0	0.6	0.1	4.5	A			
Radishes, 2 small 20 g (0.7 oz)	5	19.0	0.2	0	0.8				
Spinach Boiled, 60 g (2 oz)	20	54.0	2.4	0.2	2.4	A, K, B_1, B_2, Folic acid	Calcium, Iron		
Spring greens Boiled, 60 g (2 oz)	10	57.0	1.0	0.1	0.6	C, B_1, B_2, Folic acid			
Squash Boiled, 50 g (1.8 oz)	10	48.0	0.5	0	1.8				
Swede Boiled, 60 g (2 oz)	15	51.0	0.6	0	3.0				
Sweet potato Baked, 60 g (2 oz)	80	33.0	0.8	0.4	20.0	A			
Tomato, 1 medium Raw, 110 g (3.8 oz)	25	102	1.1	0.2	4.4	A, C			
Tomato Purée, 30 g (1 oz)	5	26.0	0.3	0	1.2	A, C			
Turnip Boiled, 50 g (1.8 oz)	10	46.0	0.5	0	1.5				
Watercress Raw, 15 g (0.5 oz)	5	14.0	0.4	0	0.2	B_1, B_2, Folic acid	Calcium		
Yam Boiled, 60 g (2 oz)	10	56.0	0.6	0	1.5				
Seaweed, Agar Dried, 30 g (1 oz)	100	3.0	0.4	0.4	24.9		Calcium, Iron, Iodine		

Fruit

Type	Energy (Calories)	Water (grammes)	Protein (grammes)	Fat (grammes)	Carbohydrate (grammes)	Good vitamin source	Good mineral source	Saturated fat	Unsaturated fat
Apricots 3 medium, 100 g (3.5 oz)	45	80.0	0.7	0.3	11.0	C			
Cherries 20 medium, 100 g (3.5 oz)	55	70.0	0.8	0.2	13.0	C			
Damsons 4–5 medium, 100 g (3.5 oz)	55	72.0	0.4	0	14.0	C			

Fruit

Type	Energy (Calories)	Water (grammes)	Protein (grammes)	Fat (grammes)	Carbohydrate (grammes)	Good vitamin source	Good mineral source	Saturated fat	Unsaturated fat
Peach 1 medium, 110 g (3.8 oz)	40	84.0	0.6	0	10.0	C			
Plums 3 medium, 100 g (3.5 oz)	60	82.0	0.7	0.1	15.0	C			
Nectarines 2 medium, 100 g (3.5 oz)	55	81.0	0.9	0	14.0	C			
Grapefruit 250 g (8.8 oz)	45	117	0.7	0.1	11.0	C			
Lemon 1 medium, 100 g (3.5 oz)	30	66.0	0.8	0.2	6.0	C			
Mandarin 1 medium, 85 g (3 oz)	35	61.0	0.6	0.2	8.0	C			
Orange 1 medium, 130 g (4.6 oz)	45	82.0	1.0	0.2	10.0	C			
Blackberries 100 g (3.5 oz)	65	83.0	1.3	1.0	13.0	C			
Blackcurrants 100 g (3.5 oz)	60	82.0	1.1	0.1	15.0	C			
Gooseberries 100 g (3.5 oz)	65	88.0	0.7	0.3	16.0	C			
Loganberries 100 g (3.5 oz)	40	85.0	1.0	0.1	10.0	C			
Raspberries 100 g (3.5 oz)	60	83.0	1.5	0.5	14.0	C			
Strawberries 100 g (3.5 oz)	40	88.0	0.6	0.5	9.0	C			
Apple 1 small, 100 g (3.5 oz)	55	80.0	0.4	0.3	13.0	C			
Avocado pear 1/2 fruit, 100 g (3.5 oz)	105	75.0	1.1	8.1	8.0	C		Low	High
Banana 1 medium, 110 g (3.5 oz)	90	75.0	1.1	0.3	22.0	C			
Dates 2 medium, 60 g (2 oz)	85	35.0	0.5	0.2	22.8	C			
Figs 2 medium, 75 g (2.6 oz)	60	58.0	0.6	0.9	14.0	C			
Grapes 20–22, 100 g (3.5 oz)	70	81.0	1.3	1.0	14.7	C			
Guava 1 medium, 90 g (3.2 oz)	55	76.0	0.9	0.5	12.6	C			
Mango 1 small, 160 g (5.6 oz)	65	81.0	0.7	0.4	16	A, C			
Melon 100 g (3.5 oz)	25	93.0	1.0	0	6.0	C			
Passion fruit 1 medium, 30 g (1 oz)	25	26.0	0.8	0	5.5	C			

Type	Energy (Calories)	Water (grammes)	Protein (grammes)	Fat (grammes)	Carbohydrate (grammes)	Good vitamin source	Good mineral source	Saturated Fat	Unsaturated fat
Pear 1 medium, 150 g (5.3 oz)	95	124	1.0	0.6	23.0	C			
Pineapple 2 slices, 100 g (3.5 oz)	55	81.0	0.6	0.3	13.0	C			
Quince Stewed with sugar, 100 g (3.5 oz)	85	76.0	0.4	0.2	22.1	C			
Rhubarb Stewed with sugar, 100 g (3.5 oz)	65	81.0	0.5	0.1	16.0	C			
TINNED FRUIT									
Apricots 2 halves, 60 g (2 oz)	50	85.0	0.4	0	12.7	C			
Grapefruit 120 g (4.2 oz)	40	109	0.7	0.1	9.1	C			
Cherries 8–10, 60 g (2 oz)	55	45.0	0.4	0.1	13.8	C			
Peaches 5 pieces, 120 g (4.2 oz)	85	96.0	0.5	0.1	22.0	C			
Mandarins 5–6 slices, 30 g (1 oz)	20	24.0	0.2	0	5.0	C			
Pears 2 halves, 120 g (4.2 oz)	80	97.0	0.2	0.1	20.8	C			
Raspberries 100 g (3.5 oz)	100	71.0	0.7	0.3	26.7	C			
Lychees 100 g (3.5 oz)	75	80.0	0.2	0.2	19.1	C			
Pineapple 90 g (3.2 oz)	35	71.0	0.4	0.1	9.1	C			
DRIED FRUIT									
Apples 35 g (1.2 oz)	105	7.4	0.5	0.7	26.0	C			
Apricots 5 halves, 25 g (0.9 oz)	65	5.8	1.3	0.1	16.3	C	Iron		
Currants 11 g (0.4 oz)	30	2.0	0.2	0.1	8.3	C	Calcium		
Dates 5–6 medium, 33 g (1.1 oz)	95	6.3	0.7	0.2	24.8	C			
Figs 2 medium, 30 g (1 oz)	80	6.9	1.2	0.2	20.7	C	Calcium, Iron		
Prunes 6 medium, 50 g (1.8 oz)	100	13.0	1.1	0.3	25.0	C			
Raisins 14 g (0.5 oz)	40	2.8	0.2	0	10.5	C			
Sultanas 14 g (0.5 oz)	40	2.8	0.3	0	10.6	C			

Meat

Type	Energy (Calories)	Water (grammes)	Protein (grammes)	Fat (grammes)	Carbohydrate (grammes)	Good vitamin source	Good mineral source	Saturated fat	Unsaturated fat
Beef, mince 150 g (5.3 oz)	390	84.0	30.0	30.0	0	A, Folic acid, B₁, B₁₂, Niacin	Iron, Phosphorus	High (high cholesterol)	High
Beef, corned Boiled, 75 g (2.6 oz)	180	45.0	15.0	13.0	0	A, Folic acid, B₁, B₁₂, Niacin	Iron, Phosphorus	High (high cholesterol)	High
Beef, hamburger (with cereal) 75 g (2.6 oz)	195	37.0	11.3	15.8	1.5	A, Folic acid, B₁, B₁₂, Niacin	Iron, Phosphorus	High (high cholesterol)	High
Beef, sirloin Roasted, 75 g (2.6 oz)	165	45.0	18.8	9.8	0	A, Folic acid, B₁, B₁₂, Niacin	Iron, Phosphorus	High (high cholesterol)	High
Beef, sausage Grilled, 75 g (2.6 oz)	210	38.0	10.5	15.0	8.3	A, Folic acid, B₁, B₁₂, Niacin	Iron, Phosphorus	High (high cholesterol)	High
Beef, steak Medium, 130 g (4.6 oz)	515	62.0	33.6	42.0	0	A, Folic acid, B₁, B₁₂, Niacin	Iron, Phosphorus	High (high cholesterol)	High
Brains Boiled, 150 g (5.3 oz)	165	120	18.0	10.5	0	A, Folic acid, B₁, B₁₂, Niacin	Iron, Phosphorus	High (very high cholesterol)	High
Brains Fried, 150 g (5.3 oz)	415	83.0	16.5	31.5	16.0	A, Folic acid, B₁, B₁₂, Niacin	Iron, Phosphorus	High (very high cholesterol)	High
Chicken (light meat) Boiled, 100 g (3.5 oz)	180	63.0	26.0	8.0	0	A, Folic acid, B₁, B₁₂, Niacin	Iron, Phosphorus	Moderate (high cholesterol)	Moderate
Chicken (light meat) Roasted, 100 g (3.5 oz)	150	63.0	31.0	3.0	0	A, Folic acid, B₁, B₁₂, Niacin	Iron, Phosphorus	Moderate (high cholesterol)	Moderate
Chicken giblets Fried, 30 g (1 oz)	100	16.0	9.3	3.3	1.4	A, Folic acid, B₁, B₁₂, Niacin	Iron, Phosphorus	Moderate (high cholesterol)	Moderate
Duck Roasted, 100 g (3.5 oz)	300	52.0	22.0	23.0	0	A, Folic acid, B₁, B₁₂, Niacin	Iron, Phosphorus	Low (moderate cholesterol)	Moderate
Kidney, beef Stewed, 50 g (1.8 oz)	110	27.0	15.0	5.0	0.4	A, Folic acid, B₁, B₁₂, Niacin, Pantothenic acid	Iron, Phosphorus	Low (high cholesterol)	Moderate
Kidney, lamb Fried, 50 g (1.8 oz)	100	30.0	13.5	5.5	0	A, Folic acid, B₁, B₁₂, Niacin, Pantothenic acid	Iron, Phosphorus	Low (high cholesterol)	Moderate
Lamb/Mutton Casseroled, 170 g (6 oz)	250	120	15.6	14.4	13.6	A, Folic acid, B₁, B₁₂, Niacin	Iron, Phosphorus	Moderate (high cholesterol)	High
Lamb, leg Roasted, 100 g (3.5 oz)	355	48.0	19.0	31.0	0	A, Folic acid, B₁, B₁₂, Niacin	Iron, Phosphorus	High (high cholesterol)	High
Liver, pig Fried, 150 g (5.3 oz)	345	81.0	45.0	16.5	3.8	A, Folic acid, B₂, B₁₂, C, D, Pantothenic acid, Biotin, Niacin, E	Iron, Phosphorus	Low (high cholesterol)	Moderate
Lamb, chops 2 (with bone) Grilled, medium, 150 g (5.3 oz)	350	57.0	18.0	30.0	0	A, Folic acid, B₁, B₁₂, Niacin	Iron, Phosphorus	Moderate (high cholesterol)	High

Type	Energy (Calories)	Water (grammes)	Protein (grammes)	Fat (grammes)	Carbohydrate (grammes)	Good vitamin source	Good mineral source	Saturated fat	Unsaturated fat
Pork, chops 1 (with bone) Grilled, 100 g (3.5 oz)	310	26.0	18.0	26.0	0	B_1, B_{12}	Iron, Phosphorus	High (high cholesterol)	High
Pork, bacon Fried, 20 g (0.7 oz)	140	2.6	4.4	13.4	0.4	B_1, B_{12}	Iron, Phosphorus	High (high cholesterol)	High
Pork, ham 60 g (2 oz)	230	26.0	9.6	21.0	0	B_1, B_{12}	Iron, Phosphorus	High (high cholesterol)	High
Pork, leg Roasted, 75 g (2.6 oz)	260	26.0	15.0	33.0	0	B_1, B_{12}	Iron, Phosphorus	High (high cholesterol)	High
Pork, sausage Grilled, 100 g (3.5 oz)	320	47.0	14.0	23.0	14.0	B_1, B_{12}	Iron, Phosphorus	High (high cholesterol)	High
Rabbit Stewed, 170 g (6 oz)	300	105	44.2	12.0	3.4	A, Folic acid, B_1, B_{12}, Niacin	Iron, Phosphorus	Low (high cholesterol)	Moderate
Tongue, ox Pickled, 60 g (2 oz)	180	29.0	11.4	14.4	1.2	A, Folic acid, B_1, B_{12}, Niacin	Iron, Phosphorus	Moderate (high cholesterol)	High
Turkey Roasted, 100 g (3.5 oz)	260	54.0	29.0	16.0	0	A, Folic acid, B_1, B_{12}, Niacin	Iron, Phosphorus	Low (high cholesterol)	Moderate
Tripe 150 g (5.3 oz)	150	125	15.0	5.8	9.3	A, Folic acid, B_1, B_{12}, Niacin	Iron, Phosphorus	Low (high cholesterol)	Low
Goose Roasted, 100 g (3.5 oz)	360	32.0	25.0	29.0	0	A, Folic acid, B_1, B_{12}, Niacin	Iron, Phosphorus	High (high cholesterol)	High
Veal, steak Grilled, 100 g (3.5 oz)	290	46.0	36.0	16.0	0	A, Folic acid, B_1, B_{12}, Niacin	Iron, Phosphorus	Moderate (high cholesterol)	Moderate
Venison Roasted, 100 g (3.5 oz)	165	60.0	30.0	5.0	0	A, Folic acid, B_1, B_{12}, Niacin	Iron, Phosphorus	Low (high cholesterol)	Low
Sweet bread (thymus/pancreas) Stewed, 100 g (3.5 oz)	180	60.0	21.9	10.0	0	C	Iron, Phosphorus	Moderate (very high cholesterol)	Moderate
Snails 60 g (2 oz)	45	48.0	6.6	0.9	1.8			Low (high cholesterol)	Low

Fish

Type	Energy (Calories)	Water (grammes)	Protein (grammes)	Fat (grammes)	Carbohydrate (grammes)	Good vitamin source	Good mineral source	Saturated fat	Unsaturated fat
Anchovy 3 fillets Canned, 15 g (0.5 oz)	25	8.9	2.9	1.5	0	A, D, E, K, B_1, B_{12}	Phosphorus	Moderate (high cholesterol)	High
Bass, fillet Steamed, 100 g (3.5 oz)	120	75.0	19.0	5.0	0	B_1, B_{12}	Phosphorus	Low (high cholesterol)	Moderate
Bream (with bone) Steamed, 100 g (3.5 oz)	65	50.0	11.6	2.0	0	B_1, B_{12}	Phosphorus	Low (high cholesterol)	Low

Fish and Sea Foods

Type	Energy (Calories)	Water (grammes)	Protein (grammes)	Fat (grammes)	Carbohydrate (grammes)	Good vitamin source	Good mineral source	Saturated fat	Unsaturated fat
Carp (with bone) Boiled, 100 g (3.5 oz)	60	40.0	10.3	2.0	0	B_1, B_{12}	Phosphorus	Low (high cholesterol)	High
Catfish, fillet Steamed, 100 g (3.5 oz)	100	62.0	17.4	3.2	0	B_1, B_{12}	Phosphorus	High (high cholesterol)	High
Caviar 1 teaspoon Granular, 5 g (0.2 oz)	15	2.3	1.4	0.8	0.2			Moderate (very high cholesterol)	High
Cod (with bone) Steamed, 100 g (3.5 oz)	70	64.0	15.0	1.0	0	B_1, B_{12}	Phosphorus	Low (high cholesterol)	Low
Cod, roe Fried, 60 g (2 oz)	120	37.0	12.0	7.2	1.8	C	Phosphorus	Moderate (very high cholesterol)	High
Fish fingers Fried, 30 g (1 oz)	55	20.0	5.0	2.7	1.9	B_1, B_{12}	Phosphorus	Low (high cholesterol)	Moderate
Flounder (with bone) Baked, 100 g (3.5 oz)	155	36.0	17.0	8.5	2.5	B_1, B_{12}	Phosphorus	Moderate (high cholesterol)	High
Haddock Smoked, 100 g (3.5 oz)	95	50.0	17.0	3.0	0	B_1, B_{12}	Phosphorus	Low (high cholesterol)	Low
Halibut Steamed, 100 g (3.5 oz)	145	66.0	25.0	5.0	0	B_1, B_{12}	Phosphorus	Low (high cholesterol)	Very high
Herring 100 g (3.5 oz)	195	63.0	19.0	13.0	0	A, D, E, K, B_1, B_2	Phosphorus	High (high cholesterol)	Very high
Herring roe Fried, 60 g (2 oz)	155	31.0	13.8	9.6	3.0	C	Phosphorus	Moderate (very high cholesterol)	High
Kippers Baked, 100 g (3.5 oz)	140	60.0	16.0	8.0	0	A, D, E, K	Phosphorus	High (high cholesterol)	Very high
Mackerel Smoked, 100 g (3.5 oz)	160	45.0	17.0	10.0	0	A, D, E, K, B_1, B_{12}	Phosphorus	Moderate (high cholesterol)	High
Mackerel Canned, 60 g (2 oz)	110	40.0	12.0	6.6	0	A, D, E, K, B_1, B_{12}	Phosphorus	Moderate (high cholesterol)	High
Mullet (with bone) Steamed, 100 g (3.5 oz)	80	47.0	14.0	2.7	0	A, D, E, K, B_1, B_{12}	Phosphorus	High (high cholesterol)	Very high
Perch (with bone) Steamed, 100 g (3.5 oz)	70	60.0	15.0	1.0	0	B_1, B_{12}	Phosphorus	Low (high cholesterol)	Low
Pilchards Canned, 30 g (1 oz)	70	20.0	5.7	4.8	0	B_1, B_{12}	Phosphorus	Low (high cholesterol)	Moderate
Plaice (with bone) Fried, 100 g (3.5 oz)	140	38.0	11.0	9.0	4.0	B_1, B_{12}	Phosphorus	Low (high cholesterol)	Moderate

Type	Energy (Calories)	Water (grammes)	Protein (grammes)	Fat (grammes)	Carbohydrate (grammes)	Good vitamin source	Good mineral source	Saturated fat	Unsaturated fat
Salmon Baked, 100 g (3.5 oz)	160	50.0	17.0	10.0	0	B_1, B_{12}	Phosphorus	Moderate (high cholesterol)	High
Salmon Smoked, 15 g (0.5 oz)	25	8.8	3.0	1.2	0	B_1, B_{12}	Phosphorus	Low (high cholesterol)	Moderate
Sardines 2–3 small Canned in oil, 30 g (1 oz)	85	18.0	6.0	6.6	0	A, D, E, K	Phosphorus	Moderate (high cholesterol)	Very high
Skate Fried, 100 g (3.5 oz)	190	50.0	12.0	13.0	6.0	B_1, B_{12}	Phosphorus	Moderate (high cholesterol)	High
Sprats Smoked, 60 g (2 oz)	160	27.0	13.2	12.0	0	B_1, B_{12}	Phosphorus	Moderate (high cholesterol)	High
Sturgeon 100 g (3.5 oz)	110	50.0	18.0	4.0	0	B_1, B_{12}	Phosphorus	Low (high cholesterol)	Moderate
Trout 100 g (3.5 oz)	115	50.0	17.0	5.0	0	B_1, B_{12}	Phosphorus	Low (high cholesterol)	Moderate
Tuna Canned in oil, 100 g (3.5 oz)	280	55.0	24.0	20.0	0	B_1, B_{12}	Phosphorus	Low (high cholesterol)	High
Turbot Steamed, 100 g (3.5 oz)	65	55.0	13.0	1.0	0	B_1, B_{12}	Phosphorus	Low (high cholesterol)	Low
Whitebait Fried, 100 g (3.5 oz)	500	23.0	18.0	46.0	5.0	B_1, B_{12}	Phosphorus	Moderate (high cholesterol)	High
Abalone 60 g (2 oz)	60	45.0	12.0	0.3	1.8	Niacin		Low (high cholesterol)	Low
Clams 60 g (2 oz)	35	50.0	5.4	0.6	1.8	Niacin		Low (high cholesterol)	Low
Crab meat Flaked, 90 g (3.2 oz)	85	67.0	16.0	1.8	0.9	Niacin		Low (very high cholesterol)	Moderate
Crayfish 90 g (3.2 oz)	65	74.0	13.5	0.5	0.9	Niacin		Low (high cholesterol)	Low
Cockles 60 g (2 oz)	35	47.0	7.8	0.3	0.6	Niacin	Calcium	Low (high cholesterol)	Low
Lobster 90 g (3.2 oz)	90	67.0	18.0	1.8	0.9	Niacin		Low (high cholesterol)	Moderate
Mussels 60 g (2 oz)	60	48.0	9.0	1.2	3.0	Niacin	Calcium	Low (high cholesterol)	Moderate
Octopus 90 g (3.2 oz)	90	72.0	13.5	1.8	4.5	Niacin		Low (high cholesterol)	Moderate

Sea Foods

Type	Energy (Calories)	Water (grammes)	Protein (grammes)	Fat (grammes)	Carbohydrate (grammes)	Good vitamin source	Good mineral source	Saturated fat	Unsaturated fat
Oysters 6 Raw, 60 g (2 oz)	40	50.0	6.0	1.2	1.8	Niacin	Calcium	Moderate (very high cholesterol)	Low
Eel 90 g (3.2 oz)	220	54.0	15.3	18.0	0	A		Moderate (moderate cholesterol)	High
Scallops 2–3 Steamed, 60 g (2 oz)	60	45.0	13.2	0.8	0	Niacin	Calcium	Low (high cholesterol)	Low
Scampi/Prawns 60 g (2 oz)	60	42.0	12.7	1.1	0	Niacin		Low (high cholesterol)	Moderate
Shrimps Steamed, 60 g (2 oz)	50	47.0	10.8	0.5	1.0	Niacin		Low (high cholesterol)	Low

Milk Products

Type	Energy (Calories)	Water (grammes)	Protein (grammes)	Fat (grammes)	Carbohydrate (grammes)	Good vitamin source	Good mineral source	Saturated fat	Unsaturated fat
Milk, cow's (whole) 150 ml (0.25 pt)	100	135	5.4	5.4	7.2	A, D, B_1, B_2, Niacin	Calcium, Phosphorus	High (moderate cholesterol)	High
Milk, cow's (buttermilk) 150 ml (0.25 pt)	55	136	5.3	0.2	7.5	B_1, B_2	Calcium, Phosphorus		
Milk, cow's (evaporated) 1 tablespoon 20 g (0.7 oz)	30	15.0	1.6	1.7	2.1	A, D, B_1, B_2	Calcium, Phosphorus	High (moderate cholesterol)	High
Milk, cow's (condensed) 1 tablespoon 27 g (0.9 oz)	95	7.0	2.2	2.7	14.8	A, D, B_1, B_2	Calcium, Phosphorus	High (moderate cholesterol)	High
Milk, cow's (powdered skim) 1 tablespoon 11 g (0.4 oz)	40	0.5	3.5	0	5.5	B_1, B_2	Calcium, Phosphorus		
Milk, goat's 150 ml (0.25 pt)	100	132	4.9	6.0	6.8	A, D, B_1, B_2	Calcium, Phosphorus	High (moderate cholesterol)	High
Milk, human 150 ml (0.25 pt)	100	129	1.8	5.3	10.5	A, D, B_1, B_2	Calcium, Phosphorus	Moderate (moderate cholesterol)	Moderate
Cream, single 1 tablespoon 20 g (0.7 oz)	45	15.0	0.8	4.2	0.6	A, D, B_1, B_2		High (moderate cholesterol)	High
Cream, double 1 tablespoon 25 g (0.9 oz)	110	12.0	0.4	12.0	0.5	A, D, B_1, B_2		Very high (moderate cholesterol)	Very high
Cheese, Cheddar 20 g (0.7 oz)	80	7.2	5.2	6.7	0.1	A, D, B_1, B_2	Calcium, Phosphorus	High (moderate cholesterol)	High
Cheese, Cheddar (processed) 20 g (0.7 oz)	70	8.6	4.4	5.4	0.2	A, D, B_2		High (moderate cholesterol)	High
Cheese, Camembert 20 g (0.7 oz)	65	9.0	4.2	5.0	0.1	A, D, B_1, B_2	Calcium, Phosphorus	High (moderate cholesterol)	High

Type	Energy (Calories)	Water (grammes)	Protein (grammes)	Fat (grammes)	Carbohydrate (grammes)	Good vitamin source	Good mineral source	Saturated fat	Unsaturated fat
Cheese, cottage 19 g (0.7 oz)	15	15.0	3.6	0.1	0	A, D, B$_1$, B$_2$	Calcium, Phosphorus	Low	Low
Cheese, cream 19 g (0.7 oz)	70	9.5	1.3	7.6	0.5	A, D, B$_1$, B$_2$	Calcium, Phosphorus	High (moderate cholesterol)	High
Cheese, Danish blue 20 g (0.7 oz)	70	8.0	4.4	6.0	0.1	A, D, B$_1$, B$_2$	Calcium, Phosphorus	High (moderate cholesterol)	High
Cheese, spread (processed) 1 tablespoon 19 g (0.7 oz)	50	8.5	3.3	3.8	0.2	A, D, B$_2$		High (moderate cholesterol)	High
Cheese, Gouda 20 g (0.7 oz)	65	7.0	4.4	5.2	0.1	A, D, B$_2$	Calcium, Phosphorus	High (moderate cholesterol)	High
Cheese, Parmesan Grated, 9 g (0.4 oz)	40	2.3	3.3	2.7	0	A, D, B$_1$, B$_2$	Calcium, Phosphorus	Moderate (moderate cholesterol)	Moderate
Yoghurt, plain (skim milk) 150 ml (0.25 pt)	55	130	6.0	0.2	7.5	B$_1$, B$_2$	Calcium, Phosphorus	Low (low cholesterol)	Low
Yoghurt, plain 150 ml (0.25 pt)	65	116	5.4	1.5	7.5	B$_1$, B$_2$	Calcium, Phosphorus	Low (low cholesterol)	Low
Butter 30 g (1 oz)	230	4.5	0.3	25.0	0.2	A, D		High (high cholesterol)	High
Margarine, pure vegetable 30 g (1 oz)	230	4.5	0.3	25.0	0.2	A, D		Low	High

Eggs

Type	Energy (Calories)	Water (grammes)	Protein (grammes)	Fat (grammes)	Carbohydrate (grammes)	Good vitamin source	Good mineral source	Saturated fat	Unsaturated fat
Hen's (whole) 1 medium Raw, 45 g (1.6 oz)	75	33.0	5.5	5.3	0.5	A, D, E, B$_1$, B$_2$, Pantothenic acid	Iron, Phosphorus, Calcium	Low (high cholesterol)	High
Hen's (white) 30 g (1 oz)	15	25.0	2.8	0	0.3				
Hen's (yolk) 17 g (0.6 oz)	60	8.6	2.7	5.3	0.2	A, D, E, B$_1$, B$_2$, Pantothenic acid	Iron, Phosphorus, Calcium	High (very high cholesterol)	Very high
Hen's Boiled, 45 g (1.6 oz)	75	33.0	5.7	5.2	0.4	A, D, E, B$_1$, B$_2$, Pantothenic acid	Iron, Phosphorus, Calcium	Low (high cholesterol)	High
Hen's Fried, 45 g (1.6 oz)	105	31.0	6.0	9.0	0.3	A, D, E, B$_1$, B$_2$, Pantothenic acid	Iron, Phosphorus, Calcium	Moderate (high cholesterol)	High
Duck (whole) 50 g (1.8 oz)	95	35.0	6.6	7.3	0.3	A, D, E, B$_1$, B$_2$, Pantothenic acid	Iron, Phosphorus, Calcium	Low (high cholesterol)	High

Cereal Products

Type	Energy (Calories)	Water (grammes)	Protein (grammes)	Fat (grammes)	Carbohydrate (grammes)	Good vitamin source	Good mineral source	Saturated fat	Unsaturated fat
Flour, wheat (white) 20 g (0.7 oz)	70	2.8	2.0	0.3	14.8	Niacin, Folic acid, B_1, E	Calcium, Iron, Phosphorus		
Flour, wheat (wholemeal) 20 g (0.7 oz)	70	3.0	2.4	0.4	14.2	Niacin, Folic acid, B_1, E	Calcium, Iron, Phosphorus		
Flour, rye (medium) 20 g (0.7 oz)	70	2.6	1.8	0.3	15.0	Niacin, Folic acid, B_1, E	Calcium, Iron, Phosphorus		
Cornflour 20 g (0.7 oz)	75	2.6	0.1	0.6	17.0	A, Niacin, Folic acid, B_1, E			
Arrowroot 20 g (0.7 oz)	80	2.2	0.8	0	18.8				
Soya flour (full fat) 20 g (0.7 oz)	90	1.4	7.8	4.2	5.0	Niacin, Biotin, E	Calcium, Iron, Phosphorus	Low	High
Soya flour (low fat) 20 g (0.7 oz)	75	1.4	9.6	1.4	6.0	Niacin, Biotin, E	Calcium, Iron, Phosphorus	Low	Moderate
Spaghetti/Macaroni Boiled, 150 g (5.3 oz)	175	108	4.5	0.8	37.5		Calcium, Iron, Phosphorus	Low	
Noodles, egg Boiled, 150 g (5.3 oz)	180	105	6.0	2.0	34.5			Low (low cholesterol)	Moderate
Rice, brown Boiled, 160 g (5.6 oz)	185	112	3.7	1.0	40.0	Niacin, Folic acid, B_1			
Rice, white Boiled, 160 g (5.6 oz)	165	115	3.2	0.3	37.0	Niacin, Folic acid, B_1			
Sago Raw, 160 g (5.6 oz)	530	18.0	0.3	0.3	131				
Branflakes 30 g (1 oz)	85	1.5	3.6	0.9	21.0	B_1, B_2, Niacin	Calcium		
Cornflakes 30 g (1 oz)	110	0.9	2.4	0.3	24.0	B_1, B_2, Niacin	Calcium		
Porridge, oatmeal 1:3 with milk Cooked, 235 g (8.3 oz)	130	203	4.7	2.3	21.0	B_1, B_2, Niacin	Calcium	Low	Moderate
Puffed Wheat 20 g (0.7 oz)	115	1.5	4.2	0.5	23.0	B_1, B_2, Niacin	Calcium		
Wheat biscuits 2 biscuits, 33 g (1.1 oz)	120	2.6	3.6	0.5	25.7	B_1, B_2, Niacin	Calcium		
Muesli 30 g (1 oz)	120	1.5	5.4	0.6	22.5	B_1, B_2, Niacin	Calcium		
Puffed rice 30 g (1 oz)	115	2.1	1.8	0.3	26.1	B_1, B_2, Niacin	Calcium		

Cakes and Puddings

Type	Energy (Calories)	Water (grammes)	Protein (grammes)	Fat (grammes)	Carbohydrate (grammes)	Good vitamin source	Good mineral source	Saturated fat	Unsaturated fat
Chocolate cake 40 g (1.4 oz)	180	22.0	2.0	7.6	26.0				
Fruit cake 40 g (1.4 oz)	170	2.4	2.4	7.2	23.2				
Sponge cake 40 g (1.4 oz)	125	11.6	3.6	2.4	22.0				
Doughnut 40 g (1.4 oz)	150	10.4	2.4	8.0	18.0				
Meringue 30 g (1 oz)	110	2.1	0.9	0	27.0				
Pastry 50 g (1.8 oz)	265	3.5	3.0	17.5	24.0				
Scones 30 g (1 oz)	110	22.0	2.1	3.6	16.5				
Jelly 100 g (3.5 oz)	100	74.0	2.9	0	21.0				
Ice-cream 60 g (2 oz)	105	40.0	4.0	5.2	10.5			High (moderate cholesterol)	High
Rice pudding 135 g (4.8 oz)	195	96.0	4.9	10.3	21.2			Moderate (moderate cholesterol)	Moderate
Blancmange 125 g (4.4 oz)	150	91.0	4.0	4.6	22.5			Moderate (moderate cholesterol)	Low
Yorkshire pudding 30 g (1 oz)	65	17.0	2.1	2.8	8.1			Moderate (low cholesterol)	Low
Apple crumble 135 g (4.8 oz)	380	53.5	4.2	10.5	66.8			Moderate (moderate cholesterol)	Low
Christmas pudding 120 g (4.2 oz)	390	32.0	6.0	8.0	74.0			Moderate (moderate cholesterol)	Moderate
BISCUITS									
Crackers, plain 2 biscuits 18 g (0.6 oz)	80	0.7	1.6	2.9	12.2				
Crackers, cheese 3 biscuits 12 g (0.4 oz)	60	0.5	1.2	2.8	7.2				
Biscuits, sweet 2 biscuits 16 g (0.5 oz)	90	0.1	0.9	4.9	10.6				
Biscuits, chocolate coated, plain 2 biscuits 20 g (0.7 oz)	90	0.6	1.2	2.8	15.0				
Shortbread 1 biscuit, 16 g (0.5 oz)	80	1.1	1.1	4.0	9.6				

Oils and Fats

Type	Energy (Calories)	Water (grammes)	Protein (grammes)	Fat (grammes)	Carbohydrate (grammes)	Good vitamin source	Good mineral source	Saturated fat	Unsaturated fat
Lard/Dripping 30 g (1 oz)	270	0	0	30.0				High (moderate cholesterol)	High
Suet 30 g (1 oz)	255	1.2	0.48	28.0				High (moderate cholesterol)	High
Sunflower oil 30 g (1 oz)	270	0	0	30.0				Low	High
Peanut oil 30 g (1 oz)	265	0	0	30.0				Moderate	High
Coconut oil 30 g (1 oz)	265	0	0	30.0				High	Low
Olive oil 30 g (1 oz)	270	0	0	30.0				Low	High

Spreads, etc.

Type	Energy (Calories)	Water (grammes)	Protein (grammes)	Fat (grammes)	Carbohydrate (grammes)	Good vitamin source	Good mineral source	Saturated fat	Unsaturated fat
Peanut butter 1 teaspoon, 7 g (0.2 oz)	45	0.1	1.9	3.4	1.2			Low	Low
Jam 1 teaspoon, 7 g (0.2 oz)	20	2.1	0	0	4.9				
Honey 1 teaspoon 7 g (0.2 oz)	25	1.6	0	0.1	5.3				
Syrup 1 teaspoon 7 g (0.2 oz)	20	1.4	0	0	5.5				
Yeast and vegetable extracts, 1 teaspoon 7 g (0.2 oz)	15	2.5	1.9	0.1	1.6				
Fish paste 7 g (0.2 oz)	15	4.3	1.3	0.7	0.3	B_1, B_{12}	Phosphorus	Moderate (high cholesterol)	Moderate
Meat paste 7 g (0.2 oz)	15	4.2	1.4	0.9	0.3	A, Folic acid, B_1, B_{12}, Niacin	Iron, Phosphorus	Moderate (high cholesterol)	Moderate
Mayonnaise/Salad dressing, 1 tablespoon 19 g (0.7 oz)	140	2.9	0.2	15.0	0.4			Moderate (moderate cholesterol)	Moderate
Tomato sauce 1 tablespoon 20 g (0.7 oz)	25	14.0	0.5	0	5.1				
French dressing 1 tablespoon 20 g (0.7 oz)	85	7.8	0.1	7.4	3.8			Low	Moderate
Sugar, white 1 teaspoon 4 g (0.1 oz)	20	0	0	0	4.0				
Sugar, brown 1 teaspoon 5 g (0.2 oz)	20	0.1	0	0	4.9				

Beverages

Type	Energy (Calories)	Water (grammes)	Protein (grammes)	Fat (grammes)	Carbohydrate (grammes)	Good vitamin source	Good mineral source	Saturated fat	Unsaturated fat
Cola type 170 ml (0.3 pt)	70	153	0	0	17.0				
Lemonade/fruit flavoured 170 ml (0.3 pt)	80	150	0	0	20.0	C if stated			
Ginger ale 170 ml (0.3 pt)	50	158	0	0	12.0				
Malted drink 1 tablespoon powder 7 g (0.2 oz)	30	0.6	1	0.4	4.9				
Cocoa 1 tablespoon powder 7 g (0.2 oz)	30	0.2	1.4	1.8	2.5				
Coffee, black 170 ml (0.3 pt)	5	179	0.1	0	0.4				
Coffee, white 1 teaspoon sugar 170 ml (0.3 pt)	35	172	0.8	0.7	5.3			Moderate (moderate cholesterol)	Moderate
Tea 170 ml (0.3 pt)	5	176	0.2	0	0.2				
Grapefruit 200 ml (0.4 pt)	85	186	1.0	0.2	20.0	C			
Orange 200 ml (0.4 pt)	100	180	1.6	0.6	22.0	C			
Pineapple 200 ml (0.4 pt)	120	180	0.8	0.2	28.0	C			
Tomato 200 ml (0.4 pt)	45	194	2.0	0.4	9.0	C, Folic acid			

ALCOHOLIC DRINKS	Alcohol (%)								
Beer 240 ml (0.4 pt)	95	3.6–4.1	0.7	0	7.2	B$_2$, Niacin			
Spirits (70° proof) 32 ml (0.06 pt)	70	31.5	0	0	0				
Liqueurs 19 ml (0.03 pt)	70	34.0	0	0	6.0				
Champagne 150 ml (0.25 pt)	115	10.0	0.3	0	2.3				
Sherry, sweet 58 ml (0.1 pt)	80	15.4	0.1	0	4.0				
Port 100 ml (0.2 pt)	160	15.6	0.1	0	12.0				
Wine, red, claret 100 ml (0.2 pt)	95	12.5	0.3	0	0.6				
Wine, white 100 ml (0.2 pt)	90	10.0	0.2	0	4.0				
Vermouth, dry 100 ml (0.2 pt)	135	18.0	0	0	1.3				

Bibliography

The following titles are suggested for further reading

GENERAL REFERENCES

Diagram Group (1976), *Man's Body*, Paddington Press. Gomez, J. (1972), *How Not To Die Young*, George Allen and Unwin. Smith, A. (1976), *The Body*, Penguin. Thomson, A. R. (1971), *Black's Medical Dictionary*, Adam and Charles Black.

WHO ARE YOU?

Barnicot, N. A., Harrison, G. A., Tanner, J. M., Weiner, J. S. (1964), *Human Biology: An Introduction to Human Evolution, Variation and Growth*, Oxford University Press. Birdsell, J. B. (1972), *Human Evolution*, Rand McNally. Bromley, D. B. (1974), *The Psychology of Human Ageing*, Penguin. Brown, R., Hernstein, R. J. (1975), *Psychology*, Little Brown; Methuen. Eysenck, H. J. (1967), *The Biological Basis of Personality*, C. C. Thomas. Eysenck, H. J. (Ed.) (1971), *Readings in Extraversion—Introversion*, Staples Press. Katz, S. H. (Ed.) (1974), *Biological Anthropology*, W. H. Freeman. Napier, J. (1971), *The Roots of Mankind*, George Allen and Unwin. Rees, L. (1973), "Constitutional Factors and Abnormal Behaviour", *Eysenck Handbook of Abnormal Psychology*, Pitman. Sheldon, W. H., Stevens, S. S. (1942), *The Varieties of Temperament*, Harper. Sheldon, W. H., Stevens, S. S., Tucker, W. B. (1940), *The Varieties of Human Physique*, Harper. Tanner, J. M. (1964), *The Physique of The Olympic Athlete*, Allen and Unwin. Weiner, J. S. (1971), *Man's Natural History*, Weidenfeld and Nicolson.

FUEL FOR THE SYSTEM

Bender, A. E. (1975), *Facts of Food*, Oxford University Press. Burnett, J. (1966), *Plenty and Want*, Nelson. Cameron, A. (1973), *The Science of Food and Cooking*, Edward Arnold. Diem, K., Lentner, C. (Eds.) (1975), *Documenta Geigy. Scientific Tables*, Geigy Pharmaceuticals. *Food Composition Table for Use in East Asia*, FAO. Guyton, A. C. (1971), *Textbook of Medical Physiology*, W. B. Saunders. *Manual of Nutrition* (1974), HMSO. McCance, R. A., Widdowson, E. M. (1969), *The Composition of Foods*, HMSO. Mellanby, K. (1975), *Can Britain Feed Itself?*, Merlin Press. Thomas, S., Cordon, M. (1970), *Tables of Composition of Australian Foods*, Australian Government Publishing Service. Warren, H. (1966), *Jainism*, Divine Knowledge Society, Bombay. Watt, B. K., Merril, A. L. (1963), *Composition of Foods*, US Department of Agriculture. *Recommended Intakes of Nutrients of the United Kingdom* (1969), HMSO. Yudkin, J. (1970), *This Slimming Business*, Penguin. Yudkin, J., Edelman, J., Hough, L. (Eds.) (1973), *Sugar*, Butterworths.

LIVING WITH STRESS

Appley, M. H., Trumbell, R. (Eds.) (1967), "Psycho-social Stress", *Research*, Appleton Century-Crofts. Benson, H. (1975), *The Relaxation Response*, Collins. Blythe, P. (1973), *Stress, The Modern Sickness*, Pan. Carruthers, M. (1974), *The Western Way of Death*, Pantheon. Dunne, D. (1973), *Yoga Made Easy*, Mayflower. Dunne, W. L. (Ed.) (1973), *Smoking Behaviour: Motives and Incentives*, Wiley. Friedman, M., Rosenman, R. (1974), *Type A Behaviour and Your Heart*, Alfred A. Knopf. Gray, J. (1971), *The Psychology of Fear and Stress*, Weidenfeld and Nicolson. Hittleman, R. (1975), *Yoga 28 Days Exercise Plan*, Hamlyn. Janov, A. (1973), *The Feeling Child*, Simon and Schuster. Karlins, M., Andrews, L. M. (1975), *Biofeedback*, Warner Books. Levi, L. (1967), *Stress Sources, Management and Prevention*, Liveright. Levi, L. (Ed.), *Society, Stress and Disease* Vol. 1 (1971), Vol. 2 (1975), Oxford University Press. Marcuse, F. L. (1976), *Hypnosis*, Penguin. McKenna, M. (1974), *Revitalize Yourself*, Hawthorn. Seyle, H. (1950), *Stress*, Acta.

EXERCISE AT YOUR OWN PACE

Baker, G. H. (1975), *Keep Healthy: Stay Younger*, Sphere. Carruthers, M., Murray, A. (1976), *F/40 Fitness on Forty Minutes a Week*, Futura. Chambers, D. (1976), *Fitness for the Motorist*, Letts. Cooper, K. (1975), *The New Aerobics*, Bantam and M. Evans and Co. *Health for Old Age*, Consumers' Association, 1972. Cooper, M., Cooper, K. H. (1972), *Aerobics for Women*, Bantam and M. Evans and Co. De Vries, H. A. (1968), *Physiology of Exercise*, Staples Press. Evans, J. E. (1974), *Service to Sport*, The Sports Council. Featherstone, D. F. (1965), *Be Fit at Forty*, Thorsons. Hettinger, R. (1961), *Physiology of Strength*, Charles Thomson. Hewitt, J. (1975), *Isometrics and You*, Tandem. Jokl, E., Jokl, P. (1968), *The Physiological Basis of Athletic Records*, Charles C. Thomas. Loken, N. C. (1970), *Gymnastics*, Sterling. Murray, A. (1971), *Modern Weight Training*, Kaye and Ward. Morehouse, L. E., Gross, L. (1976), *Total Fitness in Thirty Minutes a Week*, Hart-Davis; MacGibbon. Rankin, W. H. (1967), *The Isometric Way to Instant Fitness*, Sphere. Royal Canadian Air Force (1975), *Physical Fitness*, Penguin. Watson, B. (1975), *Tackle Weightlifting*, Stanley Paul. Watson, B. (1975), *Health and Fitness for the Over Forties*, Stanley Paul.

BASIC BODY MAINTENANCE

Brown, J. A. C. (1971), *Pears Medical Encyclopedia*, Pelham. Comfort, A. (1975), *The Joy of Sex*, Quartet Books. *The Way to Use Aspirin*, The Health Education Council. Donaldson, R. J., (1973), *The Health of Men*, British Medical Association. Gomez, J. (1971), *A Dictionary of Symptoms*, Paladin. Greengross, W. (1974), *The Health of Women*, British Medical Association. Kemp, R. (1972), *Drinking and Alcoholism*, British Medical Association. Kemp, R. (1976), *So You Need a Diet*, British Medical Association. Laurie, P. (1974), *Drugs*, Penguin. Mitchell, James (Ed.) (1977), *The Random House Encyclopedia* (UK: *Man and Society*, Mitchell Beazley). *The Concise Home Medical Guide*, (3 Vols.) (1971), Reader's Digest. Read, P., Rosenstein, H. (1969), *Foot Care at All Ages*, British Medical Association. Samuels, M. (1974), *The Well Body Book*, Wildwood House. Smyth, M. (1975), *Family Planning*, British Medical Association. Smyth, M. (1976), *Woman: The Middle Years*, British Medical Association. Stonehouse, B. (1974), *The Way Your Body Works*, Mitchell Beazley. Taylor, A. R. (1969), *Dental Care at All Ages*, British Medical Association.

INDEX

Page numbers in bolder type refer to major entries. Numbers italicized refer to illustrations.

Acknowledgements

The publishers wish to thank the following individuals and organizations for their assistance in the production of this book:

BBC: Horizon
British Family Planning Association
British Institute of Trichologists
Christine Shaw Beauty School
Consumer's Association
Drive magazine (Automobile Association)
T. Lucas & Co Ltd
John Man
Tom McNab
Nordic Sauna Ltd
Roche Chemicals
Dr Peter Sperryn
The Sports Council
Start-rite Shoes Ltd
Tate & Lyle Ltd
The Vegan Society
Vegetarian Society of the United Kingdom
M. Evans and Company, New York

Material on the BX programme is published by permission of the Queen's Printer, Canada, the Government Printer, New Zealand, Penguin Books and Simon and Schuster.

Photographic credits
Original photography by: Alan Duns 1, 2, 3, 4, 5, 6, 7, 8, 9, 10, 11, 39, 46, 47, 54, 56, 57, 62, 66, 67, 68, 69, 72, 73, 104, 105, 156, 157, 186, 187, 188, 189. John Garrett 12, 13, 14, 90, 91, 92, 93, 94, 96, 97, 98, 99, 100, 101, 112, 113, 114, 115, 116, 117, 118, 119, 121, 130, 131, 132, 133, 135, 136, 137, 138, 139, 140, 141, 142, 143, 144, 145, 146, 147, 148, 149, 150, 151, 152, 153, 154, 155, 158, 159, 160, 161, 162, 164, 165, 168, 169, 172, 173, 174, 175, 176, 177, 180, 181, 192, 193.
Cover photography by John Garrett and Alan Duns

Additional photographs: Alaska Pictorial Service 48; The Associated Press Agency Ltd 28; The Auckland Star 111; Paul Brierly 71; Camera Press Ltd 16, 29, 55; Central Press 16, 17; Colorific/Carl Purcell/John Moss 58, 82; Colorsport 76, 120, 163; Colour Library International 170/171; Cooper-Bridgeman Library/Uffizi, Florence 184/185; Gerry Cranham 42, 119; Mary Evans Picture Library 110; Susan Griggs Agency 22, 70, 163, 167; Michael Holford 89, 182, Keystone Press Agency 17, 52; Bryan Latham 29; Lehtikuva Oy, 183; T. Lucas & Co Ltd 70, 71; The Mansell Collection 110; Orion Press 183; Bury Peerless 61; Roger Phillips 63; Picturepoint Ltd 167; Popperfoto 16, 163; Shell Photo Service 70; Syndication International 29; Tate & Lyle Ltd 45.

ILLUSTRATORS
John Beswick
Chris Forsey
Rory Key
Neil McDonald
Paddy Mounter

MAKE-UP
Roy Flooks